Peoples' Spaces and State Spaces

Peoples' Spaces and State Spaces

Land and Governance in Mozambique

Rosemary Elizabeth Galli

LEXINGTON BOOKS
Lanham • Boulder • New York • Oxford

LEXINGTON BOOKS

Published in the United States of America
by Lexington Books
A Member of the Rowman & Littlefield Publishing Group
4501 Forbes Boulevard, Suite 200, Lanham, Maryland 20706

PO Box 317
Oxford
OX2 9RU, UK

British Library Cataloguing in Publication Information Available

Library of Congress Cataloging-in-Publication Data

Galli, Rosemary.
    Peoples' spaces and state spaces : land and governance in Mozambique /
Rosemary Elizabeth Galli.
        p. cm.
    Includes bibliographical references and index.
    ISBN 0-7391-0632-5 (cloth : alk. paper)
    1. Structural adjustment (Economic policy)—Mozambique. 2. Rural development—
Government policy—Mozambique. 3. Agriculture—Economic aspects—Mozambique.
4. Mozambique—Economic conditions—1975- 5. Mozambique—Social conditions—
1975- I. Title.
    HC890.G35 2003
    307.7214'09679—dc21   2003000389

Printed in the United States of America

∞™ The paper used in this publication meets the minimum requirements of
American National Standard for Information Sciences—Permanence of Paper for
Printed Library Materials, ANSI/NISO Z39.48-1992.

Contents

List of Maps

~

Acknowledgments

A book that has taken nine years to live, write, shape, and finally publish has accumulated many debts along the way. These are principally owed to the rural peoples of Mozambique who so graciously took my colleagues and I into their living spaces and homes even when they refused to take part in our proposed intervention. This book is obviously dedicated to them.

However, I also owe much to my Mozambican colleagues especially at the Instituto de Desenvolvimento Rural (INDER) who patiently but also eagerly went into the bush with me and tempered my excesses of enthusiasm over the enterprise as well as my outbursts of impatience when our training experiences did not live up to expectations. Let me mention here the support and belief in what we were trying to accomplish shown by the first president of INDER, the late Felix Mandlate, and the continuing confidence demonstrated by his successor, João Carrilho. The warmest of thanks goes to Judite Ernesto Muxlhanga, my teammate, and to Custódio dos Mocudos, our "boss" and, among our donor sponsors, Merethe Luís and Mette Maast of the Norwegian Development Authority (NORAD) and Miriam Brandão, then of the World Bank. Miriam, your generosity and openness to our tiny experiment will never be forgotten.

On the research side, I have been greatly inspired by the research work of Yussuf Adam, and many of his former colleagues at the African Studies Center of the University of Eduardo Mondlane as well as the rural historians, Gerhard Liesegang and David Hedges, also of the university. Most of all, I want to express my heartfelt thanks to António Sopa of the Historical

Archives for his untiring help to a novice in the mysteries of the Archives and also for his commitment to advancing the cause of truth in research. Talks with Julie Born, Bernhard Weimer, and the late Scott Kloeck-Jenson oriented me in ways they cannot know.

Two colleagues and friends, Len Bloom and Enrico Luzzati, laboriously read the first and second drafts of this manuscript. Thank you for your helpful comments. Mike Bell and Fred Hendricks also read different versions of part 2 and gave important suggestions. I hope I have not let you down in the final version for which I alone take responsibility.

Thanks too to Gerry Stones and Sally Graham for moral support along the way and help in the final stages of manuscript preparation.

Introduction

In 1987, Jocelyn Jones and I wrote of Guinea-Bissau in West Africa:

> No party or government, whether "capitalist" or "socialist" in orientation, can create a prosperous state on the basis of an essentially agricultural economy without taking into account the interests and aspirations of the producers. Those who have tried have found that while it is possible to impoverish peasant producers or to repress them politically, it is not possible to force them to produce for the state when the government offers too little in return. . . . This book has shown that in Guinea the policies of the party/state and the relationships of the government and international agencies toward peasant producers form institutional barriers to increases in peasant production (Galli and Jones, 1987:187).

We blamed the Guinean situation largely on its leaders' choice of an overly ambitious and inappropriate development model, which they hoped to realize through a centralized, undemocratic, developmental state. The same might have been said about Mozambique. Writing in 2002, Malyn Newitt also scored the newly independent Mozambican government for the socio-economic model it adopted, for failure to win "popular support for its policies" and, most importantly, for its resort to "repression as a means of achieving its objectives" (2002:199).

After independence, Mozambican leaders had embarked upon a Faustian project to industrialize and socialize rural areas. They created giant state farms, moved people off their lands into communal villages, and promoted cooperatives. The state farms consumed most of the resources allocated to agriculture leaving the villages and cooperatives without necessary investments or services.

1

Much of the infrastructure that was put in place suffered from the ravages of war and a lack of maintenance. Forced to abandon their original vision and to liberalize both state and economy, Mozambican leaders have still not established the infrastructure and support necessary to allow its largely rural population to realize its potential. The communications systems or credit facilities to bring into being a unified national market are still lacking. Imports feed southern regions of the country and, despite a vaunted economic recovery, Mozambique, like Guinea, is heavily dependent upon international development assistance for budget support, investment, as well as advice.

The purpose of this book is not, however, to draw comparisons between the two countries or to rehash old arguments but, instead, to suggest ways of bringing rural Mozambicans into political and economic decision making. This would, I believe, set the stage for the adoption of a model of development closer to the aspirations and needs of the majority of people and thus make it more easily realizable and sustainable.

Part 1 is an attempt to understand past and present social, economic, and political conditions in the Mozambican countryside by tracing the archival and oral histories of four rural settlements located in the northern, central, and southern regions of Mozambique. Part 1 can be read as a defense of what Newitt, quoting David Beach, has called the "little society" (1995 and 2002:186). In Mozambique these are the small and not-so-small rural settlements led by lineage-based dynasties. Remarkable has been their flexibility, resilience and, consequently, survival through precolonial and colonial conquest and postcolonial repression and warfare. This signified a measure of integrity and cohesion (in current terms, social capital) that I suggest should not be overlooked in the political as well as economic reconstruction of the country. However I do not confine my argument simply to these particular "communities."

Part 2 is an overt argument for including rural peoples, however organized, in decision making through a decentralization of government and the planning process. The argument is based upon the political debate on these topics within Mozambique since the 1990s and upon personal experience with participatory planning around the country in the late 1990s. Research into the histories of four communities as well as involvement with about twenty-five communities in a type of decentralized planning helped me deepen as well as extend Jones's and my argument.

A word about how this came about. When I arrived in Mozambique in 1991 a war of destabilization turned civil war was still in progress. Approximately 40 percent of the total population was displaced both inside and outside the country. Refugees crowded the accessible areas of Mozambique. The task that brought me as a government adviser was a project within the National Planning Commission to refocus government planning on social as well as economic needs, including safety nets for the poor and vulnerable. Since the war was directly responsible for throwing millions of people into untenable situations, the first order of government business had to be to end the war and facilitate the movement of people back to their homes and lands. Planning, under these circumstances, consisted of trying to help orient government ministries and international agencies to spend hundreds of millions of dollars on resettlement and reconstruction. However, the reality on the ground was that most of the displaced persons moved spontaneously when they were certain of security in the countryside, *with hardly any outside help.*

This book is a record of two migrations: the physical resettlement of a number of rural communities after the end of the war and the psychological migration of a few urban elites away from centralized planning. In the early 1990s, planning in Mozambique was basically understood as physical planning, the organization and development of space and infrastructures, a conception that permeated both the National Commission and the then recently created Institute for Rural Development (INDER). INDER's mission was to supervise the implementation of the rural rehabilitation projects sponsored by international donors. It somewhat complemented the National Planning Commission by having a local as well as national focus. In its early years, INDER also shared some of the personnel of the Institute of Physical Planning, nominally under the commission. In the 1980s, these physical planners had been instrumental in designing and orienting the government's communal villages. Reflecting a similar bureaucratic-technical approach, INDER organized a department of regional planning.

In 1994, I left the National Planning Commission to join INDER. As soon as the security and logistical situation permitted, INDER teams went into as many districts as possible in every one of the ten provinces in order to assess the process of resettlement. From 1995 onward, my colleagues and I visited many dozens of rural communities under the auspices of the World Bank, the International Fund for Agricultural Development, the United Nation's Children's Fund (UNICEF), French Cooperation, the Norwegian Development Agency (NORAD), among others. Using rapid rural appraisal and participatory appraisal techniques, we collected basic information and oral histories, personal and collective, from peoples all over Mozambique. In three of these donor-sponsored programs, we began something new, we began to ask people their needs and preferences, specifically where and how to organize small projects to meet their needs. In other words, we asked people to help us help them plan their space. Chapter 7 describes this informal planning process *and its limitations* in detail. The psychological migration of

INDER became complete when it abandoned the department of regional planning, along with other departments, and reorganized itself around rural priorities identified in the field and by the new head of the agency. Part 2 of the book stems from this experience.

The more I learned about rural Mozambicans the more I wanted to learn. I urged INDER to undertake complementary historical research both in the interest of deepening its field experience and as a way of buttressing its arguments on appropriate government policy. However, we could not find a donor to sponsor collective research. Chapters 1–4 are the result of my own personal research on four of the rural communities that we visited. My only criteria for choosing these communities were cultural dissimilarity and location, in the north, central, and southern regions. Most of my own field work had been in Zambézia but I eventually decided not to research Macua or Lomwé groups because of the excellent existing literature, including the works of Allen J. Isaacman (1972), Malyn Newitt (1973, 1995), Vail and White (1980), Christian Geffray (1990), and Shubi Lugemalila Ishemo (1995), among many others. I owe much to their writing and enthusiasm about rural Mozambicans but my greatest debt is to António Sopa, Gerhard Liesegang, David Hedges, Eduardo Medeiros, José Negrão, and Yussuf Adam. Because of their and others' work, I chose to research two little-known and two better-known peoples.

There is a need to change the perceptions of and discourse on rural peoples in Mozambique where it is common currency to use the term *traditional* in reference to their social organization. Strictly speaking, there are no traditional in the sense of stagnant, backward societies nor have there ever been. The story of its peoples is the search for better land, trade, and economic opportunities of all sorts. Theirs is a history of continual migrations and transformations. Yao leaders turned themselves from agriculturalists into remarkable organizers of trade, both of ivory and human beings. In the process they became Muslim and defended their people from Portuguese adventurers and British missionaries with all the means at hand, including combat and, after military defeat, collaboration and sabotage. This is recorded in chapter 1.

Gorongosa peoples (chapter 2) were elephant hunters turned farmers and, when they were finally supported by colonialism, they became producers of noteworthy quantities of cotton and maize. The Chaiva people (chapter 3) were avid followers of the Gaza empire and, through male migration to South African mines, transformed themselves into cattle owners. At first forced into cotton cultivation, Chaiva women became the most productive of their area. The people of Maputo (chapter 4) organized and reorganized themselves from elephant hunting to become the key traders between South African societies and Europeans. They also turned their mine earnings into cattle wealth. Chapter 5 gives a very general account of how twenty-eight communities presented themselves to INDER colleagues and myself during the participatory planning of resettlement projects. Chapters 1–5 (part 1) are, therefore, a record of the adaptability of rural peoples and social structures even when under the attack of conquerors, planners, and "developers" who were ever ready to grab and/or organize their living spaces.

That the assault on rural lands and institutions continues becomes clear in part 2. It is, however, not exclusive to Mozambique. The rural enclosure that began in what Immanuel Wallerstein (1975) called the long sixteenth century is now a global phenomenon. Sixty percent of the world's population is now counted as urban. Among sociologists, there are several types of response. The first takes "de-agrarianization" for granted.[1] Some who take this view feel urbanization is the basic human condition of the third millennium.[2] In this discourse, there is little room for any defense of rurality.

The second view—vociferously articulated at the Tenth World Congress of Rural Sociology held in 2000—was expressed as a worry that soon there will be no more people in rural areas to study. Some took a proactive stance urging social scientists to insist that governments and planners of all kinds stop action in order to get to know and listen to rural communities before consigning them to the rubbish heap of history.[3]

A third view sees the penetration of rural areas by nonagricultural activities, such as tourism, environmental management, processing of products, production of crafts, and so on as blurring the classical distinction between rural and urban spaces (Marsden, 1990). The following pages show that Mozambicans themselves blur these distinctions by seeking economic opportunities wherever these are present. Rural Mozambicans do not shirk the marketplace because they have a predisposed peasant or otherwise defined nature. Their struggle is not against globalization or commoditization as such but rather the current lack of opportunities to participate in global processes on reasonable terms. Moreover, they insist upon a measure of control over investment in their areas.

A long-time observer of rural societies, Bartra (2000) feels that, for the first time in human history, there does not seem to be any role for small-scale rural cultivators, not even the time-honored one of exploitation. Nevertheless, in what might be seen as one of the contradictions of global capitalism, production possibilities exist for some small-scale farmers. The question is whether Mozambican producers are in a position to take advantage of such openings as the market for high-value crops. Are such niches even made known to them?

As shall be seen in the following chapters, small-scale Mozambican cultivators have historically been underestimated as producers and have taken second place to larger-scale agriculture in the minds of economists, agronomists, and government officials. Bowen (2000) also makes this point. The potentialities of agro-ecology have not been seriously considered, studied, or explained to producers. On the other hand, in a kind of time warp, the government (and international agribusiness) sponsors Norman Borlaug to prepare a package of "improved" seeds and chemical fertilizers, pesticides, and so on in the center of the country in a renewed version of the "green revolution" for Africa. Producers have their own responses: Manica farmers take the package and use it for what suits them best, in an effort to make the best of a situation beyond their control.[4] Instead of being treated as partners in experimentation, they are reduced to sabotage. Part 1 shows that since colonial times this was one of the only alternatives open to Mozambicans. Part 2 is about changing these circumstances.

Another seeming contradiction of so-called globalization opens a possible avenue for change. This is the heralded renaissance of local life. "Globalisation not only pulls upwards, it pushes downwards, creating new pressures for local autonomy. The American sociologist Daniel Bell expresses this very well when he says that the nation becomes too small to solve the big problems, but also too large to solve the small ones" (Anthony Giddens, first Reith Lecture, 1999). In Mozambique, the debate on local autonomy, opened in the late 1980s, focused on the creation of municipalities and district governments. In the late 1990s, the government offered the possibility for thirty-three urbanized areas across the country to municipalize but stopped short of extending the process to districts. Chapter 6 reviews the climate for decentralization because of its relevance to the issue of political, social, and economic participation for rural as well as urban peoples. The challenge for Mozambicans is to discover an articulation that will allow for direct civic participation of both rural and urban peoples.

Robert Putnam (1996) offers the model of "civic community." His objective was to explain the significant differences he found in the institutional performance of Italian regional governments. His definition of institutional performance depends upon a liberal construction of governance whereby social demands are made known, through political interaction, to government that then decides and implements public policy. In order to explain why regional governments in northern and central Italy performed better, that is, were more responsive to citizen demands, than those in southern Italy, Putnam refers to the civic experience of the medieval city-states of northern and central Italy and the autocratic domination of southern Italy under the Normans. For him, the former were founded upon equality of status and power and included almost everyone in decision making, while the latter was founded on a hierarchical society that excluded the overwhelming majority.

For Putnam, these medieval "starting points," conditioned the differing responses of contemporary regional governments.

It might be argued that Putnam's reasoning ignores significant ruptures in the historical process in Italy. Greater civic participation in northern and central Italy probably has as much if not more to do with the selective modernization instigated by the Italian government after unification and the reaction of civil society actors to industrialization in the late nineteenth and early twentieth centuries than with the medieval experience. (See Gramsci, 1987, for example.) Putnam's original contribution, however, lies in making people think about the social conditions and institutional arrangements that promote inclusion and participation, which I try to do in part 2.

Judith Tendler's arguments (1997) are also germane. She sees a role for central government in promoting good governance at local levels. In a limited and inconclusive way, INDER took upon itself a similar role as described in chapter 7. Tendler's description of what motivated local Brazilian officials to move closer to their rural constituents and improve services has pertinence for the local planning experiences, sponsored not only by INDER but a number of agencies, recounted in chapters 7, 8, and 9. Nevertheless, Gramsci's analysis of the southern question in Italy and his exposition of how to bring about an articulation between north and south, urban and rural, offers greater insight and support for the arguments in chapters 10 and 11 on institutional relationships to promote civic participation and some local autonomy. If, as Mamdani avers, "peasant communities are constructed and reconstructed in practice through social struggles," then the recommendations of chapters 10 and 11 can be read as opening the possibility for rural peoples to reclaim control over their living spaces in a more propitious environment than the present one (1996:205).

Anthropological and other methodologies can be helpful in opening a sort of dialogue between urban elites with rural groups but little more. (See Chambers, 1983, 1997; Blackburn and Holland, 1998.) Since the devastating war of the 1980s, a large number of organizations have used rapid rural appraisal and participatory appraisal techniques with Mozambican communities, and chapter 8 surveys a number of the more positive experiences of the late 1990s. Just as the INDER experiments, most did not lead to empowerment. Participatory rural appraisal techniques are not designed to move people to *struggle*, that is, from passive to active resistance.

The example of the cooperatives with which Bowen worked in 1982 and 1983 was an important example of struggle. Awareness of their needs and interests and group identity enabled them to leap from dependency on the government to defiance of its price policies by selling produce at market prices.

The decision enabled them to cover their costs and have savings as well. Nevertheless, this was the action of a relatively privileged group in the 1980s context of Mozambique. Self-awareness and engagement in civic matters have, historically, been the role of upper and middle rural classes in the promotion of their own self-interests. Thus one emancipatory path for rural peoples is differentiation and a struggle focused on *individual* rights. The debate in Mozambique over individual property titles has this in view. The setting up of consultative councils incorporating "traditional" authorities, civil society leaders, and government officials at the district level of state administration could also open this path in rural areas. In chapter 10, however, I advocate another path—that of direct democracy—whereby rural communities decide and administer certain of their own affairs at subdistrict levels. If rural peoples were also able to elect district government officials, this would put them on the same civic footing as urban peoples.

Mamdani would object: for him, this would represent an incomplete democratization. He cites a number of examples of states, including Uganda and Libya, where limited local autonomy coexists with authoritarianism at national levels of government. In the Mozambican context it is unrealistic to wait for revolution at top levels of government in order to proceed with democratization. Nor has a top-down approach worked. It produced apathy: in the 1998 municipal elections only 15 percent of the registered urban voters bothered to vote in the first local elections.

The need to build from the bottom up comes from absence at central level of a mass organization defending rural community interests. It is clear that the ruling party, *Frente da Libertação de Moçambique* (FRELIMO) as a party long ago abandoned the model of "the institutions of popular participation" initiated in the liberated zones during the war for independence (Bowen, 2000:50). It is far from clear that the major opposition party, the National Resistance Movement (RENAMO), represents rural societies even though it claims to do so, while the country's most advanced agricultural cooperative, the *União Geral das Cooperativas* (General Union of Cooperatives), has more economic than political pretensions and the *União Nacional dos Camponeses* (National Peasants Union) has grave organizational problems.

Contemporary social conditions in Mozambique indicate that a more basic starting point for stimulating civic participation and organization is the life space of rural groups, first in villages or localities, then in administrative posts and so on, preferably though not necessarily in close collaboration with the lower levels of government authority. Implied in my recommendations is a concept of politics distinct from Putnam's liberal notion of governance, closer to what in Portuguese is called *trabalho de base* or grass roots organizing. Orlando Fals Borda (1987) showed that once rural communities in Latin America had resolved basic internal problems including that of group decision making they reached out to build alliances and even national social movements. In Brazil, the experience of *comunidades de base* or base communities is instructive because they were instrumental in the birth of a number of urban and rural social movements including the national *Movimento Sem Terra* (Landless Movement).

In chapter 10 I suggest that lower level state officials might help play the role of "organic intellectuals" to stimulate rural groups to engage in self-organization and development. For this to happen, however, officials at both district and provincial levels of administration need to be involved along with "traditional" and civil society leaders in awareness training, the outlines of which are discussed in the chapter. In chapter 11 I point to the civil society movement organized around the reform of the Land Law that followed a similar strategy.

The need to organize from lower levels also arises from central government's perception of rural society, which parallels that of its colonial predecessor. Because many Mozambican rural societies, especially in the north and center of the country—the most productive agricultural areas—are still primarily engaged in agricultural activities and their basic cohesion revolves around kinship, religion, and a more or less vertical gerontocratic structure, they are often seen as premodern and therefore considered atavistic. A traditional-modern or rural-urban dualism is frequent in the discourses of Mozambique's politicians and donors. The problem is not simply one of perception or discourse but also policy. The Ministry of Agriculture and Rural Development excludes small-scale rural producers from major agricultural development programs, such as those involving irrigation works. While the absorption of INDER into the Ministry, in 2000, seems at least to have stimulated an internal policy debate, the government still lacks a development strategy that encompasses the majority of producers.

The Ministry of State Administration also practices a kind of apartheid: as already mentioned, urbanized areas are included in its program of municipalization while rural areas are left under central administration. The recent recognition of "traditional" authorities as representatives of rural societies—formalized in the Decree 15/2000—is not the same as the decentralization of responsibilities or the opening of spaces for community self-management but is much more in line with the co-optation of local rulers in the colonial sense:

> the decree defines "community authorities" as "traditional chiefs and other leaders recognised as such by their respective local communities." Local state bodies are expected to articulate with community authorities and to "ask their

opinions on how best to mobilise and organise the participation of local communities in the realisation of plans and programmes for economic, social and cultural development." The decree goes on to say that "the objective of this collaboration between local state bodies and community leaders is the mobilisation and organisation of the population for their participation in implementation of local development tasks." Collaboration with community authorities is to be in a wide range of areas (European Parliamentarians for Southern Africa, no. 25:4).

Note well that the decree says nothing about deliberation or decision making but emphasizes mobilization for implementation of public tasks, true to the colonial style of administration, amply described in part 1.

Until recently, the Ministry of Plan and Finances (which absorbed the National Planning Commission in 1995) did not consider small-scale producers as economic agents. Ministry officials characterized the smallholder economy as "informal" and excluded its production from the national accounts. This exclusion ignored the integration of members of Mozambique's rural societies in the national economy (as workers in national industry, on national plantations, as informal economic agents in peri-urban settings), in regional enterprises (as miners and illegal immigrants), and even in the global economy (as cashew growers and cotton growers).

The government's disregard for the smallholder economy was most clearly seen in 1996 when it badly let down Mozambican producers. Many farmers were celebrating their first abundant harvest after the disruption of civil war and four to five years of drought but they were not able to realize any profit from their backbreaking work. Echoes of this are found in chapter 3. Some background is necessary to appreciate the situation.

The flight of the majority of small colonial traders during and after the war for independence left the countryside without a secure marketing system. The postcolonial government initially tried to substitute state marketing for private trade without much success. Under a structural adjustment regime, it slowly began to liberalize commerce and equally slowly itinerant traders began to replace the more or less organized colonial system of local shops linked with wholesale traders. In the 1990s, a government-sponsored Cereals Institute functioned as a buyer of last resort at a minimum price. When they could obtain credit, its outlets bought grain from small and intermediate traders. Nevertheless, because of bad debts and the general lack of agricultural credit, the outlets mainly did not have access to sufficient credit to keep pace with demand and, even when credit was forthcoming, it often arrived late in the season. This situation was particularly damaging to small traders who bought early, had few storage facilities for crops, and depended on a quick turnover in order to continue buying from producers.

At the beginning of the agricultural season in 1995–1996, the government announced a minimum price of 1,500 *meticais* (approximately 15 cents at the time) per kilogram of white maize, the staple food. This was a reasonable price and raised farmer expectations. However, when it became clear that all of southern Africa had had regular and abundant rainfall and that there would be a bumper crop in the region as a whole, the government decided in mid-season that it could not afford to support the announced price. The result was chaos. In surplus-producing northern and central regions, prices plummeted to 500 *meticais* and less. Farmers were in despair as this price did not cover their costs. Many boycotted the market. In the next year, agents from the Malawian State Marketing Board appeared as active buyers in northern regions of the country and drove white maize prices up to around 1,000 *meticais* per kilo. However, this only slightly improved the unfavorable terms of trade and did nothing to ameliorate the lack of readily available consumer goods in rural areas.

The disappearance of local shops meant that people had to take long, arduous trips to the nearest town with basket loads on their heads or, in the case of the more prosperous, on their bicycles. The prices received for produce and those paid for goods were extremely prejudicial. The deficient marketing system was officially recognized and commented upon in the agricultural season of 1999–2000 (Mozambique-On-Line, 28 November 2000).

Given this unfavorable political-economic context and a discourse that demeaned them, it was no wonder that rural peoples lacked appreciation of their latent force. While rich in multiple identities as individuals, they did not realize their potential as a group. The histories collected by INDER teams from 1995–1999 record cooperation within family groupings and conflict among rival groupings at community or inter-community levels (chapter 5). They found high levels of cooperation among members of a religious group, and non-cooperation based on exclusion between religious groups within the same community. They found trust and reciprocity (social capital) as demonstrated by local rotating funds but a refusal to join producer cooperatives. In general, colonization, the almost continual state of war from the 1960s onward for the peoples in northern and central Mozambique, as well as discrimination in policy, practice, and discourse, have reduced rural societies across the country to minimal forms of social organization.

In Mozambique, the historical battleground of inclusion-exclusion is land. Land is what Mozambicans identify with and fight over and it is the issue that most clearly pits the interests of politicians and government officials against those of rural peoples. In the recent reform of land law, legislators refused to cede state control over land either to a private property regime or to community control. Community management was, however, conceded under certain conditions, one of which being recognition by the cadastral agency. The final chapter discusses the land question as it is the ultimate battleground for the assertion not only of rights and citizenship but also identity and, finally, power and authority.

A Word on Source Materials

Apart from the surveys undertaken by INDER colleagues and myself, my other major source of information has been the Historical Archives of Mozambique, and consists of colonial company reports, mission reports by colonial inspectors, district administrator reports, and so on. This has meant looking at peoples' histories through the eyes of oppressors, which requires being sensitive to the notions of "we" and "they" and to what was not reported as well as what was reported. It also means trying to discern what part of the colonizer's perceptions became internalized in the colonized's self-image.

One of the interesting lessons from these records is that the longer an administrator stayed in one district, the more aware and sympathetic he became to the situation of its constituents. The "fellow-feeling" that developed was in a real sense the colonization of the colonizer by the colonized but it also had to do with the frustrations of administering a territory without the necessary resources, of knowing full well the potentialities of an area and a people and not being able to see these come to fruition. It also came from an understanding, born of experience, of the injustice and counter-productivity of such practices as forced labor, beatings, and cheating. And it bore the hallmarks of the humiliation administrators felt as their proposals to change policies went unheard. As a keen observer of the recent years of Mozambican history and as a government adviser, I often felt the same helplessness. Moreover, it is uncanny the extent to which local officials today encounter the same problems: inadequate resources and infrastructure, a lack of vision especially at central level, and the inability to establish horizontal relations with rural communities because of vertical power structures and prejudice.

For a large part of colonial history in the areas chosen for study, companies governed rural Mozambique. In Niassa this was the Companhia do Niassa and in Sofala and Manica, the Companhia de Moçambique. They were licensed to rule from 1894 until 1929 in the first case and until 1942 in the latter case. The records of the Companhia do Niassa no longer exist in Mozambique whereas many records of the Companhia de Moçambique do. In regard to Maputo province, occupation and administration was only possible after 1896 and the Archives have a few administrators' reports up until the 1940s. This meant filling in a number of blanks with other source materials. Despite the often patchiness of the archival record, there is enough of a pattern in civil administration and what was called native policy to be able to make comparisons in the four areas covered by the study.

Precolonial history is another matter. Here I have relied upon the work of historians and the bits of oral history gathered in conversations with descendants of founding fathers or with elders in the settlements visited.

It was not possible to gain access to relevant primary source materials for the period 1975 to 1991. Moreover, a number of key rural informants preferred to maintain silence on this period. Bowen's work (2000), a case study of one of the more privileged rural areas in the period 1950–1984, partially fills the gap. Its focus is on FRELIMO government policies. Moreover, Bowen provides valuable insight into a much-neglected category of rural producer that she calls "the middle peasantry" but would qualify as "upper peasantry" in comparison to the majority of smallholders visited in the course of this study.[5]

The war that began in earnest in the 1980s and ended in October 1992 wrought havoc with local record keeping and meant dislocation for all of the populations visited and studied. It was a time of vivid memories many of which were full of anguish. The history of the war needs to be told from the point of view of the displaced and those who accommodated them,[6] but I made a deliberate choice to concentrate on the process of resettlement after the war and to try to understand it in the light of an albeit incomplete history. But then, information is never complete nor history ever completed. It must, however, be confronted.

Notes

1. This term appears in Deborah Fahy Bryceson, ed., *Disappearing Peasantries?* (London, ITDG Publishing, 2000), 3.

2. For example, Ladislau Dowbor, a Brazilian planner and one of the foremost proponents of decentralization in his country, made this argument in his presentation to the *Escola de Formação dos Governantes* (Local Official's Training School), Fortaleza, Ceará, 18 September 2000.

3. This was essentially José de Souza Martins' appeal in his plenary address reproduced in *Estudos Sociedade e Agricultura* 15 (October 2000): 5–12.

4. Interview, Chimoio, Manica, October 1999.

5. For a brief discussion of Bowen's terminology, see Galli, H-Net Review, 25 October 2000.

6. JoAnn McGregor (1998) does this for the people of Matutuíne district and I have relied heavily upon her material in chapter 4.

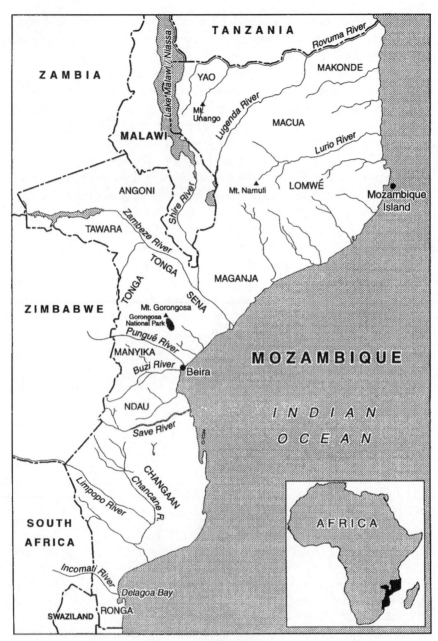

Map 1.   Some of the Major Peoples of Mozambique

PART ONE

⁓

Organizing Rural Space

Located in southern Africa, Mozambique has a coastline that extends more than two thousand kilometers along the Indian Ocean forming the country's eastern border. To the north is Tanzania and to the south, South Africa. In the northwest are Malawi and Zambia while the central-western border is with Zimbabwe. Swaziland lies to the southwest. (See map 1.) The 1997 census estimated the population at slightly over 16 million people of which 7.4 million made up its workforce. Eighty-one percent were active in agriculture, 6 percent in industry, and 13 percent in the service sector.

As in many African countries, the population is ethnically diverse with more than twenty languages spoken. Map 1 shows the general spatial location of most of the large population groups. Where these groups came from and how they got to Mozambique is hard to determine. There are few written records before the fifteenth and sixteenth centuries and oral tradition is only reliable for about one hundred years. A common hypothesis is that hunters and gatherers initially inhabited Mozambique and were displaced by a number of Bantu-speaking agricultural societies.

The history of the country can be read as a series of migrations or intrusions (invasions) depending upon one's perspective, as migrant or settler. The following chapters note the Marave expansion from what is now Malawi into northern Mozambique, the waves of Karanga (Shona) migrants from what is now Zimbabwe to the center of the country, the bands of Nguni warriors, originating in the south, that terrorized much of the country and later dominated southern regions and the succession of Muslim, Swahili, Portuguese, Afro-Portuguese, Goan, and East Asian traders who spread across the country. Natural disasters such as drought, flooding, and, as a consequence, famine as well as the general search for better opportunities motivated much of this movement.

Malyn Newitt summarizes the cultural history of the country on the eve of the Portuguese campaign for effective occupation of the country:

> In the immediate precolonial period dating from the middle of the nineteenth century the country was dominated by three powerful and expanding cultural systems; the Islamic expansion north of the Zambesi carried by the Yao and the coastal Swahili and underpinned by the slave trade; the movement of Afro-Portuguese out of the Zambesi valley in search of slaves, ivory and land; and the conquest of much of the area south of the Zambesi by the Gaza state bringing with it an overlay of Nguni military, cattle-owning culture. Although these established a kind of cultural hegemony that appeared to divide the country roughly into three zones, there were always underlying survivals of past regimes and older cultures which made Mozambique a palimpsest, resisting simple description (2002:187).

The next four chapters look in some depth at the recorded experiences of four communities. Kalanje, in Sanga district in northernmost Niassa province, is an example of the Yao, the first cultural system noted. (See map 2.) Kanda in Gorongosa district in central Sofala province, and Chaiva in Mossurize district in Manica province, were founded by different waves of the Karanga peoples. The impact of the Afro-Portuguese expansion was felt by Kanda while the influence of the Gaza "empire" is an intimate part of Chaiva's history and that of Massoane in Matutuíne district in southern Maputo province.

Continuities and Discontinuities

Two important considerations should be kept in mind in reading the stories that follow. The first is the *contrast* between pre-colonial and Portuguese rule. The powerful systems just described normally left subject populations—the so-called little society—to govern themselves in their own territories. While those subjected might assimilate to the dominant culture, it also happened that the "invaders" adopted local customs or that a fusion occurred between cultures.

When it became effective, Portuguese rule was dramatically different and, in many respects, destabilizing. In the process of occupation, the Portuguese adopted the tactic of "divide and rule." Whenever a centrally organized kingdom resisted, its territories were divided into smaller units and those who had paid tribute to a paramount ruler were recognized as chiefs (*régulos*, later designated as *regedores*). Whenever any ruler or chief gave the Portuguese administration or its surrogates trouble, he was beaten, fined, jailed, or deposed and a Portuguese-appointed person put in his place.

In order to subjugate Mozambican communities, the administration took away their sovereignty. Manuel Gomes Amaral, a former administrator in Yao territories, put the matter clearly: "The extension of Portuguese law to the country altered the situation; the Sultans [which is how the Yao termed their leaders] lost their rights of sovereignty as well as their land rights but maintained their authority with respect to customs and norms, within reasonable limits (1990:16)." Chapters 1 to 4 also show how each of the four rural societies was reduced from self-management and/or self-government to submission. As a reaction to the loss of sovereignty as well as other colonial impositions including taxation and forced labor, many families fled into the bush or across borders. Chapters 1 to 4 record massive migrations that had a devastating impact on population growth. In three of the four areas, the effect was temporary although at times long-lasting. For Niassa province, described in the next chapter, the result has been depopulation.

Portuguese rule reached all the way into individual households by extracting labor from both males and females, unsettling gender divisions of labor and placing unduly heavy burdens on female workloads. In order to comply with work obligations and taxes, males absented themselves for months, even years from the household. Females became entirely responsible for subsistence production, on top of which administrators placed the obligation to produce commercial crops in some areas. This is most clearly seen in chapter 3 in relation to Chaiva females and cotton cropping.

The second consideration has to do with what might be called the colonial legacy, that is, the several aspects of colonial rule that not only influenced the political-economic destinies of the four communities described in the following chapters but also continue to affect Mozambique as a whole. If *contrast* characterized precolonial and colonial rule, then *continuity* marks certain aspects of colonial and postcolonial practice. The first aspect has to do with the already noted regionalism of the economy and society. Portuguese "rule" reinforced this regionalism, in part, because Portugal was initially unable to govern the whole of Mozambique. Consequently Portugal gave the Niassa Company the northern part of the country to administer (chapter 1). The Mozambique Company received the central territory of Manica and Sofala (chapters 2 and 3). Until 1929, Portugal only directly ruled southern parts of the country and a few other areas (Tete and Bàrué). Portuguese direct administration is described in chapter 4.

Although there were many similarities in these different administrations, which are underscored in the narrative, the three regions continued as separate areas even after Portugal was able to assume direct administration of them all. "The isolation of the various regions from each other was accentuated by the location of the capital city in the extreme south in a spit of land that is virtually an enclave in South Africa and in most respects belongs to the communications system and economic structure of that country" (Newitt, 2002:186). Taken together the four chapters show an imbalance in the economic development of the country with southern areas in a privileged position. Niassa, a prime agricultural area, is still the least favored province in the country while the area around the capital, Maputo, continues as the area most favored by investment.

Regionalism continues to have both an economic and political impact in the country today. For example, the social bases of the leadership and basic constituencies of the two major political forces, FRELIMO and RENAMO, reflect the split between south and northern and central regions.

The second aspect also has to do with Portugal's initial inability to field enough people to man a colonial service. Until the 1930s, Portugal left colonial administration in the hands of adventurers, traders, and military men, as well as companies. People came to the colony to make their fortunes. The following chapters give many examples of the predatory nature of the ruling companies and also individual officials and administrators, but chapter 3 illustrates most clearly the cupidity of the Mozambique Company and some of its personnel. One important consequence of this lack of capacity was the need to make tax-farming arrangements with local people. Tax farming turned into an insidious form of co-optation of local rulers. In 2000, tax farming resurfaced under the FRELIMO government just as "corruption" became widespread after the economy was liberalized. These points are taken up in part 2.

In the second period of colonial rule, when, in the 1930s and 1940s, Portugal was ready to assume direct control over Mozambique, it adopted a highly centralized administrative style and eventually instituted central economic planning in the colonies. As already noted in the Introduction, FRELIMO, in its initial period of rule, adopted this style of rule although, in this instance, the influence of its Eastern European allies was undoubtedly stronger than Portugal's. Bernhard Weimer (2002) makes the point that one of the major reasons for the spread of opposition to FRELIMO after independence was this highly centralized style of government. Chapter 4 shows that even some local FRELIMO officials resisted, along with their rural constituents, some of the central government's policies. When, after the most recent war, FRELIMO began to modify government to allow for a measure of local autonomy in urban areas, rural areas were left under a centrally controlled administration. This was true to the pre-1961 colonial legacy, a point that is also discussed in part 2.

The fourth legacy touches upon one of the most ambitious of Portugal's rural policies: the attempt to mold Mozambicans into a kind of Portuguese peasantry by moving dispersed rural people into village settlements. In certain parts of the country such as Niassa and upper Zambézia, the intention was to bring commodity producers closer to access roads and markets. In other parts, people were encouraged to move onto plantations to serve as a labor force. In still other parts, settlements were part of development schemes established near irrigation works and so on. Finally, the Portuguese forcibly moved people to make way for major hydroelectric schemes and, in the end, to remove them from FRELIMO influence. Chapter 1 provides the most vivid example of the negative impact of this policy upon the social organization of rural societies. The establishment of *aldeias comunais* (communal villages) also became one of the cornerstones of the first phase of FRELIMO rule. Here, too, the influence of the Soviet Union and Tanzania was certainly crucial but Portugal had set a precedent and FRELIMO took over many of the same village settlements left by the colonial government. Opposition to this policy made evident before and during the most recent war was crucial to the government's decision to revoke the obligation to live in communal villages. This opposition is most clearly seen in Chaiva's and Massoane's stories (chapters 3 and 4).

Taken together, chapters 1 through 5 vividly illustrate how rapidly rural people responded to economic opportunities when and wherever these were opened to them. They also show a collective resentment of FRELIMO's failure to provide incentives for small commodity producers and traders, one of the most evident *discontinuities* between late colonial and postcolonial rule.

On Terminology

Most of the historical information on Mozambican rural peoples is from Portuguese explorers and officials who often adopted names used by such other "intruders" as the Maraves and Nguni. Names also changed from author to author, and from place to place. I have generally followed the names and spellings of places and people in current use in Mozambique.

When I use the term "rural community," I am referring to a self-defined aggregate of people living in a commonly recognized space and having a decision-making structure. "Commonly recognized" means simply that neighbors more or less agree on boundaries.[1]

Note

1. In a perceptive critique of community-based approaches to development, Woodhouse, Bernstein, and Hulme questioned three common assumptions: "that a 'community' is readily defined; that it will produce consensus rather than conflict over the use of local resources; and that the community's knowledge is sufficient to manage their environment" (2000:14). In the following pages, it will become obvious that "communities" as such are in constant flux. For this reason, preconceived and static notions are useless. In regard to the issue of consensus, the fact that communities have decision-making mechanisms means that decisions are possible but not necessarily on the basis of consensus. Conflict is an intimate part of community life. When conflict is serious, groups break away and form new "communities." The conversations with the Chaiva people in chapter 3 illustrate most clearly people's eagerness for outside "knowledge" in managing their environment.

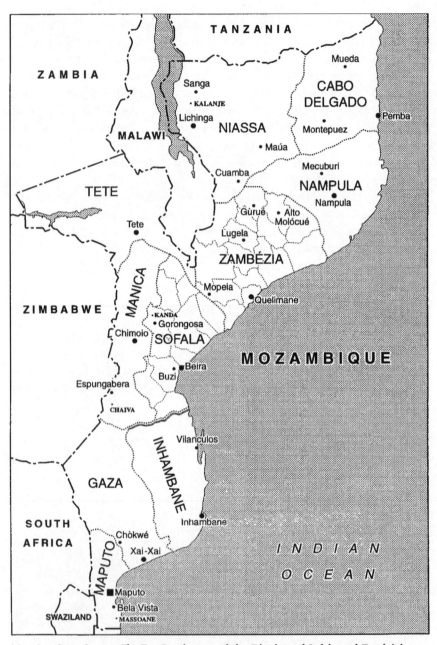

Map 2. State Spaces: The Ten Provinces and the Districts of Sofala and Zambézia

CHAPTER ONE

∽

In the Shadow of Unango Mountain

The northern Yao peoples, to which Kalanje pertains, were a dominant force in the pre-colonial ivory trade. After gold, ivory was the second most sought after commodity from Mozambique. Ivory was in great demand in the Far East and both northern and southern Mozambique exported elephant tusks, rhinoceros horns, and hippopotamus teeth. Many peoples were involved: in the north, the Maraves facilitated trade from its source in Tete to the port areas where Portuguese traders took over.[1] While the Portuguese feared the Maraves, they traded freely with them and sent ivory traders through their lands in an effort to keep them from migrating southward.

The Yao were known to be involved in the ivory trade as early as 1736[2] when a French trader noted their presence along the coast, but there is speculation that the Yao became involved in long-distance trade even before the arrival of the Portuguese in the late fifteenth and early sixteenth centuries (Amaral, 1990:212). It can only be stated with certainty that Yao caravans with as many as one thousand porters became important in the ivory trade north of the Zambeze river and that they eventually eclipsed the Marave traders.[3]

Origins and Political Relationships

The Yao are known as an Eastern Bantu people, a matrilineal society that depended economically on shifting agriculture, hunting, iron working, and trading (Hafkin, 1973:76). There is one seventeenth century text by a

Portuguese explorer, Gaspar Bocarro, who traveled from Tete to Kilwa and described a people he called Nguru who may have been the forebears of the Yao.[4] These people were living in relatively extensive population groups rather than in small clans. On the basis of this evidence Liesegang thinks that the Yao did not share the clanic structure of their neighbors, the Macua and Nyanja, but rather formed regional groupings, which took their names from the mountains where they lived.[5] (See map 1.) By the time explorers and missionaries reached them in the nineteenth century, the Yao were living in dense populations governed by powerful ruling families.

Most of the written records on the Yao date mainly from the nineteenth and twentieth centuries and many are memoirs and diaries of English explorers and missionaries, such as David Livingstone. These people were part of the British effort to make inroads in Yao territory through the establishment of Anglican mission stations. Sensitive to this British challenge to what it considered Portuguese territory, Portugal sent a number of expeditions to try to convince local chiefs to accept Portuguese sovereignty. Later, there were a number of exploratory and military expeditions. While the reports of these various expeditions abounded in the names and locations of the principal rulers of the time, there is little detail on the people themselves. One of the first descriptive texts was written by a Yao, an Anglican priest, Yohanna Abdallah, and published in 1919.

"We know little in detail about Yao leadership until the 19th century, when a whole new generation of Yao trading chiefs emerged to establish the dynastic lines which dominated subsequent Yao history" (Alpers, 1969:407). Abdallah's narrative relates the founding of two of the most important ruling families, the Makanjila and Mataka dynasties. Even though Abdallah was stationed in Unango and worked among the people who are the focus of this chapter, he has relatively little to say about the major dynasties there, Kalanje and Nampanda, probably because they were relatively minor in comparison with Makanjila and Mataka.[6]

Trading, raiding, and military prowess were essential ingredients in the rise of these dynasties (Alpers, 1969; Abdallah, 1983; Ishemo, 1995). Abdallah also mentions the importance of travel in the prestige of chiefs. Trade goods from India probably induced them to organize the caravans to the coast for which they became famous. At first they brought hoes, tobacco, and skins to exchange for salt, cloth, and beads; then they traded ivory and, by the nineteenth century, slaves. Still, the origins of long-distance trade among the Yao are lost.

Abdallah suggests that adverse environmental conditions facilitated the rise of Makanjila and Mataka, specifically drought. The first drought in 1831 sent Macuas into Yao territory in search for food, then in 1845, a drought turned the Yao into raiders attacking their Yao neighbors for sustenance (1983:60 ff). The Yao also suffered attacks by Nguni peoples[7] which some say were responsible for their militarization and subsequent transformation into great slave raiders (Liesegang, n.d., chapter 3; Ishemo, 1995). Weaker chiefs submitted to the stronger and some even sought their protection.[8] Abdallah emphasizes the fierce aggressiveness of the greatest of the dynasties, Mataka, who began his ascent by raiding his neighbors for food and then slaves (1983:82 ff). He instilled great fear in them and his name still inspires awe: this was clearly heard in a taped interview with a Unango schoolteacher made in 1981.[9]

The acquisition of slaves added greatly to the numbers of people in the followings of the dynastic chiefs, to their armies, caravans, and even their immediate families. Whereas male slaves were often sold, women could be married, sometimes to the chief himself, and their children were adopted, thereby strengthening the patrilineal lineage to the detriment of matrilineal organization (Alpers, 1969).

The various upheavals forced people into even denser concentrations and led to undue population pressure on the land, yet another reason for frequent moves. One of the more stable territories of the Yao, Unango also suffered a number of attacks and population pressure (Peirone quoted by Wegher, 1995:113, 114).

Trade introduced the Yao to many innovations, such as fruit and coconut trees, rectangular houses with verandas, the construction of boats with wooden planks, the use of Arab secretaries, Arab dress, the Swahili language and custom, and Islam. Originally the changes in habit were confined to ruling families but later became commonplace. Trade also introduced new crops, new carpentry techniques and a written language but, as Liesegang reminds us, a certain underdevelopment also occurred. The importation of cloth and iron goods made weaving and iron-working all but disappear as important skills from 1850 onward (Liesegang, n.d.: chapter 5).

According to Alpers, the rule of the dynastic chiefs was fluid. No formal territorial administration developed; no tribute was collected[10] and there were no standing armies. *Local rule continued in the hands of lineage headmen.* The headman had both judicial and religious functions: he and the elders tried all cases; he conducted initiations with his eldest sister and he made offerings to his ancestral spirits.[11]

The paramount chief was in a constant struggle with headmen over followers[12] and it shall be seen that this struggle continues today between Che Kalanje and Headman Ilinga and within Ilinga itself. The paramount chief (known as Che) was headman for his kinsmen and lineage; he administered them and performed such religious functions as intermediary with the founding ancestors, and so on. Moreover chiefs often gave their daughters in marriage to unrelated headmen as a way of exerting control and extending their lineage.

The great Mataka developed a rudimentary three-tiered government: he placed the people he most trusted in positions of authority over lineage leaders as intermediaries. Those nephews or sons considered potential rivals found themselves in the geographical areas farthest from his court. At his court, he had a number of advisers as well as a "minister" of trade and a "minister" of defense. The two most powerful holders of the title, Mataka I and Mataka II, ruled with an iron fist. They razed and burned villages in their slave raids and did not hesitate to mutilate and kill their enemies. Abdallah talks of the cutting off of heads, castration, and even cannibalism in relation to an unsuccessful attack by Portuguese soldiers (1983:90, 100). Makanjila, the leader of the rival dynasty, was also known for his cruelty.

The Unango Peoples

The peoples of the Unango region were not only subjected to Nguni attacks but early on found themselves in a vise between the two leading dynasties. In one version, Mataka and Makanjila were in a contest to unite the Yao and each tried to subordinate as many of the other territorial chiefs as possible (Amaral, 1990). Unango, in between Muembe (the home of Mataka) and the Lake area (which Makanjila came to dominate), was in a strategic but vulnerable position. (See map 3.)

Dominated by the twin-peaked mountain of the same name, Unango's valleys and minor mountains can support a large population due to high annual rainfall (over one thousand mm), the existence of several important rivers and their affluents, and generally good soils. Mbembas from the mountain range immediately to the southwest of Unango came there between 1850 and 1860.[13]

Oral history says the Mbembas migrated because water was scarce in their mountains and also because of Nguni attacks. Since Unango was higher than Mbemba, its peaks served as a lookout, and the Mbembas camped there for a number of years. The most important chiefs of the Unango region, Kalanje, Chipango, and Nampanda, probably came from Mbemba and were of the same dynasty. In the memory of the fourth person to hold the dynastic title of Nampanda, they were all related through Nampanda's mother. Kalanje was Nampanda's nephew and Chipango was their cousin, all of them from

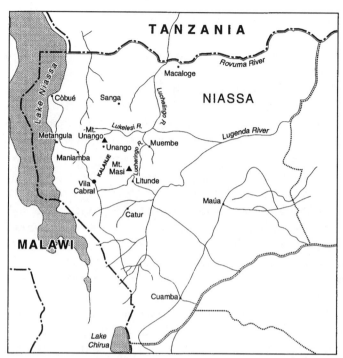

Map 3. Some Important Administrative Divisions in Niassa under Late Colonialism

the same uterine group, a primary relationship in this matrilineal society. The present holder of the Kalanje title corroborated this story (see the last section below).

The first time Abdallah mentions Kalanje and Nampanda is in regard to Makanjila's successful bid around 1870 to become dynastic ruler of the Lake area. The story was that these chiefs fed the great warrior on his way to battle near the Lake indicating that either they were under his influence or just did not want to face his aggression (Abdallah, 1983:64–67). Kalanje and Nampanda appear not to have fared any better against Mataka. In the wars to establish his hegemony, Mataka beheaded Makanjila and raided Unango. Abdallah says it was in an effort to enlarge his great city, Muembe, by taking slaves. At about this time, 1870–1880, one of the early holders of the title, Kalanje, is said to have sent Mataka a bull in homage and probably submission (Liesegang, n.d.: chapter 5). According to oral history, Mataka also attacked the Unango chiefs' caravans but the caravans were able to defend themselves.

Both Kalanje and Nampanda were active traders in ivory and slaves and oral accounts have them raiding other villages for slaves much in the same manner as Mataka. Unango was recognized on the coast as an important trading partner. Bishop Chauncy Maples, who visited Unango in 1893, noted that "Kalanje's ivory caravans are among the very largest and most important of those that pass from the lake districts to the coast. In past years, many and many a time have we fallen in with them" (1899:245).

In regard to population size, W. P. Johnson, who traveled to Unango two times in the 1880s, thought he saw as many as nine thousand dwellings which would have meant a population well over twenty thousand, but Liesegang considers this a gross overestimation and calculates it to have been in the range of ten thousand people. Perhaps the problem is the difference in period in which the two calculations were made. Johnson came during the time of Nguni raids when a number of peoples had sought refuge in Unango, including Mataka's people for a time. Liesegang's own estimation is based on an 1894 estimate when the situation had normalized, when people felt safer, had come down from the mountains and settled in the valleys.

At some point, the Unango people had to abandon the mountainsides because of soil depletion. Fields for cultivation had moved farther and farther and forestland had all but disappeared requiring women to walk four to five kilometers to the north and seven to fourteen kilometers west of the mountains for firewood (as per the accounts of Johnson and Maples). After coming down from the mountains, the peoples of Kalanje lived on the southern side of the mountain and those of Nampanda on the northern side where the third ruler, Chipango, had lands as well. There was land for everyone and no need to fix limits as there were miles of territory. Nampanda's land stretched to today's border with Tanzania while Kalanje's touched the border with what is now Lichinga district. (See map 2.) People spread out. There is no record of land disputes among these chiefs or their subordinates who headed up various subgroups of people. It was only in colonial times that boundaries were set for these territories.[14]

Probably, there were disputes over who was paramount ruler. Abdallah recounts a story of a dispute between Kalanje and Nampanda over a leopard or lion's skin. Since these skins were the symbol of chiefly authority, it may be that the disagreement was over who was supreme. In 1902, the governor of the Niassa Company reported that Nampanda tried to stage an uprising against Kalanje and so terrified the Anglican missionaries in Unango that they contacted the colonial administration. When Nampanda heard of possible intervention he fled to join Mataka, whose dynasty was in open rebellion against the colonials (Vilhena, 1905:264, 265). Liesegang, however, thinks that Nampanda, being the elder, was probably paramount at least in the beginning of their settlement in Unango. It may be that Kalanje had accumulated more wealth, slaves, and followers and became paramount by the time of the governor's report. I asked the present Che Kalanje which ruler was paramount and his answer, reported below, reconciled and put these various points of view in perspective.

Company Rule: The Companhia do Niassa

By 1906, neither Kalanje nor Nampanda opposed the advance of the Portuguese surrogate administration, the Niassa Company (Companhia do Niassa). Liesegang speculates that Father Abdallah, resident at that time in the Anglican mission and mindful of the futility of opposing the colonists, advised the course of diplomacy. Unango was made a military post. Company rule, however, meant taxation and forced labor, which caused much unrest and, in protest, emigration.

The migration of Unango people between 1906 and 1912 formed part of a massive exodus of Yao. Forever spying on the Portuguese colony, the British Admiralty calculated that forty five thousand people went to Tanzania in 1912, and one hundred thousand people to Nyasaland (Malawi) before 1919 (Neil-Tomlinson, 1977:118). According to Medeiros, the first figure refers to Mataka's followers who took flight with him after his last campaign (1997:91). Because the Niassa Yao had never been a very large group, *these migrations signified the depopulation of Niassa,* a fact that is still very much in evidence today. In Neil-Tomlinson's words, what occurred was the "complete dispersal of those large settlements of up to 5,000 people [and more] which had clustered around once powerful chiefs" (1977:118). The following chapters show that all the peoples under study followed the same pattern of massive flight during the conquest of their leaders.

Portugal ceded what are today Cabo Delgado and Niassa provinces to the Niassa Company (map 2) on the condition that it would create a viable economic and administrative infrastructure within thirty-five years. Heavily in debt to international bankers, the Portuguese government had no capital to invest in the area. (In what seems an ominous repetition of the past, the present Mozambican government ceded parts of Niassa to the Mosagrius Development Corporation and later to the MADAL Company. See below.) With over eighty thousand square miles to govern, the Niassa Company was never able to raise sufficient capital on international markets to provide investment for infrastructure. The initial capital of around four hundred thousand pounds sterling was a mere fraction of what was deemed necessary and was frittered away on speculative stock manipulation. In the thinking of the time, the key to profit making was the opening of a railway linking the coast to Lake Niassa, in order to attract outside investment in mines and agriculture. However, the cost of the railway was estimated at three million pounds sterling, not including the costs of bringing the vast area under Company rule. The most the Company was able to do in its turbulent, short life was to bring first the Macua to heel, then Mataka and finally the Makonde just before its Charter ran out in 1929. With each campaign it ruthlessly exacted a heavy and ever increasing burden of taxes on each people it forced into submission.

Taxation

In 1921, the hut tax was two *escudos*, and kept rising dramatically. In six years it had reached fifty *escudos*, and in the last year of Company rule it was eighty-five *escudos*. Some of these rises had to do with the falling value of the Portuguese currency and a diminishing number of taxpayers. To give some idea of the burden upon the population, it was estimated that a tax of fifty *escudos* was the equivalent of three month's paid labor (Neil-Tomlinson, 1977:123). The British Vice-Consul estimated that, after taxes, the population had a *per capita* disposable income of only sixpence (Neil-Tomlinson, 1977:123 and Vail, 1976:414).

The so-called hut tax was in reality a tax on all adults. Men began paying at the age of eighteen and they were expected to pay for their wives as well. Single women also had to pay. Here the burden theoretically fell on the uncle or brother. In the words of the Unango people, the taxes were at first paid in kind with maize meal (which was the form in which women paid for themselves), sorghum, goats and thatch for Company officials' huts. Later men seasonally migrated to Tanzania and Malawi to earn cash with which they could pay taxes. They worked not only on tobacco plantations in Malawi and sisal plantations in Tanzania but also as porters and bearers of merchandise, as guards, any and all odd jobs. As the tax burden increased, the time away became longer, increasing the burden of agricultural production upon women.

The Company used pernicious methods of tax collection. A British consular official noted that the tax was "collected by the simple expedient of sending out the native soldiers from the posts at collection time to round up all the women on whom they can lay their hands. The women are brought to the posts and kept there until the husbands and fathers rescue them by paying the tax" (Vail, 1976:400). This may be the situation that one of the Unango people referred to when he stated that women were the first to pay the hut tax. Only later men paid.

If a person did not have the means to pay, s/he was put into forced labor as a form of payment. According to a group of Unango elders, one type of labor consisted of carrying cargo and people from Unango to Metangula or to Macaloge. Round trip to Metangula equaled a tax chit worth twenty *escudos* but to Macaloge it was only seven and one-half *escudos*. Map 3 gives an idea of the distances involved.

Labor Conscription

While the hut tax was the major source of revenues, the Company also made money exporting male labor to the South African mines. In 1903, the Company signed a contract with the Witwatersrand Native Labour Association to supply labor for the Rand mines but by 1908 only 764 "niassas" were in the mines. The Association then took over the recruiting and the Company began an aggressive campaign. Along with growing numbers came an extraordinary rate of deaths: seventy out of every thousand workers, and, in 1913, the South African government ordered an end to recruitment in the North. The Company then exported labor to the Katanga mines, to sugar estates in Zambézia, and to Mombasa for the port development project.

Recruitment for the mines reached Unango. In the memory of some of the elders, an official they called *Abatamar* came from Pemba to register people for work on one-year contracts in the mines. However, many died. In their words, many went but few came back. Nevertheless, there were survivors among the people interviewed who had worked not only in South Africa but in Katanga and Zambia as well.

As the bulk of the male population was exported to other parts of Africa, the local population was largely women and children. The abuses against them were reported to be horrific, as all means possible were embraced to compel the people to work. Rape was so common that it was accepted without surprise, and an observer could remark with justice in 1914 that "so far as natives are concerned, this is a land of blood and tears, where the most brutal ill-treatment is no crime and murder a slight indiscretion" (Vail, 1976:401).

Male labor was also conscripted for work on the few small and medium-sized agricultural concessions granted by the Company. This included Company officials who had their own, illegal, plantations. "The standard practice was for the planters to place their orders with the *chefe de posto*, who then supplied that labor, for a fee, by force and at a wage which was either non-existent or well below the voluntary rate" (Neil-Tomlinson, 1977:124).

The Yao are said to have greeted the German army with open arms in the hopes of being liberated from Company rule and practices (Pelissier, 1984:695). Presumably, they willingly supplied the German troops with rations and porters just as the Macua had done in Montepuez (in Cabo Delgado) and the Lomwé peoples in Alto-Molocué and Namacurra (in Zambézia).[15] However, the memory of some of the Unango people is more of fleeing than welcoming the Germans, although one old woman remembered seeing them living in huts in Unango. They all remember supplying the British who had come to fight the Germans but could not say whether the British paid them.

It is no wonder that the collective memory is one of flight because the conflicts between British, Germans, and Portuguese troops (the bulk of which were African auxiliaries) were very costly to the peoples of Niassa, Cabo Delgado, and Zambézia where the major battles were fought over a period of a year and a half. The Portuguese estimated that fifty thousand Africans who served as porters and laborers in the war effort died thus adding to the depopulation of the region but Pelissier says the total may have been as high as one hundred thousand people (1984:684).

In his history of Cabo Delgado and Niassa, Eduardo Medeiros sees Company administration as a bridge between mercantile capitalism based on mere extraction of gold, ivory, and slaves and colonial capitalism that stimulated smallholder production of crops, rubber collection and plantation agriculture of sisal and sugar cane which exploited migrant labor. The elders of Unango noted that the men were especially involved in seasonal migration to plantations and also collected rubber, generally outside of Mozambique. Nevertheless both men and women participated in the production of beeswax, oil crops such as groundnuts and sesame seed, and such other crops as sorghum, rice, and beans. Apart from beeswax, the latter were mainly for domestic consumption. There was no organized marketing system or stores to buy crops so that whatever surplus production people had they traded locally or across the nearest border. The one commercial crop that the Unango elders remember being traded in an organized way was tobacco, which they carried to Quelimane. Moreover, dynastic leaders continued to send their caravans of ivory to trade clandestinely with the Germans in Tanzania for consumer goods, firearms, and gunpowder. Caravans also went to the Zambézia Company to the south and to Porto Amelia (Pemba) on the coast. Slave traffic also continued until the advent of the German invasion (Medeiros, 1997:101 ff).

Emigration and forced labor decimated the Yao populations. The dense settlements of the nineteenth century gave way to dispersal and local settlements of women, children, and older people. Still the dynasties persisted and organized life, including their trading caravans. Fragmentation nevertheless continued and worsened under Portuguese state administration.

Portuguese Administration

One of the characteristics of Portuguese state administration was frequent and confusing change in organizational setup. Niassa was created as a District (*Distrito*) in 1929 but, five years later, an administrative reform did away with Districts and instituted Provinces. Mozambique was then divided into three provinces: Sul do Save, incorporating southern areas; Zambézia, which included Beira, Tete, and Quelimane; and Niassa, including what is today northern Mozambique (Niassa, Cabo Delgado, and Nampula provinces).[16] The provincial capital of Niassa Province was the city of Nampula. Over the next thirty-four years, Unango, an administrative post, was placed under at least three rural districts, including Lago, Maniamba and Sanga. Sanga was created in 1963 when Maniamba was divided between Lago, and Sanga. (See map 3.)

In part, these changes reflected the availability of more manpower to administer the colony. From 1928 civilians replaced military personnel as heads of administrative posts and new positions opened at local levels. At the end of colonial administration, Niassa was again a separate District with two municipal (urban) areas, seven rural districts and, under them, thirty-one administrative posts, and an area of 123,000 sq. km. *Then, as now, it was the most neglected region, lacking personnel and especially trained officials.*[17] (See chapters 8 and 9.)

With the growth of bureaucracy came the need to increase state revenues. One of the first things mentioned by the Unango elders in regard to the transition to Portuguese administration was that taxes increased. The taxpayers in Niassa were less than eager. Tables for 1930 to 1938 showed that, in every year, the number of taxpayers who were supposed to pay taxes was larger than the number who actually paid (Colonia de Moçambique, 1938–40: Volume I).

Nor did cruelty cease. One of the Unango informants in the 1981 interviews focused on the cruelty he witnessed: "When I was young I saw the Unango *chefe de posto* [administrative head], someone called Luwala, having people tied up and beaten until they paid their taxes." Because of the difficulty people have in recalling specific times and dates, it cannot be stated categorically that this was under state administration or under the Company. From the context of the interview it had to be at least in the late 1920s. Abuse of the population became one of the specific problems for which the Portuguese government came under international scrutiny after World War I. "The threat of having its colonies included with those of Germany under the Mandate system was only just avoided at the Versailles Peace Conference" (Newitt, 1995:470). A new labor policy, announced in 1928, abolished forced labor, ended state recruitment, and initiated pay for work for the administration. Nevertheless, violence continued.

Along with the new policy, the state instituted a system of inspection, which was carried out to the level of administrative post. The inspections were periodical, although not necessarily regular and included meetings—the so-called *banjas*—with indigenous authorities. Niassa received its first inspection in 1938. In his report, the Inspector noted that the beatings of chiefs and the population continued. Moreover he reported large-scale migrations, which he attributed to beatings, the lack of marketing facilities, and employment opportunities that forced people to emigrate in order to earn tax monies. People were also reacting to higher taxes in Mozambique than in neighboring territories, to forced labor for road building and work on colonists' plantations, to the spread of the tsetse fly, and to problems caused by wild animals (Colonia de Moçambique, 1938–40:125). Not very much had changed from the time of the Company, at least in these early years.

In the 1940s, Inspector Jones da Silveira also found brutality (Colonia de Moçambique, 1944:39). He advised that abuses be stopped: "we have a lot to learn in terms of relationships within these societies and we must stop thinking that a beating will resolve everything" (Colonia de Moçambique, 1944:32). In the memories of the Unango elders, the major difference between the time of the Company and that of state administration was the near elimination of forced labor, with the exception of road building. In the 1950–1951 inspection, the Inspector found that violence was finally diminishing. The Unango elders were unanimous in their opinion that the outstanding abuse perpetrated on them was compulsory cotton cropping, which was also imposed on all northern and central farmers. The Inspectors' reports are revealing.

Cotton
Compulsory cotton growing was initiated in Niassa in the period 1937–1940 and not under the Company as Mamdani incorrectly states (1996:162). Medeiros suspects that the Niassa Company's lack of interest in propagating this crop was one of the major reasons that its lease had not been extended beyond 1929. The Portuguese government gave concessionary companies thousands of hectares for the production of cotton. The government fixed the dimension of cotton plots at sixty square meters. A company agent measured the plot for each farmer. Policemen supervised cropping. The concessionary company bought all the cotton at a fixed price, ginned it, made cotton seed oil and exported the refined cotton to Portugal. The first company to operate in Niassa was João Ferreira dos Santos but its lands were trans-

ferred to the Sociedade Algodoeira do Niassa, Ltda. or SAN. There was a second company known as SAGAL.[18]

Inspectors reported many abuses. In 1940, the inspector found that in one area the company agent was doubling farmer's plots, which caused the flight of many families (Colonia de Moçambique, 1938–40:12). At marketing time, sellers waited in line three or more days because there was only one scale or not enough workers to weigh, register, and classify their cotton and pay them. Sometimes the companies did not have sufficient funds or the correct change and used chits, eventually to be exchanged for money or they paid three or four people at the same time with one note. (Colonia de Moçambique, 1938–40:92). In another area SAGAL only paid the harvest of 1937 in the second half of 1938 (Colonia de Moçambique, 1938–40:98)

Cultivators were not informed until the last moment about the classification of their cotton. Sometimes they were paid the price of second quality when the cotton was first quality. Prices were not remunerative considering the time and effort cotton required. In neighboring countries, the prices were two or three times higher than in Niassa (Colonia de Moçambique, 1938–40:94). The concessionary companies did not give technical assistance; the few agents that they had knew nothing and explained nothing. There were reports that the time normally spent on food crops was being usurped. "The villages which had a year of famine were not few" (Colonia de Moçambique, 1938–40:98). These same observations were repeated in subsequent reports. (See, for example, Colonia de Moçambique, 1944:48–51.)

In the meetings with various chiefs in the early 1950s, complaints were almost entirely on cotton. The inspector concluded that the Niassa population had experimented twelve years with cotton with nothing to show for it. He went out on a limb when he openly criticized the system of the concessionary companies: "I cannot agree with how cotton cultivation has proceeded" (Colonia de Moçambique, 1950–51:175).

Cotton cultivation lasted only a short time in the Unango area because the people sabotaged it but they saw even the three or four years of cotton growing as years of suffering. In the peoples' own words:

When the government came, there were works to be done such as building roads and bridges and working in the administrative post. But above all, there was cotton cropping. In Lumbiza, a village in Nampanda's area, it was a productive crop but we were not happy with cotton. No, the policeman (*cipaio*) came and measured a field for every family. The machambas were on the average very big; we were paid little; we only cultivated cotton for about three years and then resisted.

We would boil or fry the seed so that it would not grow. The *cipaios* did not discover this because they were on the side of the Portuguese. We, the people, had our own secrets. The system was like slavery. We were like prisoners. The *cipaios* would go into the fields and shout "Hurry up" and beat people so that they would work faster (Arquívo Histórico de Moçambique, 1981).

The people in Kalanje's area described their experience in this way:

The head of the administrative post received white people who wanted cotton planted so he called the population together and explained. People asked for seeds because they expected money for their efforts. Each person had a measured plot of seventy or eighty *passos*. . . . People from here began to flee from cotton cropping; they went to Mbagalila where it was not compulsory and they also cooked the seed in order to prove that this was not a good cotton area. . . . Cotton was not remunerative for the work it gave. It was forced labor; the prices were miserable, there was no gain. Three or four *cargas* only fetched fifty *escudos* because they said that the quality was bad. Kalanje did not react to people fleeing to Mbagalila's land because he considered that area his land (Arquívo Histórico de Moçambique, 1981).

Neglect under Portuguese Rule

That the Portuguese government was only interested in extracting commodities, taxes, and labor is reflected in the otherwise general neglect of northern Niassa. A glimpse of what became the administrative seat of Sanga rural district shows this. Under the Niassa Company, Macaloge, at the confluence of the Rovuma and Lucheringo rivers, was made a frontier post. It had been the site of a fierce battle between the Portuguese and the German army in World War I and was considered a strategic area. When Portugal took over the area, it moved the seat to an area sixty kilometers southward and two years later, the head of the post moved the seat once again southward to the area called Sanga, one hundred kilometers from the frontier. (See map 3.) When, in 1935, he was transferred, no one else was posted there! The place fell into ruins.

There was little in the way of any kind of infrastructure in the whole of northern Mozambique. The roads were precarious and impassable during the rainy season; there was no public transport. This situation prejudiced agricultural marketing and made the provision of social services nearly impossible. In all of Lago district, the only commercial outlet was a tiny shop near the Catholic mission, Sant'António de Unango. In Lago there was a health service of some kind, but only one doctor and he had been sent to combat the problem of sleeping sickness. Lago also had a school. The only other school in the whole of the area was at Sant'António de Unango.

When Inspector Teixeira arrived in the 1950s, he lamented: "In this most backward district of the Colony, the number of roads has actually decreased" (Colonia de Moçambique, 1950–51:154). In the Unango area, the Unango-Macaloge and Unango-Muembe roads had ceased to exist. Nevertheless, there was a good road connecting Unango with the Vila Cabral (now known as Lichinga), the most important "urban" area in northern Niassa, and consequently there were now four stores for an area that covered close to three thousand square kilometers. Unango now had a sanitary post and the missionary school was still in operation. Given that the majority of the population was Muslim, the school served only a minority of the population. The Portuguese did not register the Koranic schools so it is not possible to know the extent of their dissemination.[19]

In the Inspector's opinion: "The worst difficulty that the indigene has and the one that stands most in the way of his raising productivity is the lack of commercial outlets, principally in Maniamba district; for the indigene this means having to travel great distances in order to sell his products" (Colonia de Moçambique, 1950–51:170). For the Yao male travel was a way of life, an adventure as well as the securing of a livelihood. Nevertheless, retail outlets or regularized marketing would have stimulated production and the commercialization of domestic food crops such as maize, rice, and potatoes and this would have alleviated the search for basic necessities such as salt, soap, cloth, matches, and so on, simplifying everyday life. It would not have eliminated the production and commercialization of tobacco by men and their three-month or more journeys to Cabo Delgado and Quelimane in order to sell this product but it would have immensely helped the women in the community, responsible for basic agriculture. Teixeira recommended the setting up of monthly or biweekly fairs, which Vila Cabral merchants could attend. *The situation concerning commercial outlets in the Unango area never did change during Portuguese rule; the elders interviewed in 1981 could remember only four stores.*

In 1963, the rural district of Sanga was created and the seat of Macaloge moved again southward to an area by the name of Miranda. Soon thereafter the war for independence began and everything got much worse.

The War for Independence

By 1965 the war for independence caught up with Unango and the overwhelming majority of people took flight. Of the 22,580 inhabitants in Sanga district, by 1966 there were only 5,627 (Portugal, Província de Moçambique, 1971:3). Those who did not flee into the bush, to Tanzania or

Malawi, were rounded up and placed in what the Portuguese called *aldea-mentos*, or concentration camps. I use this word advisedly because, according to those who lived in them, the camps were encircled with barbed wire. In 1971, the Sanga population was still only 11,467 almost all of whom were in the camps. This figure included the Unango peoples who numbered 10,491 divided between five camps (Província de Moçambique, 1971:53).

The policy of grouping people together in settlements or villages had been discussed for at least thirty years and apparently some administrators had tried a few experiments along these lines.[20] *Aldeamentos* were seen as an efficient solution to governing low-density areas with widely scattered populations, allowing not only control over the movements, lives, and "security" of people but also provision of essential services such as water, health, and education. Village settlements also made the building and maintenance of roads easier as well as facilitated the provision of transport and communications. James C. Scott (1998) characterizes such social engineering as the creation of state spaces at the expense of what I have called peoples' spaces.

Aware that they were profoundly altering the structure of people's lives and society, the Portuguese justified their actions in this way:

> The concentration of these populations has as its consequence a profound transformation of the conditions of life of the so-called rural populations. . . . All that we have accomplished, and it is not little even though far less than is necessary, can be seen as social advancement, economic development and self-defense. For the purpose of consolidating this achievement, it is imperative that the aldeamentos be given political-administrative structures; that is, that each settlement, the embryo of a future town, has its own proper governing body. And this, because of the upheaval caused by the eradication of the traditional hierarchy. We have tried to deal gradually with this problem by placing a regedor [this was what the Portuguese called headmen] in each aldeamento (Distrito de Niassa, 1970:18).

Thus, rural society was forcibly urbanized, on Portuguese, rather than on Yao terms. The fact that the Yao had historically lived in large groupings (before the Portuguese conquered them) was not taken into consideration in the organization of these camps. Nor, probably, was it even known by these professional administrators. People were thrown together with people from many different areas and backgrounds. Territorial chiefs were removed from their territories. Everyone was disoriented.

An attempt was made to put a water point, school and health or first aid post in each aldeamento. The Portuguese message to the world was that villagization was rural development, and among those who believed it was their archenemy, FRELIMO, which as soon as it was in power adopted this as one of its primary policies towards rural peoples.[21]

The Treatment of "Traditional" Authority

For the first few years of direct administration, the Portuguese were willing to tolerate a number of powerful, relatively equally balanced, chiefdoms in Niassa so long as no charismatic leaders were available to unite them and foment rebellion. Medeiros records that the Portuguese recognized Kalanje in 1929 as a Sultan in the company of the other greats, Mataka, Makanjila, Mponda, Ntalika (or Mtarica), Napulo, Catur, and Kandulu, and as having a territory that encompassed the Cimoso, Njile, Maniamba, Mapanje, and Lichinga mountains (1997:94).

The Portuguese were not, however, above interfering in the selection of successors to a title in order to arrange an amenable ruler nor to the breaking up of territories.[22] Yet at a certain point, at least among those most concerned with the question of administration, the awareness grew that the breaking up of kingdoms and the reduction of the role of the "ruler" to an errand boy was counterproductive to Portuguese policies. More and more orders had to be enforced through police rather than the chief. This concern was evident in the Inspection reports on Niassa. Already in 1938, Inspector Pinto Correia remarked:

> The traditional hierarchy seems disaggregated, without authority, heterogeneous and without effectiveness or prestige. The old social organization has been fragmented in thousands of regedorias, some with only twenty huts and at the leadership of these artificial groups have been put insignificant figures, rulers by chance. . . . Nevertheless, within black society, there exists a real hierarchy, mainly ignored by us, but the only one recognized by the natives (Colonia de Moçambique, 1938–40:69).

In 1944, Silveira commented: "It is rare to find a régulo with the old authority" (Colonia de Moçambique, 1944:39). Inspector Teixeira found one in Kalanje. "The *régulo* Calange is the most important of the region, having many people [under him] and a lot of prestige" (Colonia de Moçambique, 1950–51:35). In 1947, Kalanje had 38 *cabos* under him and governed 6,019 inhabitants while Chipango had only 9 cabos and 1,410 inhabitants and Nampanda had 9 cabos and 1,893 inhabitants (Manuel Simões Alberto, 1947:114). Teixeira added "it is a shame that he does not carry out orders the way he should and does not give them much importance" (Colonia de Moçambique, 1950–51:35). He concluded his report with the admonition: "In the midst of a great number of existing *régulos*, there are some who are real leaders; such as . . . Malingalira and Calange of Unango post. . . . Even though they are prestigious *regedores*, Mataka and Calange are not being used well, their prestige is largely ceremonial" (Colonia de Moçambique, 1950–51:196).

The forced concentration of all the Yao into camps significantly reduced Kalanje's authority. In 1971, Kalanje, two cabos, and 887 people were confined to the concentration settlement at the Unango post. (See Che Kalanje's story below.) The encampment was noted to be large, very well cared for, well ordered, and properly zoned (Província de Moçambique, 1971:44). This situation did not fail to have repercussions on the subsequent organization of the Unango Yao.

The War Itself[23]

In Niassa, FRELIMO opened up a front in the Lake area on 25 September 1964, the anniversary of its foundation. It was supported by the Nyanja population, which had been psychologically prepared for independence by its proximity to the liberation struggles in Malawi and Tanzania in the late 1950s. Never favorable to the establishment of the Anglican missions in Niassa, the Portuguese blamed them for propagandizing the Nyanjas against the Portuguese (Distrito de Niassa, 1971:183). In preparation for its activities, FRELIMO launched an intense propaganda campaign, then an attack on Còbué administrative post, followed in December 1964 by a second attack on another post. (See map 3.)

FRELIMO succeeded in creating bases all over Niassa, and especially in the north. Its method of attack was both direct by bombing military bases but also indirect through ambushes, the destruction of bridges and so on.

The Portuguese Armed Forces installed themselves mainly in district and post seats; in Unango post, they took over the residence of the administrator. They then rounded up suspected "terrorist" elements (Distrito de Niassa, 1971:183). The Portuguese accused FRELIMO of extracting populations from their control not simply by conversion but also by intimidation when local groups did not respond immediately to their cause. The acts of intimidation supposedly included kidnapping people and murdering traditional authorities faithful to the Portuguese and ordinary people as well. This resulted in the flight of the majority of Nyanjas and Yao (Distrito de Niassa, 1971:184).

By 1966, FRELIMO had made inroads everywhere except in the southern part of Niassa. The conflict intensified with attacks on civilian as well as military targets, on commercial establishments, and on settlers in order to drive a wedge between civilians and military. FRELIMO's military strategy was to capture the area linking Vila Cabral, Catur and the frontier of Malawi where it had support (Distrito de Niassa, 1971:185). As the Portuguese stepped up defensive activities, people began to return from the bush where they had fled and the Armed Forces attempted to establish safe zones, including the *aldeamentos*, grouped around their military bases.

1967 brought a series of reversals: the Portuguese army succeeded in destroying a number of FRELIMO bases but, just as one was razed, another one was established. However the Armed forces had FRELIMO temporarily on the run. The hold on the Vila Cabral–Catur axis was also broken but when FRELIMO was able to regroup, the level of violence increased. In 1969 it was even attacking *aldeamentos*. In 1970, the last year of information, FRELIMO succeeded in inflicting eight hundred or more attacks and was attempting to make headway in the south of the Province. One of the most affected areas in 1970 was Sanga (Distrito de Niassa, 1971:192).

The War in Unango
The elders of Unango remembered the war in this way: when the war broke out in 1964, the officer at the post called all the authorities together and told them to tell their people to kill any strangers they found lurking around using whatever weapons they had at hand: spears, nets, hatchets and so on. The *cipaios* came and did a house-to-house search for anyone who might be hidden. Then FRELIMO came (the elders called them *camaradas* [comrades], FRELIMO's preferred greeting) and also tried to mobilize the régulos with these words: "Hey, this is our country, and we want our country now . . . we need unity . . . but this is our secret and not to be spoken anywhere." They asked the régulos to send young men to join the cause. The régulos spoke to the young people in secret because the Portuguese were sending troops, sometimes at night, to look for enemies.

The elders stated that the Portuguese even killed régulos and burned reserves of maize. The war broke out in the Lake region; mines exploded. The next year it reached Unango. The comrades came and took everyone to the bush. Then a Militia Group by the name of *Roxa* (or *Wayiyovololo* because of the purple color of its uniform) came and killed lots of people. Many fled by night to Tanzania. Some trained to fight for FRELIMO, others fled. There were many bases (each group of elders interviewed named many different sites) and after a number of massacres at some of the bases, people moved from base to base.

The elders affirmed that some régulos were with FRELIMO and some with the Portuguese. When FRELIMO contacted Kalanje, he accepted and went to live in the bush where he died of a sickness. In the bush the Unango people suffered a lot of hunger because the Portuguese burned their stocks. The elders remembered having only sweet potatoes and bananas to eat.

FRELIMO had few arms to begin with but this situation improved over time and then they had anti-aircraft weapons, bazookas, and so on. When these weapons arrived people were able to fish and plant. FRELIMO distributed fishing nets and there was a cooperative for the exchange of goods where the people sold fish and sesame and received goods including clothing in exchange. There was enough food produced for both the population and the fighters. People were not allowed to sell food but could eat it with the soldiers.

The elders noted that when people left the bush, the Portuguese either put them in *aldeamentos* or killed them. The lucky ones went to the camps, one of which was Waya where life was hard. It had barbed wire to keep people in. At first people were only allowed out with armed guards and then afterwards, they were allowed to go, accompanied, into the fields. There was no store, no soap, no cleanliness, and at first no schools. Wood and water came in by vehicles.

They also recalled the barbed wire around Cantina Dias, which concentrated people from Unango, Macaloge, and Likwanyile. The people were able to plant fields of maize and cassava but only with guards around them. *Many people did not return from Tanzania after independence.*

Unango in the Late 1990s

In the late 1990s, I found Kalanje and the remains of his people clustered in communal villages around the seat of Sanga district which had moved yet again, this time as a result of RENAMO attacks. It was now located in the installations of a failed agricultural project of enormous dimensions locally known as *Empresa quatrocentos mil hectares* or the Four Hundred Thousand Hectare Enterprise. This giant project had been instituted in the early 1980s under the FRELIMO president, Samora Machel, with the collaboration of Eastern European technicians who brought with them heavy agricultural equipment in order to implant large-scale socialized industrial agriculture.

Sometime, also in the early 1980s, the community of Ilinga left their home and fields in the area of Masi mountain to occupy a small part of the lands ceded to the project. It is not altogether clear whether the community moved in order to provide agricultural labor to the Empresa or whether it was fleeing RENAMO attacks upon its homelands. In any case, RENAMO attacks eventually forced the closure of the Empresa. Along with most people, Ilinga's population was forced to flee yet again to Tanzania, Malawi, or into bush land. Not all of its population had returned by the time of the INDER visit in February 1998 to help local government officials begin participatory planning exercises with this and neighboring communities.

Ilinga was loosely organized along the lines of an aldeamento or FRE-LIMO communal village, and was located two kilometers from the district seat still on Empresa lands. It was designated a *bairro* of the administrative post of Sanga. The people who came to the inaugural meeting with INDER identified themselves primarily as Yao and Muslim. They appeared to be more or less organized on a "traditional" basis, that is, the elders identified a *régulo*, Paca Alifa, as their ruler along with six *ndunas* (settlement heads). This "traditional" structure worked in close collaboration with the civil authorities. Paca Alifa, and the nduna of the settlement where the meeting was held, presided over the meeting. What the INDER teams did not recognize on this first day was that the community was suffering from a number of internal conflicts.

On closer examination, the teams found an ethnically mixed population and, as a consequence, a certain amount of social friction. There were Macua, Makonde, Nyanja, and Changaan peoples in Ilinga because of an early FRELIMO policy to rid urban areas of political dissidents and undesirables, designated as unproductive members of the population. In the late 1970s, there were regular checks of the population; those found without the proper identification papers were taken to areas such as Niassa where they were expected to "rehabilitate" and transform themselves into productive members of society. Among twenty-four known re-education camps established by the government, Niassa had nine camps, one of which was in Unango (Cabrita, 2000:97). In 1983, the IV Party Congress of FRELIMO decided to put into effect *Operação Produção* (Operation Production), which removed forcibly unwanted people from cities and dumped them in Niassa (Cabrita 2000:214). This partially explained the presence of "outsiders" in the Ilinga population.

There were other contradictions within the community as well. It was not until the second day of the visit, in interviews with individual families, that the INDER teams were told that Paca Alifa was subordinate to Che Kalanje. Apparently he was a lineage headman. Yet, the elders had not mentioned this nor did the map they drew show them as part of Kalanje's territory. (See appendix for a reproduction of the sketch map.) Maps from the Portuguese era did not show a *regedoria* (native administrative unit) named Ilinga but did suggest that the lands identified by the elders had been part of a larger territory. One could only suppose that the 'traditional' hierarchy had broken down.

Moreover, it became obvious that Paca Alifa himself was having great trouble exercising his authority. He had decided that the best thing for the people was to leave the district capital of Sanga and move back to the 'original' upland homelands, more or less bounded by three rivers, the

Lucheringo, Lukelesi, and Luchimua. In 1998 we verified that a small part of the population had already followed Paca Alifa. When I returned a year later on another mission, I found that even more of the population had followed him but the majority was still in the bairro. Ilinga was an example of both the centrifugal forces in the Yao political setup, reinforced by villagization, *and* the intergenerational conflict, which plagued a number of Cabo Delgado and Niassa communal villages visited by INDER (described in chapter 5). The elders admitted in 1998 that, even though they wanted the community to move, the young people felt that they had a better chance of finding employment if they stayed close to the district capital.

The community recognized some of these internal splits and insisted on respecting them. After the inaugural meeting, the INDER teams asked the community to divide into three groups, of women, elders and young people in order to interview them separately. During the planning exercise on the third day, the community insisted that each group again meet separately to prioritize what it considered the principal community problem before meeting altogether as a committee of the whole to make a final decision. This was the only community that organized itself in this manner during the participatory planning exercises. It did not hinder and may actually have helped the community reach a final consensus on its priorities.

Social Organization

The community identified itself as matrilineal but individuals spoke of a minority that followed patrilineal norms. In regard to marriage customs, the young men as a group said they no longer followed all of them. For example, they admitted having sexual relations without the benefit of engagement or marriage. Should the girl become pregnant, they said that they were either fined or obliged to marry her. Once marriage took place, however, the young man left his family to stay with his in-laws and worked alongside his bride in her mother's fields, a typical matrilineal custom. Should either the bride or groom die unexpectedly, their children were given to the mother's family and the maternal uncle took charge of their education.

Ilinga residents complained that divorce was frequent. Women complained most of polygamy and the man's consequent neglect of his wife/wives since equal treatment was expected. When there were marriage problems, the brothers of the bride and groom got together to try to resolve the situation. Otherwise, families appealed to the *régulo* for his advice and, in very serious cases, the matter was passed to the civil authorities.

The elders spoke of Muslim marriage ceremonies but said that these occurred only after the formal traditions were followed, which included the presentation of bride and groom to the *régulo*. Normally there was no marriage payment but in the cases of marriage between Makonde, Nyanja, and Changaan, the patrilineal custom prevailed. Trouble and misunderstanding arose in the cases of mixed patrilineal and matrilineal marriages. It was not possible to investigate the relative influence of matrilineal and patrilineal customs; that is, whether patrilineal influences were gaining ascendancy (as suggested by Alpers and Amaral).[24]

Among other rituals still respected were initiation rites for both boys and girls. When natural disasters occurred, the *chiombo* ceremony was performed and at harvest time, the *sadaca* ceremony. There was also a ceremony at the time of death.

Economic Organization

In Ilinga, the principal occupation was farming *but people said that they were not giving their full time or energies to it for lack of formal marketing outlets*. They could and would produce more if they had regular buyers. In 1998, they were dependent upon itinerant traders, especially from Malawi, to buy their crops but this was too uncertain to invest extra effort in producing large surpluses. At times, they themselves launched caravans, but contemporary caravans consisted of bicycles, rather than slaves, loaded with produce to sell in Malawi.

The whole family, including children, worked together in family fields of, on the average, one and one-half hectares in dimension. In their upland fields, they generally planted maize and beans in association and also groundnuts, sorghum, cassava, sweet and regular potatoes, and garlic. In lowland fields, they cultivated a large variety of vegetables. Some families were again experimenting with tobacco as a commercial crop because of an assured buyer in the provincial capital. They did not fertilize their crops but moved to new fields when the original soils were exhausted.

Land was abundant and when a family came from outside the community it was able to gain access to land by talking with the owners and/or neighbors, the head of the settlement and finally the lineage head. Land was never given or sold but rather lent for an agreed length of time. During the interviews both the elders and women, in separate groups, mentioned the survey of their fields by the National and Provincial Geographical and Cadastral Service (DINAGECA) in 1997. They were worried because the surveyors had come unannounced, did not ask permission to visit people's fields, trooped all over them and then laid down concrete markers. A delegation of the community including Paca Alifa visited the district administration to find out what was going on but the administration was only partially informed. It had only received information that a survey would take place. Together the *régulo* and his men and some district officials went to see the markers in Ilinga fields. They also showed them to us during the INDER visit.

In the district, it was known that the survey had to do with an agreement between the Mozambique and South African governments to set up a joint venture known as the Mosagrius Development Corporation. They had no other information. On 9 July 1997, the Mozambican news agency, AIM, reported:

> The Mozambican and South African governments own the Mosagrius Corpo-
> ration, and under its auspices South African farmers are to settle in the north-
> ernmost province of Niassa. Fourteen South Africans are already present in the
> provincial capital, Lichinga. Technical teams are busy demarcating plots of
> land in the districts of Majune and Sanga. At the same time, contacts are un-
> der way with international organisations and financial institutions to raise
> funds to finance those farmers who have expressed interest in taking part in
> the programme, but do not have enough money of their own. About 30 South
> Africans are ready to join the first 14, and about 200 Mozambican farmers have
> been enrolled. The programme will start with a small number, in order to en-
> sure close follow up and assistance. The Mozambican government has decided
> to exempt the South African farmers participating in Mosagrius from customs
> duties on agricultural and other equipment to be used in the programme (AIM
> report, 9 July 1997).

The district tried unsuccessfully to get further information at provincial level of what the markers signified. By the time we reached Ilinga in 1998 the elders were very concerned that the Government might be *giving their lands away.* (Chapter 11 discusses the issue further in the context of the reform of the Mozambican land law.) We were also told about the behav-ior of a Boer farmer settled near the neighboring village, Miala: he had contracted a number of men to open his fields including the uprooting of trees but had not paid them. The elders said that they were ready to ac-cept Boer settlement, but only if it was done in the spirit of cooperation and collaboration.

Individual Voices: An Outsider and an Insider

Jenela Mohamade Benamulu
Benamulu was a middle-aged man and a *forasteiro*, an outsider. He had been born along the Rovuma river but did not specify on which side of the border. He left his first wife there and came to Ilinga where he met his current wife.

His second family consisted of two adults and nine children, three of whom were his wife's by another man.

They had only one family field planted in maize, beans, potatoes, and garlic (a commercial crop in neighboring Lichinga district) yet they were able to produce about one hundred kilograms of maize for sale and enough reserves to last the family until the end of the year. To supplement his income and food budget, Mr. Benamulu traded fish for maize flour. Because he had a modicum of success in trading, he felt singled out for criticism by his neighbors. His business had enabled him to buy wrappers, the object of envy. Benamulu said he had already picked out a new terrain where he would move his family in order to get away from these neighbors. The Benamulu family had two of their school-age children in school while a girl had to stay home to care for the small children as her mother was unwell.

Pretis Macambate Jete

Jete was a young man of twenty-three, born in Tanzania where his parents, a local family, had fled during the war for independence. His uncle was one of the six ndunas. Jete had already lived with his in-laws but had now struck out on his own with his two wives and two tiny children. They all lived together but each wife had a separate field where he worked with them. Together the fields were three hectares in dimension and Jete had obtained them by negotiating with his neighbors. In 1996–1997 he had been able to sell around a ton of maize as it was a good agricultural year, but 1997–1998 was not promising because of excessive rainfall. Jete was forecasting a shortfall of food. To make up for this he had planted half of his fields with tobacco and also had potatoes growing in the garden around the house to exchange for maize.

Pretis Jete had made a contract with a tobacco company in the provincial capital, which had sent him an extension agent and inputs. The cost of these was then discounted from his proceeds at harvest and, although he was unhappy with the size of his profits, Jete felt that he was still learning about tobacco cultivation.

Neither Benamulu nor Jete had any intention of going to live in the Ilinga mountains as neither had a living memory of or attachment to this homeland. For them the communal village was home.

Che Kalanje

In 1999, I went to visit the current head of the Kalanje dynasty, an elderly man who, at the time of the visit, was suffering from a bad case of bronchitis. Minutes before I entered his compound in Miala, a communal village also close to the district seat, he had presided over a ceremony to intercede with the spirits of the ancestors to halt the rains, which threatened the crops of Miala and neighboring settlements. Because of his illness, I felt uncomfortable about tiring the Che with many questions so I concentrated on the origins of his dynasty.

Stambuli Amade, the present Che, said the founding father was a certain Nyanjawili. When he died nobody replaced him. Wars for primacy and dominance brought a number of invaders including Mataka and Makanjila to the homelands in the Mbemba mountains. The name Kalanje comes from this time: it was derived from the word to roast. When the people fled Mbemba to get away from the dynastic wars, they carried their maize stocks on poles and created a kind of smokescreen by firing the corncobs. For this reason their leader became known as Kalanje. He had brought with him earth from the tomb of the founding father in the Mbemba mountains and buried it in a sacred place near a river at the base of the Unango mountains. The area is still a shrine.

According to Amade, the first Kalanje was a nephew of Nampanda. The greatest chief at the time, Nampanda divided the land with Kalanje and two other nephews, who became his chiefs. Kalanje was given Unango. When the Portuguese came, Nampanda refused them land on the suspicion that they would seize his lands, while Kalanje, who was younger and less experienced, welcomed them.[25] The Portuguese thus favored him.

Stambuli Amade, the sixth and current person to hold the title, became régulo when the fifth Kalanje was still alive but very old and ill. Both of them fled into the bush during the war for independence. When he returned, Amade was interned in the camp at the base of the Unango mountain, which had been a Portuguese military outpost. After the war he came to Miala and has not since moved even during the conflict with RENAMO. Although there had been difficulties after independence, FRELIMO did recognize him as chief (*régulo*).

Asked to comment on the postcolonial period, he hesitated then declined. In the one comment he made about the post-independence era, Stambuli Amade considered the Four Hundred Thousand Hectare Enterprise to have been a blessing as compared with the present situation. The Enterprise had afforded people employment and all kinds of goods, including soap, sugar and cooking oil. There was a health post and so on. The people did not suffer privations. However, the project was closed after RENAMO killed twelve of the foreign technicians assisting the Enterprise and also destroyed many infrastructures. The village of Miala was, however, saved from RENAMO because the spirit of Kalanje protected it. Whenever RENAMO people wanted to enter, they were discovered.

Later I was informed that the spirit of Kalanje had protected Miala and the surrounding areas from the heavy rainfall of 1999.

Notes

1. Arab penetration of the coastal and interior regions was known as early as A.D. 700; they established the port of Kilwa at the end of the twelfth century. Control over this port fluctuated between the Arabs and the Portuguese (Mitchell, 1956:22). The Maraves brought ivory to the ports of Kilwa (in Tanzania) and Mozambique Island (Ilha de Moçambique) in the seventeenth century.

2. Historians with the Arquívo Histórico de Moçambique (Mozambican Historical Archives, AHM) place the date even earlier, around 1696, but there are few records for this period.

3. Yao caravans traveled at least two routes: through Yao territory across the Lugenda river up to its confluence with the Rovuma and on to Kilwa; and through Macua territory east of Lugenda river, across the Lurio and Macuana rivers, and on to Mozambique Island (endnote, Abdallah). (See map 1.) Eduardo Medeiros adds another two routes to Quelimane and to the ports of Cabo Delgado (1997:86).

4. Mitchell found Nguru peoples in Nyasaland and noted their cultural and structural similarity to the Yao and Nyanja peoples. They spoke a different but "mutually intelligible" language (1956:16).

5. Abdallah names ten such groupings, which he says are the most well known (1983:7–9).

6. Father Abdallah was pastor of the Anglican mission in Kalanje's lands. It is therefore odd that he did not record the history of the Unango peoples including Nampanda, Chipango, as well as Kalanje. Sometime in the period, 1875–1890, the Nguni attacked Unango and the area may have, for a time, paid tribute to the invaders. According to Liesegang, the lacuna in Abdallah's account in regard to these and other events may have been related to some prejudice on his part (chapter 3, note 98).

7. From 1830 to 1860, the Nguni moved north into Malawi, east of Lake Niassa, into the Rovuma valley and as far south as Mount Namuli, substituting themselves for the Marave whose empire had disintegrated (Newitt, 1995:259).

8. In his fascinating history of the peoples of the Mueda Plateau in neighboring Cabo Delgado, Harry G. West describes a similar process of consolidation (1988:145).

9. In 1981, the historian G. Liesegang led a team of researchers to Niassa and interviewed people from Unango. The results of this research are noted throughout this chapter. It is because of this invaluable research that the narrative of this chapter can be organized first with the discourse of the historian and/or colonizer and then, in counterpoint, with the experience of the Unango people.

10. Alpers' affirmation should probably be taken to mean that there was no formal tax collection. His assertion was backed up by Duff MacDonald's account of the

Yao around Blantyre in 1882. Nevertheless, in the area under study, subordinate and allied chiefs offered gifts to the territorial chief. Newitt, for example, says that the Manganja [Maganja?] population was paying tribute to the Yao in 1861 (1995:278).

11. Mamdani is thus incorrect in attributing judicial powers to the colonialist's expansion of chiefly powers (1996:109 ff).

12. "The chief was therefore in direct competition with his subject village headmen, and involved in a constant struggle with them for followers" (Mitchell, 1956:34 confirming MacDonald's observations).

13. Another group, the Makale, from the north also came.

14. The rural district of Sanga, created in 1963, was 12,161 sq. km. Unango, one of its three administrative posts, had an area of 2,379 sq. km. (See map 3.)

15. Pélissier is the best source of information on this period and he laments the lack of records on the extent of the Yao-German collaboration but there is no doubt that the Yaos were in open rebellion (1984:695–697).

16. The Territory of Manica and Sofala continued under the administration of the Mozambique Company until 1942.

17. See the inspection reports for details, Colonia de Moçambique, Inspecção da Administração Civil e dos Negócios Indígenas, 1938–40:5; 1944:12; 1950–51:125; and Governo do Distrito do Niassa, 1971:1.

18. For an interesting comparison of how cotton was organized in Nampula, see M. Anne Pitcher (1998).

19. In Niassa as a whole the Inspector found only two official schools for indigenous people but there were twenty-five Catholic schools, of which six were considered well organized, and one Anglican mission school. The mission schools also provided some literacy training. Because of the problem of religion, the most frequented of the Catholic schools was the one teaching trades such as carpentry, masonry, and so on (Colonia de Moçambique, 1950–51:148, 149). The five missions run by the Consolata order in Cuamba, Mecanhelas, Unango, Maúa, Massangula and Vila Cabral also had small first aid posts. By 1951, health services showed a distinct improvement. There were three rural hospitals, in Vila Cabral, Cuamba and Maniamba. The hospital in Maniamba, however, was designated for Europeans only. Maniamba provided a maternity ward for the local population and a sanitary post in Metangula, Còbué and Unango. There were also three rural health posts (Colonia de Moçambique, 1950–51:158).

20. In 1951, Nampanda confessed to Inspector Teixeira that his people had already abandoned the aldeamento (Colonia de Moçambique, 1950–51:33).

21. According to Cabrita, the first communal villages established by FRELIMO were the Portuguese-inspired aldeamentos (2000:117).

22. Pélissier states that after Mataka V was on the run and migrated to Tanzania, the Portuguese elected the new Mataka, Salange, who never gave them any trouble (1984:301) but Abdallah says he was elected by the people (1983:10).

23. The information for this section comes from two sets of documents: the first is the Governor of Niassa's annual report for 1970 and the second are the oral inter-

views of Unango elders in 1981. Because there is a remarkable similarity in the history recounted by these two groups, I did not feel it necessary to consult further documentation.

24. Amaral found the Yao paying a symbolic *ndoua* to the father of the bride; he recognized that this was not lobolo but wondered if this signified a trend towards a patrilineal regime. His feeling was "possibly, yes, because many Yao seem little in conformity with the matriarchy, which is shown by the frequency with which they are choosing wives of ethnic origins in which lobolo is permitted" (1990:71 and 72).

25. This story is backed up with Maples' account that "Kalanje sports the Portuguese flag on his hill, and his caravans also find their way to the Portuguese coast possessions" (1899:245).

~

CHAPTER TWO

Gorongosa: Mountain Rebels

Gorongosa derives its name from the majestic yet mysterious mountain range that dominates the area. Goro means mountain range and Ngozi means danger; thus, Gorongozi signifies danger in the mountains, a sacred place inhabited by diviners, but also a place for hiding and subterfuge, as shall be seen. The range rises above two relatively high plateaux and the bottom extension of the Rift Valley. Altitudes, higher than those of surrounding districts, modify the climate and temperature and heighten the incidence of rainfall near the mountain. The entire area is covered in forests and irrigated by numerous rivers, most of which emanate from the sierra. Before the civil war, there was an abundance of wildlife, including lions and elephants.[1] This chapter traces the history of a community living in the foothills on the western side of the mountain, in an area they called Kanda.

Beginnings

According to the people of Kanda, their dynasty began in Mbire in what is now Zimbabwe.[2] And indeed there were Shona migrations from the heart of the Monomotapa kingdom in the northern end of the Zimbabwe plateau to what is now Mozambique. In his outline of Shona history, David Beach says that these migrations came in at least two phases; the first one lasted several hundred years and is dated roughly between the thirteenth and sixteenth centuries (1980:161). Map 4 shows the direction of these migrations. Just as in the case of the Yao, it is impossible to know with any exactitude the origins of the migrants and the dates of their movements.

Shona-speakers came to Mozambique for many reasons. The people of Gorongosa said that they used to come to this area to hunt elephants. They were also attracted to the natural seaports of the central coast where they traded ivory and gold from their mines. Today, the Beira Corridor from the major seaport of Mozambique to Harare is the modern version of this same linkage.

The Karangas, as eastern Shona migrants called themselves, settled from Tete to the mouth of the Zambeze river and southward throughout the area that became known as Sofala and Manica. In the sixteenth century, they created a number of states in this space, including Báruè, Quiteve, Quissanga, Manica, and Sedanda. (See map 4.) Báruè's rulers assimilated the culture of the Sena-speaking Tongas who were living there, including, in part, their language.[3] Remarkably, Báruè survived, more or less independently, over four centuries.

Tonga dynasties are also said to have come from Mbire and one hypothesis is that they were driven from Zimbabwe during the secular advance of the Karangas. Some of the Tonga peoples successfully resisted the Karangas but in Báruè they established a close relationship to its ruler. This was institutionalized by the appointment of one of their chiefs from the *tembo* totem to sit on the highest council of government as senior adviser. He was known as the *Mukomowasha*. Many Gorongosans identified themselves with the *tembo* totem, including Kanda and a number of the other rulers.[4] In 1999, Celestino Tsacaune Kanda, a member of the Kanda dynasty, confirmed this but did not describe the relationship of Kanda to Báruè as particularly friendly or close even though they shared a common border.[5] The relationship he described was more akin to that of an ant to an elephant.

Oral history placed the first immigrations to the area known as Kanda in the early nineteenth century. The migrants are said to have left the Monomotapa kingdom during one of its many wars of succession. They came to the uninhabited land where they had previously hunted elephants. Celestino Tsacaune recounts that there were three migrating groups: the one led by Sadjunjira arrived before the others, the second group was headed by Mazausiso, and the third by the person who later received the name *Kanda*. Along the route, Mazausiso's group found a dead elephant and decided to feast on it and so made an encampment. When Kanda's group arrived, they were asked to join the celebration but decided instead to continue the journey. They asked Mazausiso for some parts of the animal in order to feed themselves en route. Mazausiso gave them a leg and some skin. With these provisions, they arrived first. When, at last, Mazausiso's group arrived, and the first harvest was in, they held a big celebration during which Mazausiso

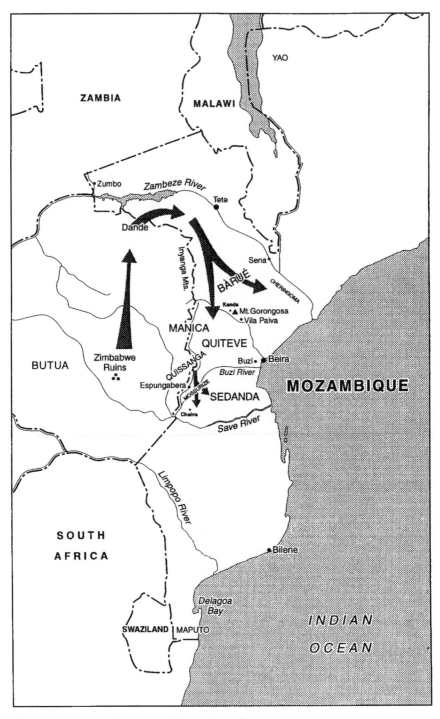

Map 4.   Kasanga Migrations and State Formations

gave Kanda his name meaning "elephant skin." Kanda's group also brought with them *Nhamadzi* or lion, which is connected to the spirit of its ancestors. Today, the administrative post of Kanda is known officially as Nhamadzi.

When, in the 1850s, another powerful neighbor, a Goan by the name of Manuel António de Sousa, began to carve his domain on the northern side of the mountain, the first Kanda had already died. Sousa was remembered by the name *Gouveia* and as a fugitive from a war with Báruè. He later became a ruler as powerful as Báruè. Legend has it that he gave two red berets to loyal chiefs, one of which was used in their crowning and the second for everyday usage.[6] I found no evidence to show whether Kanda was among them.

Kanda's history resembled Kalanje's in that both peoples found themselves in the middle of at least two opposing powerful forces—Báruè and Gouveia in Kanda's case. Both maneuvered as best they could to maintain as much independence as possible. The major difference between them was that the people of Kanda *openly* opposed those representing Portuguese rule as they later opposed FRELIMO restrictions on their livelihood.

The Portuguese

Portuguese penetration of African territories was originally driven by gold lust. From the ninth century Swahili traders had traded cloth and beads all along the coast and the Zambeze river for gold from the mines of Manica (Gorongosa's neighbor to the south). In the sixteenth century, Portuguese and Afro-Portuguese traders replaced them. In the 1570s Portugal tried to wrest control over the gold mines from the Shona but this was a futile attempt. After that it sought to control the flow of trade goods. (Trade goods passed through many lands whose rulers exacted a percentage on goods in transit.) In this it was more successful but only because it was willing to rely on the greed of individuals (among whom Gouveia) whose private interests at times coincided with Crown interests. Such buccaneers were at times rewarded with land grants known as *prazos*. But mainly they seized lands.

By the seventeenth century, with the aid of large slave armies, prazo-holders were in a position to negotiate with paramount chiefs. In order to maintain independence from these acquisitive land/warlords, Báruè played one prazo-holder off against another. However, in the nineteenth century, the ruler of Báruè was outmatched first by the Nguni leader, Soshangane (sometimes spelled Soshegane), and then by Gouveia.

In the 1830s Soshangane was able to put Báruè and Gorongosa under his power. In the 1850s his son, Umzila, attacked Gouveia and his slave army in their fortress built in the Gorongosa mountains, and he eventually sacked it.

In response Gouveia built stockades throughout the surrounding areas to link his home base with the Pungué River to the south and the upper waters of the Luenha (Newitt, 1973:314). He was then positioned to help the ruler of Báruè defend his territory. By the 1860s, when Umzila left the area to establish his capital at Mossurize (chapter 3), Gouveia had not only recovered his authority but, through a series of political maneuvers, he succeeded in controlling Báruè. "The free inhabitants of Báruè were regrouped in settlements near the aringas [stockades] and new chiefs were chosen under Sousa's supervision and had to reside where the captains could keep an eye on them" (Newitt, 1973:317). These settlements could be considered the precursors of the *aldeamentos*, described in the last chapter.

Fifty years afterward, the people of Gorongosa recalled Gouveia and the Nguni invasions in somewhat less glorious terms. What they remembered were Gouveia's stockades. They said that because Nguni warriors preferred open combat they did not attack the mountain forts. The Nguni accused the Gorongosans of running away and being cowards. Their riposte was that the Nguni were cowards for not coming up the mountain. In the opinion of the historian that collected oral history, "Gorongosa was the only area in the whole Territory of Manica and Sofala that never paid tribute to the Vatuas."[7]

Gouveia put his forces at the service of the Portuguese Crown, and for a very brief time was lionized by Portuguese society. He became a close friend of Joaquim Carlos Paiva de Andrada, a freelance concession hunter with no money (Newitt, 1973:312). Together they hatched a number of schemes to acquire the mineral rights of what was soon to become the Territory of Manica and Sofala, which included Báruè, Quiteve, Sedanda, and parts of Quissanga and Manica as well as the Gorongosa-Cheringoma complex. In March 1888 Andrada launched the idea of the Companhia de Moçambique (Mozambique Company) and was able to convince a number of investors to put up money for the enterprise, which was granted a charter in 1891.

Andrada and Gouveia had designs on areas also coveted by Cecil Rhodes and his backers but they were no match for him. Rhodes' British South African Company (BSAC), which had won its charter two years before the Companhia, successfully courted the chiefs of Mashonaland. When Andrada, Gouveia, and Baron Resende made a special trip to the area to claim the loyalties of Chief Mutassa, BSAC policemen arrested them and took them to jail in the Cape, causing a diplomatic scandal. Their absence was the occasion for a falling out among Gouveia's captains and the beginning of the end of his personal empire. He died trying to reclaim Báruè in 1892.

The Companhia de Moçambique was launched with a capital of only twenty thousand pounds sterling and in 1896 it gave Gorongosa in concession to the

Companhia de Gorongosa. Neither company began with effective control over their respective concessions. Two of the captains, Luís Santiago and Cambuemba, played an important part in the struggles of Gorongosa and Báruè to remain independent during the ten years following Gouveia's death.

The Administration of the Mozambique Company

In 1893, Luís Santiago invited the Companhia de Moçambique to establish a post in Gorongosa and agreed to supply policemen to collect taxes but only from the villagers around the post. Cambuemba, however, opposed any intervention by the Company and raised a force with which he attacked Company posts. A number of Gorongosa chiefs collaborated with him, refusing to pay taxes. Santiago was generally blamed for this revolt, which occurred in 1895, but the next year the Companhia de Gorongosa gave him a job. The sub-concessionary company pretended to collect taxes on an even wider basis, which provoked an even greater reaction from the chiefs.

Sometime during the same year, 1897, ten chiefs, among which was Kanda, left their homes and took refuge in the mountains.[8] They "rejected all political overtures made by the company, they broke all external commercial relationships and they effectively closed all lines of communication between the Pungwe and Zambesi rivers which passed through Gorongosa" (Neil-Tomlinson, 1974:171). About a year later, the ten chiefs were forced by hunger to abandon the mountains and called for a formal meeting with Company officials.

In attendance were chiefs Kanda and Sadjunjira and eight others. Representing the Gorongosa Company were the chief of post, four other employees and another of Gouveia's captains, the ancient Chitengo and some of his followers.

> The chiefs claimed that although they had withdrawn into the mountains they had never taken part in the attacks on the company. They declared that they now wanted to come down out of the mountains in order to begin preparing their fields in time for the approaching rains, without being pursued, harassed and attacked by the company. They wished therefore to make their submission of vassalage and they expressed their willingness to open the roads which they had closed, to obey all orders and to pay head tax, not only for 1898 and all the following years but also for the past year of 1897 (Neil-Tomlinson, 1974:174).

This capitulation did not signal the end of resistance. Despite its victory, the Gorongosa Company was not a viable enterprise. There was a quick succession of Company administrators. In July 1900 the Company invited Gustavo

Bivar Pinto Lopes to take over and he quickly found himself involved in the continuing rebellion.

Báruè never stopped defending its sovereignty but its forces were divided at the turn of the century because it was in the midst of a succession struggle. Even so, many of the chiefs who objected to the Company saw in Báruè a leader. Moreover, Gouveia's captains, with the exception of Chitengo, kept up the pressure on Company posts. In 1901, the Company called upon Captain Azvedo Coutinho to put down Báruè[9] and in the process he also eliminated the rebellious captains. When the military column incorporating Gustavo Bivar and the auxiliaries of Gorongosa defeated Macossa, the head of the southern branch of the royal family, a frontier was drawn between Gorongosa and Báruè at the Vunduzi river. The border divided Kanda from Báruè but proved no barrier to the people on either side. The Company claimed that it could not pay the expenses of the war so Portugal put Báruè under direct administration. This did not spell the end of Báruè or rebellion. What then followed was the calm before the storm.

In protest to Company rule, Gorongosans went en masse to Báruè but many returned. Gorongosa's abundance of water, forestland, and wild game tempted them back. The Gorongosa Company was well aware of these assets and the industriousness of the people. An early expedition pointed to "a strong African agricultural economy with widespread market oriented production, making for potentially lucrative trading opportunities. The expedition reported that beeswax, groundnuts, and oil seeds were the most widely produced and traded products with a large profit margin between the buying price in Gorongosa and the selling price at the coast" (Neil-Tomlinson, 1974:123). The historical tragedy is that it took almost fifty years for Gorongosans to be able to realize their potential because neither the Gorongosa nor Mozambique companies invested in the necessary infrastructure to bring agricultural products to the markets developing on the coast and in Rhodesia.

When colonial administration began, there were no roads except for footpaths. Transport was essentially by foot, with cargo and passengers carried by bearers. During the rainy season, travel was impossible in many areas because there were no bridges over the many rivers and flooding occurred. The Mozambique Company rushed to build a railway between Beira and Southern Rhodesia but took thirty years to complete an all-weather connection to it from the administrative seat of Gorongosa. The first telephone installation was in the 1920s. For most of the years under Company rule, there were *only three retail shops* in the entire area. Gorongosa was virtually an island, renown for its rebellious people.

Bivar gave his superiors a picture of people's lives at the turn of the century. He described how people managed their resources and what little was needed in the way of investment to make the area flourish. Farming practices were rudimentary and he felt that there was little variety in the crops cultivated: mainly sorghum and maize with some rice as far as cereals were concerned. Complementary to this were legumes, squash, cucumber, cassava, and sweet potatoes. Because Bivar did not find groundnuts he tried to introduce them.[10] Cultivation was extensive and itinerant. Whole villages moved on a regular basis in order to take advantage of fallow lands. People had few animals. They made most of what they needed with the help of a few blacksmiths and carpenters. One of the people's greatest concerns was co-existing with the wild animals; lions and elephants often plagued their lives. Another was the need to go to Rhodesia, first of all, to find markets as there were almost none in Gorongosa, secondly, to obtain more favorable prices and, thirdly, to find work in order to pay taxes. Bivar reported that about 50 percent of tax collected was in gold which could not have been obtained in Company territory.[11]

The three paramount rulers (nhacuáuas) of Gorongosa were Tambarara, Sadjunjira, and Kanda.[12] In 1907 Bivar noted emigration from Kanda to Báruè but he did not worry because tax collections were increasing.[13] He reasoned that the exodus from Kanda was nothing more than the Báruès returning home "now that there are no more causes for flight" and that this exodus was counterbalanced by the immigration into Gorongosa of people from Buzi and elsewhere south of the Pungué.[14] (See map 4.) However, Bivar's assistant revealed a more accurate reason for the emigration to Báruè:

This is a point that I don't know how to describe to your Excellency: it is the bane of my existence as head of this district, because I don't know how to explain the resistance to the service in Macequece.[15] I have to get used to this passive war, and still furnish serviçães [workers] to Manica in homeopathic doses, using a mild manner in order not to compete with the emigration that has developed in Maringue. What is the cause of this resistance and repugnance to the service in Manica: several nhacuáuas whom I interviewed said that the work in Macequece is very heavy and the Company pays very little in relation to the private sector and, above all, men cannot stay four months away from their fields, especially in the planting season. Others say that in Báruè, people have to pay mussoco [tax] but don't have to go to forced labor and they prefer to live there for this reason. The horror of forced labor makes people hide in the forests as soon as they see the cypães [company policemen] for recruitment and they hesitate to come to pay the mussoco for fear of being grabbed for Macequece.[16]

Gorongosa was forced to send, on average, twelve hundred males per year to labor mainly in Manica mines and plantations. This was around 18 percent of the fit male population not counting those conscripted for work inside the circumscription.

In spite of forced labor and emigration, Kanda grew and prospered. People made the best of a bad situation. In 1916, Kanda's population was close to five thousand people out of the district total of approximately twenty-four thousand. Households owned 787 goats and 416 pigs, double the amount of the year before and by far the largest number of small animals in Gorongosa.

The Revolt of Báruè

Without any doubt, the Báruè revolt of 1917 took everyone and certainly Bivar by surprise: his reports gave no hint of anything brewing. The following résumé of the revolt relies mainly on war dispatches in the records of the Government of Mozambique Province and Pelissier's account (1988).[17]

Putting aside their rivalry, the feuding branches of the royal family recruited allies amongst the peoples surrounding Báruè for a last desperate fight against the Portuguese. They even tried to enlist Great Britain to its cause. Apparently there was little difficulty in forming a coalition of neighbors, including the peoples of the district of Tete on the west, the Tongas to the north, the Gorongosans and Senas to the east. Relationships had already been cemented with Gorongosa by intermarriages. Kanda gave a daughter in matrimony to Macossa, and, according to Pelissier, also to the other branch of the royal family led by Ngongwe-Ngongwe (1988, vol. 2:350).

The Báruès organized for battle. In the south, Macossa and his war chief, Ngaru, led warriors from Báruè, the northern prazos, Sena, and Gorongosa. Ngongwe-Ngongwe led the coalition of forces from Tete and the northeast including the Tawaras. They opened two fronts beginning in March 1917. There were wild, sometimes unconfirmed reports, particularly from informants to the British authorities, regarding the successes of the Báruès. One of the first engagements of the war was a clash between the Portuguese and the Báruès near Tete city around the middle of April with the Portuguese reported to have suffered heavy losses.[18] A British report out of Beira recorded the fall of the administrative capital of Gorongosa, known as Vila Paiva de Andrada, in early April.[19]

At the end of April, the Resident Commission in Salisbury queried the Governor-General of Mozambique on how Portugal was going to respond. He replied:

> The military strategy is as follows: three columns have been organized under the direction of the Tete governor and will be deployed from Tete to the south

in the direction of Báruè; from Sena along the Zambeze in order to defeat the
rebels of Chemba to Tambara and then moving on Báruè; from the South and
Southeast toward Manica and Gorongosa and then moving on to Báruè. These
columns are made up of regular troops and auxiliaries and are commanded by
the Governor of Tete himself for the Tete Column, by Captain Rodriguês for
the Sena Column and by Major Graça for the Gorongosa Column. Each column is accompanied by a functionary who has prestige among the population
and knows well the region where the columns will operate. . . . Besides these
preparations, the armed steamship Salvador and a new one will be outfitted to
control the Zambeze River.[20]

Pelissier calls the Portuguese plan similar to the successful one executed by
Coutinho in 1902: to strike at the heartland of Báruè and to protect the railway and the southern bank of the Zambeze river (1988:362).[21]

The Gorongosa column led by Major Alberto Graça consisted of a native
company and five pieces of artillery supplemented by auxiliaries led by Gustavo Bivar. It crossed the Pungué on 29 April, established communications
with Vila Paiva on 5 May and seemed to win against Macossa's forces on 7
May. Combat occurred in Kanda in the serra da Gorongosa in August or early
September (Pelissier, 1988:363; Nogueira, 1963:170). Nogueira reported the
settlement destroyed by Gonçalo Amado da Cunha e Vasconcelos with the
help of sixty cipais.

Eventually, Bivar and his auxiliaries went to join the auxiliaries of Tete led
by his brother Rafael with the objective of moving toward the center of
Báruè, where they apparently put Ngongwe-Ngongwe to flight. By November 1917 Rafael Bivar routed the northern coalition. In the meantime, Macossa declared himself ruler and the rebellion continued in Gorongosa and
Cheringoma (Pelissier, 1988:375, 376). From the war dispatches, it is apparent that the Portuguese focus in 1918 was on the pacification of Gorongosa
where the remaining rebels held out.[22] In March, the wounded Macossa was
forced to flee to Rhodesia. The Portuguese allowed soldiers to have their way
with Gorongosans in their path. The women of those who were seized were
distributed among the fighting men.[23] Some slaves were taken and huts and
fields were burned to the ground.[24] The punishment for Gorongosans who
surrendered was twelve months forced labor with only food rations.[25]

Pelissier records 25,929 deaths in just the Company's territory (1988:381,
footnote 118). Thousands also fled. The Company itself registered a 20 percent drop in population from three hundred thousand to two hundred and
forty thousand. Báruè itself was depopulated, with twelve thousand people
fleeing to Rhodesia (Pelissier, 1988:382). The 1918 census for Gorongosa
showed a drop of more than seven thousand people. Kanda's population was

decimated. From almost five thousand people in 1916, the first census after the revolt showed Kanda's population to be at 2,411 people in 1920. Over twenty years were necessary for Kanda to regain its population and relative prosperity.

The Aftermath of the Revolt
The Company acted quickly to punish the Gorongosans for their participation in the revolt and to make up for lost revenues. Conscription of workers for Manica nearly tripled in the year after the revolt ended. Fully 28 percent of the male population was forced to the mines and plantations while another 10 percent worked in Gorongosa itself. 1919 was not a good year for Gorongosans. In the aftermath of the war, the harvest did not go well; there was hunger and many people contracted influenza and died. Vicente Bandeira da Lima, the new administrator, vividly described the war's impact:

> The old villages are mainly gone. The Gorongosans, properly speaking, are almost all living . . . in groups of three, six, or eight people, in general hidden as much as possible, each group as far away as possible from the others in every way, in the flimsiest provisory straw housing hedged around with thorny bushes for protection from wild animals. Those formerly belonging to established villages are dispersed throughout the district.[26]

As an example, the administrator described the plight of one family where the father was living by himself in a mountain shelter, while a younger son was found in Maringué and two older brothers were in another area. The mother and two younger children were in Sanhaxoco without any knowledge of where the others were.

In order to deal with this situation, Lima reported that he with a contingent of his policemen grouped families together in order to make a reasonably sized unit with a minimum of seven men. He designated this grouping a village, indicated a locale where the families could settle, near water and their fields, and also appointed a headman. He also said that he gave instructions as to how the village was to be constructed but did not expect that this would happen until 1920 because so many men had been taken away by the labor recruitment. He further reported that many of the former headmen had disappeared, fled, or died, and that many of the chiefs had died.

When he got to Kanda, Lima found:

> Everyone fled on that first day but when I got to the area of Kanda's family compound and of his companions, I sent the guards and his sons to call the people and on the third day they came, singing and dancing. Everywhere I

camped, at the end of the census, I would join together the natives and make them see the error of following and being a part of the last revolt, telling them what their future conduct should be and reminding them of the abundance they had and the misery they now found themselves in. . . . In general both women and men wore sacks and monkey or other skins, bark cloth and some were nude. . . . The population still thought the war was on. There was a lot of hunger everywhere because when the 1916 reserves were finished there were few seeds to plant and even what was planted was swept away by floods.[27]

As far as Lima could determine almost two hundred Gorongosans had died of starvation but large numbers of children were only skin and bones and expected to die. As a result of tiger attacks, over forty people had died and lots of others were wounded. In Pungué-Urema people began dying of Spanish flu. In general, the administrator predicted that resettlement and reconstruction would take two years. He was wrong and the policies he carried out were partially responsible for the difficulties of the situation.

One of the first policies Lima suggested was to replace the rebellious chiefdoms, with Kanda topping the list. According to oral history, this suggestion was followed and proved infelicitous for the people of Kanda (see note 39). Under Lima's administration, Gorongosans continued to suffer massive conscription: of all the rural districts in the Territory, it provided the greatest number of men in this period. Understandably, between 20 and 30 percent of Gorongosans moved out of the district. They were fleeing both labor recruitment and hunger, as droughts continued. In 1923 Lima reported that ten thousand people had left Gorongosa. This figure did not include the labor conscripts.

Lima was sensitive to the negative effects of the forced labor system and complained particularly about the one-year contracts. "One-year contracts are prejudicial to the social system; a man returns to find his wife with another man."[28] He saw long absence as responsible for the loosening of moral values and gave, as an example, the 904 single women, many of whom had children by unknown fathers. One-year contracts also gave rise to falling birth rates, alcohol abuse, and divorce.

On a more positive note, Lima built five of the six bridges needed on the main road to Pungué and began a program of road building. He succeeded in getting a Fiat truck purchased and a telephone line installed for administrative purposes. For the first time in over twenty-five years of Company rule, Gorongosans began selling their goods in Beira. Lima mentioned that rice, some tobacco, sorghum, and bananas had been sold.[29]

Gonçalo Amado da Cunha Vasconcelos, the man who had destroyed the area in the revolt, was called to be its administrator in 1928 but little

changed during his term of office. From 1928 the Company no longer recruited labor; workers had to find their own jobs. Because of the Great
Depression, there were more people looking for work than there were jobs
available. As a consequence men returned to farming and agricultural productivity rose notably. Nevertheless, people were prevented from realizing
income because the roads had once again deteriorated to the point that bearers were the main form of transport. People experienced great difficulties in
paying their taxes.

In 1930, when Pedro Carmona e Silva took over, the Company began
buying people's crops. When the Company made cotton a compulsory crop
in the district, production grew dramatically: from approximately fifty tons in
1936 to eight times that amount in 1939 and to approximately 1,749 tons in
1940. Maize production was estimated at an annual average of ninety tons
and much of it was converted into maize flour and commercialized. Since the
estimates of production do not correspond to the amounts of exported flour,
it is certain that administrators grossly underestimated harvests. The conditions were finally being put into place to allow Gorongosans to begin to realize their agricultural potential.

In summary, under the Mozambique Company, just as under the Niassa
Company, agricultural development had never been the main emphasis. The
Mozambique Company profited mainly and considerably from tax collections: in most years in Gorongosa it made, at the very *minimum*, a *100 percent return* over expenses.

Portuguese Administration

Portugal took over Manica and Sofala on 18 July 1942, and began to make
noticeable improvements both in terms of economic conditions and
infrastructure in a drive to promote agricultural production. The campaign to
promote cropping began with a regulation fixing a minimum number of
hectares for each person over the age of eighteen to farm, including an allotment for cotton cropping (*Nota circular número 2*, 16 November 1942).
This campaign had a number of objectives, the most obvious of which was to
raise cotton yields for Portuguese textile factories. However, much more was
at stake.

In areas of significant emigration, such as Gorongosa, Portugal thought
that a commercial crop would fix the male population and thus stem rural exodus. Having a commercial crop to sell would provide an alternative to mining wages as a means of paying taxes. However, Kanda and Xicari told a Portuguese inspector that young men still preferred working outside Gorongosa

as a way of earning money for marriage payments and taxes while family men were happier staying at home and planting cotton.[30]

A further reason behind the cotton campaign was the desire to demarcate land. Portugal found it difficult to administer people who moved to new fields every four or five years and it also wanted to make land available to potential immigrants. In Manica, Portuguese and other European farmers had spontaneously and successfully established themselves as comparatively large-scale maize producers in the early part of the twentieth century. The administration wanted to replicate this experience in Gorongosa by demarcating areas for concessions to Europeans as well as native reserves. Finally, more or less fixed native settlements corresponded to the Portuguese ideal of rural development[31] and to the Portuguese mind brought the administration a step closer to the realization of *aldeamentos*. As noted already, Scott is highly critical of this bureaucratic conception of settlement:

> This process has often been described as a "civilizing process." I prefer to see it as an attempt at domestication, a kind of social gardening devised to make the countryside, its products, and its inhabitants more readily identifiable and accessible to the center. Certain elements of these efforts at domestication seem, if not universal, at least very common, and they may be termed "sedentarization," "concentration" and "radical simplification" of both settlement and cultivation (Scott, 1998:184).

In Gorongosa, the National Cotton Company (*Companhia Nacional Algodoeira*) became the principal buyer of cotton. In 1942–1943, it had 4,376 growers who together produced slightly over one thousand tons,[32] somewhat down from previous yields but by 1962 Gorongosans were producing two and a half times that amount. By this time also, they were producing abundant yields of cereals, which then eclipsed those of cotton. In the agricultural year 1963–1964 under good climatic conditions, they produced twenty-five thousand tons of sorghum, fifteen thousand tons of maize, and 1,377 tons of cotton.[33] Gorongosa then had a maize mill with a capacity to manufacture sixteen tons of flour daily. The mill was a secure outlet for the producers and there were other buyers as well, including the railway, government departments, the growing population of Beira, municipal departments, and the Port authority. By the end of the colonial period, Gorongosa was the most productive area of Sofala. It exported up to two thousand tons of maize a year, which was the equivalent of 15 percent of all the marketed maize in the country (Price Waterhouse Agriculture, 1993).

In the 1960s, roads and transport as well as telecommunications improved. There were three classified roads and five hundred kilometers of access roads, a daily bus service, bridges over the Pungué and some other rivers, telephone service, and mail three times a week. There were also three airstrips, one of which served the game reserve that had been carved out of district lands in 1949. There were *thirty commercial establishments*, thirty-one missionary schools, and three public schools. In Vila Paiva, there was running water and electricity. Medical care, in general, had not improved.

Kanda, by now designated as an administrative post, was somewhat exceptional in that it had a well-maintained health post. Moreover, in the 1960s, it had eight schools, four stores, and three small-scale maize mills. It was also recognized as an official market. Kanda had the largest number of registered cotton growers in the entire district, slightly over one thousand farmers, while eighty-eight grew maize as a commercial crop. Its population had grown to 11,102 people. As a whole, Gorongosa more than doubled its population in the 1960s, from 24,000 to almost 52,000 inhabitants and its population density went from 3 persons per square kilometer to 6.7 persons.[34]

In May 1967, the governor of the District of Beira, encompassing Gorongosa, wrote to the treasury director of the colony that its mountains could serve as a hideout and base for the liberation movement, FRELIMO, given the fertile lands surrounding it.[35] In that same year, a surveillance mission came to inquire about people's receptivity to subversion. While noting many existing contradictions due to Portuguese meddling with indigenous political structures, the mission report found most people in a "natural" state, that is, very much attached to their customs and traditions and hardly spoilt from contact with the rest of the world, meaning, apparently, that FRELIMO had only limited penetration at this point in time.

Nevertheless, the governor's warning was not only accurate but prophetic. Guerrilla activity reached central areas in the 1970s. (It never reached the south of the country.) André Matsangaice is said to have known the mountain area when he was a freedom fighter for FRELIMO. After independence, when FRELIMO created re-education camps, it established three in Gorongosa. One was in Kanda and another in Sacudzo. Matsangaice, who in the meantime had become a dissident, was interned in Sacudzo. He later broke out and fled to Rhodesia. In May 1977 he returned to Sacudzo to liberate its inmates, twenty-eight of whom became the original core group of the National Resistance Movement, RENAMO. In September 1979, Matsangaice returned once again to the area and established Gorongosa "as the movement's central base" (Cabrita, 2000:135–155).

The surveillance mission of 1967 made a radical suggestion: to give community leaders "a greater hearing and participation in the management of problems affecting native life as a whole and of their group in particular."[36] It even recommended allowing natural leaders full reign over their people.[37] Needless to say, this advice was not taken, but it foreshadowed the recommendations to a FRELIMO government published thirty years later by an international seminar convoked by the Ministry of State Administration, most of which have gone unheeded.

Gorongosa in the 1990s

I made three visits to Gorongosa in the 1990s: in 1995 to help train district officials and the project personnel of a local project, sponsored by German Technical Cooperation, in participatory rural appraisal techniques; in 1996 to help lead the INDER training program and participatory planning exercises; and in 1999 to help evaluate the INDER planning exercises.

Gorongosa in 1995

My first impression of Gorongosa was of a sun-baked, dried, and dusty land due to the unusually severe drought affecting the district as a whole in 1995. Resettlement had begun but few people had returned by then. The district's total population was roughly estimated at 56,327 people, 70 percent of whom were still crowded into the district seat, now simply called Gorongosa city. Kanda held only 10,304 people. The war had left both Kanda and Gorongosa as a whole with the population of thirty years before!

Committed to giving emergency relief to the resulting famine, project personnel and district officials needed to know what people needed. Teams were organized to visit several settlements. One of the areas visited was Bazarangoma, a dependency of Kanda, with the small population of 845 people. We were told that the people were organized both under Kanda as *régulo* and the government *bairro* Secretary. Even though there were only 153 families, they had a *juiz* (judge) and adjunct *m'fumo* (assistant settlement head), both of whom responded to Kanda. The secretary defined his role as intermediary between this indigenous structure and the government at large.

Cut off from easy communication with the outside world because of mines on the access road and the lack of a bridge over the Nhandare river,[38] Bazarangoma took its name from a near-by outcropping where wildebeest had roamed in early times. *Bazarangoma* was the Portuguese adaptation of the local language name meaning 'house of the wildebeest.' The area was mountainous, which made agriculture difficult under any circumstance but, during the war, land was subject to overcrowding. Being close to the district capital, Bazarangoma had become an accommodation center for displaced people.

People had been confined to the same plots for ten or more years and many of the displaced people had only small ones, which they were forced to cultivate as intensively as possible. The terrain showed all the signs of soil degradation and was a prime example of the civil war's impact on food security.

It was no wonder that one of the major problems people talked about was land conflict, due to the great pressure on the land and a lack of virgin lands. Despite the end of the war, people from the district capital were still coming to this area looking for land. Moreover, many of the displaced people had not returned to their homelands. Original owners were reclaiming their lands and, due to the drought, people were coming from even worse off areas in search of water as well as land. Problems arising from this demand were first taken to the juiz, then to the adjunct m'fumo and then the régulo. If none of these authorities could elicit agreement between the contending parties, the problem was referred to the civil authorities.

Neither of the two heads of family that I personally interviewed was native to Bazarangoma. Their situations were typical of the problems of the settlement. Senhor Mello had formerly lived in the district capital but was a descendent of natives and Sr. Maibeque originally came from Sacudzo. After the death of his parents, Sr. Mello came to take over his grandparent's lands. He was a relative newcomer while Sr. Maibeque had actually occupied the lands he was cultivating for more than ten years. Now, however, the original owner had come back to reclaim the best part of this land. Despite occupying inherited lands, Sr. Mello was worse off, in the short term, than Sr. Maibeque because he had only his wife to help him. His sons were either too young to farm or physically handicapped. Moreover, he had just suffered the loss of all his farm animals.

Sr. Maibeque had three wives and six sons, five of whom were at home. His eldest son had sent him construction materials and this had much improved his family dwellings. The Maibeques along with all the people in the area farmed mainly maize and sorghum. In good years, they even marketed maize and in 1993–1994, they were able to market around half a ton. However, in 1994–1995, Maibeque had nothing to show for his efforts because of the lack of rainfall. Moreover his soil was beginning to show signs of serious erosion, especially as his fields were on the slopes of a hill. He said that several of his neighbors had already left the area because of the generalized erosion. He hoped to feed his family at least partly on the produce grown in the second season on some lowland property along the riverbanks. Because his maternal uncle was the ruler of neighboring Sacudzo, he felt that one day he would probably return to his lands there.

Because of crop failure in the first growing season, both families in 1995 were eating only one meal a day. Sr. Mello had become a fisherman in order to make ends meet. Sr. Maibeque's wife was making pottery, which she hoped to sell. Others were cutting wood and bamboo to sell in the town.

Kanda in 1996

My second visit in April 1996 was to Kanda proper, delimited by the confluence of two rivers, the Nhandare with the Vunduzi, while a third river, the Nhandue traced Kanda's eastern border with Macossa in Manica province. See the sketch map designed by the population in the appendix. Kanda's 1,158 square kilometers, traversed by numerous small rivers that flow from the mountain, make it one of the most fertile lands of Mozambique. These rivers did not dry even in times of drought. The timing of our visit was propitious in that the first harvest was in progress and it was an especially abundant one, the first good harvest since war's end.

Kanda's major problem was lack of access. First of all, to reach the district capital one had to cross three rivers, none of which had a bridge over it. The first vehicle our team used was not able to ford the Nhandare so we switched to another four by four van, which sustained damage on the final day. We were lucky to have been able to make the three, day trips to Kanda.

Two weeks before our arrival, the people of Kanda had found themselves with a new régulo due to the death of the fifth titleholder, Almeida Charamanza Kanda. Not more than a month after our visit, however, the sixth titleholder was not deemed fit for the task; the people deposed him and elected a new ruler. This was not the first time they had done so.[39]

On the occasion of our visit, the elders told us that the people were governed directly by m'fumos of whom there were more than twenty (including that of Bazarangoma) and they were subordinated to four chefes directly under the dynastic ruler, Kanda. Problems were first raised with an m'fumo and made their way up the chain of authority when necessary. The only government official in the area was the head of the administrative post of Nhamadzi and, therefore, the counterpart of the dynastic ruler. However, it was very apparent that the "traditional" structure ruled the area.

The elders complained that, over the years, many people had died of war and famines and mentioned, in particular, the 1973 famine, the one in 1979, the great famine of 1983 and the one of 1991–1992 that desolated the entire country. Kanda suffered thirteen years of war between RENAMO and FRELIMO and most people had fled either to Zimbabwe or Chimoio, the capital of Manica Province. In 1996 more people were still outside Kanda than had returned. The elders said that under normal circumstances men had, on average, two wives and the general rule was between fifteen to twenty people per family.

Kanda had no visible land problems and both men and women had the right to tenure on the land. Fields were generally two hectares in dimension but some were even larger. All of the families that I visited had several fields over four hectares in total. People cropped maize and sorghum together in the same field. This very unusual practice was very much appreciated by the Price Waterhouse consultant agronomist contracted by the German Technical Cooperation-sponsored project. Billing noted that the maize and sorghum combination was very well adapted to the climatic conditions and the constraints of a limited work force. Because of tsetse flies, there were no animals for traction. Therefore, "the opening of fields consumed the principal part of the time of the work force and the association of maize and sorghum both optimized the work force and guaranteed the maximum possible food security" (Billing, 1993:12). Kanda's families habitually employed seasonal workers to assist family labor and paid them in some combination of money, food and clothing.

Moises Carlos

This young man lived with his two wives near a crossroads area, known as Cruzamento. In 1996, he was in the process of building his compound on the top of a small hill, which gave magnificent views of the Gorongosa mountain range on one side and the valley all around. He had encircled his house with banana trees. Sr. Carlos had a somewhat unusual background. During the war, he had been "recruited" by the government army (recruitment was done by press gangs) and spent eight years as a soldier. Then he was captured by RENAMO and spent another five years fighting for them. It was during this period that he met his second wife, Teresa Rodriguês, whom he married during the last few years of the war. She was from the neighboring district of Cheringoma. His first wife was from Kanda. They all lived in the same compound with four small children, one of whom he had adopted during the war.

Because of his location at the crossroads, Sr. Carlos was in the process of opening up a small shop. He had received training in small business management from a German Technical Cooperation program for demobilized soldiers and had been promised credit to stock his shop. He was also a farmer as were his wives and there were three large granaries in his yard. They all cultivated maize with sorghum while he alone planted cotton. During the season of 1994–1995, Sr. Carlos was able to sell eight sacks or around three-quarters of a ton of cotton to a company by the name of Moçambique Industrial that paid him 200,000 *meticais* (somewhat over U.S.$20 at the time). In 1995–1996 he desisted because the price was too low. Together the family had four and a half hectares of land under cultivation. It was all rain-fed and upland. On the weekends, Sr. Carlos was leader of a congregation of the Apostolic Zion Church of Mozambique, which also had branches in Zimbabwe, Malawi, and South Africa. He had thirty church-going members.

Fatima Vulande

Senhora Vulande was the next person we met, a widow with two adult daughters who did not live at home but came to farm with their mother. Sra. Vulande hired other workers to help her and her daughters. She was also a traditional midwife and had recently taken a course sponsored by UNICEF to assist midwives identify complicated pregnancies. She proudly showed us her certificate.

Sra. Vulande had eight hectares of land, both upland and moist lowland. We visited them with her and it was like going into a magical world of lush green fields filled with maize and sorghum, banana, sugar cane, melons, bean-stalks twining around the cereal stalks, tomatoes, cabbages, sweet potatoes, and groundnuts. Every inch was planted. Sra. Vulande's compound was crowded with granaries. On the day we arrived, workmen were building a third large one. All were bursting their seams with maize. Sra. Vulande explained the situation. The government had set a minimum price of 1,500 *meticais* per kilogram of white maize but when the harvest proved abundant, it abandoned the guaranteed price, which came tumbling down to 500 *meticais* per kilo. Sra. Vulande and many farmers of Kanda were boycotting the market at that ridiculously low price and were fixing to store the grain until a buyer appeared offering more. She was not particularly unhappy about storing maize because the two previous years had been disastrous and her family had been reduced to eating mangoes, a wild fruit in Mozambique. Her grandchildren went to school as did the nephew that lived with her.

Vasco Frose

This middle-aged man headed the third, large family of twenty persons my group visited. He had four wives, each having her own fields and granaries. Together there were fourteen children, eleven of whom were male. They had a very large and beautifully spaced compound and were evidently prosperous. Each field was one and a half hectares in dimension, making a total of seven and a half hectares.

The family recalled drought in the last three agricultural years, and felt that 1996 was a season for celebration. They were sure that they had enough food even though the locusts were eating the sorghum crop. They had planted maize, sorghum, cassava, sweet potatoes, sesame, groundnuts, different varieties of beans, bananas and sugarcane. Sr. Frose also was boycotting the market but not so much for economic reasons, rather he was being very cautious and wanted to be sure to have enough seed to plant in the coming season. He said that many of his neighbors had sold much of their reserves because of enthusiasm at finally having something to sell.

The Frose family also had a visibly large array of small animals, from chickens, to goats, doves, dogs, cats, pigs, and ducks. His wives were jointly responsible for their care. Six of his children were in school, the others being too young.

With such a good start to the agricultural year, what then were Kanda's problems? As was to be expected, the first three priorities people identified had to do with marketing. People asked for a maize mill, for stores, that is, commercial outlets and a means of transporting goods and people to market in the district capital. The fourth priority was for employment, then schools to complement the few they had, wells for clean water, and farming implements.

The last time I visited Gorongosa in 1999, I was not able to cross the Nhandare. There was still no bridge and the river was on a rampage; no vehicle could pass. I noted however that the agricultural year was again very promising and when I arrived in March people were already marketing maize. Globalization had reached the district capital: Coca-Cola had come to Gorongosa with a vengeance. There were small stalls lining access and main roads selling warm Coke, Sprite, and Fanta. Since I could not go to Kanda, I did the next best thing. I went to see a man who was part of the dynastic line. Celestino Tsacaune Kanda, catechist for Cristo Rei mission, lived on the church's compounds. He was very happy to talk about Kanda though not much impressed with the bottles of Fanta, Coke, and Sprite that I offered.

Celestino Tsacaune Kanda[40]

As a young man, Sr. Tsacaune had studied with the White Fathers who opened Cristo Rei mission in 1957. Among the priests he remembered were Adriano Brusciotti, who knew all the spiritual secrets of Gorongosa mountain, Cesar Capanelli who built seven schools, and a certain Father Bertuli. At about the same time, Protestant churches began to penetrate the district. First was the Assembly of God mission and then Zion. They were not welcomed by the Portuguese.

I asked Sr. Tsacaune to tell me the story of the dynastic line and especially to explain the most recent removal of the titleholder. He confirmed that the Kanda lineage came from Mbire in Zimbabwe near Mount Inhamcungo. He called the clansmen Zimbas or descendants of Zimbas and said that they had been forced to leave because of the Monomotapa wars of succession. One group went to Malawi, others to Gorongosa and the third to the south. (His version of how the lineage received the name, Kanda, is described in the beginning of this chapter.) The second Kanda was Umbawara, the brother of the first; he was contemporaneous with Gouveia. The third king was Araiva, ruler at the time of the first World War and the Báruè revolt. Araiva lent soldiers both to the Báruè ruler and to the Portuguese. Kanda found itself in the middle of these two warring parties and although it respected Báruè, it was to some extent its victim because the Báruès were cruel and grabbed what they could from Kanda including its women. The Portuguese expelled Araiva for his part in the revolt and installed Quembo, known as "Canhoco." This ruler did not respect the women of others and, according to Sr. Tsacaune, the population complained about him to the Portuguese who then replaced him with Vijarona.

Vijarona Charamanza Kanda was Sr. Tsacaune's uncle. He died in 1963 or 1964 and was succeeded by Almeida Charamanza who died in 1996. When Micalete Almeida, who was living in Chimoio in the neighboring province, came for the funeral he tried to assume the title by force without the benefit of an election. (He was the person with whom the INDER team worked during their visit.) The population quickly expelled him and elected Sr. Madeira, the current Kanda.

From 1953 to 1955, Sr. Tsacaune lived in Zimbabwe. During the war for independence, he was held prisoner five times by the Portuguese. After the war, FRELIMO invited him to be a part of the "dynamizing" group of cadres (*grupo dinamizador*), but he did not assume this position. Nevertheless he collaborated with FRELIMO until 1990.

His view on FRELIMO as a governing party was that it should not be condemned for the mistakes of individual members. *Its greatest fault lay in abolishing the marketing system, and commerce in general, in the name of socialism.* However, he recognized that there were also people who took other people's goods and that there was a general lack of control. For these reasons rebellion began. Most people remained on the sidelines but their children went to fight. There were many atrocities on all sides. People did not respect each other and grabbed everything they could from others, even their clothes.

At the war's end, the administrator gave Sr. Tsacaune permission to begin the mission once again and ended up praying there as did the present Administrator. Sr. Tsacaune also helped organize a cooperative of maize farmers, which affiliated with the National Union of Peasants (*União Nacional dos Camponeses*). There were problems because the vice-president, secretary and treasurer had stolen cooperative monies. The union set up a commission of inquiry, the wrongdoers admitted their guilt and promised to reimburse the cooperative.

Liberalization had brought Gorongosans the freedom to organize politically, economically and religiously as they pleased but by the end of 1999 the very basic infrastructures and/or commercial system to realize fully these freedoms had not yet been put in place.

Notes

1. The Portuguese created a hunting reserve that eventually covered approximately fifty-three thousand square kilometers. In 1953 the total area of the rural district of Gorongosa was 75,740 square kilometers. (*Boletim Oficial* no. 15, 11 April 1953, III Série).

2. In his 1980 work, David Beach refers to three different locations for Mbire depending upon the period; in 1994 he called into question oral traditions regarding the founding of the Mutapa state and says that there is no clear picture of where the capital was located (1994:101).

3. "Just where Sena borders Shona is a matter of dispute, complicated by the existence of the large territory of Barwe, lying between the northern end of the Eastern Highlands and the lower Zambezi, with a political existence spanning four centuries" (Beach, 1994:26). The Portuguese saw Báruè as divided between Shona-speakers in the south and Sena-speakers in the north separated by a dry zone with Shona-speakers on both banks of the Pungué toward the Zambeze.

4. Portugal, Serviços de Coordenação e Centralização das Informações, 1967:1.1.8.

5. Interview with Tsacaune Kanda, March 1999.

6. Colonia de Moçambique, Província de Manica e Sofala, Inspecção dos Serviços Administrativos e dos Negócios, *Relatório da Inspecção Ordinária às Circunscrições de Buzi, Chemba, Cheringoma, Chimoio, Gorongosa, Manica, Marromeu, Mossurize, Sena, Sofala,* 1943–1944:6.

7. Companhia de Moçambique, *Respostas ao Questionário Etnográfico,* 1928:14. Celestino Tsacaune's father told him that the impis (Nguni warriors) reached Kanda and grabbed clothes and bangles that people, by the sweat of their brow, had acquired from trading with Asian (Goan?) merchants.

8. This information comes from Barry Neil-Tomlinson's Ph.D. thesis and unfortunately it was not possible to ascertain whether the retreat of Kanda coincided with that of Cambuemba. In any case, the ten chiefs completely disassociated themselves from Cambuemba.

9. Apparently, sometime in 1901 the Governor of the Companhia de Moçambique received information that the Báruè royal family was willing to submit to the Company and he wanted to verify this before sending the military expedition that was already planned. Company headquarters was not ready to delay and refused permission to allow the Governor to check the information and the expedition went ahead. Companhia de Moçambique, *Relatório do Governador do anno de 1901:77.*

10. Companhia de Moçambique, 1906:27.
11. Companhia de Moçambique, 1906:6.
12. At this point in time, the district also included Pungué, Maringué and Santa.
13. Companhia de Moçambique, Circumscripção da Gorongosa, *Relatório do mez de Maio de 1907*:7.
14. Companhia de Moçambique, *Relatório da Circumscripção da Gorongosa do anno de 1908*:2.
15. This was where a road was being built.
16. Companhia de Moçambique, *Relatório da Circumscripção da Gorongosa do anno de 1909*:11, 12.
17. Also consulted was Barbara and Allen Isaacman, *The Tradition of Resistance in Mozambique* (1976) and various documents from the records of the Companhia de Moçambique in the AHM. The report of Major Graça was missing and various files including the Commission of Inquiry documentation were very skimpy. From the present state of records in the AHM, there was no way to confirm or deny Pelissier's assertion that the Commission's report was never published and is missing.
18. Telegrams, 16 and 21 April.
19. Telegram, 11 April.
20. Governo-Geral, Quartel-General no. 5, Processos, Telegram of 25 April 1917.
21. See also Armando Guedes Nogueira, 1963.
22. The First World War was in progress and the Portuguese had an Expeditionary Force in the north of the country collaborating with the Allies against the Germans. In February 1918 the Supreme Commander of the Allied Forces in Africa, General Van Deventer, urged the Portuguese to take all measures to put the rebellion down as it could create an opening for the Germans. The Portuguese Commander took this advice very seriously and conferred with the Governor-General on the situation. The reply on 25 February indicated that the various columns had matters well in hand. Telegram, 25 February.
23. Telegram, 5 June, from the Governor of the Territories of the Companhia de Moçambique.
24. Telegrams of 24, 29 June.
25. Telegram, 5 June.
26. Companhia de Moçambique, *Relatório da Circunscrição de Gorongoza, ano de 1919*:1–7.
27. Companhia de Moçambique, *Relatório, 1919*:4.
28. Companhia de Moçambique, *Relatório do recenseamento da população indígena do ano de 1923*.
29. Companhia de Moçambique, Circunscrição de Gorongoza, *Relatório Anual de 1923*.
30. Colonia de Moçambique, Inspection report, 1946.
31. Zamparoni describes the model of rural development in this way: "What surely passed through the head of the reformist administrators was the transfer to the

colonies in the midst of the twentieth century of a pre-industrial revolution and rather romanticized model of Portuguese smallholding. . . . Land and family, values that were profoundly rooted in western culture, constituted the icons of colonialism." (2000:209).

32. Colonia de Moçambique, 1946:94.

33. Colonia de Moçambique, *Relatório da Inspecção Ordinária à Circunscrição da Gorongosa*, 1967:57.

34. Colonia de Moçambique, 1967:14.

35. Fundo do Governo do Distrito da Beira, 1967.

36. Portugal, 1967:57.

37. Portugal, 1967:64.

38. One of the highlights of this visit was the fording of the river on foot. The current was strong and the waters at least three to four feet high.

39. After the Báruè revolt, Lima removed the dynastic ruler Araiva and replaced him with Quembo Chaneca Kanda but he had to be removed, at the behest of the people, because of his excessive philandering among Kanda's women.

40. I have kept as much as possible the flow of Sr. Kanda's interview.

CHAPTER THREE

⁓

Mossurize: Gungunhana's Men

The specific Karanga migrations that settled the southern highlands of Zimbabwe and south-central areas of Mozambique, such as Mossurize, appear to have been different from the ones that settled Gorongosa. They are said to have been sparked by the Monomotapa's decision in the mid-seventeenth century to rid his kingdom of the Portuguese. The Monomotapa asked his sometime rival, Changamire, to assist him whereupon Changamire raised armies from among the many different clans of the central *moyo* area.[1] Then, at the end of the century, Changamire rebelled against the Monomotapa and led his followers to southwestern regions between the Save and Limpopo where he founded a state called Butua. Another group led by Mutema, who may have been Changamire's relation, went to the southeastern highlands where the *moyo* superimposed themselves on existing populations.[2]

Mutema founded the state of Quissanga, which initially owed tribute to Butua. From Quissanga the *moyo* flowed into the area now known as Mossurize, the valley complex south of Gorongosa, just above the Save river that divides central from southern Mozambique. (See map 4.) Chaiva (Chaibva), the smallest of the four communities described in this book, seems to have been involved in these migrations.[3] The following textbox illustrates the hierarchy under Quissanga. Under its protection, the *moyo* enjoyed almost one hundred years of freedom and peace until the Ngunis arrived.

Nxaba's Nguni took Mutema's territory in 1826 and for the next ten years raided the lands of Manyika, Teve and the Sofala hinterland. They were driven out by Soshegane's Gaza Nguni, who remained in the south-eastern highlands for another two years before returning south (Beach, 1994:133).

Life under the Gaza State

A Gaza state—consolidated by Soshegane's grandson, Gungunhana—superimposed itself on the Quissanga hierarchy. The Chaiva people did not fail to be influenced by Gaza. Even to-day old men identified themselves as Gungunhana's men and sported pierced ears, a visible sign of allegiance to Gaza. According to Chaiva elders, inter-viewed in 1995, Gungunhana held court in Chinguno, immediately to the north, and recruited his armies from Chaiva and other areas. Subject chiefs sent their daughters to court and gave hospitality to Gungunhana's representatives known as *indunas*. It is interest-ing to note that the title of *induna* has survived into the 1990s, even as far away as Ilinga. The current Chaiva titleholder called the deputy who assisted him, *induna*. See the last section below.

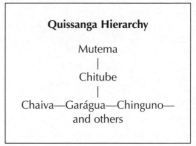

Quissanga Hierarchy

Mutema
|
Chitube
|
Chaiva—Garágua—Chinguno—
and others

According to Rennie (1973), there were three orders of people in the Gaza state: the Gaza aristocracy, the subject peoples who adopted Nguni cul-ture, and the subject people who preserved their old ways. Chaiva may have belonged to the second group. Never-theless, the rule of Gaza was not easy for any of its subject peoples. According to one description, the state, which cov-ered the whole of the southern Mozam-bique and much of the center as well, was divided into districts that were dis-tributed to royal and warrior houses, as the textbox shows. Each district had a number of resident *indunas* and warriors

Gaza Hierarchy

Gungunhana
|
Majobos (indunas, mofanas)
|
Subject chiefs

(*mofanas*), both called *Majobos*, who lived off monthly tribute. Between July and October, large groups of *majobos* traveled the empire to collect the yearly taxes for Gungunhana; they were backed by the sanction of the regiments (*mangas*) who would crush any resistance (Neil-Tomlinson, 1974:12–13).

Two Portuguese sources of the time suggest that the Nguni aristocracy were outrageous in their imperious treatment of and demands on all of their subject peoples, including the Ndau, the name the Nguni gave the clansmen of the area under study. Baptista[4] (1892) describes his own embarrassment at the manner in which Mexameja, king of the Buzi region, was treated in his presence. After witnessing the pomp and ceremony with which the Council of Elders treated their old sovereign, Baptista was pained to see the arrogance and meanness with which the Gaza ambassadors treated him. In order to underline his point, Baptista cited a section from an account by Paiva de Andrada who testified to similar humiliations in the state of Quiteve (Baptista, 1892:80 ff). While it is beyond present knowledge to describe how Chaiva's people were treated, it is certain that a part of their agricultural produce and game hunting was taxed and, as we have seen, their sons yielded up to the Gaza armies and their daughters for marriage. (This is reminiscent of the homage paid by Kanda to the Báruè rulers on the eve of the revolt of 1917.) Perhaps their lot was somewhat easier because as they themselves told us, "they allied themselves to Gungunhana's cause."

In another important aspect, Chaiva was affected by Gaza rule: this was in regard to the dispatch of its young men to the Transvaal and Southern Rhodesia mines. Gungunhana encouraged this as a way of gaining revenue from the migrants at the end of their contracts. Migration to the mines continued long after the demise of Gaza in 1895 and on a minor scale exists even today among those lucky enough to find work in South Africa. The current Chaiva titleholder along with a number of the older men told us of their time in the mines. Mining wages proved to be one of the greatest sources of tax revenue for the subsequent ruler, the Companhia de Moçambique.

It is almost certain that when Gungunhana moved his court from Chinguno to Bilene on the coast hundreds of kilometers away (see map 4), he took the people of Chaiva with him. The march in June 1889 right across the country from the highlands to the sea just north of the Limpopo included tens of thousands of people and thousands of cattle driven by men separated from their families. Many people died of hunger and thirst along the way. Chaiva disappeared from the map and only reappeared in the 1904 population census carried out by the Companhia de Moçambique. While it is not possible to know how large Chaiva was during the reign of Gaza, it may be a consequence of the march to and from Bilene that the total number of huts in Chaiva was quite small, signifying a population of fewer than three hundred.

When the Companhia de Moçambique tried to initiate its regime, Gungunhana was still in power. His chiefdoms refused to submit. As a

Company document put it: "On the other hand, the country obeyed the vatuas and did not pay tribute, nor did it obey orders that did not come from Régulo Gungunhana" (Companhia de Moçambique, 1902:286).

A shortage of personnel forced the Company to negotiate a tax-farming arrangement with Gungunhana regarding the use of his tribute collectors. *Indunas* and *mofanas* became Company agents and were paid a portion of the taxes that they collected for the Company. This measure reduced considerably not only revenues but also the Company's authority over the Territory of Manica and Sofala. In 1894, receipts were a mere 11,178 *mil reis*; in 1895, they rose slightly to 11,915 *mil reis*. In 1896—after the defeat of Gungunhana—the Company began its own collection and revenues jumped to 63,564 *mil reis* (Neil-Tomlinson, 1974:65). Tax farming, however, continued with chiefs eventually taking over the position of Gungunhana's collectors.

Company Rule

Gungunhana's downfall was disastrous for the whole population of Mossurize. They scattered and a terrible drought accompanied by locusts brought famine in 1896. The Company and the administrators of the British South African Company worked out a *modus vivendi* in regard to borders and, as just noted, the tax collection began. These events did not, however, defeat or make people compliant. There was resistance of many kinds, including hiding in the bush to avoid being registered.[5] This may be another explanation for the non-appearance of Chaiva between the years 1896–1904 and for its low population in the early years.

In 1897, the Company administrator, Anibal Machado, reported:

All the populations that I encountered on my trip are insignificant and miserable even those that belong to régulos and these, in general, are not more than eight to twelve huts. The whole region is depopulated for the well-known reason of Gungunhana's move to Bilene. Presently, many families are moving back to find their former lands and a large number of indigenes are coming back to this area and many more would come if the lack of rainfall had not put them off. The harvests having been destroyed by locusts, the people are walking three and more days looking for water which has led to the death of many, above all children . . . many people at the Save frontier are only waiting for the harvest in order to continue their walk home.[6]

Perhaps Chaiva's people straggled back, as so many others did, resettling in a disorganized manner, which would have made it easier to hide their presence until they were of such a number that they could not help being no-

ticed. Chaiva was one of the last regulados to be recorded.[7] In 1902, the agricultural season went well and more than 3,300 people returned to the district
from Bilene. This was a huge increase given that the total population of the
district was only 7,900 inhabitants in 1900.

The Physical Setting

From the very beginning, Company administrators recognized Mossurize as
an area of great potential. The following description is freely translated from
an 1896 report:

> The Mossurize valley . . . is 120 kilometers in length and 10 kilometers in width;
> it is irrigated by the Buzi, Mossurize, Xinhica, Morungueze and other rivers, and
> should be good for agriculture, similar to the land in Manica. It is not very wooded
> and is almost a plain and does not have swamps . . . around Chibabava and Chi-
> tobe, subject to the flooding of the Buzi river, the vegetation is extraordinary; the
> opposite is true on the right bank of the Buzi, two or three km. inland, which is
> dry and lacking humus. The region between the Buzi and Lucite rivers until the
> Buzi's confluence with the Mafussi is more or less a flat plain and is either similar
> or better than that of the Mossurize valley. . . . The region, which extends from
> the banks of the Save to its confluence with the Lundi until its mouth, is not good
> for agriculture according to the Boers. . . . Then there is the mountainous region
> formed by the ranges. . . . This is the most excellent agricultural region of all the
> lands of the district. Here all kinds of cultivation should be attempted from wheat,
> maize to rubber, coffee, cocoa, and so on . . . if the natural frontier, which is the
> river bed of the Save, is respected as per the treaty, then Mossurize should be the
> number one region of the Company from an agricultural perspective, especially
> given its position close to the Transvaal.[8]

Contemporary scientific surveys also divide Mossurize into three simplified
agro-ecological zones. The upland and plateau zones correspond roughly to the
mountainous region described above. The escarpment and valley zones include
a part of the Mossurize valley and the region between the Lucite and Buzi rivers.
The third zone consists of the low valley of the Morungueze, Mossurize, and Buzi
rivers, one part of which falls into the above description of the Mossurize valley
and the other part, that of the Save to the Lundi rivers. Crossed by the Mossurize, Morungueze, and Chirera rivers, Chaiva falls mainly into the low valley
zone.

As shall be seen, the administrator's dream of turning the district into the
prime agricultural area of the Territory was never realized, because, as noted
in the previous chapter, the Mozambique Company was not interested
enough in agricultural development to invest in the necessary infrastructure.

It also ignored the area's mining potential. Much to the frustration of the administrators it abandoned there, the Company left the region mainly the way it found it. During most of its fifty-year rule, Company's directors went after quick profits, including speculation on European stock markets, tax collections, and commodity extraction.

Rubber and Ivory Collection

From 1894 to 1910, the Company made rubber collection its primary activity in Mossurize. The Company busily encouraged the bleeding of the wild rubber that grew in the Mafussi and Madanda forests, in an area that in 1902 covered approximately seventy thousand hectares. Supervising the extraction were régulos bordering the forests.[9] Chaiva was not directly involved in extraction but may have contributed to the hundreds of men forcibly recruited for transporting extracted latex to Beira. At the height of extraction, around twelve hundred men were involved in the exploitation and transport of rubber. By 1913, extraction stopped altogether.

While it lasted, the rubber trade yielded enormous profits. The Company sold the commodity for a 50 percent profit after expenses were deducted (Neil-Tomlinson, 1974:282–4). Mossurize produced a large share of these profits. Exports reached a high of twenty-two tons in 1910 and expenses were the lowest in the Territory.

A number of problems with rubber collection in Mossurize came to light when a new administrator was appointed. Luciano Lanne immediately called attention to extraction methods and called for help from Company agronomists. Extractors were using machetes to slash the trees rather than making precise incisions with knives. In 1907, the agronomist came and recommended new techniques. In 1909, Lanne recommended even more protective measures but he never received authorization for these.[10] Company profits took precedence over both the environment and people.

Ivory replaced rubber as the commodity of extraction. In 1909, Administrator Lanne organized a regular Company hunt, which, for most of his time in office, did not yield much ivory, mainly because he was a conservationist. Once he left Mossurize, things changed considerably. Between 1931 and 1940, around twenty-eight tons of ivory were sent to Beira for export, surpassing by twenty tons the amounts exported previously, during Lanne's more than twenty-year administration.

Forced Labor

Rather than invest in the district, the Company preferred to exploit Mossurize as a labor reserve for the mining enterprises and settlers' agriculture elsewhere in its territory. In the earliest years, labor was conscripted for work within the district, such as building a few rudimentary dirt roads, cultivating Company rubber plantations, and maintaining Company property. Thereafter, labor was sent to the private enterprises of the Manica and Chimoio areas, referred to in the last chapter as models of Portuguese colonization:[11]

> Large blocks of land on alternate sides of the [Beira] railway were surveyed and sold/leased to individuals or companies. These blocks of land were of some ten thousand hectares, or more, and formed the basis of many of the future farms in the Manica and Chimoio District (Bannerman, 1993:10).

Labor on these farms was paid at a miserable rate. As in Gorongosa, the impact on the Mossurize male population was very significant. Lanne was not the first Mossurize administrator to understand the consequences of such exploitation.[12] He reported a mass exodus to British territory: the population of the district had increased rapidly from 12,007 in 1902 to a high of 26,643 in 1911, but then it dropped significantly reaching a low of 16,331 in 1922, mainly as a protest against the forced export of men to the Manica mines and plantations but also because of drought (see below). When the Company changed its labor recruitment policy in 1928, the population began to increase. By 1930, it again reached more than 26,000 and thereafter the population climbed steadily.

Mossurize's labor was even more heavily exploited than Gorongosa's. In 1911, nearly one-third of the male population was coerced to work for pitiful wages. A breakdown by area showed that in the rubber collection areas, 28 percent of the male population was involved but, in other areas, the percentage recruited was as high as 41 percent. The year after Lanne made his calculations the percentage of the male population coerced into the labor force rose to 36 percent, after which it fell. Only in 1918, 1922, 1924, and 1925 did it again reach 30 percent or higher.

One fundamental reason why the population did not join the Báruè revolt in 1917 was the existence of escape routes to the Transvaal and Rhodesian mines and plantations where conditions and pay were superior. These ways out still exist. For example, during the most recent conflict, Zimbabwe was the preferred refuge.

In 1921, Lanne's secretary calculated that about one-third of the male population was either in the Transvaal or Southern Rhodesia. When drought struck in 1922, it was reported that half of all the able-bodied population was out of the district (trying to survive). As shall be seen, the emigration to the mines grew considerably throughout the colonial period.

During his more than twenty years as administrator, Lanne was surprisingly outspoken in regard to the labor regime. In 1909 he offered the following suggestions for improving the situation: that salaries be at the same level as in Rhodesia; that wages be paid in gold as in the Transvaal; that there be no advance payments and only a final payment; that a Labor Bureau be institutionalized and that food rations be one kilogram of maize meal and include salt and meat or dried fish every day. Then he reminded his superiors that, at the prevailing salary levels, "if all the men of Mossurize went to Manica to work they would not gain enough to pay taxes!"[13] Needless to say, the directors did not heed Lanne's advice.

Men followed the well-worn path to the Transvaal where they earned three pounds in gold per month in mines that were very dangerous, two pounds in dangerous mines, one pound in mines that were relatively safe, and ten to fifteen shillings for agricultural work. They could not make these wages anywhere in the Territory. In fact, the Company, hoping to attract international investment, advertised that its wages were 30 percent lower than in Rhodesia and 50 percent lower than in the Transvaal. In 1935, the discrepancy was even larger: the minimum wage in the Transvaal was equivalent to 13.5 *escudos* whereas it was only 3.37 *escudos* in the Territory.[14] In 1936, the then Administrator estimated that two-thirds of the fit male population was in the Transvaal making seven times what they could in Manica and Sofala.[15] This was probably no exaggeration.

Wages were not the only problem for those Mossurize males unlucky enough to be caught in the recruitment net. In terms of other working conditions, Neil-Tomlinson noted that, in the period 1894–1910, food and shelter were of poor quality, work was ten hours per day, six days per week, and beating and abuse were commonplace (1974:282). In 1913, Lanne asked for the investigation of the deaths of 6 percent of the people that he had sent to work in Manica. He also noted that nearly three hundred people went voluntarily to the Buzi sugar factories because treatment and salaries were better. However, by the 1920s, mass desertions were reported among Mossurize males being transported to these very same sugar fields.[16]

By 1922, the Buzi sugar company, which had offered a salary of one pound per month, dropped salaries to fifteen shillings. This was at a time when the neighboring Rhodesian district, Melsetter, was experiencing a wave of white farmer settlement and the demand for a labor force was so great that agricultural wages were reportedly up to two pounds per month. In his annual report for 1923, Lanne noted that about 30 percent of those recruited for the Buzi Company had fled.[17] In 1924 the Company reduced agricultural wages even further to twelve shillings per month. Lanne protested: "in the last two years three régulos attempted suicide due to the opposition of their people to the labor recruitment."[18] And he went on to underscore the strong propaganda from the British side against forced labor, spread through Church missions, and visits by various European and American commissions to Southern Rhodesia.

The Great Depression beginning in 1929 hit all areas hard, including Mossurize. Even the well-beaten path to the Rand was blocked. In 1931, the Administrator calculated that 20 percent fewer males were making their way to the mines. There was no agricultural work available for them in Manica and Sofala either. In 1935 things picked up a bit as Portugal negotiated with South Africa an agreement that allowed the colonial government to earn gold for each Mozambican mine worker. Twenty percent of the male population of Mossurize was in the Transvaal in 1935 and, by 1938, 70 percent were out of the district.[19] By 1942 there was also a significant migration to the Rhodesian mines.

Gold and Hard Currency

While the mass migration of Mossurize males from the Territory was a disadvantage for Manica and Sofala employers, the Company gained significant sums of gold and hard currency for its treasury. Lanne was one of the first to point this out to his superiors who constantly plagued him about filling the labor quotas. In 1916 he renewed his plea to reduce the number of workers recruited by the Company and cited the fact that almost all taxes were paid in gold—six to seven thousand pounds annually—because of the migration to the Transvaal.

It is not possible from administrator's reports to calculate just how much the Company received in gold but there is no doubt that the majority of hut taxes were paid from the wages of the Transvaal miners. As late as 1935, the Administrator mentioned that 90 percent of the taxes collected in that year—about eleven thousand pounds—had been paid in English money. In the 1940s, the total amount of hut taxes reached over eighteen thousand pounds. These amounts were not inconsiderable.

The General Welfare under Company Rule

Up to this point, the chapter has focused on what the Company got out of the district. It is time to ask what the people got from Company rule. Did they receive any benefits from the taxes they paid, the labor they were forced to give, the rubber they collected, the ivory they hunted and so on?

One of the reigning myths is that colonial rule brought peace to African populations. What the Companhia de Moçambique did was to substitute itself for the Gaza state in Mossurize. Gaza was a centralized state with more than fifty years of peaceful rule in the Mossurize area, just as Quissanga, before it, had had nearly a hundred years of peace. Even though Baptista states that local populations confessed "spontaneously" to him that they would prefer "whatever European dominion to that of Gungunhana," this does not seem to have been the case in Mossurize (1892:84). As already noted, for almost ten years after the Company had established its rule, people did not rush back from Bilene. Those who came back were uncertain whether to settle on the Portuguese or British side. Anibal Machado's reports are full of suggestions about what to do to attract people.

Still the myth persisted. When the régulos of Mossurize ignored the Báruè ruler's call for recruits for the revolt, Lanne offered the opinion that they did this because they remembered the difficulties they had had under Gungunhana and thus preferred Portuguese to Báruè rule.[20] Nevertheless, the harsh treatment meted out by Gaza was not replaced by gentleness on the part of the Portuguese administration.

Barry Neil-Tomlinson, who made a thorough study of the Company from 1894 to 1910, showed that brute force was used to establish its rule. When the Company began to collect taxes, its soldiers and *cipais* forced people to pay by burning huts and food reserves, and grabbing everything in sight. Just as in Niassa, women and children were imprisoned until the hut tax was paid. Eventually the Company evolved a system incorporating local chiefs and régulos as tax farmers and intermediaries. "The incorporation of the chiefs into the administrative structure was probably the single most important factor, apart from the straightforward use of force in the company's growing control over the population of its territory" (Neil-Tomlinson, 1974:181). When it began to recruit labor, its agents flogged, executed or imprisoned rebels, and deposed chiefs. Neil-Tomlinson reports even one incident of decapitating heads and parading them around (1974:265). These were some of the ways in which the Company established its authority in the very early years.

Between 1898 and 1910, *cipais* were sent out with rifles and rounded up workers at gunpoint (Neil-Tomlinson, 1974:265–267). Machado reported trying to end violence yet there were complaints about him and his men. It is not easy to know how Lanne treated people but we do know that his officers were not necessarily kind and that he tolerated some outrageous behavior. In 1908, a young official under him, António Fernando Armas, accused Lanne of certain irregularities in a hand-written note to the governor of the Company. These included mishandling small amounts of money and goods. In the long and thorough investigation, Lanne was exonerated but it came to light that Armas had squandered his family's money in Portugal and received his post out of pity. An abuser of alcohol and apparently Mossurize women, he used violence in his relations with the local population. Although Lanne was cleared of the original charges, it does not speak well for his administration that Armas continued in his post once his conduct was known. This may be due to the fact that Armas apparently had a well-placed patron in the governor.[21]

In 1935, Administrator António de Lima Correia was dismissed from his post and put before a military tribunal to face the following charges: first, he did not follow normal procedures in paying Chibabava régulos their commissions on tax collections. Second, only a small part of the one hundred sacks of maize seed designed for local distribution in a year of hunger was distributed. Third, old people, blind people, and children were forced to pay taxes. Fourth, régulos were forced to say each taxpayer's name and, if they forgot any, they were fined. Fifth, régulos were forced to pay the taxes of those who fled to Rhodesia. Sixth, old widows were charged taxes. Seventh, he seized women at will. Eighth, women prisoners were obliged to produce his personal crops in the two years of his administration.

Twenty-one régulos of the total fifty-one confirmed these accusations.[22] There were also a number of other administrative irregularities. The only positive thing to be said of this sad story was that Lima Correia was removed rather quickly. However, his crimes were blatant as well as numerous and could not have been hidden easily. One can only wonder whether other officials were not also guilty of one or more of such acts in the course of their duty. Inspections made in the late 1940s and 1950s showed that even when the Portuguese state took over beatings still took place.

Drought

Besides Company exploitation, the people of Mossurize also had to battle the weather. From 1908 until 1943 administrators reported seventeen years of bad agricultural conditions, nearly half of the time in this thirty-five year span. Drought was the most frequent calamity and hit hardest the southern part of the district. Only a few years saw relentless torrential rains. Droughts were often accompanied by plagues of locusts. The period, 1912–1922, was probably the worst, when starvation struck.

In 1912, people from southern areas were driven to forage the forests for food and then to move to upper Mossurize, which had some crops. Lanne distributed eighteen tons of maize seed. The population statistics of 1913 revealed a loss of 12 percent of the population, not all of whom died from starvation yet the census attributed the disappearance of 903 huts to deaths. Chaiva lost around one-third of its population, but one does not know how many of these succumbed to the famine. People ate their animals and régulos distributed the harvests of the dead to the most needy, thus saving some people's lives.[23]

Moreover, Chaiva did not do well in the next two agricultural seasons. Because of hunger, the population had to eat all the maize seeds distributed for planting. As a consequence they were only able to plant eleven hectares, two-thirds of the area cultivated in 1912. The sorghum they seeded developed a disease and insects ate crops.

1916 was the fifth year of hunger for southern populations. Lanne urged people to go to another district, Moribane, in order to avoid starvation and he distributed about three hundred pounds of food rations. Again the population fell by slightly over nine hundred huts. According to the census report, the people of Chaiva complained that it had not rained in more than three years and that there was insufficient drinking water. They had not had a cereals harvest for more than twelve months and were eating wild roots and fruit. In this year, they were only able to plant ten hectares.[24]

The next agricultural year was reportedly even worse but this time because of torrential rains affecting mainly those in upper Mossurize. However, Chaiva along with neighboring settlements lost all crops. Spanish influenza began to affect a sizeable number of people. The population of Chaiva dropped by 20 percent.

The worst seemed to be over as the agricultural years of 1919 and 1920 were very good. However, this was only a respite: drought hit again in 1922 and Spanish flu and small pox took a large number of children's lives. Chaiva's population decreased by 5 percent, its goats by more than 50 percent, and its cattle by 60 percent. Over the next four years, there were two more bad agricultural years. During this time Chaiva lost all of its cattle (that is, its savings).

A good agricultural year in 1929 led to a significant climb in Chaiva's population, which reached 407 in 1930. Thereafter it began to climb, in spite of bad agricultural years, until it reached 856 people in 1942, the last year of Company rule. It had not yet regained its cattle but the goat population soared to a high of 207.

On both sides of the border the population experienced remarkable growth from at least the 1930s. Regarding the Rhodesian Shona, Beach commented: "Of all the developments which have taken place during the past century, the most important has been the increase of population. . . . We do not yet know exactly how and when this remarkable change began . . . the origins lie in the first three decades of this century, but at present its history remains unclear" (1994:171 ff). The growth of the Mossurize Ndau was noteworthy from 1931 onward. By 1941 the population had risen 74 percent. The leap in Chaiva's population began in 1930 and increased by about 110 percent in the same ten-year period. By comparison, the Gorongosa population increased only slightly. While growth came in the same period as some significant changes in infrastructure in both rural districts, it is hard to know what sparked the extraordinary rates of growth among the Ndau, for, as shall now be seen, the impact of medical services, to cite one salient example, was negligible.

Infrastructural Development

In 1912, Administrator Lanne began seriously to agitate the Company to provide a minimum of infrastructure and he used what must have seemed a radical argument: it is time to think about improving roads and population centers *because the population is paying taxes! It is out of date to understand development only in terms of milking populations for taxes and labor.*

Mossurize had only a few dirt roads connecting it to the rest of the world and these were generally in poor condition and hardly passable in the rainy season. Lanne knew that, just as in Gorongosa, a link to the Beira railway was the primary way to stimulate agricultural development. He also felt that a telephone/telegraph line was essential: the administration had to cross the border to ask the British administration for use of its lines. It must have been embarrassing to ask such favors. This bother lasted until 1939 when the first telegraph line was mounted and inaugurated. A railway link never happened but a road that could carry vehicles was finally constructed in 1925 although it only went as far as Chibabava. Moreover, there was trouble in maintaining it due to a lack of an adequate budget.

By way of contrast, Mossurize's neighbors on the Rhodesian side of the border had had a road for transporting goods to the major market town, Umtali, since 1907. Trucks plied this road while in Mossurize the transport of persons was still by hammock and goods by individual porters. In 1930, Administrator Santos announced triumphantly that the days of the hammock were over; two motor-worthy roads now linked the district with the district of Buzi (and thus Beira, the capital) and with the southernmost outpost of the district (and South Africa). Whereas transport had taken ten to fifteen days on foot, it now only took two days by car. His optimism was not warranted because, by 1936, the roads could only be traversed by porters bearing people and goods.

In 1930, the Company deposited some medicines in each of the administrative posts, for distribution by the heads of post. This was the only medical service available until 1937 when a health post was finally established. *Until that time, Mossurize, the largest district of the Territory, was the only one without a doctor or nurse.*[25]

In 1927, the first school in Mossurize opened. It was an American mission school that had been built in 1915 only to wait twelve years before the Company authorized it to give instruction. This was mainly because it was a Protestant mission and Portugal regarded such missions with suspicion. Schools were few in the Territory as a whole; in 1928 there were only seven.[26] It was only in 1930, in the wake of the Protestant school, that three Catholic primary schools were opened in Mossurize. In 1931, a trade school was also opened. By 1944, there were nine schools; in 1957 twenty-five; and in 1967, the last year of available information, there were thirty-seven mainly missionary schools.

The number of commercial establishments went from *three to six!* Almost at the end of Company rule in 1942, there were three motor-worthy roads, from Espungabera (Spungabera, the district seat) to the south, to Buzi and to the east. There were four transport services serviced by ten trucks and five administration vehicles as well as vehicles from Govuro and Buzi. The infirmary had three pavilions, a pharmacy, and electricity.[27] However, this somewhat rosier situation was not sustained and suffered some decline during the early years of Portuguese state administration. A report in 1962 affirmed that Mossurize was practically cut off from the rest of the district and that to reach Manica it was still necessary to go through Rhodesia.

Between 1933 and 1940, agricultural production did not advance due in part to uncertain agricultural seasons. Yet, despite the risks and the lack of incentives, Mossurize's women were significant agricultural producers. Taking population differences into account, they produced much larger quantities than Gorongosa did. The one exception was in 1933 when both districts produced around two thousand tons of grains.

Cotton was also imposed on Mossurize and the cotton growers were mainly women. By 1966, cotton production registered an export of 667 tons, small in comparison to Gorongosa's sales. Nevertheless, Chaiva's women produced almost 10 percent of this cotton and when production per capita is estimated, Chaiva became Mossurize's largest producer with thirty-six kilograms per person. As in Matutuíne, described in the next chapter, emigrant male salaries were invested in cattle. By 1966, there were 4,575 heads.

Communications improved in the 1960s but not to the same extent as in Gorongosa, and this seriously undermined agricultural sales and exports. Population, however, continued to climb in leaps and bounds. From 46,322 inhabitants in the last year of the Company administration, the population grew to 66,566 inhabitants in 1954 and to 97,334 inhabitants by 1966. In that year, there was a regional hospital but only two other health posts, all reported in poor condition. There were, however, *forty-one commercial outlets* and two trucking lines, one of which went to the dropping off point in Massagena where Transvaal labor recruiters picked up emigrants.

From the point of view of the ordinary person, the opening of the roads and transport services in Mossurize was probably the most important development of colonial rule as a whole. Transport meant the possibility of receiving merchandise, of carrying produce to market and travel. The increase in commercial establishments made a small but important impact. However, they did not initially buy crops, which had to be smuggled across the border where small commercial establishments mushroomed. Ndaus, many of whom had originated from the Mozambican side, ran these shops alongside of Boers. While it is impossible to know just how many tons of crops the Mossurize peoples carried to Southern Rhodesia, it is easy to concur with her administrators that Mossurize could have produced large exports had there been a link to the Beira railway or good roads to Buzi, *a conclusion that is still pertinent today.*

The Role of Protestant Churches

Rennie's dissertation (1973) explores the impact of Protestantism on the Ndau of the Melsetter highlands, across the border from Espungabera. He details the growth of a petty bourgeoisie mentality and lifestyle as well as beginnings of nationalism. For the period of Company rule, there was only one such mission in Mossurize, in Gogoi near Espungabera—too far for Chaiva and other lowland communities to benefit. Another American Protestant mission was planned for an area on the Buzi river but never implemented.

Rennie makes the point that the emergence of an Ndau elite was much more rapid in the Melsetter highlands than in Manica and Sofala. In 1950 in the Territory as a whole, there were only around 600 *civilizados* out of a population of 294,000 and in the whole of Mossurize there were only 28. In contrast, the Ndau educated elite was about 1 percent of Melsetter's population. Christian marriages had led to separate villages with permanent brick houses and the desire for individual freehold tenure (Rennie, 1973:523). "This new elite occupied a strategically important place in the economic changes occurring in African society in this district, particularly after 1914" (1973:525).

Despite the physical absence of mission churches and schools, returning migrants brought to their communities the Protestant and nationalist ideas that blossomed in and around the mining camps of Rhodesia and the

Transvaal. Thirty independent African churches were finally implanted in the Territory of Manica and Sofala. According to Arnold (1991), the Igreja Fé dos Apostolos, a Zionist church, had nearly three thousand members. Also eminent was the Igreja Zion Apóstolo em Moçambique with over two thousand in the congregation. The church of Johane Marangue, another Zionist offspring, had over one thousand members, as did the Igreja de Cristo. Still another, the Zion City of Jerusalem church, took root in Chaiva in the area of Paunde. Pedro Pambanhe, an adviser to Regedor[28] Chaiva, was one of its active members. It was one of the ten Protestant churches established in Mossurize in the late 1960s.

According to Rennie, the Zionists offered their services against witchcraft and sickness, much in the way that the customary medicine men and women did. However, they did not charge for their services (1973:485). This must have been one of their great appeals. Another of their attractions, according to Arnold, was that they served as an outlet for discontent with the hardships and injustice of colonialism. The independent churches promoted African values and a sense of identity and self-respect in contradistinction to the Catholic mission schools, which, Arnold argues, "contributed to the retardation of Black education, emancipation and progress" (1991:3, 4).

The independent churches were kept under surveillance and political activities were restricted. Despite rather than because of these precautions, Mossurize was exempt from national liberation front activity. When FRELIMO finally entered the area now known as Manica province, in July 1972, it apparently was confined to northern zones (Cabrita, 2000:chapter one). Nevertheless, one of the leading figures in the liberation movement throughout the 1960s and 1970s was Ndau, the Reverend Uria Simango,[29] as was the future leader of RENAMO, Afonso Dhlakama.

By contrast, RENAMO's presence was very much in evidence in the 1980s. Although RENAMO made Gorongosa its headquarters for most of the war, it was forced to flee the base in 1980. It then established another one in Garágua (Chaiva's immediate neighbor to the south). From there RENAMO regrouped and sent battalions southward. In a counteroffensive, government forces operating out of Espungabera pushed the local population into communal villages, which caused a massive exodus into Zimbabwe. Many of Chaiva's people emigrated.

In late 1982, FRELIMO was said to have conducted an operation it named *Operação Cabana*, the objective of which was to create a killing field on both sides of the Save river. In the first phase it initiated a huge relocation of villagers from the areas now known as southwestern Manica, where Chaiva is located, and northwestern Gaza. In later phases, it hoped to herd RENAMO forces into the area and then kill them. Apparently, the operation failed. RENAMO reestablished the Gorongosa base (Cabrita, 2000:182–209). However, for the locals, the damage was done as they had been forced yet again to abandon their lands. They only began to trickle back once they felt secure in the middle 1990s.

The following comes from field diaries that I made during a rapid rural appraisal of Chaiva undertaken in 1995 by the Provincial Directorate of Agriculture to train its rural extension workers. German Technical Cooperation sponsored the training under its Manica Agricultural and Rural Rehabilitation Program and invited INDER's participation.

Mossurize, September 1995

It was still necessary to use Zimbabwean roads in order to reach Mossurize from the capital of Manica province under which Mossurize was designated a district. (See map 2). The only other alternative was to have turned off the Save–Inchope road onto a dusty dirt road opened after the war by the United Nations High Commission for Refugees, a tortuous five-hour drive. The closure of this road during the war between FRELIMO and RENAMO had isolated Mossurize from the rest of the country. We therefore followed our provincial counterparts through the then relatively prosperous Zimbabwean villages and towns.

Espungabera, on the other side of the border, presented a rather poor aspect in comparison. Unpaved streets were full of potholes; the market was an unruly gathering, the buildings very much decayed with signs of neglect everywhere. On the other hand, people were gentle, curious, very observing, picking out every new car that came their way and helpful if one had a question or got lost. One physically redeeming feature was the very large green area, a park or public garden, which separated the dusty main street from the public buildings. Also the old colonial house being restored for the district administrator lent a grace and elegance hard to find at first glance.

Nestled in the mountains, Espungabera attracted morning mists and drizzles, while Chaiva, an hour's descent on the Espungabera–Machaze road, was situated in a very dry plain, with only slight undulations near the many almost all dry river beds. 1995 was yet another year of drought. Three rivers separated Chaiva from Espungabera, but the only one with water was the Xinica. Crossing the Mossurize river marked entry into the area of Chaiva. In this descent we transected the three topographic and agricultural zones of the district: the mountain slopes, the mid-level rather well watered terrain and the semi-arid river valleys. In 1995 the lowlands had the look of open savannah.

In the middle zone was Chiurairue, home to the São Leonardo mission and the administrative post under which Chaiva and surrounding areas were officially subordinate. It had a health post. In 1995, the mission also served as *the* trading post for the valley that had no commercial or other infrastructure. Although agriculturally very productive, the middle zone suffered severe problems in marketing its produce.[30] Chaiva in the third zone had no market system whatsoever, only barter trade, unless a producer traveled on foot to Zimbabwe. Because very dry conditions and irregular rainfalls in the early and mid-1990s had curtailed production, the population was suffering from a lack of food and other very primary necessities, such as clothes, soap, cooking oil, matches, and so on. In contrast, the middle zone was replete with many unlicensed merchants in roadside stalls.

Cut off from the rest of Mozambique because of war, Chaiva was under RENAMO influence but its people seemed very independent of any political ideology. They appeared to be their own people. One got the impression that the Chaiva people did not want to be dominated by people of any color. However, political realities in September 1995 meant that they not only took orders from the RENAMO military commander, still headquartered in Sita close to the mountains, but also responded rather grudgingly to the head of the administrative post in Chiurairue.

People told us that the name Chaiva was a clan name. Janson Chaiva was the fifth such titleholder or *mambo*. He had inherited his position from his father. However, in the 1960s, the colonial administrator had removed him from his position because he is illiterate and had given the title to his uncle.[31] This was not a popular move and the population restored Janson after independence. He normally was assisted by an adjunct (*induna*) that substituted for him and by the literate registrar or scribe (*mabalane*). He also had five policemen of his own and twelve headmen, who led the various population settlements. The headmen were known as *sabucos*, a name derived from the tax books they were supposed to keep during colonial times. Each had a policeman also known as *induna*.

Chaiva divided its lands into twelve zones: Chaiva where the clan leader lived; Bapha where Janson's father, the former leader, lived; Mabonjo; Seven; Jutas; Guende; Johane; Machacuri; Mapembane; Dheme; Paunde; and Jona. Within these areas, people lived in widely dispersed households. In Mabonjo and Seven, which I visited, people lived one to two hours apart. This was only partly due to preference. Given that the area was semi-arid, it was necessary for people to hold large areas in order to secure their livelihood. Being a year of drought, people had moved as close to a water source as possible. The great distances between households recalled the situation of Bazaragoma in Gorongosa, which we had visited earlier in the same year.

Seven, headman of the area of Seven, was Janson's uncle and an ageless person, spry, lean, of medium height, pierced ears, steady gaze. He related that he had lived in many places, among them South Africa as a miner, and that he spoke a number of languages.

Mabonjo and Seven

On my visit to Mabonjo and Seven I was accompanied by Taimo, a former district director of agriculture now working in the provincial directorate of agriculture, a likeable reserved man of forty something, knowledgeable but not given to many words, and Valentim, an extension worker with responsibilities in Chiurairue, trying hard to learn the rapid rural appraisal methodology, to please his supervisors, a bit timid, very respectful, thoughtful, a bit melancholic (the extension workers had not been paid in three months). Our guide turned out to be the son of Seven's policeman, Samson. He was eighteen years old, very reticent, very kind, a bit overwhelmed. He said that he was not interested in getting married at the moment because it cost five hundred Zimbabwean dollars, which was not easy for a young unemployed lad to accumulate. Like many others, he and his family had fled to Zimbabwe during the armed conflict where he had worked as a shepherd and later as a worker on a tea plantation.

Six Young Men

From the meeting place in Bapha, our team took a one-way dirt road opened by people working in the South African mines that was said to run the length of the area all the way to the border of Gaza province and from there to South Africa. The people had opened it because the old road, to which it was somewhat parallel, was still mined. On the road we met six young boys aged eight to sixteen years old. They were from Maracote (which we later learned was also the name of the headman of Mabonjo) and were accompanying a donkey cart to the Espungabera–Machaze road. One of the young men was on his way to Machaze.

We talked mainly with Dickson, the fourteen-year-old who "managed" the donkey cart. His job was to transport people and goods to Espungabera (about thirty-five miles) at a cost of sixty Zimbabwean dollars (U.S.$7.50). Apparently all the boys had been in Zimbabwe until recently where they attended school but there was no school in Chaiva. They all hoped to be able to return to school some day.

Lyson Sithole took care of about ten cows: he explained that his father had many more before the war but that they had been stolen (on the second day, we went to his father's home). Lyson also fetched water in the morning and he had his own fields. His family used donkeys for ploughing and the usual hand tools, the hoe and machete. When I asked the boys to speak about their dreams for the future, Lyson monopolized the conversation. He talked of having a shoe repair business, of owning cattle and fields and of going to South Africa before he settled down and got married. Johane, the only other boy to speak, said he dreamt of having a school near him.

Senhor Dada

At a certain point in the road, we turned west and traveled another forty minutes or so until we reached Mr. Dada's compound. The day before we had been taught how to approach a family in this part of the world, what words to say, what attitude to take, in general how to behave and now was the moment of truth. Before actually reaching a compound, a few yards away, one should shout a greeting to ask permission to approach; as one approaches, there was another greeting, *Macadini,* to ask how people are. Simultaneously one clapped. If one's attitude was found respectful and non-threatening, one was invited and given a place to sit. Generally we found many guard dogs warning of our approach, but we always found a warm welcome.

As it turned out, Mr. Dada was the poorest man we visited. His compound consisted of only one house, an open-air pavilion, a covered storage facility, and a kitchen. He was sitting in the middle of his compound weaving baskets, which he sold to supplement his income. He was a thin, wrinkled man of around forty-five years old, with a kind, wizened face. His ears were pierced and he had copper wires through them and a copper bracelet. His offspring, four women and one man, were grown and lived away from home; he had only one wife and probably a niece or a grandchild living with him (at least at that moment). His wife was not to be seen on this day but on the next day we met her and her sister on their way back from Zimbabwe so we visited Mr. Dada on two consecutive days.

Mr. Dada was not born in Chaiva but came from neighboring Garágua during the war to ask headman Maracote for land. Mabonjo has an abundance of land. He mentioned that a number of people from Machaze district had also come to Chaiva to settle since the end of the war.

Because he had no other farm hands, Mr. Dada and his wife worked together in one big field (*machamba*), about two hectares in all, and planted all their crops side by side. This year they also planted another field in the riverbed because of the prevailing dry conditions but lost their crops when the rains came and washed them away.

All Mozambican producers had fields in what are called *sequeira* or dry lands, which meant that the crops were rain fed. Whenever feasible they had fields in areas called *baixas*, literally lowlands, generally along the margins of rivers. In drought years, the only hope for producers was to plant in the riverbed itself. This solution saved many families from starvation in the terrible drought of 1991–1992 but the risk was great. One heavy rainfall and the crops were wiped out which was what happened in Chaiva to many producers in 1995. Those who produced alongside the river were much more fortunate.

Mr. Dada said that he and his wife normally planted their crops all at the same time at the end of October or beginning of November. They weeded in December and harvested from March until May. The crops included the usual maize, sorghum, squash, and pumpkin.

Maria Muiambo

Sra. Muiambo was the sister of Nekwasi Muiambo, Mr. Dada's wife. She stopped to visit with Mr. Dada on the second day and agreed to talk with us. Nekwasi prepared a kind of local popcorn for us to eat while we chatted.

Maria was much younger than Nekwasi, also prettier and very vivacious. She seemed robust and her conversation was intelligent, dynamic, and animated. Wearing a new wrapper, she had a beaded necklace and bracelet. Maria was Samuel Sithole's second wife and it was obvious from talking with her that Mr. Sithole was much better off than Mr. Dada. Maria and her sister had tattoos on their face and chest as beauty marks. Maria has two children.

Maria was born in Mabonjo and explained that the great distances between families was the result of their search for water and land near rivers. Samuel, her husband, was one of the few left with animals for animal traction. This gave them the possibility to farm much bigger fields. Maria and Samuel's other wife have their own fields in the dry lands while Samuel had his fields in the lowlands. The wives' production was used for family consumption while Samuel's crops were held in reserve and in good years sold. They too planted maize and sorghum and had been using two types of hybrids introduced in 1992–1993 as well as four local varieties. They planted sorghum alone but associated maize with *nhemba* beans. They also grew pumpkin, groundnuts, sesame, and other beans. The Sitholes asked other families to help out during weeding time and offered drinks. Mutual help was a common practice in the area.

It had been a bad year also for the Sithole family and their reserves would only hold out until November. Samuel planned to try his hand at hunting and to sell the meat locally or at the São Leonardo mission, three hours walk away. They raised chickens and goats for food and also had burros and dogs.

Among the problems of the area, Maria mentioned the scarcity of water. Both she and her sister had been reduced to going to a swampy area once a day. For Nekwasi this was an hour's walk. Other problems included the lack of a store, flourmill, and school. These used to exist in an area called Gapara and her hope was that they would be rebuilt now that the war was over.

Headman Maracote's Household

Probably it was more correct to say households because headman Maracote had four wives, and the compound we visited was that of one of his wives, Nhokwasi. On this day she was with her daughter-in-law, Violet. There were no men in sight. Nhokwasi called to another of the wives, Muchada, who lived in close proximity and she and her daughter-in-law Berita soon joined us.

Nhokwasi and Muchada were older women, maybe in their fifties. Their husband had died a while back and left the oldest son as head of the household/s and head of Mabonjo. Nhokwasi was dressed in rags. However, two days later when we went to a funeral ceremony she appeared in a proper dress (maybe her best dress). There was a general lack of clothing. Of all the regions visited in 1995, the Chaiva population had the oldest clothes.

Nhokwasi with her very lively eyes was the obvious leader of this group of women; she did almost all of the talking. The problem that worried her the most was hunger; production had been very poor this year and her family were reduced to one meal a day. She and Muchada showed us their fields, which seemed enormous for strictly hand-worked fields. Each woman had her own fields both in the dry lands and lowlands. Their husband's fields were not now being cultivated but Nhokwasi said that their sons planned to open up these fields. She confirmed that both husbands and wives planted the same crops and whereas the women's crops were for domestic consumption, the husband's were for food reserves and for market. The wives helped each other as necessary in each other's fields. They raised chickens and turkeys.

Nhokwasi also mentioned the hybrid seeds distributed in 1992, which were good only for 1992–1993 and then did not produce well thereafter. She told us that for this next planting season (fast approaching) they would need seeds as well as tools because they only had old worn-out tools.

Nhokwasi mentioned something that many people of the area talked about: before the armed conflict the harvests were generally abundant but ever since people fled their homelands there had been hunger. Although she did not say so, the general feeling was that, by leaving the land, they had left their ancestors and neglected the ceremonies connected to them and the land.

Headman Seven

It took over an hour and a half to reach the headman's house. On the way, we stopped for about ten minutes to look at the swamp, which provided water for Mabonjo. There were cattle drinking from one end and women filling cans at the other end. There was no protection from dirt or feces. Around the swamp were planted very tiny plots of vegetables, the first green vegetables we saw or heard about in Mabonjo.

The hike to Seven was across the snaky Chirera river. We crossed it many times as we went uphill. Seven lived on a plain just beyond the Chirera, not high but higher than Mabonjo in the delta where the Mossurize river crosses the Morungueze.

Seven's place was very spacious; a very neat, nicely swept courtyard around which there were many buildings. We were greeted by two of his sons, Johane and Simon, robust lads, who told us that their father, Seven Combura, was the head of Chirera, which bordered on Maracote, which bordered on Bapha. Seven's policeman was Samson, who lived close to him.

As I was curious about the role of a headman, I asked information from the sons, one of whom would inherit this role. They told me that a headman resolved conflicts among the people living in his area, and distributed land to strangers after a gift or offering was made, which he, in turn, offered to the régulo. In terms of the ceremonies connected with farming, Seven met with the heads of families to hear their concerns, which he then presented to the régulo. Régulo Chaiva then consulted his right hand man, who lived in Chinguno, about weather predictions and, when necessary, authorized rain ceremonies to be held locally. Each area collected money, which was given to the oracle/medicine man (*curandeiro*) in Chinguno. The local oracle then conducted the ceremonies, if I understood correctly.

When Seven arrived, we talked mainly about agricultural problems. Seven also reiterated that these last few years had been unusually dry and he calculated that his own reserves would only last until December. He, too, was very interested in having access again to hybrid seeds and mentioned R501 maize and a sorghum variety known as *Cegaulene*. While we talked his wife prepared a dish for us of red sorghum meal with a sauce made of ground beans and leaves. It had a wonderful nutty flavor. Producers grew four kinds of sorghum in Chaiva.

Seven also stressed the need for help in repopulating the cattle that everyone lost in the war and for animal traction in order to open even larger fields. He took us to see two of his fields and also the natural spring from which his area draws water. It seemed to be much cleaner water than the previously visited waterhole. Seven also emphasized the need for rebuilding the schools in the area.

Robert Sithole

The next day, we were taken to see Robert Sithole, who, as it turned out, was the most enterprising of the farmers that we met with comparatively large resources. His compound had eight constructions with a very big storage area in the middle. Storage areas also doubled as meeting places as they are round, thatched constructions without walls. The roofs, where grain was stored, were very low so that one stooped to slide in and sit in the cool and shade, so desperately sought in the hot afternoons. Robert Sithole showed us a number of stored sorghum stalks and categorized various storage problems. Most prominent was the insect, which bored inside the grain, commonly known as *gorgulho*. There were several storage methods, including the construction of a cone-shaped receptacle mounted high off the ground in which seeds were kept.

Robert Sithole had been using both regional maize and sorghum seeds but also a maize hybrid that he identified as 207. He planted the regional maize in dry lands and the hybrid in his lowlands. He also showed us a sorghum seed with a short cycle and said he would like to grow only this kind of sorghum. Unlike farmers in Gorongosa, he and his wives put the maize and sorghum crops in separate fields and planted them in different sequences. Sorghum was planted at the end of September whereas maize at the end of October. The women also combined sorghum with sesame and maize with beans and pumpkins. He himself did not recommend association and prefers to have separate crops. He said that his wives also grew some vegetables such as tomatoes, cabbage, onions, and the like—but in small quantities.

The most obvious difference between the Sithole household and that of the neighbors was his abundant labor force. There were four young wives and eleven children. We sat with three grown men who worked on the farm but it was not clear if they were Sithole's sons. Dickson and Lyson, whom we had met on the road the day before, were his adolescent sons and there were many little children.

The wives had their fields and Sithole had his. The young men were in charge of the cattle and donkeys used for transport and for plowing. The young men plowed for the women and their father. However, Mr. Sithole also mentioned that the women had a pair of bulls for animal traction, which they had learned to manage by themselves. His herd was small because he lost most everything in the armed conflict and was in the process of reestablishing his enterprise. In 1995, his family also raised chicken and goats, which he sold because there was nothing else to sell at the moment. One of his wives prepared for us, white maize meal and grilled chicken; it was a feast!

Robert Sithole was born in Mabonjo as were his parents; his father was a headman and the registrar and he himself was the policeman for Maracote in the area of Mabonjo called Matoma. Matoma was very close to the juncture where the Morungueze and Mossurize rivers cross, prime agricultural land because of the proximity of vast lowlands. Despite the irregular rainfall during 1993–1994 Sithole had been able to market three and a half tons of maize; however, this year, production was particularly bad and he would only have enough reserves to last through the agricultural season.

Robert Sithole sent even his girls to school. Because of the lack of schooling in Chaiva, he had to send three children to live with their aunt and uncle in Chimoio. He put the need for a school high on his list of priorities, which also included access to short cycle seeds and replacements for his plows and donkey carts. He also mentioned the need for a health post because of the expense and risk of sending people by donkey cart to the post in Chiurairue. A flourmill was also high on the list and also a store.

Robert Sithole was the only producer who said that he had had contact with an extension service. (There was no service for Chaiva at present.) Someone known as Joseph who had organized a network of model farmers had contacted him.

A Ceremony of the Dead

On our final day in Mabonjo, we were told that we would be meeting with a group of people but did not realize until we got there that the meeting was a ceremony related to the recent death of a woman in Thousand Muiambo's family, apparently one of his wives. The ceremonies, which included speaking with the dead person, took place in her house on the edge of Mr. Muiambo's large compound. Mr. Taimo compared this ceremony to the Portuguese custom of placing flowers on the grave seven days after the death of a beloved.

Mr. Muiambo's compound seemed to be very near the Morungueze river near the frontier with Garágua. Visible were the palm trees, which divide Mabonjo from Garágua, on the southern border with Chaiva. Mr. Muiambo was the only person in our sample who mentioned having fruit trees on the margin of the river: banana, orange, tangerine, and mango. On our way to his compound we saw an exceptionally large field recently plowed by tractor but, under the circumstances we did not talk to Mr. Muiambo about agriculture.

Thousand Muiambo was a very tall, greying dignified man, every inch the host. He wanted to make us as comfortable as any of his over one hundred guests. He would not let us just ask a few questions of his neighbours and then slip away. We had to share in the feast, of goat meat sauce over a mixture of white maize and sorghum meal, which was delicious, as well as plentiful home brew. That he even let us ask our questions was quite a concession. Seven appeared and helped along in the discussion.

We were able to test with the larger group some of the perceptions we had gathered from individual households. One of the most interesting revelations was that before the armed conflict everyone in the area had cattle. This was not hard to imagine because the area is nothing if not a natural grass area. At this point in time, only about ten families had cattle for animal traction. Some had cattle and no plows; others had plows and no cattle. Some rented cattle to their neighbors. All wanted to be included in a credit program to repopulate cattle.

We also clarified the situation regarding the 1994–1995 harvest: the first planting had failed while the second was better but then the third planting had also failed. We also learned that there was a practice of planting sunflower seeds in between rows of maize. We confirmed that those with animal traction have big fields and divided these, by planting a single crop in each division. Otherwise, the smaller fields mixed all the crops. The only people with reserves sufficient enough to last the season were those with animal traction.

Besides the current food insecurity due to lack of rains, the other problems people raised were water scarcity, lack of hybrid seeds, lack of transport and easy access to markets, no school and no clinic. Women voiced their need for a mill because of the very heavy burden of grinding cereals; they usually used stones or a large wooden mortar and pestle.

A Political Meeting

It was normal to end a rapid rural appraisal with a meeting of community leaders in order to present a preliminary analysis of the findings upon which they are asked to comment, correct, and discuss. When the exercise is participatory and used for planning rather than simply research, one attempted to get as many people together as possible, in a community meeting, to list priorities and to begin thinking about feasible solutions to the most common problems.

Our team leader was not very experienced and made a grave tactical error by inviting two local government officials, the chief of the administrative post of Chiurairue and the district director of Agriculture and Fisheries under whose auspices the rapid rural appraisal had been conducted. These two gentlemen proceeded to turn the meeting of community leaders into a political event in which they both tried to impress FRELIMO government authority on Chaiva. It was the wrong message at the wrong time. Certainly the effect was to discourage discussion. Janson Chaiva's response to the visit was that he had seen nothing bad about our work but that it wasn't worth talking further. "Hunger was already being felt and would make itself known even more so before long." This was probably a polite way of saying "We have already wasted enough time with you since all you bring us is speeches." We all left, I with a big sigh at this lost opportunity.

FRELIMO rule had not left the Chaiva people any better off than during colonial rule, either in terms of infrastructure or respect for their political structure and economic potential.

Notes

1. *Moyo* meaning heart was the totem of these clansmen.

2. Rennie talks about a process of layering whereby immigrant and ruling groups were on top of earlier groups who then exercised ritual authority (1973:73).

3. Only by 1912 were there slightly more than three hundred people registered in Chaiva. Even, in 1929, Chaiva's population was only 296. There is no reason to assume that Chaiva was ever a big settlement, although its territory covered 732 square kilometers. The majority of rural communities in Mossurize had fewer than two hundred huts. The largest ones were those of Chaiva's neighbors in the dry lowlands.

4. J. Renato Baptista was an engineer hired by the Companhia de Moçambique to do a survey of the lands between Beira and Manica for the purpose of building a railway.

5. "In a similar way, villages in Buzi and Mossurize withdrew into inaccessible forest retreats (Neil-Tomlinson, 1974:171)." Neil-Tomlinson also noted that some villages moved constantly to avoid tax, some chiefs accommodated but concealed villages, and some failed to obey orders (1974:172).

6. Companhia de Moçambique, Secretaria-Geral, Circumscripção de Mossurize, *Relatório Annual de 1897.*

7. Machado listed forty-nine régulos in 1901 and there were never more than fifty-one registered régulos before 1923 when Alto Save and Chicuala-cuala were added to Mossurize circumscription.

8. Companhia de Moçambique, Secretaria-Geral, Circumscripção de Mossurize, *Relatório, 14 July 1896.*

9. Companhia de Moçambique, Secretaria-Geral, Circumscripção de Mossurize, *Relatório Annual de 1906.*

10. Companhia de Moçambique, Secretaria-Geral, Circumscripção de Mossurize, *Relatório Annual de 1909.*

11. See page 64.

12. Companhia de Moçambique, Secretaria-Geral, Circumscripção de Mossurize, *Relatório Annual de 1911.* Anibal Machado had noted this problem for the administration, even before Lanne. (See *Relatório Annual de 1902.*)

13. Companhia de Moçambique, Secretaria-Geral, Circumscripção de Mossurize, *Relatório Annual de 1909*.

14. Companhia de Moçambique, Secretaria-Geral, Circunscrição de Mossurize, *Relatório Anual de 1935*.

15. Companhia de Moçambique, Secretaria-Geral, Circunscrição de Mossurize, *Relatório Anual de 1936*:87, 88.

16. In the 1920s, recruitment from Mossurize supplied mainly private farms in Manica, Chimoio, Neves Ferreira, and Buzi and still later the sugar plantations of the Companhia Colonial de Buzi. Desertions were another form of resistance to forced labor and were not new to Mossurize males. As far back as 1902, Anibal Machado reported that many Mossurize workers fled the employment of abusive bosses; this in regard to the Manica mines. (See *Relatório Annual de 1902*.)

17. Companhia de Moçambique, Secretaria-Geral, Circunscrição de Mossurize, *Relatório Anual de 1923*:41.

18. Companhia de Moçambique, Secretaria-Geral, Circunscrição de Mossurize, *Relatório Anual de 1924*:36.

19. Companhia de Moçambique, Secretaria-Geral, Circunscrição de Mossurize, *Recenseamento da População Indígena e Arrolamento de Palhotas*, 1938:6.

20. Companhia de Moçambique, Secretaria-Geral, Relatórios, *Relatório Anual de 1916*.

21. Companhia de Moçambique, Secretaria-Geral, Processos Confidenciais.

22. Companhia de Moçambique, Secretaria-Geral, Processos Confidenciais, Director de Negócios Indígenas, carta ao Governador da Companhia de Moçambique, 22 November 1935.

23. Companhia de Moçambique, Secretaria-Geral, Relatórios, *Relatórios de Segundo e Terceiro Trimestre*, 1913.

24. Companhia de Moçambique, Secretaria-Geral, Relatórios, *Relatório do Recenseamento e Arrolamento do Ano de 1916*.

25. Chimoio, Manica, Neves Ferreira, and Govuro had hospitals; Buzi, Cheringoma, Mocoque, Marromeu, and Sena had a health center; and Gorongosa, Sofala, and Chemba had health posts. Companhia de Moçambique, Secretaria-Geral, Relatórios, *Relatório Anual de 1936*:119.

26. Companhia de Moçambique, *Respostas ao Questionário Etnográfico*, 1928:12.

27. Governo do Território de Manica e Sofala, Companhia de Moçambique, Direcção dos Negócios Indígenas, *Relatório da Inspecção Ordinária a Circunscrição de Mossurize*, Setembro de 1940.

28. Regedor was the title given to Régulos after 1933. See chapter 6.

29. According to Cabrita, Simango was expelled from FRELIMO in 1970. In 1974 FRELIMO arrested him and his wife. Both were later executed along with other dissidents, Simango in 1979 and his wife in 1982 (Cabrita, 2000:101, 102).

30. An Italian non-governmental organization was trying to change this situation by constructing two warehouses in the vicinity of Chiurairue.

31. This was later verified in the 1967 surveillance report (Portugal, 1967).

CHAPTER FOUR

~

Matutuíne: Living with the Elephants

Of all the peoples so far described, the Ronga in the southernmost tip of Mozambique had the longest continuous contact with Europeans.[1] From the sixteenth century onward Ronga chiefs met not only Portuguese but also British and later Dutch traders and explorers on a more or less regular basis. Trade with the Europeans encouraged political expansion and large-scale organization and, as a consequence, one of the chiefs, Maputo, became "south-east Africa's first great ruler."[2] His dynastic line still exists today in attenuated form. How the Maputo Ronga first gained eminence, maintained rule, and then lost their independence and, in the case of Massoane, even the means of sustenance is the subject of this chapter.[3]

The Ronga people are classified as part of the linguistic group known as Southeast Bantu, which also includes the Nguni, Venda, and Sotho peoples, and were probably a fusion of these and other peoples. The Portuguese ethnographer Alberto saw them as resulting from the integration of the Karanga and Tonga peoples. Another theory was that they were a blend of agricultural people and the pastoral Nguni (Dias, 1964). Smith noted that their own traditions allege that migrations by Sotho or Shona peoples over a considerable period of time were instrumental in the formation of their local chiefdoms (1973:570, 572).

Their earliest contact with Europeans appears to have been before the middle of the sixteenth century when Lourenço Marques, a Portuguese adventurer, was said to have arrived in the area. He was credited with finding the mouth of the Espirito Santo River (the Tembe River) at Delagoa Bay, a natural harbor, and with trading iron, beads, and other goods in exchange for ivory (Theal, 1898:267). Later, annual trading ships came to Delagoa Bay, in search of ivory. From then, Ronga fortunes were intertwined with those of the Europeans traders. Just as the Yao chiefs, Ronga chiefdoms expanded and contracted depending upon their leaders' commercial and diplomatic prowess in dealing with the traders and their military skills in dealing with each other. At the acme of their powers, in the late eighteenth and early nineteenth centuries, Maputo chiefs controlled coastal and interior areas south of Delagoa Bay all the way to Saint Lucia Bay (now in South Africa). They were bounded on the west by the Libombos and on the east by the Indian Ocean. In this area huge herds of elephants grazed and watered all along the river, which bore Maputo's name. (See map 5.)

Early Ronga Chiefs

Sixteenth-century Ronga chiefs included Cherinda, Magaia, Inhaca, and Tembe. Relying on Lourenço Marques' and Perestrello's accounts among other's, Hedges (1978) argued that Inhaca persuaded shipwrecked Europeans to stay with him so that he could collect a ransom for them and gain access to their goods. These he traded with other chiefs assuring for himself the role of intermediary, the key to his success (1978:113). In addition to the Portuguese, the British also sent trading ships, as early as 1597. By the late seventeenth century they outclassed the Portuguese traders because of their better and cheaper exchange goods (Smith, 1970:39, 40).

Inhaca's kingdom, south of Delagoa Bay, was fairly extensive. Perestrello encountered his settlement on the Umbeluzi River and said that his people controlled access to the Espirito Santo River, which was navigable and on which trade goods could be transported. Tembe later pushed Inhaca back beyond this river, which thereafter became known by his name and marked the boundary between their lands. About then the Dutch East India Company sent a trading ship to Delagoa bay to investigate the possibilities of setting up an enclave. According to Smith, the Dutch were not simply interested in ivory but also wanted to find a way to the kingdom of Monomotapa and his gold (1970:xviii).

The Dutch were only able to maintain their colony in the bay area from 1721–1730 (Hedges, 1978:120). They too were outmaneuvered by British traders who paid better prices for ivory. The Dutch left their historical mark by becoming the first to engage in slave trading from Delagoa bay. In 1726, a war for cattle and control over trade among the local chiefs forced the Dutch to leave the bay in search of a more peaceful site. The war continued

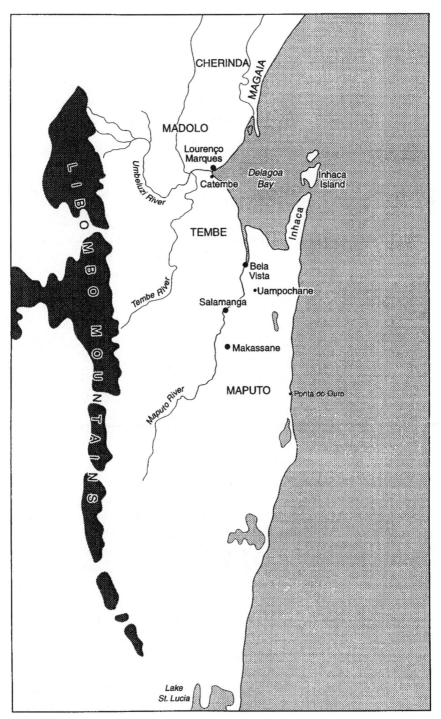

Map 5. The Delagoa Bay Area

as the chiefs regrouped and switched alliances. The Dutch eventually abandoned settlement in favor of sending trade ships.

During this period, Tembe expanded his territory to twenty-seven provinces, which he divided into districts and then into villages (Smith, 1973:572). By the mid-eighteenth century, Tembe had eclipsed Inhaca in power and territory. He was able to capture the ivory trade by also controlling access to the Maputo river, the second of the two navigable rivers on Delagoa bay and the one that became more important. Tembe extended his territory southward and brought the southern side of Delagoa Bay all the way to Saint Lucia under his control. (See map 5.)

Tembe placed his sons, including the enterprising Maputo (Mabudu), in charge of the newly acquired areas. In that period, another leader, Mattoll (Madolo) dominated the areas surrounding the bay. Now the greatest of the Ronga chiefs, Tembe became an important figure in determining the balance of power among the numerous chieftains all vying for a share of trade.

During the 1770s, the Austrians competed fiercely with the British and the Dutch for trade. According to Smith, from 1777–1780, the ivory trade reached one hundred thousand pounds annually, although Hedges put the amount at seventy-five thousand pounds (1978:129). In 1782, the Portuguese sent settlers to the bay but were ousted by the French who were only able to raise their flag temporarily. The Portuguese returned at the end of the century.

The Rise of Maputo

Rivalry and jockeying for position were not exclusive to the Europeans. In the late eighteenth century Maputo began to increase his influence and loosen his ties with his father Tembe. He was able not only to fend off attacks from other Ronga chiefs but also to neutralize the Nguni now on the move. Nevertheless, in 1823, Maputo's grandson, Makassane, the second dynastic ruler, fell under the control of Shaka Zulu. He, however, turned this to his own advantage and secured for Maputo an era of peace and prosperity. Not so Tembe who saw his territory sacked and pillaged by the Zulu. The reason Makassane was successful had to do with being able to control the access to European trade goods. He was able to furnish the Nguni with a regular supply of brass (used for neck collars by the aristocracy) and glass beads (for ornamentation).

The British eventually came to Tembe's aid and also made a treaty with Makassane. Nevertheless, the Portuguese, rather than the British, became the principal European protagonist in the struggle with the Nguni and Ronga for control over the bay. The British pulled out in order to concentrate on the areas south of Maputo as well as on Swaziland to the west. Britain's success in these areas came later to influence the Maputo chiefs' efforts to maintain independence from the Portuguese.

The Portuguese eventually subjugated a number of Ronga chiefdoms but not Tembe or Maputo or those in the interior under Nguni domination (Smith, 1970:288). In 1834, Shaka's successor sent Zulu forces to the Portuguese colony to kill its governor. At the same time, various Nguni forces moved northward to take over vast areas of Mozambique, Rhodesia, Zambia, Malawi, and Tanzania (see previous chapters).

According to Smith, the flourishing ivory trade transformed the Ronga from elephant hunters to middlemen and then into aggressive professional traders looking for other potential trade goods. As early as the nineteenth century they began to take up residence in the Transvaal to facilitate trade. Smith reasoned that they did not turn to the slave trade because the Ronga did not capture other Rongas as prisoners, nor did they war against the northern Tschopi once the latter began to defend themselves. The entry of the Brazilians and French into the market for slaves, however, changed the nature of trade temporarily. The Nguni did not share Ronga compunctions and were willing to supply the Portuguese with slaves for a short time after 1810. This put pressure on the Ronga to do the same. Nevertheless, the slave trade diminished after 1830 probably because of the continuing flow of ivory (Smith, 1970:353).

Internal Social Relations

While Smith concentrated upon the international relations of the ivory trade, David Hedges (1978) turned his gaze upon the internal workings of Ronga and Nguni society. The Maputo plain, coast, and river areas were "said to be fertile and highly populated" (Hedges, 1978:61). The main occupation of ordinary people was a combination of agriculture, cattle raising, hunting, and fishing. All engaged in hunting small game to supplement their diet and some people specialized in hunting elephants, hippos, and the like. The basic staple was a kind of millet, *pennisetium*, but a variety of cereals was grown depending upon soils and microclimates. People took advantage of the varied terrain and range of microenvironments and diversified their crops and activities accordingly. Hedges noted that the Ronga-Nguni territory was divided into three main eco-systems, including coastal lowlands, the drier sandy lowlands, and the uplands (Hedges, 1978:61).

People organized themselves along patrilineal lines. The *sibongo* was the patrilineage and it grouped family members in a geographical space. The head of the founding or dominant lineage was known as *Inkosi* or king and he supervised and controlled the *abanumzane* or subordinate lineage heads. The two-tiered hierarchy described by Hedges was three-tiered in larger kingdoms as the Inkosi divided large lands into "districts" and put his relatives in charge to govern in his name. This was the case with Tembe and later Maputo and is still followed today as the information from Massoane showed (see below).

Each lineage designed its living space (*kraal*) in the form of two concentric circles. In the middle was the cattle-grazing area and around it in a circle were the family dwellings. These were then fenced together in a circular fashion. People did not marry within their own lineage; men acquired brides from other lineages by transferring cattle to the bride's lineage. Cattle were the measure of value and necessary not only for marriage but also other important ceremonies, subsistence, and exchange.

Lineage heads coordinated the activities of their settlements. One of their tasks was to guard long-term grain supplies to which each household contributed. Another was to maintain the division of labor. Women did not own cattle but they were responsible for cultivation. Young men were organized from about the age of ten to do a variety of tasks, as described in the following account:

> It is their custom when their sons are 10 years old to turn them into the woods; they clothe themselves from the waist downwards with the leaves of a tree like the palm and rub themselves with ashes till they look as if they were painted. They all assemble in a body but do not come to the kraal, their mothers taking them food. Their duty is to dance at weddings and feasts, which it is the custom to hold, and they are paid with cattle, calves and goats where there are any. When one in this way has got together 3 or 4 head of cattle and has reached the age of 18 and upwards his father goes to the (*umnumzane*) and tells him that they have a son of fitting age who by his own exertions has gained so many head of cattle and the said father or mother is willing to help him by giving him something further and they further request the (*umnumzane*) to give him a wife . . . he arranges the payment the husband is obliged to make to his father-in-law, and in making these contacts something always falls to the share of the (*umnumzane*) (D'Almada, 1623, cited by Hedges, 1978:97).

These groups of young men were also used for hunting and fighting.

The dominant lineage organized big game hunting which was external to settlement life; the spoils were divided among the hunters and elders. The Inkosi was also responsible for defense of the settlements, which according to Hedges was organized along the same lines as the hunt (1978:74). Lesser lineages gave tribute to the dominant one. The Inkosi and headmen were the links between ordinary people and the ancestors. The founding father was invoked in ceremonies that celebrated all major events of settlement life and a person's life. Some of the most important ceremonies had to do with management of the agricultural cycle.

The royal lineage controlled external trade which included cattle, game, skins, pelts, ivory, copper, brass, tobacco, and beads. As already noted, Maputo became the bridge between the bay and Zululand and therefore access to European exchange goods.

Maputo's lineage began with Mangobe (chief of the Tembes) who was his father. Maputo's son was Mwali but he died leaving his son Makassane, the second titleholder, to inherit the kingdom. Missongue succeeded Makassane and was succeeded by his son, Guanazi.[4] From Makassane onward they gave tribute to the Nguni.

Nineteenth-Century International Relations and the Gradual Rise of the Portuguese

The Boers entered the fray for command over the bay area in the 1830s. They had moved from the Cape Colony to the Transvaal, and in 1838 sent a scouting party to Delagoa Bay because of their desire to establish an opening to the sea. A plaque and small monument in the Mozambican capital now commemorates this particular trek. The party was defeated by exhaustion, malaria, and sleeping sickness but this did not inhibit Boer attempts to open a trading station. In the 1850s, they succeeded in establishing a colony in Zoutpansberg and from there forged ties with several Portuguese traders, among whom was João Albasini, the most successful of his time, and key to access to the port. In 1868, the Boer president Pretorius claimed that the frontier of the Transvaal extended to the coast. In 1869 the Portuguese signed a treaty with him that gave themselves possession of Delagoa Bay and the coast as far south as 26 degrees and 30 minutes latitude (that is, in Maputo's area). The eastern frontier of the Transvaal was set at 36 degrees and 50 minutes south along the ridge of the Libombos. Both parties agreed to build a road linking the bay to the Transvaal.

The success of British settlements in Natal, Johannesburg, and the Transvaal, however, threatened not only the Boers but also the Portuguese because the British once again claimed the bay area. In 1871, the Portuguese suggested to the British that their dispute over the bay area and over Bolama in West Africa be submitted to the French president, Marshall MacMahon, for arbitration. On paper, MacMahon's decision divided Maputo's kingdom between the Portuguese and the British. In the meantime, work on the road began and in 1873 the Portuguese signed a free trade agreement with the Boers.

The Zulus who saw the British colony of Natal as a menace to their sovereignty began to use the Portuguese against the British. They sent an order to Maputo's chief, Missongue, to deny a British settler permission to establish a plantation on the island of Inhaca (the much reduced base of Inhaca, over which Maputo laid claim). Fernando da Costa Leal, who was secretary to the Portuguese mission to the Transvaal at the time, interpreted this action as support for Portugal in its claims against the British.[5] Nevertheless, neither the Zulus nor Maputo proved certain allies. Moreover, Portugal itself was not above playing the Zulus against the British. It courted the paramount Nguni chiefs north of Delagoa Bay, Umzila and later Gungunhana, in order to forestall British expansionism in Manica and Zambézia.

Even though MacMahon awarded Delagoa Bay to the Portuguese, the British came to exercise economic domination over the entire southern region. Lourenço Marques was little more than a fortress: it enclosed a mere 127 houses.[6] A number of minor chiefs paid tribute to Portugal but the major chiefdoms, Moamba to the west and Maputo to the south, continued to refuse to recognize Portuguese sovereignty. Eventually a British company constructed the railway line between the Transvaal and Lourenço Marques. Natal colony and the British gold, coal, and diamond mines in the Johannesburg area and the Transvaal attracted Ronga emigration. In 1877, the Portuguese representative to Maputo alerted his superiors that a great number of Maputo people were immigrating to Natal by land and returning after a few months of employment by sea. They came back with English sterling, new clothes, beads, blankets, copper, and other articles. Over one thousand emigrants returned with enough money to be able to contract marriages, arrange their dwellings, pay tribute to their chiefs, and buy armaments and alcoholic beverages.[7]

José Fialho Feliciano (1998) put the beginning of Ronga migration to Natal as early as the 1850s and to the mines in the 1860s, thus antedating the Mossurize Ndau by several decades. He affirmed that in less than thirty years the migration had become a "tradition" for the entire male population of southern Mozambique (not to mention Mossurize and other areas). Contemporaneous with this migration and perhaps stimulating it was the decline in the elephant population. This forced young men, who formed the hunting parties, to search for alternate ways of earning lobolo (the marriage payment). Both young and old also used their salaries to stock cattle.

At the Berlin Conference of 1884–1885, the European powers staked their claims to Africa. Britain pretended sovereignty over a wide area, including such areas in southeastern Africa as Matabeleland, Mashonaland, Malalakaland, Zumbo, Shire, Nyasaland, Zambézia, and Manica. As previous chapters have shown, this left the Portuguese scrambling to make their occupation effective in the contested areas. One of the reasons for Britain's success in establishing a foundation for its claims was the rapidity with which colonization occurred. For example, in 1877, Natal had 27,654 white people, 12,823 Indians, and 290,036 Africans. In contrast, Lourenço Marques had only 93 Europeans and a total population of 458 people.[8]

Settlement in the British colonies was facilitated by government investment in public works, including ports, roads, bridges, and railways. As already noted in previous chapters, the Portuguese were never willing or able to match this effort, much to the chagrin of its administrators. Each new governor of what became the District of Lourenço Marques lamented the state of the "colony" and had many proposals. Even the military was in a deplorable state. In 1882, the governor, Sebastião Chaves d'Aguiar, reported that the police force was composed of only one European soldier and that there was little training for native soldiers. The sergeants and corporals, he affirmed, used an inordinate amount of alcohol, gambled, and had many other bad habits. The force was stationed in Inhaca, Bembe, Catembe, and Marraquene.

In April 1882, Aguiar gave a detailed report on relations with the surrounding chiefdoms. In regard to Maputo, he complained that the people of Maputo considered themselves independent. The territory of Maputo extended to Catembe across the bay from Lourenço Marques, which made the Portuguese residents of the capital anxious. Moreover, Aguiar felt harassed because the rulers of Maputo were making it difficult to set up a proper military barracks in Inhaca. He expressed humiliation at having to give gifts in order to assuage them but resigned himself because "Maputo is a vast and well populated area that could bring in a large amount of taxes once pacified."[9]

Later in the 1880s, rumors began to circulate that the Portuguese were about to depose Missongue's heir and put Missongue's brother in his stead. Maputo's legitimate rulers, the regent Queen Zambili[10] and her minor son Guanazi, the fourth titleholder, asked the British for protection and offered a small piece of territory north of the Umkosi river in return. In effect this was formal admission that Maputo no longer controlled the territory below this point. Zambili signed a treaty to this effect on 29 November 1887.

The rumors about Portugal even reached Pretoria, which questioned Portuguese intentions. Portugal sent a mission to the queen and her son to clarify the situation. Diplomats arrived in time to witness a rain ceremony and hoped the fact that rains came would be taken as a good omen (Machado, 1889:12). Indeed, the queen accepted Portugal's offer of protection in exchange for arms.

There was some question as to whether this meant that she had ceded sovereignty over the entire territory of Maputo. A further meeting amended the treaty to read that the rulers ceded only that part of Maputo awarded by the MacMahon decision (slightly below Salamanga, see map 5). By this agreement, Portugal gained the right to send a resident to the kingdom. The residency, placed on Salamanga's (Guanazi's brother) lands was named "Bom Sucesso" or Good Success. The question is, whose success?[11]

In 1890, the British sent two tax collectors whereupon the queen informed them of her treaty with Portugal. In 1891, the Portuguese sent their tax collectors and the queen reminded them that Portugal had not yet satisfied its treaty obligations, namely, delimitation of borders with Swaziland; delivery of flags; installation of a resident in the south for protection against attacks; and opening schools.

In response, the Portuguese established another residency in the lands called Matutoine, at Bela Vista (which is today the seat of Matutuíne district). This was in northern rather than southern Maputo. In regard to schools, the British anticipated the Portuguese by sending three missionaries to set up a school, a challenge to which the Portuguese responded by sending two teachers. One left and the other did nothing because she had not been paid. The queen asked for her removal. Mission schools, both Catholic and Protestant,[12] eventually became the sole sustainers of education in the colonial period (and even today in Massoane, as shall be seen). The Portuguese seemed either incapable or unwilling to fulfill most of their treaty obligations: invasions into Maputo from the Transvaal were frequent, the frontier remained unmarked, and there was no school for the eighty students the queen had arranged. There were also bad relations between the rulers and the resident at Bela Vista.

In 1894, the Portuguese faced an imminent uprising among the Rongas[13] and asked for Guanazi's help in putting down the other chiefdoms. When it appeared that Guanazi was ready to accept this role, the governor sent his secretary, Joaquim José Monteiro Liberio, to thank the people of Maputo. Liberio reported that during the audience both the regent mother and her son denounced the resident, Simão Gomes, for withholding gifts sent by the governor and for not responding to British settlements on their land. Eventually he was withdrawn but not before Guanazi had publicly humiliated the Portuguese.

As the Portuguese requested, Guanazi mobilized a party of five thousand warriors for the defense of Lourenço Marques and sent them to Catembe. He made a number of demands including food for the troops and the delivery of Martini Henry rifles, reputed to be the best available. The Portuguese, however, offered Albani rifles whereupon the *indunas* showed their disappointment. An emissary from Gungunhana arrived and the indunas went into council.[14] Meanwhile, the soldiers settled on the beach, eating and drinking, presumably waiting for transport to Lourenço Marques across the bay. However, when morning dawned, the beach was empty! The Maputo warriors had deserted the Portuguese cause. They had gained the best of the situation because they left with the Albanis.[15]

Throughout 1895, Guanazi refused to pay tax to Portugal, demanding that the borders with Swaziland be demarcated. Even though Guanazi was related through the queen to the Swazi kings, this did not prevent him from having disputes and conflicts with the Swazis. Moreover, there was famine in Maputo. The administrator gave the following condescending description of Guanazi that included a warning:

> The king is a child, not simply because of age, but in how he thinks, and he is surrounded by old people who hate us and by children who are indifferent. The grandees are from Missongue's time and this king did not allow white people to settle here. The grandees feel that the present king has lost his authority and respect.[16]

The administrator regretted the absence of Queen Zambili who had always been able to reconcile differences among the counselors. He also speculated that Guanazi's difficulties with the Swazi were related to the queen's absence.

Taxes were delivered to the Portuguese in January 1896 but the amount was so small that this was taken to be a sign of rebellion. Flushed with military victory over Gungunhana, General Mouzinho de Albuquerque now moved on Maputo. In February, he led an expeditionary force to Bela Vista, then to Salamanga, and finally to Makassane, the seat of the king. The general ordered Makassane to be burned and then proceeded to the queen's settlement in hot pursuit of Guanazi. Not finding him, he burned this village and seized cattle.[17]

Guanazi's brother, Mpobobo, then betrayed him. Armed by the Portuguese, Mpobobo delivered Guanazi's war chief, Chibite, to them. At the time, Chibite was carrying two letters that showed that Guanazi had never lost contact with the British. Guanazi himself was never captured; he and the chiefs loyal to him fled from Maputo to Zululand with a majority of the population.

Mpobobo replaced Guanazi as chief of Makassane and the kingdom entered into a process of disintegration. The Portuguese finally succeeded in their design to divide and rule but they did not inherit the well-populated land of before. Maputo became the fifth *circumscripção* (rural district) of the District of Lourenço Marques and Bela Vista became its seat. The resident representative was now known as "Administrator of Maputo Lands" but *most of its people were in Zululand*.

Portuguese Administration

From 1897 the independent kingdom of Maputo ceased to exist. The administration split the fifth district into four administrative units, Catembe, Matutoine, Makassane, and Libombos. Now subordinated to Portuguese-approved régulos, the *indunas* delivered another installment of taxes in December 1896 and again in January 1897. The first tax census estimated that there were 2,234 villages in the entire area. Two years later, a new census showed 2,907 villages and 9,576 dwellings. Some of the Maputo people had returned.

Compared with the three previously described communities, Maputo had much more in the way of infrastructure in this early period of colonial rule and it shall be seen that the district developed to a degree not seen in Sanga, Gorongosa, or Mossurize. Roads had been built both for military and fiscal purposes. There were several military posts and a Catholic mission and school in 1896. In 1898 there was a health post in Makassane. In 1899 the Swiss Romande Mission was authorized to establish itself in the district.

One of the first measures of the Portuguese was to forbid labor recruitment to the Transvaal. The administration tried instead to stimulate agricultural activities among the male population, first by establishing a small agricultural plantation of sixty hectares in Bela Vista. The administrator tried, with limited success, to experiment with new crops such as wheat, cotton, tobacco, maize, groundnuts, sweet potatoes, white potatoes, cassava, garbanzo beans, peas, white beans, fava beans, and various vegetables. Of all these crops, potatoes gave the best yields. Nevertheless, the years, 1898–1900, were not good agricultural years because of irregular rain and the men, always more involved in cattle raising than agriculture, were having a lot of difficulty in restocking their cattle. Forced labor was also imposed, mainly for the construction of public works, military service, agricultural labor on official and unofficial plantations, and porterage. People, however, continued to trade, now illegally, and to emigrate without much interruption.

Clandestine Emigration
So-called clandestine emigration was the major headache for Portuguese administrators. Emigration to Natal, the Transvaal, and other mining areas had

become a ritual for the male population, as already noted. The Portuguese considered this illegal because it was done without authorization and obviously signified a lack of manpower for Portuguese projects. Each successive administrator noted the problem and had his own explanation. For example, João Bravo Falcão felt that the administration lacked a clear native policy. Writing in the first decade of the twentieth century, he denounced the hut tax as too high and said that it forced people to crowd into huts in order to avoid tax payments. This, in turn, had ill effects on health and morality. Falcão suggested instead a head tax.[18]

Viana Rodriguês blamed emigration on drought[19] but he also felt that people were being encouraged to cross borders because of the influence of the foreign missionaries who spread British influence and inculcated a preference for British goods. (This preference, as has been seen, was of very long-standing.) Also, Viana Rodriguês agreed with Falcão that there was a lack of clarity in Portuguese policies:

> the numerous promises that are never fulfilled and the increase in taxes without improvements, are, in my opinion and to the best of my knowledge, the factors, along with the political situation, that have contributed the most to the dissatisfaction of the natives of this district. . . . If we add to this the inconstancy of our laws, mandates and orders and the disorganization of our services compared to those beyond our borders, it is easy to conclude that if they [the Ronga] are not right, then we also have no right to be surprised at the state of things.[20]

In 1943, José Franco Rodriguês made a government inspection of Maputo. He felt that the fact that Maputo had been split between the Portuguese and the British was responsible for the mass migration of peoples. He calculated that 90 percent of the male population from Catuane had left for the Natal plantations while the majority of the population of Changalane went to the mines. Others went to Natal and still others to Lourenço Marques from the district. He said that Maputo reminded him of the other frontier areas that he had visited where the men were on one side of the border and the women, children and elderly were on the other side, in the fields.[21] *As shall be seen, the same situation continues today in an aggravated fashion.*

Writing in 1950, Inspector Vaz Spencer felt the problem arose from the creation of the Game Reserve (1932). Just as it did later in Gorongosa, the Portuguese administration superimposed the Reserve onto native lands, including Massoane. This action forced the population of these areas to move. Adding insult to injury the animals, mainly elephants, began to run amuck and invade cultivated fields, destroying everything in sight. People had nowhere safe to hide or to cultivate. Their only option was to emigrate.[22] This was another situation created by colonial policy that continued today.

In 1954, Inspector Mendes Gil estimated that 80 percent of the total male population left illegally to work in South Africa because "the people are in a critical situation." Native authorities asked Gil for help in presenting their case for the elimination of the Elephant Reserve. Gil conceded that the hunting brigade established earlier had not been sufficient to resolve the problems caused by the rampaging elephants (Província de Moçambique, 1954:43).

Mendes Gil made another inspection of Maputo in 1960 and reported that the district was continuing to lose population due to the recurrent drought, the lack of salaried employment in the territory, and the scourge of the elephants. A number of chiefs requested permission to kill the animals, which he considered a "just request" (Província de Moçambique, 1960:22). A fence was built in 1965 to block the elephant's movements. The local chiefs called for its reinforcement and for greater vigilance over the elephant's movements. The Reserve itself was a failure as it was not attracting visitors.

Mass emigration due to the lure of South Africa, continuing drought, the constant destruction caused by elephants, high taxation, and forced labor had a striking influence upon Maputo's rate of population growth. If one omits the figures of 1896–1898, which represent a significant loss of residents due to the subjugation of Maputo, one begins to get a better idea of the negative impact of colonial administration. Between 1899 and 1964, the number of inhabitants increased by only 130 percent which equaled an annual growth rate of 2 percent.

Growth rates of Mossurize and Gorongosa were notably higher. In 1904 population records were available for all three districts. In the period, 1904 to 1966, Mossurize experienced the extraordinary increase of 546 percent or an annual rate of 8.6 percent. The comparable figures for Gorongosa are 176 percent giving an annual growth rate of 2.7 percent. Maputo, however, still had an annual growth rate of only 2.07 percent.

As in the case of Mossurize, annual migrations to South Africa were a mixed blessing for the Portuguese. For one thing, the administration gained access to gold bullion through its collections of hut taxes even though it lost gold on those contracts it had not directly negotiated with South Africa. The gold revenue was not inconsiderable. Between 1896 and 1916, the fifth district contributed around eighty-five thousand gold pounds. In 1916, alone, taxpayers yielded over nine thousand gold pounds. In the same year, Mossurize taxpayers were contributing between six and seven thousand pounds.

For Ronga males, work in the mines and on the sugar plantations had some rewards. The temporary loss of human population was accompanied by the spectacular rise of cattle. Miners' and sugar plantation workers' gold earnings were transformed into the walking capital of agrarian society. The first estimates of cattle appeared in the administrator's report of 1913–1914 when the total was 6,720. It increased to 19,100 beef cattle in 1943 and leapt to 39,000 by 1954 and to 66,406 in 1965.

Settlement Schemes
The colonial administration's answer to mass migration was, as noted above, to exhort the male population to engage in farming in lieu of salaried employment and, to that end, it not only established agricultural farms but also agricultural schools. In the late 1950s, the administration opened commercial farming opportunities to the native population. It also campaigned the population regarding the benefits of agricultural cooperatives. Two cooperatives were started in Salamanga with thirty-two families in each. Two more were begun in Santaca.

The administration gave the cooperatives parcels of land along the Maputo river, built a dike, and installed pumps in order to combat drought and help the cooperatives get a head start. Furthermore it distributed rice and other seeds and established rules regarding the proceeds of agricultural production. The response of those participating was enthusiastic in the beginning and there was interest in extending this type of productive organization in the 1960s.

This initiative was undoubtedly influenced by the administration's success in attracting European migrants, particularly on small plantations. The administration had prepared parcels of land of about three hundred hectares in size along the banks of the Maputo River. A number of European rice plantations were launched and by 1960 produced an annual total of five thousand tons of rice. Some of the immigrants combined rice growing with cattle raising and a number of ranches also sprouted. In 1960, Europeans owned almost ten thousand head of cattle but this was still only about one-fourth the number owned by the Ronga.

Tourism
Tourism became a major source of revenue for Maputo as crowds of South Africans and Portuguese flocked to the long extension of beaches from Catembe to Ponta do Ouro near the South African border. (See map 5.) Private and public investment created a minimum of infrastructure. A hotel sprang up on Inhaca island and a smaller one in Catembe. Beaches were dotted with

restaurants. There was one gasoline station, several post offices with public telephones, two bus services, and two national roads, one of which linked Catembe with Ponta do Ouro.

Maputo experienced the throes of urbanization. By 1950, over twenty thousand people were concentrated in Bela Vista, that is, over 40 percent of the district's population. In recognition, Maputo was elevated to the status of Concelho, reserved for areas that had a significant "civilized" population.

Infrastructural Development in the 1960s

Most of the investment in infrastructure was designed for the urban "civilized" population but not all. Already mentioned were the experimental farms and two agricultural schools. To attend to the area's cattle, a veterinary center was instituted and eleven dip tanks scattered around the Concelho. A minimal number of rural industries, such as a cal factory, a rice-husking mill, a sawmill, a dairy, two brick-making enterprises, and a salt extraction plant, sprung up. Four companies provided river transport from Catembe to Lourenço Marques and a railway ran trains from South Africa. A small boat workshop offered services of construction, maintenance, and repair. There were thirty primary schools, although most were annexes to the three Catholic mission schools. Protestant missions included Swiss Romande and the Anglican and Wesleyan missions. Besides the two national roads, a number of unclassified roads existed and there were *101 commercial outlets* supplying the Concelho. This compared very favorably with the four stores in Sanga, the thirty-odd outlets in Gorongosa, and the forty-one in Mossurize during the same period.

Matutuíne under FRELIMO

Matutuíne did not see military action in the war for independence but it suffered its aftermath with the flight of European settlers, European and South African tourists, and the owners of the industries and commercial enterprises that served them. All services and infrastructures suffered degradation from a lack of maintenance.

After independence the first priority of FRELIMO was to establish its own administration in Matutuíne. JoAnn McGregor notes that, while FRELIMO took control from régulos and excluded them from any position of authority, it incorporated both former colonial officials and lower-level indigenous authorities into its administrative system (1998:41). In line with its agricultural policy and plans, it took over the settlement schemes and consolidated them into two state farms and tried to villagize the rural populations. It also encouraged agricultural cooperatives among producers. According to McGregor, this last measure was received with some enthusiasm, which is consistent with what was reported in colonial times, but the population fiercely opposed the policy of communal villages. After a few years FRELIMO proved unable to give support to the cooperative movement and the peoples' expectations quickly turned to disillusionment. Moreover, the state farms were badly managed and "abysmal conditions prompted a high turnover" among the workers (McGregor, 1998:46). In the case of Massoane, 75 percent of its workers deserted the Salamanga state farm in 1982.

The government's willingness to use force in regard to villagization also turned the population against it. Between 1975 and 1983 the people of Matutuíne along with their local FRELIMO administrators successfully resisted central government dictates to move into villages. McGregor singles out the role that Protestant religious leaders took in the resistance (1998:43). One of the tactics that the population used was to threaten massive migration to South Africa or Swaziland, *a tactic used before and still, as we shall see, today.*

McGregor argues that the failure of the state farms and cooperatives along with the halving of mine contracts by the South African government contributed significantly to the opening of clandestine trade between South Africa and Swaziland and the Mozambican capital. Given the long history of such trade, it is doubtful that it had ever stopped but the economic crisis that gripped the area must certainly have given it renewed vigor. McGregor shows that it became a mainstay of the area. What was new was the wholesale export of forestry products, in the form of charcoal, an activity promoted by government troops to their own advantage.

Consonant with previous periods of turmoil, people began to flee, particularly when RENAMO began to establish bases. The district became a special RENAMO target and, by the end of 1984, it established bases in Bela Vista, Salamanga, and Ponta do Ouro (Cabrita, 2000:248). (See map 5.) In response, the government used force to crowd the remaining population into 'protected' communal villages in order to remove people from RENAMO influence.

RENAMO followed two strategies in Matutuíne: one was to establish alliances with indigenous authorities, even soliciting régulos to perform ceremonies in order to appease the spiritual founding fathers. The other strategy was to destroy as completely as possible FRELIMO infrastructures including the state farms and communal villages. RENAMO also cultivated the informal trading networks and used indigenous authorities to link itself with the refugee population as one way of continuing necessary supplies to its troops.

Not surprisingly, one of the major trade goods was *ivory*. According to Mc-Gregor, "Matutuíne's pre-war elephant population of 350 was depleted during the war to an estimated 30–55" (1998:55). Likewise, the cattle population was decimated.

Massoane and the Elephants in the Late 1990s

Massoane is a community of farmers, petty traders, fishermen, and cattle raisers, the latter having lost most of their cattle in the war. It lies more or less half way between Bela Vista and Salamanga (see Uampochane on map 5). The center of Massoane is about twelve kilometers north of Salamanga and is bounded on the north and east by the Elephant Reserve, in which lies part of its territory. On the west is the Maputo river and on the south, the neighboring community of Madjajane. The Futi river traverses the entire community. See the sketch map in the appendix.

Administratively, the community pertains to the locality of Salamanga under the administrative post of Bela Vista, seat of Matutuíne district. Massoane divides itself into four settlements, Nkangazine, Buingane, Lihundo, and Nwaxinengane where the *régulo* Massoane lives.[23] The name Massoane first appeared in the inspection report of 1950, where it was listed as a commercial village, that is, the site of a store run by António Pereira Frazão. It appears to have kept this status throughout the remaining colonial period.

Massoane never had a school or health post, the nearest being in Salamanga or Madjajane. Even in 1998 Massoane had no local primary school or treatment center, although it appeared that a local Presbyterian church was about to finance a local school built out of wooden poles and bamboo. The people availed themselves with great difficulties of social services in Salamanga, three hours away on foot. During the war, the majority of the population fled to Natal. Many, especially the younger people, have not returned.

In twentieth-century Portuguese documents, Massoane appears as Uampochane, from whom the community of Massoane traced its history all the way back to Guanazi's treacherous brother, Mpobobo. It will be recalled that Portuguese awarded the lands of Makassane to Mpobobo. According to local oral tradition he had a son, Madjajane, who succeeded him, and a daughter Mimpowowo. Uampochane pretended Mimpowowo for his bride and negotiated a marriage settlement with Madjajane, which included a grant of northern territories from which he could collect tribute, a part of which he then passed on to Madjajane. These subject northern territories became known as Uampochane. Uampochane's son, Massoane, succeeded him. See the following textbox. Massoane's son, Viana Tembe, the current régulo, succeeded him in 1954.

Mabudu (Maputo)
↓
Makassane
↓
Missongue
↓
Guanazi → Mpobobo
↓
Madjajane—Mimpowowo+ Uampochane
|
Massoane

When I interviewed Viana Tembe in 1998, he was already eighty years old. Because of ill health and frequent absences, he was assisted in his own village by Jameson (or Jemissene) Tembe, a younger brother. In the dynastic hierarchy, Massoane was a lineage chief, also called *induna* and subordinate to the *Inkosi* Madjajane. The *abunumzane* below Massoane included Jameson, another younger brother, Baiano, Massoane's eldest son and the settlement headmen who turned out to be Massoane's sons-in-law. They were each assisted by one or more policemen. In principle, Massoane was subordinate to Madjajane but, at the time of my visit, all of Madjajane's heirs were in exile in South Africa. Moreover, there were no FRELIMO officials in the area except for the locality president, Sr. Dambo, in Salamanga. Thus, "traditional" authorities were more or less in charge.

With the aid of the healers/diviners, of which there were three, Massoane and the elders were responsible for evoking the spirits of their ancestors in the sacred forest in times of trouble, including drought and infestation by insects. Massoane was called upon to resolve serious conflicts over land, divorce cases, land requests, thefts, and the like. These problems were first brought before the *abunumzane* and only referred to Massoane if they could not be resolved at this level. Civil matters of even greater dimensions were taken up with the locality president in Salamanga or with the district administration in Bela Vista. As shall be seen, the Massoane population faithfully respected these procedures.

My INDER colleague and I came to Massoane as part of an effort to train the staff of the Swiss nongovernmental organization, HELVETAS, which had been working in Mozambique since 1979 and had begun work in Matutuíne in 1994. They had never before used participatory methodologies in their work with Matutuíne communities and wanted training in them. The training, which took place in April 1998,[24] began with gaining permission from

Massoane leaders to interview their community. Thereafter, my colleague and I gave the HELVETAS personnel a brief introduction to the notions of participatory rural appraisal and discussed with them which participatory techniques we would use. The following day we made our way to Massoane where people were waiting for us. Some background is necessary before recording what then happened at the community meeting.

Massoane had in its midst a South African entrepreneur, Fizar Koekemoer, who had set up a kind of "store" in Massoane's compound and was involved in marketing fish and providing transport to Bela Vista. In my interviews I found that Koekemoer had established a cordial and collaborative relationship with the people.[25] He had taken up residence in what had been his family plantation, a land concession ceded to his father in the 1960s. Both Koekemoer senior and a Portuguese by the name of Lazaro had requested a concession from the local administrator. Once the governor granted permission, a topographer had surveyed and delimited the area. Viana Tembe also recalled the event and noted that his community, upon whose land these settlers camped, had never been consulted. Massoane also remarked that the Portuguese gave the best lands to white people and moved the original inhabitants to higher, drier lands, in obvious reference to the creation of the Elephant Reserve and encouragement of European settlement.

Koekemoer showed us the original pillars demarcating his plantation and, not far from them, an electrified fence. This fence has replaced the colonial one that had demarcated the Elephant Reserve. The difference between the two fences was that the new fence was at least six feet high, was made of barbed wire, was electrified and was not in the same place as the old one. Koekemoer even showed us where the old fence had been built. The new fence cut off between four and five kilometers more of Massoane's territory. Moreover it blocked pathways between the four settlements, effectively dividing the territory in two. The fishing communities were barred from direct access to markets, the school and health post in Salamanga. The other communities no longer could enter the areas where they normally procured kindling and wood for their fires and charcoal making, found the plants for "traditional" medicines and bamboo for their homes, fished, and extracted salt. Entirely aware of the distress caused to the community, Koekemoer felt that the government should remove the fence.

The National Directorate of Forestry and Wildlife under the Ministry of Agriculture and Rural Development, which controlled the Elephant Reserve, had authorized the new fence but this was not all. The fence was part of a much larger agreement (1996) between the government and James Ulysses Blanchard III to exploit the reserve for big game hunting and tourism. The agreement gave the Blanchard Mozambique Enterprise the entire district of Matutuíne and part of Inhaca island in concession. The Blanchard Mozambique Enterprise then created the Elephant Coast Company for the purpose of publicizing its plans and attracting foreign investment in them.

The Elephant Coast Company had promised to consult with the communities of Matutuíne before putting infrastructures and tourist enterprises in place and to discuss with them how best to manage natural resources. In regard to the reserve, the Elephant Coast Company subcontracted "Nkomati Safaris" to build the fence, supervise the movement of elephants and game, and manage eco-tourism. When the HELVETAS training came to Massoane, most of the fence had already been completed and, through some terrible blunder, a number of elephants had been left on the wrong side of the fence and were blocked off from entering the reserve. These elephants were on the rampage in the surrounding communities, especially Massoane.

The population was in both revolt and despair. More than a year before, they had received a visit from Blanchard himself and government representatives who had promised them that they would be consulted before any investments affecting their territory were made. They had not been consulted about the placement of the fence. Soon after the elephants had made their appearance, the population sent a delegation to Salamanga, and then to the director of the reserve and finally to the district administrator. In all cases, they had been turned away.

Our community meeting of 14 April 1998 comprising seventy people, mostly women, was emotionally charged. One person after another spoke of the severity of the problem that they were facing. The following is an almost literal transliteration of my field notes. It concords with the much more synthetic report produced by HELVETAS.[26]

The first person to speak, a man, said that the principal problem was how to communicate community concerns to Blanchard.

> He [Blanchard] was supposed to have spoken to us before even asking for the concession. Blanchard and the Administrator, between themselves, decided the concession; they closed our access roads. Ever since colonial times, the area of the Reserve was well known but now it isn't. Blanchard said that the elephants belong to the white people but they are God's creatures. The copper wire fence is not in the agreed area. Our healers cannot go to find their medicines.

Another person complained that Blanchard had come to talk with them and had promised a school and health post but nothing had come of it. "He has not come back to speak with us since the fence went up. . . . We are poor and no one looks out for us."

A woman said that the people had prayed for the end of the war to come but a new war has begun, that of the elephants. "The elephants don't give us peace, they invade our fields and now we do not sleep at night because they lift our thatched roofs with their trunks in the search for food and they rob our pantries."

Another person said: "We are ready to tie up Blanchard in order to get heard." A woman lamented that the people do not laugh any more. The land may appear to be bush to outsiders because it is uncultivated but this is because people are sick of fighting these problems. Another community member noted that as a community they have tried all channels of communication without success. "Now we are ready to ask the Administration for permits to leave Mozambique for South Africa and Swaziland because in Mozambique animals are treated better than people!"

Another woman noted that the community's children are outside the country with no intention of returning because of these problems. Yet another woman stated that she had written her son who was coming to care for her but she does not know what he will do once he arrives. In all probability he will take her back to South Africa with him.

At this point there was an outcry among the women to tie Blanchard and bring him before the community.

Another woman brought up other relevant worries including the drought and corruption at border posts where the guards confiscate the gifts sent to them by their children. "We do not know where to complain. When we try we are sent away like donkeys."

Still another woman mentioned that during colonial times communities had the support of the settlers in questions relating to the Elephant Reserve. A man, who identified himself as a former government-licensed hunter during colonial times, confirmed this. "Now," he said, "we don't have bullets or weapons."

The fourth man to speak said that the people were fed up with the way both the Blanchard people and the present administration were fleeing their responsibilities. "Now we are ready to tie up our trousers and skirts and create confusion." The last woman to speak compared these times to the end of the world found in the Bible.

Jameson Tembe spoke of how things were better during colonial times. "Nowadays armed guards shoot at people who even approach the electrified fence." The last person to speak was Viana Tembe who said that he confirmed what his people said:

> We don't have a problem with the government; when we fled to Swaziland during the war, President Chissano called us to come back but his government

doesn't support us in anything. The Administrator should not take Blanchard's money and leave us to die. There is no richer land than this one. It has fish, everything. We are not cultivating because the elephants are destroying everything. The people have said all there is to say. I am sad. I am going to die here.

The HELVETAS report circulated government and international agency circles. It caused quite a stir: the governor of Maputo province called the administrator of Matutuíne to explain the situation and what he was doing about it. The administrator called upon HELVETAS to explain its actions. The governor then called HELVETAS to see what could be done. It was agreed that Massoane should receive another visit of government, Blanchard and this time HELVETAS personnel. At the meeting, the Blanchard representatives spoke of the various efforts to round up the elephants to bring them into the reserve. They also promised to build ladders over the fence so that both sides of Massoane could communicate with each other.

A month after we left Massoane, the South African *Mail and Guardian* newspaper reported:

> In mid-April, four hundred peasant farmers, some armed with pangas, threatened the reserve's administrator, Paulo Tomas, and demanded a solution. Tomas defused the crisis, but the problem remains: at a recent meeting in Massoane, the first problem raised was the destruction of crops and huts by elephants (15 May 1998).

The Blanchard concession was finally canceled. However the electrified fence was still in place and *the ladders never constructed*. Two and a half years after our visit, Massoane and the other surrounding communities were still unhappy. The government was apparently still looking for foreign investors for Maputo.[27]

Of the four communities described in this book, Massoane was materially the worst off.[28] Mass emigration had decimated the area and continued to do so. Massoane was composed mainly of elderly women, both single, married and widows, struggling to bring up minor children, including grandchildren, who when they became of age would also leave. In 1998, there was not even the possibility to farm. People subsisted on remittances from their relatives from South Africa. The South African rand was the effective currency of the community. People engaged in informal border trade or made and sold charcoal for use in Catembe and the capital, Maputo. Still others worked on the few farms left or for their wealthier neighbors in exchange for food. The poorest foraged the forests for wild fruit and tubers. It was difficult to imagine a bright future for the community. In many ways, its location in an area rich in forests, game, fish, and riverine lowlands—the object of national and international envy—has proved to be its scourge rather than its advantage. Massoane, just as Ilinga, faced the prospect of losing access to important parts of what remained of its resources.

Notes

1. For convenience sake I use the terms "Ronga" (also known as Tsonga or Thonga) and "Maputo" throughout although I try to note other spellings used in various historical texts.

2. Stephen Taylor, 1995:35–37.

3. Roland Brouwer (1998) has written an account of the peoples on the Machangulo peninsula adjacent to what was Maputo.

4. The spellings of Missongue and Guanazi vary according to texts. Missongue is also spelt Msongi and Nozinguele. Guanazi is also spelt Nguanazi, Unguanazi or Ngwanase.

5. *Boletim Oficial* (B.O.), no. 11, 18/3/1871:46.

6. B.O., no. 47, 19/11/1877:340.

7. B.O., no. 45, 28/10/1877:324.

8. B.O., no. 52, 30/12/1878:299, 300.

9. B.O., no. 15, 1 April 1882:138.

10. Also known as Zambia and Zambi in certain texts. See, for example, Newitt (1995), Pelissier (1988), Brouwer (1998), among others.

11. Guanazi's own settlement at Makassane was twenty kilometers south of Salamanga.

12. The Portuguese looked upon the Protestant schools as "British" and were deeply suspicious of them, as already noted in the last chapter.

13. During this period, the Portuguese had divided the lands subordinated to them into four *circumscripções* (later spelled *circunscrições*, signifying rural districts). One of them, Magaia, was in open revolt.

14. At this point in time, Maputo was under the Gaza empire. It may be that what then happened was due to an order from the emperor who was never on really good terms with the Portuguese.

15. Eduardo Noronha, *A Rebelião dos Indígenas em Lourenço Marques*, Lisboa, 1894, gives the details.

16. Governo do Districto de Lourenço Marques, Fundo do Seculo XIX, Caixa 107, 12 September 1895.

17. Governo do Districto de Lourenço Marques, Fundo do Seculo XIX, Caixa 107, 27 March and 1 April 1896.

18. Distrito de Lourenço Marques, *Relatório das Circumscripções*, 1909–1910:120.

19. Distrito de Lourenço Marques, *Relatório das Circumscripções*, 1911–1912:48 and Distrito de Lourenço Marques, *Relatório das Circumscripções*, 1913–1914:64.

20. Distrito de Lourenço Marques, *Relatório das Circumscripções, 1913–1914*:50.

21. Colonia de Moçambique, Inspecção dos Serviços Administrativos e dos Negócios Indígenas, *Inspecção Ordinária às Circunscrições de Marracuene e Maputo, ano de 1943*:147.

22. Colonia de Moçambique, *Relatório da Inspecção Ordinária ao Concelho de Lourenço Marques e Circunscrições de Marracuene e Maputo, 1950*:166.

23. In our interview with the community women, they identified seven *zonas*, including those mentioned above and Mutxai, Nhakeni, and Nwadomani.

24. See HELVETAS, 1998. Later in the year, the Agronomy and Forestry Faculty of Eduardo Mondlane University conducted a rapid rural appraisal in Massoane and confirmed all of the information that we gathered (Universidade de Eduardo Mondlane, 1999).

25. The Massoane population also testified to the Boer's collaboration.

26. See HELVETAS, 1998.

27. The source of this information is an e-mail communication dated 13 October 2000 from the USAID officer on environmental affairs stationed in Maputo. Her information came from her counterpart at the World Bank office in Maputo who reported that there have been various interested parties in reviving the concession of whom the most environmentally minded was Morris Strong (Earth Summit, Co-chair of World Economic Forum, advisor to Koffi Anan). Strong submitted a proposal to set up a Trust Fund for the area and discussions were held about linking the Reserve to the Futi Corridor to a Trust Fund Concession Area. The private concessions that already exist in the area would have to comply with government regulations. In my interview with Koekemoer, he expressed a similar sentiment, that is, he suggested a Trust Fund with a steering committee comprising government, concessionaires and communities to administer the area, including the Reserves and its profits. Nevertheless, the government hesitated to commit itself, and as of the date of this writing in May 2002, the fate of Matutuíne has not yet been settled.

28. The survey of the Agronomy and Forestry Faculty referred to above compared Massoane with three other communities in Gaza, Tete, and Nampula and also found it to have the lowest level of consumption of the four communities (Universidade de Eduardo Mondlane, 1999:26).

CHAPTER FIVE

~

Resettlement, 1995–1999

In the period following the war's end in 1992, the Mozambican government told the millions of displaced persons that they were free to resettle wherever they liked: no longer were they obliged to return to communal villages. This chapter records how and where people resettled in the period 1995–1999, or to be exact, how they presented themselves to teams from the Institute for Rural Development (INDER). The purpose of the chapter is to give an overview of the problems of resettlement as people themselves perceived them and gave voice to them.

The following information derives from open-ended interviews with groups of elders, women, young people, and others and also individuals from twenty-eight communities[1] in Cabo Delgado, Zambézia, Manica, and Sofala provinces. (See map 2.) Information was also included from a few other communities in Niassa and Maputo provinces as appropriate. People were asked to consider their physical environment, including the extent of their territory and its borders, the population, the community's history, customs and traditions (normally understood as ceremonies), political and social organization, economic activities, physical and social infrastructures, and principal problems. The narrative covers these points.

A few caveats are in order: first, raw information obtained in short visits, from three to five days, cannot be more than preliminary and superficial. Second, combining information from at least twenty-eight sources leads to a high level of generalization. Third, the context of the interviews—introducing a participatory planning process—also colored people's responses, a point made again in chapter 7 that analyzes the process. The teams tried to verify, whenever possible, important information through crosschecking, triage, and direct observation.

Size and Types of Communities Visited

Guided by the choice of district administrators, INDER teams visited communities of varying sizes and types. Kanda, for example, was one of the largest; it covered the administrative post of Nhamadzi, the government unit that supervised a number of localities and was directly subordinate to the Gorongosa district administration. Kanda covered over 1,100 square kilometers. In other areas, people were characterized as communities but the administrative units into which they had been divided were smaller than their "traditional" territories. They were, in effect, "sub-communities" of a larger lineage-based community. This was the case of Dugudiua in Nicoadala, Natelaca in Alto-Molocué, and Hapala in Ile, all three in Zambézia. They were being governed by Samassoas, the second in command in the hierarchy of the Lomwé people. This was also the case of Massoane, in principle subordinate to Madjajane. At the end of the colonial period, Madjajane with 1,327 square kilometers had an even larger territory than Kanda.[2] In all of these cases, however, people recognized their governing structures as legitimate.

Other communities included four communal villages, some of which had been the product of Portuguese and later FRELIMO social engineering. They consisted of a conglomeration of different populations and were the sites of frequent conflict between older generations who wanted to return to their homelands and the young who appreciated the social advantages of urbanized rural life, that is, the benefits of close contact. As noted, Ilinga typified this situation.

Two other communities had been refugee centers of very mixed populations. After the war, these had taken on the life of small villages. They were known as *bairros*, a Portuguese term more commonly used in reference to subdivisions within urban centers. Their physical layout, and that of the communal villages, conformed to an urban plan.

Six other settlements had the aspect of "company towns": they were formed under colonialism by the influx of migrant plantation workers. Two others were frontier areas with a mixture of peoples from both sides of the border. The communal villages, former refugee centers, "company towns" and frontier areas were distinct from the more "traditional" communities in that the latter acknowledged a common origin or ancestor, had a self-governing structure and lived in a space with more or less recognized boundaries.

At the time of INDER's visit, however, the lineage-based communities also fell into several groups in terms of their governance. Eight of them were ruled by authorities backed by RENAMO and did not recognize the jurisdiction of the government at the time of the INDER visit. Sometimes, INDER was mistaken for a nongovernmental organization and was tolerated as such even though preliminary introductions tried to make the origin and mission of INDER clear to communities. In two communities there was open division and conflict between the representatives of the two rival parties, also making it impossible for government structures to govern. In four other communities, there was open and free collaboration between government officials and "traditional" ones. In one community, Pungué, there was utter confusion: it had been divided by FRELIMO between two districts, Gorongosa and Nhamatanda. However, its problems had begun even earlier, under the Portuguese. The colonial administration had deposed the dynastic ruler, Sanhaxoco, and made him a chief under a new régulo of its own choice. Moreover, it had moved the people of Sanhaxoco from their original homelands. When the INDER teams arrived in 1996, they found Mendes Sanhaxoco, a member of the ruling lineage, administering the area on the Gorongosa side without the help of government structures. The teams were told that his return to rule had been a demand of the community. However, this did not resolve the situation of the people on the other side of the border.

The former refugee centers, communal villages, frontier areas, and "company towns" were all administered by officials recognized by the government. In the communal villages of Niassa, these were also "traditional" leaders as has been seen in the cases of Ilinga and Miala.

The physical sizes of the communities varied enormously from 1,158 square kilometers (Kanda) to 38 square kilometers (Maleia in Nicoadala, Zambézia). In general, the size of the communities in Zambézia was small whereas the dimension of those visited in Sofala and Manica was relatively large. Chaiva, for example, a tiny community in demographic terms, covered 732 square kilometers.

Mapping

The INDER teams asked communities about their physical environment, including their land area, water, and forestry resources. They suggested communities try to map the areas they considered their territories and to identify in the maps their natural resources and basic infrastructures. Without any hesitation, the elders or oldest members of the community produced sketch maps of their areas on the ground, which were then reproduced on paper by a member of the visiting team and presented to the community as a whole for verification. This presentation was, without a doubt, one of the highlights of each visit and evoked great attention and discussion within community meetings. The appendix has the examples of the sketch maps of the four communities described in the previous chapters. In most cases, the maps were carefully reproduced for publication and general distribution together with the reports of each visit. Only the map of Massoane preserves the original drawing.

In 1998, I tried to match the sketch maps with maps produced at various times during the Portuguese administration in order to ascertain whether the memory of the elder reflected the *regedorias* established in 1933 or the earlier rural districts (*circunscrições civis*), the boundaries of which were supposed to coincide with "traditional" boundaries. However, the Historical Archives of Mozambique did not have adequate maps for this purpose and it was not possible to enter the archives of the Geographical and Cadastral Service of the Ministry of Agriculture to ascertain whether they had the appropriate maps. As far as I was able to determine, the Portuguese only published the result of their demarcations of the regedorias in the 1970s and, from the maps that I was shown, which were much reduced photocopies, the lines they drew of the boundaries were often straight rather than following natural ones.[3] Communities, on the other hand, generally used natural features such as rivers or mountains to mark their frontiers.

The names of the territories of the "traditional" communities normally came from the family or person recognized as the founding member or leading member of that community. Thus the name of leader, community and territory was the same.[4] Sometimes the people themselves named their leaders because of a special quality they wanted to recognize. For instance, the first Dugudiua was known as a very hospitable person. *Dugu* in Lomwé means "reception hall." Intama was known as the protector of his people. During World War I fighting between Portuguese and German soldiers caused these Lomwé peoples to flee; at a certain point they were surrounded by Germans and Intama faced them saying that his people were not going to move from this spot, that they were tired of fleeing. The word *Intama* means moving and the ruler was attributed this name to commemorate the event. The people chose the name *Maleia*, which means "have the power," for their leader because when the original dynastic ruler and his family proved to be corrupt under colonialism, the people threw him out and gave Maleia the power.

The names of the territories of most of the other communities were related to a prominent geographical feature, particularly a mountain or nearby body of water. However, this was not the case in three of these communities: one

named itself after the date of the end of the war between FRELIMO and RE-
NAMO while another, Block Nine (*Bloco Nove*), was named by the sugar es-
tate whose land it occupied and a third inherited the name of the person who
had built an access road from his home, on community lands, to the national
highway. These three communities were in Sofala province. The first and
third communities were *sui-generis*, that is, they were groups of displaced persons who had decided not to return to their native lands due to the advantages offered in the former accommodation centers, where they were staying.
Benefits included schooling, medical assistance, and perhaps most important
of all access to the Beira Corridor (following the rail and motorway between
Beira and Harare, Zimbabwe). It was not uncommon to find groups of displaced people along the Corridor even in the late 1990s. The second community was a "company town." Since our visit to Block Nine in December
1995, the sugar company has reclaimed its land and the people, mainly cane-
cutters and their families, have had to move.

Population

The populations of the communities varied considerably ranging from a little over one thousand inhabitants to as many as twenty-eight thousand
dwellers. A significant number were small communities below three thousand members. Since returning from the war, the general pattern of settlement has been dispersed and in some cases exaggeratedly so because recurrent drought forced people to spread out in search of water, as was the case
of Chaiva. Another factor in this dispersal may have been the collapse of organized marketing systems. The previous chapters showed that wherever and
whenever desirable trading opportunities were present, people tended to organize and population densities increased accordingly.[5] The notable exceptions to dispersed settlement were the communal villages, the former refugee
centers, and some of the company towns where people lived in neatly aligned
houses with little space between them. The majority of people in the communities visited lived under a patrilineal organization but twelve communities identified themselves as matrilineal. In general there were more women
than men in the communities.

History

All of the communities spoke of the influence of Portuguese occupation and
colonialism upon their lives. The Cabo Delgado communities remembered
vividly the various cotton regimes and at least one of them had been created

as a village of workers for Portuguese cotton growers. In this village, the men said they were happier growing cotton now because they were their own bosses but they recognized that, in the later years of Portuguese rule, they had better terms of trade than they did at the time of our visit in 1996. Others talked about the hardship of forced labor as a reason for migration to South Africa or in relationship to building public works or, as in the case of Cocorico, Mopeia, Zambézia, in regard to work on the Sena Sugar Estates. The various large-scale plantations, particularly in Zambézia, were the raison d'etre for six communities, as already mentioned. World War I and the German invasion held vivid memories for at least two Zambezian communities. The "socialization" of the countryside under FRELIMO affected those in the communal villages and in a few other communities as well.

However it was the war between FRELIMO and RENAMO that was the single most significant moment for all of them. For the majority, that experience meant the death of family members, migration, life in crowded camps, or as strangers in a foreign land. For a few it meant receiving a large number of strangers in their midst and the need to try to accommodate them with food, housing, and land. For most it was a time of suffering, for many hunger, but some populations benefited from the professional training and services provided in the refugee camps in Malawi. In 1995 and 1996 many people had still not yet returned mainly because of their fear of insecurity in the countryside at large. In Massoane, as just seen, they may never return.

Formal and Informal Political Structures

Whether or not they were living under "traditional" rule, all but one of the twenty-eight communities described the indigenous pattern of authority. That is, they had a living memory of how they had organized themselves in the past and, for at least half of them, in the present. Although not all communities still maintained this elaborate organization, all but one spoke of a three-layered structure of chiefs aided by advisers, judges, and policemen. In the one exceptional case in Cabo Delgado, there were only clan heads.

The Portuguese, as has been seen, called the highest level of authority, *régulo* and after 1933 *regedor*. (The next chapter has a fuller explanation of colonial administration.) Each group of peoples had their own titles. In the Macua and Lomwé areas that were visited, the paramount chief was known as *Muene*; in the Magorongosa and Sena areas that were interviewed, he was known as *Nhacuáua*; in Ndau, he was *Mambo*; and *Che* in Yao territories. The adjunct to the paramount chief was called *Samassoa* (Macua/Lomwé), *Sapanda* (Magorongosa/Sena) and *Nduna* in the Ndau and Yao areas.[6] The level of chiefdom closest to the people was often called *Cafumo, Camfumo, M'fumo, or N'fumo* (also known as *Nihimo, Mahumo, or Humo* in the Macua areas visited in Cabo Delgado), *Muene* in some Sena areas and *Sabuco* in the Ndau area visited. These chiefs had responsibility for a certain number of families in their areas. They had assistants known as *cabos da terra* or policemen, in some areas still called by the colonial name, *cipaios.*

The government structure established by FRELIMO showed a parallel organization. In the case of Kanda, the parallel government authority was the head of the administrative post (*chefe de posto*). Most of the communities visited were, however, localities, such as the Zambezian communities of Muagiua, Intama, and Natelaca, or even lower level units. The equivalents of most of such chiefs were locality presidents. Under them were secretaries. The secretaries were heads of administrative units known as *bairros* (this was the designation of Ilinga, for example) and *circulos*, terms that had an urban ring to them. For example, *bairro* was generally translated as suburb, quarter, ward or even district, while *circulo* was translated as circle or club. A more rural term, *povoada*, was sometimes used, meaning settlement or village. Under secretaries were adjuncts and under them were the heads of *quarteirões*, which was the Portuguese equivalent of "blocks of houses." This office was closest to the level of M'fumo, the lowest level of "traditional" chiefdom but these structures were not always present. However, in some communities, party organization went even lower, consisting of the heads of ten houses (*chefes de dez casas* or *chefes de comissões de moradores*). What was striking was the lack of uniformity of official structures. Not all levels were present and the various levels had a variety of names.

The basic functions performed by "traditional" authorities were similar in all areas. M'fumos were responsible for resolving conflicts between families, that is, in keeping social order as well as helping with family problems such as divorces. They also were the first to receive requests for land from families and "strangers" wanting to settle in their areas. All problems not able to be resolved at this level were referred to the level above and upward to the highest authorities. Intractable problems and those that involved another community were automatically turned over to civil authorities. Settlement heads were expected to make regular reports to the adjuncts or to the Muene himself. We met only one female M'fumo in all of the twenty-eight communities. She was related to the ruling dynasty and had been chosen by her people because, while others fled, she had stood up to the armies of both FRELIMO and RENAMO during the recent war.

The Muene (Nhacuáua, Mambo, etc.) was the coordinator and organizer of community-wide activities. He had advisers, generally among the elders of the community. In some Macua societies, there was a parallel female author-ity known as the *Apuiamuene*. In the three Cabo Delgado villages included in this sample, the INDER teams met only one Apuiamuene and, unfortu-nately, did not gather specific information regarding her role. The Muene was responsible for convoking important ceremonies such as the rain cere-monies. These were vital for agrarian areas periodically affected by drought and sometimes excessive rainfall as in the case of Niassa. At times people came to the Muene through their M'fumos with requests for these cere-monies and other times the initiative came from above.

The Muene arranged with the local diviners, made the necessary prepara-tions, and presided over the ceremonies. He presided over such other events as the ceremonies launching the agricultural season, those related to initia-tion rites, harvest celebrations, thanksgiving to the community spirits, inter-cessions with the dead, and other religious rituals. The chief authority was consulted on land allocations for which his permission was sought as well as on marriages and divorces. He was responsible for harmony among the fam-ilies and for the well-being of the community in general. He was also the rep-resentative of the community to the external world. His adjunct took deci-sions in his absence and also resolved problems in the area in which he lived and he supervised the lower level chiefs and referred their outstanding prob-lems to the paramount chief whenever necessary.

Social Organization

As in all societies, the basic unit is the family. How the family was consti-tuted and who governed the family was an important part of the conversa-tions between the INDER teams and the people they met. It must be recog-nized that the descriptions of marriage customs that people, mainly women, gave us was, in many respects, idealized, that is, a description of procedures, rights, and obligations that were respected when circumstances permitted them to be respected, that is, in the absence of war, displacement, drought, and so on.

In all communities, men were the recognized heads of families. However which male succeeded to this position varied according to whether the fam-ily was organized along a patrilineal or matrilineal pattern. As already noted, of the twenty-eight communities, sixteen were patrilineal and twelve de-clared themselves matrilineal.

There were many similarities in how marriage was organized under the pa-trilineal system. The would-be groom generally took the initiative and de-cided upon whom he would like to marry, although in at least one community in Pebane (Zambézia), people said that the family decided for the young man. Contacts were made with the family of the pretended bride. Generally the young man was officially presented to the bride and her family at which time he might present gifts and a small amount of money. (In most communities, whether or not patrilineal, the young couple already knew each other, having met at social gatherings.)

The most important step that followed was the marriage payment, *lobolo*, the amount of which varied considerably from community to community. Today money is the main component of the marriage payment. In frontier areas or those, which did commerce with neighboring countries, the amount might be determined in the "harder" currency of the other country. The payment of this amount signified the commitment to found a new family. There might or might not be a feast. In some communities, there were even more steps and ceremonies accompanying marriage. In some, tests of virginity and/or virility were demanded.

In patrilineal societies, polygamy was frequent. In general, families were made up of husband, wife, and children. In cases of polygamy, each wife lived separately in her own house with her children. Her husband visited her regularly according to a program that he established with his wives. The program was considered sacrosanct and was a matter of pride for each wife. Each wife received one or more plots of land to farm from her husband's allotment of land. This allotment was normally a designated portion of land received from the father of the husband. It was her responsibility to produce on it food for herself, her children, and her husband when he visited.

In the patrilineal society, the children of the marriage belonged to the man's lineage, and the inheritance of land and goods were from father to the children. (In Kanda, it was stated that the children belonged to the wife until a certain amount of money was paid to the bride's family, after which the children belonged to the husband. Whether this was a second form of *lobolo* or just a prolongation of the payment of the first one, was not specified. This norm was only mentioned in Kanda.) When the husband died before the children were grown, they generally passed to the husband's family, often in the person of a brother. In this case, the widow could be given the option to marry him or another one of the husband's family. If she refused, she had to leave her home, children, and goods and return to her family.

In matrilineal communities, the head of the family was the maternal uncle. When a young man decided to marry he consulted his family and the intended fiancée advised hers. In the formal presentation of the would-be groom to the fiancée's family, his maternal uncle accompanied him. Then, the bride's family consulted their uncle. The uncles of both families then negotiated the marriage and became its sponsors. If approved, the young man went to live with the bride's family where he was under observation for a number of years. (In some communities it was mentioned that this probation might last as long as two years.) During this period, the bride's family paid attention to how the young man tended their fields, how he comported himself, whether he drank excessively, went after other women, whether he treated their daughter with respect and so on. Only after he passed examination was he officially the groom and presented as such to the M'fumo or even to the Muene.

The land given to the new family was from the uncle of the bride and remained in possession of her lineage. The children also belonged to the wife's lineage. There was no marriage price, although practicing Muslims might make a symbolic payment to the bride's family. Polygamous marriages were also contracted in matrilineal societies. Extended families were more common in matrilineal than in patrilineal communities.

In both societies, people mentioned that polygamy was often problematic for women and could be the cause of divorce especially when the man violated the established routine and showed preference for one or another woman. Not surprisingly, polygamy was not common in the more impoverished communities, such as those with very limited land or where people were still essentially displaced. This was the case in one of the former refugee centers and four of the "company towns." The same was true of three of the lineage-based communities.

Divorce was common to all of the communities and among the reasons most often cited were abandonment of the wife and children, misuse of financial resources on drinking and debauchery, wife-beating, adultery by wives, infertility, and incompatibility. Adultery on the part of wives could be disastrous for women in both patrilineal and matrilineal communities if the husband wanted to press charges because, if the wife were found at fault, she risked losing everything and being sent home in disgrace. Nevertheless, in matrilineal society, the children remained with her.

Family problems were generally resolved between the families or marriage sponsors. In matrilineal communities, the maternal uncle of the wife was particularly responsible for trying to reconcile husband and wife. When this was not possible, then the problems were referred to the clan head or M'fumo and grave problems were referred to the adjunct and/or Muene. A formal divorce decree was a matter for the civil authorities.

In all the communities visited, Christianity was represented by a multitude of churches, and in a few communities Islam was a major influence. In a number of communities, it was mentioned that the Christian ban on polygamy had helped somewhat toward diminishing the practice. Religious practices integrated themselves in both the marriage and divorce proceedings. In the case of marriage, this meant that after complying with the customary procedures, the couple underwent a church ceremony. Often the churches were involved in trying to solve problems between husbands and wives.

The war between FRELIMO and RENAMO had a great impact on social organization. There was a larger than normal number of widows and orphans. There was, moreover, a large number of abandoned wives and unmarried young women with children. The plight of the female-headed household was deplored in a number of communities. Yet there was a lack of organized community-based support for these vulnerable members. The last section of this chapter explores the general social problems afflicting communities in the process of resettling their homelands or places of accommodation.

Economic Activities

In all the communities, people cited agriculture as their principal economic activity. In the first instance, it served to feed the family after which production was sold in order to obtain basic consumer goods and to cover the expenses of education, health care, burial, marriage, and investment goods such as agricultural implements, carts, bicycles, and cattle.

In theory, everyone was said to participate in cultivation and family land was divided accordingly, to provide fields for husbands, wives, and children above the age of twelve or fourteen. In some matrilineal societies, such as Ilinga, there were family fields where men, women, and children cultivated together. In communities that had formerly supplied a male workforce to nearby plantations, mills and factories, or to far off mines, more often than not, agriculture was the basic responsibility of women. In all cases, as just mentioned, it was her responsibility to provide food security for her husband and children.

Normally, each member of the household had his/her own separate fields and was responsible for working them but, as just noted, there were the exceptions where husband and wife worked one or more or all of the family fields together. In general, especially within extended families, people gave each other a helping hand in their fields. Between families, there was also the general custom to provide labor in peak periods in exchange for food and drink but there were communities where mutual aid did not exist (or no longer existed). And there was the widespread practice of *ganho-ganho* (also spelled *ganyo-ganyo*) among poorer members of many communities who worked in the fields of the richer ones or in nearby private small-scale plantations in exchange for a part of the harvest or some money (Massoane is an example).

Newcomers to a community, that is, people who were not yet integrated into it through marriage, were able to ask for land to cultivate and to build their houses. During the war, as noted before, communities accommodated large numbers of people fleeing from the battlefield. In all cases, the stranger needed to get permission from the family holding the piece of land he/she would like to occupy and this request had also to be submitted to the chief of the area, the M'fumo, who was responsible for making the Muene aware of the particular transaction. Generally speaking, the land was on loan for a set number of years.

The principal crops for domestic consumption were cereals such as one or more varieties of maize (white maize being the preferred one), several varieties of sorghum, millet, local grains, and rice. Cassava was also a mainstay; in certain areas it was the basic food and the cereals grown were then marketed. In most other areas, it was a crop held in reserve to cover supplies when drought had killed the other cereal crops.

The second most basic set of crops for family diets were legumes, including a wide assortment of beans and groundnuts. Then there were the condiments, which consisted of garlic, onion, and tomatoes. Oilseed crops included sesame and sunflower. Finally, in order to vary the diet, families tended to grow an array of vegetables such as squash, eggplant, melon, cabbage, lettuce, cucumbers, and many sorts of greens. Potatoes and sweet potatoes were grown in appropriate soils. These foods served to enrich the relish, which accompanied the basic cereal. In the case of maize, millet, sorghum, and other more local grains, the core of the grain was ground into flour and cooked into porridge.

Almost all communities had access to fruit trees; some actively cultivated them. From these trees, they extracted bananas, oranges, lemons, mangoes, tangerines, papaya, and other tropical fruits. Sometimes pineapples were grown. Sometimes the communities harvested wild sugar cane and other times they planted it. In appropriate areas, they also harvested cashew nuts and coconuts. Among the crops grown for market were the cereals already mentioned, cotton, beans, groundnuts, cashew nuts, fruits and vegetables, and even cassava.

In general, large families with over four working family members had the largest number of fields and the largest amount of land under cultivation. They commonly planted one crop per field and practiced crop rotation on these fields, which could be as large as two or more hectares in dimension.

Families with animal traction, a rarity among the communities INDER met, were able to cultivate even larger tracts of land. Smaller families with fewer and smaller fields (one-half hectare or less per field) would often associate two and three crops in one field. However, these were gross generalizations since planting practices varied from location to location as well as from family to family.

There were at least two growing seasons. Where maize and other cereals were always grown in the first season, legumes were normally planted in the second season. Vegetables and sometimes cereals and sugar cane were planted in the second season on low-lying moist lands or around perimeters of cereal fields. Wherever practicable, it was not uncommon to find families with the two kinds of lands, the high ground where rain-fed crops were grown and the lower grounds where moisture would collect or along river banks but not everyone had access to both kinds of land. When the agricultural season turned bad, for lack of rainfall or irregular rainfall, people not only planted cereals in the low-lying lands, but also in river beds, and they tried their luck regardless of season.

Almost all work in the fields was done by manual labor because most families in cattle-raising areas, such as Massoane and Chaiva, had lost their cattle during the war between FRELIMO and RENAMO. However, most of the communities visited were infested with tsetse flies making cattle raising impossible.

There was a notorious shortage of farm implements including hoes, spades, machetes, hatchets, and so on because most families lost everything when they fled their homelands. Some had received emergency help upon their return but these fortunate ones generally received only one or two of some of these implements, not enough to go around the family. Moreover, the relief agency of the Ministry of Agriculture was well known at the time for its inefficiency, often importing the wrong type of instrument and delivering it well after the agricultural season had begun, and for its corruption, that is, nondelivery of donated goods. During the emergency relief operation, there were few items for sale on markets, when there were markets. When the agency was disbanded, the prices of farm implements rose to prohibitive levels.

It was not only difficult to get implements but also seed and, when it was available, it was not necessarily good quality seed. Both of these problems were presented energetically by communities to INDER, as shall be noted below. Most families tried to save seed from their harvests to plant in the following season but this was not always possible under drought conditions.

Gender Divisions of Labor

In some communities, it was stated that there was no significant division of labor between men and women in terms of crop production, whereas in others men grew a commercial crop while women grew subsistence crops. In all communities, men were responsible for cutting down and uprooting trees in order to open a field for planting. Roots and remaining vegetation were burnt in August on all fields in order to provide fertilizing ash material to enrich the soil. Men also generally turned the soil in preparation for planting but a lone female head of a household would do this work herself or, when she had the resources, would hire young men to do it for her. In the communities where men actively farmed, both men and women planted while women and children were responsible for weeding. Both men (in the areas where they farmed) and women harvested crops.

To supplement family diets, men as a rule hunted usually during the months of August and September, when burning fields flushed out the game. In one community, Marruma, in Mopeia district, Zambézia, women also hunted. Where there was a near-by body of water, men and sometimes women engaged in fishing both to enlarge food supplies and also to sell in local markets.

Almost all families raised some kind of small animals. Those most frequently mentioned were goats, chickens, ducks, pigs, rarely sheep,[7] rabbits, doves, and so on. These, too, enriched diets and were sold locally to raise money for family expenses, mainly emergency expenses such as medicines, health care, and burials. Generally the care of animals fell to wives and children but they were not allowed to sell them unless authorized by husbands who also had authority over the money obtained. In Ngongote, Sanga district, Niassa, this gender division was reversed.

Only two of the twenty-eight communities, Muchenessa (Buzi, Sofala) and Chaiva raised cattle and only the richest families because, as noted above, most cattle had been killed during the war. Massoane was another area where a few rich families were beginning to reaccumulate cattle. Cattle served mainly as a family reserve (savings) and for animal traction, ceremonies, milk and sale on local markets, but only as a last resort. Men and young boys tended cattle.

All families engaged in handicrafts for domestic use and for sale. Generally men wove baskets and mats and made furniture while women manufactured pottery. Most communities brewed local alcoholic drinks such as beer from cereals, rum from sugar cane, and palm wine. In some cases, this was women's work and, in other cases, men were involved. These drinks were both for feasts and for sale. Charcoal making was another remunerative activity and this, too, could involve a division of labor. Whereas men cut wood, women and children gathered it and carried it to where men would make and sell the charcoal. In communities near district capitals, working plantations, South Africa, Zimbabwe, or Malawi, it was common for men to migrate to seek salaried employment and many times the remittances from these salaries were essential to maintain the families left behind. In Massoane, they meant the difference between the life and death of the community.

Where men and women worked together in family fields, the harvest was common. In most other cases, men and women had separate granaries. In polygamous marriages each wife guarded her own production. In these marriages, the husband's harvest was destined as a reserve to supplement deficits in his wives' reserves and also for his own personal needs. The production from children's fields often went to defray educational expenses.

The INDER teams did not uniformly investigate the question of family budgets and who had authority over them. In some cases, it appeared that the husband had ultimate authority, but at times it was stated that there was joint consultation between husbands and wives on the question of sales and the use of the money obtained from them. The exception of Ngongote in Niassa was already mentioned.

The INDER teams did ask families and groups to distinguish the general tasks of men and women in each community and to describe a typical working day for males and females, sometimes for children. Men and women worked on the average between fifteen and one-half and seventeen hours per day. Mostly women got up a half an hour to an hour earlier than men in order to prepare breakfast, get children ready for school and arrange the house. Rising time was normally at 5:00 A.M. for men and 4:00 or 4:30 A.M. for women. Women also left for the fields later than men, generally one hour later, and they returned home one hour earlier in order to begin to prepare the main meal of the day. In the afternoon, women might not return to the fields, depending upon the domestic work they had to complete. In the evening, men rested and took their bath, while women prepared the meal. The wife was also responsible for heating water for her husband's bath. The family ate and went to bed around 8:00 to 9:00 A.M.

Besides opening and working in fields, men generally had obligations to procure building materials, build and repair family dwellings, hunt, fish, and raise cattle, where these applied, engage in handicrafts, market goods, help educate and discipline the children, and resolve family problems. Women were expected to plaster the walls of family dwellings after her husband put up the structure, to keep dwellings and the yard clean, carry water to the house, fetch kindling for cooking, wash clothes, bathe children and her husband, generally take care of children and the sick, find the makings of family meals, cook it, work in the fields, fish, wherever appropriate, build granaries, do handicrafts, and take care of the family's small animals. One of the most time-consuming and strenuous tasks was crushing cereal grains and grinding flour. Female children helped their mothers in the household chores while male children helped in raising the small animals.

The Question of Stratification

In all communities, there were marked socio-economic differences among families. There was a clear distinction between the poor and the majority of families. The poor, in this postwar period, were widows and widowers, abandoned women, abandoned old people, middle-aged couples with no grown children to help them, single mothers with small children, and so on. These people lacked a sufficient labor force to sustain them and also lacked remittances from better off family members. To a great extent, they were the casualties of the war and the social disintegration that occurred with dislocation and the tearing apart of families. Families had split into parts as some fled before others and settled in different areas. Some never returned to their homelands. Moreover, many soldiers brought home another wife or wives, *if* they returned home at all. Many did not return to the countryside. As shall be seen below, there was little or no community support for the vulnerable community members. In part this was because most returning families were hard pressed to feed and clothe their own members during resettlement.

Nonetheless, in some communities, there was a wealthy group of families and, in all communities there were the better off, or middle group. The wealthy were those with cattle, mentioned above, and therefore access to animal traction as well as those able to rent animal traction, and those able to contract seasonal workers (and not simply to host *ganho-ganho* workers). The better-off families had a large number of working family members, both on and off farm. Access to remittances from regularly employed family members also made a big difference. New clothes, radio-cassette players, furniture were some of the most visible signs of relative affluence in this postwar phase.

Three to five-day stays in the communities were not long enough to be able to observe the significance of these structural differences on community life, especially on matters requiring community solidarity.

Links with Urban Areas

Although all communities described themselves as essentially agrarian, there was no doubt that links to urban areas were crucial and in some cases, such as Massoane, vital. These links made the difference between mere subsistence and a measure of comfort: in the first instance, they meant marketing outlets for agricultural and other production, second, they meant access to consumer goods and services and, in the last instance, employment. People of both genders were constantly on the move in order to reach markets, obtain services and secure jobs. Many communities asked for factories to be established in their areas because they accepted the fact that many of their young would not farm. Moreover, as already mentioned, in many communities men "traditionally" worked off-farm. The last section of this chapter demonstrates that rural peoples demanded the same services and economic opportunities available to urban-based peoples. *They* did not see themselves as inferior or as deserving anything less than their cousins, brothers, sisters, uncles, husbands and others living in cities and towns.

Religion and Customs

As can be seen from how they described marriage customs, people, in general, and women in particular, consciously identified with "traditional" ways and had an emotional attachment to them even though they accepted new ways and ideas, such as organized religion. One of the reasons most commonly mentioned in regard to the old ways was that their revival was necessary for the survival of communal life and in order to educate the young. During the 1970s and for most of the 1980s, FRELIMO had banned "traditional" practices including polygamy and initiation rites but in the late 1990s these seemed to be coming back with a vengeance. Similarly Christianity frowned upon such customs but rural peoples found ways to accommodate both outside strictures, emotional needs, and cultural bonds. Syncretism marked the religious life in all communities.

In all the visited communities, organized religions were present. Christianity was dominant but, in the communities of Cabo Delgado and Niassa, Islam was also a potent influence. Besides the Roman Catholic Church, inherited from colonialism, denounced by FRELIMO in the early years of independence and now rehabilitated, there was a great variety of Protestant churches, many of which derived from Zimbabwean and South African congregations. Among the latter were the numerous forms of Zionism, Johane Malangue, and the Assembly of God. A list of some of the better known Protestant churches found by the INDER teams included Bethany, Pentecostal, Union Baptist, Convention Baptist, Seventh Day Adventism, Jehovah's Witnesses, Nazarene, Evangelical, Methodism, and Anglican. There were also many individual churches including those headed by entrepreneurial pastors. Some of these were Salvation of Christ, Love of God, the International Body of Christ, the Church of Christ, the Gospel of Christ, New Apostle, Apostles' Faith, Jesus' Path, New Birth, Sendiluca, Church of St. Luke, New Alliance, Twelve Apostles, and the Complete Church of God.[8]

In terms of "traditional" religion, people showed great respect for ancestors and prayed to them to intercede on their behalf. In many areas, family spirits were considered the protectors of the family and the ancestors, particularly of the founding family, were considered guardians of the land. The various family and community-wide ceremonies, conducted by local diviners and presided over by the heads of households, the chiefs, and the paramount chief, were ritualized forms of communication with and appeasement of the spirits.

Besides the community-wide ceremonies mainly following the agricultural cycle and its hazards, there were family ceremonies accompanying the most important moments of an individual's life such as birth, puberty, marriage, and death. In most of the non-lineage-based communities and in some of the lineage-based ones, these ceremonies as well as the community ones were not followed with the same assiduity of former times and some people mentioned this with regret. It was probably fair to say that in these communities, the organized religions played a greater role in the lives of their members. Apart from the marriage procedures, the one ceremony that appeared to be most common and still widely respected even in some of the non-lineage communities was initiation, expected of adolescents of both sexes. The duration of these rites, the purpose of which was to teach young people the duties, responsibilities, and pleasures of adulthood, varied considerably among populations. In some areas young men were also circumcised while the girls might be tattooed and taught to elongate their clitoris. The time periods mentioned were from three days to three months. Some of the other ceremonies still respected had to do with purification after giving birth or after the death of a spouse.

"Traditional" medicine was practiced in almost all areas and in some the healers were attempting to organize themselves and institutionalize their practices on the model of the Zimbabwean healers.

Although mentioned in only three communities, the belief existed that some people practiced witchcraft in order to cause misfortune to others. There were diviners and ceremonies to deal with this problem and "traditional" authorities were asked to pass judgment on wrongdoers.

Economic and Social Infrastructures

Each community was asked about its access to such basic economic and social infrastructures as primary schools, health or first aid posts, safe water, access roads, grain mills, and stores (marketing outlets). When the INDER teams arrived, they generally found a bleak situation. *Only one of the twenty-eight communities had a store within easy reach.* Only one had access to safe water. A grain mill serviced only two. The majority lacked a health post or first-aid post and for most a sick person had to walk several miles before reaching a post. Half of the communities were served by a decent access road. However this was probably atypical because district administrators generally sent INDER teams to communities within easy reach of some kind of road. Almost all communities had primary schools within two kilometers but the majority of these were built of precarious materials and some were open-air schools, under a shady tree. The following section looks at what the communities themselves felt were their principal problems.

Principal Problems

After two days of interviews with groups and individual families, INDER teams compiled a list of the principal problems people talked about and presented the list to the entire community on the third day. After an explanation and some short discussion of each problem, community members were asked to prioritize the problems in order of urgency and/or preference for solution. By far the top priority of the twenty-eight communities was health care. The second greatest concern was that a primary school be built in conventional materials so that it would last at least a generation. Schools built of locally fired bricks lasted only five years at the most. Moreover, many communities did not have the soils appropriate for fired bricks and some lacked the techniques to make them. In these communities, schools had to be rebuilt every two or three years.

In third place were marketing facilities, safe water, and a grain mill. In fourth place was a supply of farming implements at reasonable prices, and in fifth place, a supply of seeds.

In terms of frequency of citation: twenty-four of the twenty-eight communities listed the lack of medical assistance as their principal concern, twenty-three mentioned the need for improved school buildings, twenty-two complained about the lack of marketing facilities and twenty, the need for access to safe water. As just seen, the other most frequently cited problems were the lack of a grain mill, agricultural implements and seeds. Moreover, the lack of employment, unfavorable terms of trade, insufficient roads, and transport were also noted.

It does not require much analysis to realize that this list corresponded to the situation of war-torn communities undergoing resettlement and demonstrated that, *given the opportunity to do so,* rural peoples had no trouble defining their needs. Chapters 7 and 8 address how some of these needs were met by INDER and other state and international agencies.

Social tensions
Not addressed by the INDER planning exercises were the social and emotional needs of these communities. Although actively voiced by individuals and groups and sometimes listed among their principal problems, INDER teams did not feel it appropriate to underscore social conflicts in open community meetings as INDER had nothing to offer in consolation nor did the teams have the power or skills to engage people in a healing process. Among the most frequently mentioned problems was the presence of large numbers of vulnerable people with little or no support. A number of communities also spoke of physical insecurity, including attacks on women, and crimes of various sorts. Theft was rife in seven communities, one-fourth of the sample.

Land conflicts and land insecurity plagued many communities due mainly to the continued occupation of land by displaced people. Generally, this was due to the attribution of lands by local government authorities, which had ignored customary practices and/or previous owners. When "traditional" procedures were followed, these conflicts were seemingly resolved. Another reason for conflict was the arbitrary demarcation of land by national and provincial government officials without consulting local populations, as was the case of Ilinga and Massoane. Within communal villages, there was soil erosion especially around the villages due to intensive cultivation. In some other non-lineage-based communities, there was land shortage for various reasons. Many of these situations resulted from government intervention in land questions, discussed in chapter 11.

Inter-generational conflict particularly afflicted communal villages usually over the question of returning to homelands but also over initiation rites and respect for older people. As already mentioned, there was tension between formal and informal authorities; in some communities, this led to chaos. In a few communities there were tensions and rivalries between churches. In a few cases, people mentioned the practice of premature marriages, one explanation for which was the inability of the girl's family to sustain her during times of stress.

There is no doubt that "traditional" structures and procedures have emerged weakened, transformed and, in some cases, seriously undermined through colonialism, FRELIMO prohibition, and two successive and bitterly divisive wars. Nevertheless, where these institutions still existed, they embodied long-standing ways of resolving differences and were, for the most part, still respected. On a more symbolic level, they represented social cohesion and a measure of identity. On a political level they represented authority and power. This did not make them perfect or even recommendable institutions. On the other hand, they were meaningful to the people who lived under them.

Notes

1. There were no written questionnaires guiding the interviews, only topics. People were encouraged to speak freely about whatever concerned them.

2. Província de Moçambique, Direcção Provincial dos Serviços de Planeamento e Integração Económica da Província de Moçambique, *Estudos 13: Divisão Administrativa de Moçambique, por Regedorias*, 1970. Information received in 2001 indicated that, after a number of years of dormancy, a new titleholder was to be installed. The former Madjajane and his heirs had fled to South Africa during the most recent war.

3. Província de Moçambique, *Estudos 13: Divisão Administrativa de Moçambique, por Regedorias*, 1970.

4. Harry West also found that on the Mueda Plateau of Cabo Delgado "each group referred to itself by the name of an elder who led it to a new home and who founded the settlement in which they would live" (1998:144).

5. See West, 1998:145 for a description of this process of population concentration in Mueda in response to the opening of marketing opportunities.

6. As already noted, the title *nduna*, which was derived from the term used by the Nguni for their chiefs, also appeared in Ilinga and Massoane, at the two extremities of Mozambique demonstrating the far-flung influence of these people.

7. Here Niassa was the exception.

8. These names have all been literally translated from their Portuguese names, with the exception of Sendiluca, which was the name given by community members.

~

Creating Democratic Spaces

Part 1 described how the "little society" was weakened through the loss of both land and governance in what might be seen as the conquest of peoples' spaces by state spaces, a modern version of enclosure. Part 2 is about regaining some of what was lost.

To summarize: colonial and postcolonial rule undermined, in similar and dissimilar ways, the institutions of rural Mozambicans and also prejudiced their livelihoods. Loss of the best lands and the lack of the physical, economic, and commercial infrastructures necessary for facilitating commodity production put rural peoples in their present precarious position. In the post–civil war period some infrastructures have been replaced in some areas through governmental and nongovernmental projects. Chapters 7 and 8 examine the process of reconstruction from 1995 through 1999 and the role rural peoples played in it.

The following chapters are about finding a balance between state spaces and peoples' spaces. Chapters 10 and 11 argue that the only way rural communities can gain what they need—not simply to survive but to flourish—is to reclaim, to the extent possible, their lost sovereignty. Rural communities need to recover and make their voices heard in the present cacophony of elite discourse not through the co-optation of their leaders, which seems the government's preferred course of action, but by organizing to take control over some part of their lives and destinies. The interesting experiments in community planning of infrastructures that took place in the late 1990s under governmental and international agency sponsorship did not lead to empowerment, as chapters 7 and 8 show. Chapter 10 suggests institutional arrangements that would promote a measure of community self-management while chapter 11 discusses the issue of community land management. The next chapter explores some of the obstacles to decentralizing governance including the colonial legacy, which continues to shape the relationship of the state to rural Mozambicans despite the massive intervention of international and multinational agencies since 1987.

CHAPTER SIX

~

Governing Mozambique

The Weakening of Lineage-Based Authority

As previously noted, Portugal initially had neither the physical power nor the manpower and, much less, the legitimacy to establish an effective central authority of its own and so was forced to rely on adventurers to secure its "colony." For at least the first four hundred years of its presence in Africa, de facto decentralization marked Portuguese "rule."

Beginning in 1505, a stream of military men and traders paraded across Mozambique under the not so watchful eye of the Estado da India, Portugal's outpost in the Far East and the governing body of the colony. The captain of Mozambique Island with his trade monopoly, the handful of great prazo-owners on the Zambeze, the captains of the trading fairs and the bush traders in search of gold, copper, or ivory, all had one thing in common: they opposed closer royal control which would have meant regulation and taxation, and had no wish to share the profits of their Africa enterprise with settlers or anyone from outside. In this regard they made common cause with African chiefs and headmen when they could not conquer them.

As the adventurers gained a foothold in Mozambique, however, they began to enrich themselves at everyone's expense. Private individuals appropriated government for personal gain. Newitt calls this indirect form of government "proprietorial office-holding" and estimated that even during the earliest captaincies, officeholders garnered three-quarters of the trade for themselves (Newitt, 1995:27). No one exemplified this double aspect

of public office and private gain better than the prazo-holders.[1] They accumulated enormous wealth.

Newitt saw this regime as counterproductive to trade over the long run.
He contrasted monopoly control of trade for short-term gain with Dutch and
English systems of administration that relied upon soundly financed joint
stock enterprises that could afford to nurse markets rather than take quick
gains (1995:168). Also struck by the "informality" of the arrangements under which private gain was endemic to the system, Barendse asserted that
from about 1630 the main source of gain for both the state and the adventurers was no longer trade but land revenues.[2] The previous chapters have
shown how—after the effective occupation of the country—tribute and later
taxes were forcibly extracted from smallholders via the régulos. For the Niassa and Mozambique companies, neither of which was on a secure financial
footing, taxes became a major part of their revenues. And it was the prize the
Portuguese administration long sought but only gained by subduing Maputo
and routing the Gaza empire.

Control over the land chiefs rather than control over trade became the
major source of Portuguese gain. As has been seen, one of the principal in-
strumentalities of this style of governance was tax farming, which meant
splitting revenues with those able to extract taxes. The prazo-holders
used slaves to collect taxes, the Companies used their own police force
but both they and the Portuguese (in the areas administered) co-opted
local authorities. Co-optation was now again public policy. Speaking
to the newspaper *Noticias* (Maputo) on 10 July 2000, Minister of State
Administration

> Chichava . . . stressed that "community authorities" would be involved in tax
> collection, and that any income they received would be based upon the
> amount of tax they collected.[3]

This form of co-optation had seriously undermined the authority of such
rulers in their own communities during the colonial period and worried colonial administrators.

The Evolution of Colonial Native Policy

Cunha (1953) taught Portuguese administrators at the colonial school that
there were three phases of colonial policy in Africa: the first he termed *subjection*, during which the colonies existed simply for the profit and prosperity
of Portugal and indigenous peoples served to furnish raw materials and markets. During the second phase from 1820 to 1910, policy was based on what

he called *uniformizing assimilation*, under which Lisbon made no legal distinction between the colony and the Metropole or between Portuguese citizens and native populations. For the greater part of the first two periods, such policies were limited to a few pockets of Mozambican territory because, as seen, the Gaza empire only fell in 1895, Mataka in 1912, and Báruè in 1917, and the Makonde people in the late 1920s.

During the third period, the Portuguese turned to brute force to impose itself on the various rural populations. During this phase, which lasted until 1961, Portugal turned to what Cunha called *long-term assimilation* and *indirect administration*, but which is better characterized as apartheid and co-optation. Under this policy, natives were classified as "uncivilized" (*não civilizado*) in order to distinguish them from "civilized" Portuguese citizens.[4] While Portuguese settlers were citizens under the law of Portugal, native peoples were subject to a separate regime based on what was defined as customary law. After 1961, customary systems were incorporated into the administration yet even then and only under certain well-defined circumstances could some natives assimilate and qualify as Portuguese citizens.

Mahmood Mamdani (1996) shows that Portuguese rule was far from singular in its development. Both British and French colonial systems underwent similar phases, moving from subjection to indirect administration. In South Africa, for example, "1910, 1927, and 1951 stand out as three pivotal points, each the bearer of a key principle in a growing consensus that would eventually be summed up under apartheid as a unified and generalized policy of native control" (Mamdani, 1996:65). The British, French, and Portuguese learned from their Asian colonial experiences that assimilation led to political demands for autonomy so they turned to indirect administration as a means of pacifying the great majority of rural peoples (Mamdani, 1996:83). Mamdani errs, however, in characterizing the Portuguese administrative setup as the last to institute indirect administration, as shall now be seen, and in his description of some of its details, as has already been pointed out in previous chapters (1996:87).

Armando Marques Guedes (1965) also defined three periods of colonial administration in Mozambique.[5] Guedes dated the introduction of a separate administration for rural peoples from the second Administrative Reform of 1907 that created two administrative units, *Concelhos* (municipal councils) and *Circunscrições Civis* (rural districts). Wherever two thousand or more "civilized" persons resided, the colonial state constituted a Concelho and gave it a measure of self-government while keeping rural districts under close supervision. The boundaries of the rural units were supposed to coincide "in so far as possible, with native boundaries, in such a manner that the administrative authorities can easily take advantage of, absorb and *substitute* the native authorities" (article 87 of the Reform, emphasis mine). A special department was set up in each of the African colonies to supervise native affairs.

Newitt feels that the foundation for separate administrations came even earlier, in 1899, when Governor-General Enes introduced the Colonial Labor Law that distinguished two classes of Mozambican citizens (1995:384). Zamparoni documented a series of measures instituted in the colonial capital between 1904 and 1908 in such areas as health, transport, marketing, recreation, and disparities in salary levels, all designed to separate whites from non-whites (2000:199–207). Apartheid thus came early to the Portuguese colonies.

The advent of the Republican regime codified the system of apartheid. The 1911 Constitution conceded that each of the colonies could have their own special laws depending upon their "state of civilization" (Article 67). Law no. 277 of 1914 referred to the need to maintain but also "perfect" native traditions and customs. Decree no. 3983 of 16 May 1918 distinguished native reserves from lands under State dominion. The Political, Civil and Criminal Native Statute of 1929 enshrined the distinction between indigenous and non-indigenous peoples. These were the legal foundations of what the Portuguese called "native policy."

The coming to power of Salazar initiated an era of tight control from Lisbon. The major pieces of legislation included first, the Colonial Act of 1930 which, among other things, abandoned the creation of new *Companhias Majestaticas* and reinforced the intervention of the Minister of the Colonies in provincial affairs; second, the Constitution of 1933; and third, the Overseas Administrative Reform (promulgated in 1933), which in Mozambique transformed native territories into *regedorias*. (See figure 6.1.) The dotted line in the figure represents the measure of self-government enjoyed by the urban *Concelhos*. The *Estatuto dos Indígenas Portugueses das Províncias da Guiné, Angola e Moçambique* (1954) incorporated all native lands under state dominion.

The administrator of a *circunscrição* was expected to define the boundaries of regedorias with the approval of his superior who then communicated them to his superiors. As in the previous Reform of 1907, Article 93 of the new Overseas Administrative Reform recommended that "delimitation should be made with information from the populations, respecting, as far as possible, local traditions." Nevertheless, as before, administrators did not hesitate to disregard community living spaces when it suited either commercial or administrative needs. The Portuguese were only able to organize and publish a map

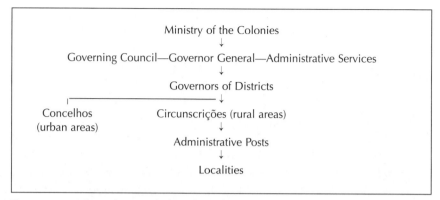

Figure 6.1. Schematic Description of Administrative Units under the Estado Novo

showing demarcation in the early 1970s, a few years before decolonization.[6] As shall be seen in chapter 11, the question of delimiting rural communities has again become an important legal issue and for the same reason: the generalized and blatant disregard of community rights to land.

There was lively discussion and serious concern both inside and outside Portugal regarding the evolution of native policy. Cunha worried "that the laws are not being carried out. In the selection of the native authorities, it is rare that habits and customs are respected and administrative authorities rarely, with some honorable exceptions, worry about defending the prestige of native rulers. . . . The result is that chiefs recognized by Portuguese authorities rarely have effective control over their populations" (1953:196). During the war for independence, the administration's own surveillance team also admonished the colonial administration to work with "natural" community leaders in order to gain the confidence of rural peoples and went so far as to recommending that they have full reign over their people.[7]

Under international as well as internal pressure especially from the national liberation movements in all of its African colonies, a more open-minded Caetano regime abandoned the native policy. The Estatuto was revoked as well as all provisions for native reserves. Legally, apartheid ended and assimilation was once again officially promoted. The regedorias were incorporated under Portuguese administrative law as local autarchies (*autarquias locais*). Decree no. 43,896 of 1961 integrated the regedores into the Portuguese administrative system. Property and land rights were the last to be modified to allow for conversion from communal to individual property rights (only after ten years with the permission of the Governor-General and the Governing Council).

In the first phase of government after the war of independence, the new government under FRELIMO direction decided not to follow this trend but to re-centralize power. It stripped the régulos of their formal powers and nationalized land. It subjected some régulos to imprisonment and treated all of them to ridicule and debasement. Nevertheless, the new government, just as Portugal, was never able completely to ignore the political role and influence of dynastic lineages. Nor did it have enough cadres to substitute for them. In certain places, therefore, a modus vivendi and division of power took place between community leaders and FRELIMO government and party officials as exemplified in the histories of Kalanje, Celestino Tsacaune Kanda, and Matutuíne. This was not always an acceptable arrangement as Kanda's story showed.

Depending upon time as well as place, upon the extent of exploitation as well as the opening of opportunities, Mozambicans expressed themselves in many ways, as the experiences of the four communities showed. When things got really bad, people migrated and some openly rebelled. In other words, at certain times and in certain places, the modus vivendi broke down, as, for example, in the areas which openly supported RENAMO in the last war.

RENAMO re-instituted customary authority in the areas it controlled. However, this too came with a high price as RENAMO leaders also subordinated customary rulers to *their* authority. INDER teams saw numerous examples: for instance, when the RENAMO commander called Janson Chaiva to Sita on the very day he was to open and thus legitimize the rapid rural appraisal of the community. Or when the RENAMO-approved leader of Sacudzo refused to vacate his position upon the return of the former ruler from exile in 1995 and the people of Sacudzo asked INDER to ask the district administrator to intervene as they considered the former ruler their leader. Or when régulo Muagiua of Gùrué district in Zambézia died and a new successor was elected locally. More than a year later, in 1999, the new Muagiua was called to RENAMO area headquarters to receive its seal of approval.

At the end of the civil war, the government, elected in 1994, lifted the prohibition against "traditional" organization but ambivalence continued both within and outside FRELIMO regarding the role indigenous institutions should play in governance. In part, the hesitation reflected the fact that RENAMO had, from its first political program in 1979, championed and continues to utilize "traditional" authorities in its struggle against the government. In part, it reflected the undisguised urban, modernist bias of elite circles and their genuine repugnance for the negative aspects of "traditional" rule but ambivalence was also a psychological manifestation of the undeclared struggle over legitimacy and sovereignty, a point taken up again in chapter 11. As one observer put it, "there is little apparent movement by the elite civil society for broader democratization."[8]

At local levels in the late 1990s, there was both hesitation in dealing with local rulers and collaboration with them as shown in this example from Catandica district, in Manica Province:

> While some government officials are still reluctant to grant customary author-
> ities any formal recognition others have arranged formal meetings with them,
> for example in Catandica in January 1999. In the meeting, which was con-
> vened by the District Administrator, customary authorities were allocated
> various tasks, and their role as local representatives of the government was em-
> phasised. The tasks included land use management, prevention of uncon-
> trolled bush-fires and poaching, and conflict resolution (Artur and Virtanen,
> 1999:4).

In Nampula, M. Anne Pitcher found: "Occasionally, government officials recognized the continuing importance and legitimacy of *régulos* in particular communities. As a consequence, they collaborated with them or invited them to join government and party ranks. For example, there is a chief in Mecuburi who is also a Frelimo secretary, and in at least five zones of Mecuburi district, there has been a history of collaboration between the Fre-limo secretary and 'traditional' authorities" (1998:129). Our fieldwork in Niassa, in Lichinga and Sanga, showed that district administrators there worked directly through régulos but this was not common practice in other provinces we visited where we found both caution and hostility.

An antagonism towards the so-called traditional authorities also appeared in the texts of some international commentators on Mozambique, among whom, Bowen (2000), O'Laughlin (1992), and Mamdani (1996).[9] Mamdani, for example, characterized indirect administration as decentralized despot-ism. There is no doubt about the harshness and injustice of the regedoria sys-tem. It must continue to be decried along with the individuals that profited from it. Nevertheless, it is vital to recognize the historical legitimacy of "tra-ditional" authority as well as the fact that in certain areas of the country "these structures constitute the real governance system" (Jackson, 2002:8).

INDER's fieldwork showed conclusively that indigenous structures still have currency in people's minds.[10] In all but one of twenty-eight communi-ties described in chapter 5, people described chains of command even when they were no longer governed by them. "Traditional" communities continued to identify with a dynastic lineage and had their own systems for selecting titleholders and procedures for removing bad or illegitimate rulers. Previous chapters also showed that once the Portuguese and later FRELIMO (and RENAMO) relaxed or disbanded rule, people tended to restore the rulers they considered rightful. And they created new dynasties when the old ones were found lacking. These communities still accorded lineage leaders with allocation rights over land, with judiciary powers over intra-group disputes, and with representation to the outside world.[11] However, internal power struggles within communities provided a further reason why their members must be the ones to decide who governs them rather than national governments armed with decrees on uniform systems of governance or pronouncements on who should or should not hold office in rural areas. On this same point, M. Anne Pitcher's research showed: "Whether *régulos* had legitimacy in the eyes of the regime or in the eyes of their own people depended very much on what they did and on how they were chosen" (1998:121).

In 2000, the Ministry of State Administration issued Decree 15/2000, which promoted a form of collaboration between local administrators and what it called "community authorities." This category included lineage-based leaders, local officials such as the secretaries of *bairros* and *aldeias*, and religious and other civil society leaders.[12] The context for "collaboration" was, however, the centralized chain of command of state administration and the decree did not specify at what level of administration there was to be communication and/or participation. Although the community authorities were recognized as representatives, this was largely a ceremonial role and had nothing to do with decision making and everything to do with political and economic mobilization at local levels, including tax collecting and labor recruitment. In effect, the authorities were to be "support mechanisms for the work of the state local bodies" (Samaje, 2002:15). This distinctly colonial position, was a giant step backwards from the stance taken by the Ministry's own Nucleus of Administrative Development (*Núcleo de Desenvolvimento Administrativo*), in 1993. An international seminar sponsored by the Nucleus not only recommended recognition of "traditional" authorities but also went so far as to recommend that

> the community grass-roots institution commonly known as "traditional authority" be considered in the decentralization process, which is occurring through the setting up of municipalities. It recommends that . . . the insertion and role of traditional authorities be established in symbiosis with the municipalities.[13]

These words were written at war's end when it seemed as though Mozambique was moving along the road of decentralization and democratization. What actually happened is the subject of the rest of this chapter.

The Post-Independence Climate for Decentralization

Immediately after independence in 1975, FRELIMO not only attempted to re-centralize power but also assumed an assimilationist attitude towards rural societies through the promotion of communal villages, which aimed at urbanizing as well as socializing rural society. This policy corresponded roughly to the period of leadership under Samora Machel.

Yet, even under Machel's period of presidency, FRELIMO began to admit that it had concentrated too much power at the national level. Decentralization was, however, slow in coming, confirming Judith Tendler's contention that central governments do not easily give up power (1997:197). What has mainly taken place is the transfer of functions (deconcentration) rather than the devolution of policymaking areas (decentralization).[14] A summary follows of the most important moments in postcolonial administrative history.[15]

The post-independence government eliminated municipalities in favor of a unitary government, consisting of three hierarchically subordinated administrative levels—the nation, the province, of which there are 10, and the district, of which there are 128. As early as 1983, the fourth Congress of the FRELIMO party admitted that government was excessively centralized. This opened a debate on decentralization and local autonomy. However, moves toward deconcentration of central government powers did not occur until the late 1980s when, in an effort to resolve the economic problems of the country, the FRELIMO government cut its ties with the Soviet Union and other socialist allies and applied for membership in the International Monetary Fund and World Bank. These and other agencies as well as governments urged a program of both economic and political liberalization. This opened the possibility for a new round of private-public appropriation of the commonwealth.

In January 1987, the Popular Assembly approved a law allowing experimentation with forms of financial and administrative autonomy in pilot districts. Within the Ministry of State Administration, a Program for the Reform of Local Authorities was set up and given the task to transform districts into local governments with a distinct juridical status and financial and administrative autonomy. With World Bank financing, a team from Portugal produced the groundwork leading to the *Quadro Institucional dos Distritos Municipais* (Legal Framework for District Municipalities).

In August 1994, the framework became law. However, dissenting voices in the first democratically elected Assembly—constituted in 1995—halted this process. The Assembly revoked the law and put in its place a constitutional amendment that distinguished between *Poder Local* (Local Authority) and the *Orgãos Locais do Estado* (State Local Bodies). Law no. 9/96 approved the creation of municipalities but limited this status to 23 cities, 68 towns, and, in some undetermined future, the 393 administrative posts. This meant that provinces and districts would remain administrative entities subordinate to central government.

The thirty-three new local authorities included the twenty-three cities and only ten of the sixty-eight towns. Established in 1998, their primary objectives are "the organization of citizen participation in the resolution of community problems, the promotion of local development, the deepening and consolidation of democracy in the framework of a unified Mozambican state."[16] Areas of decision making included local economic and social development; environment, basic sanitation and quality of life; food security; health; education; culture, sports and leisure; local police forces; urban planning including construction and housing.[17]

To a remarkable extent, the government seemed to be repeating the colonial pattern of apartheid by giving relative autonomy (represented by the dotted line) to urbanized areas through the municipalities while leaving rural areas under state administration. (See figure 6.2.) It recreated two classes of citizenship: first-class "urban" citizens who vote for local representatives and second-class rural citizens who have no voice in selecting their local administration.

Despite the opening of democratic spaces for urban people, the local elections in 1998 of thirty-three autarchic assemblies, councils and presidents throughout the country aroused little enthusiasm. The electorate hardly participated.[18] One consequence of the apathy was the attempt by the new local authorities to prove themselves responsible to their constituencies. One of the first activities was to examine the tax rolls and improve tax collec-

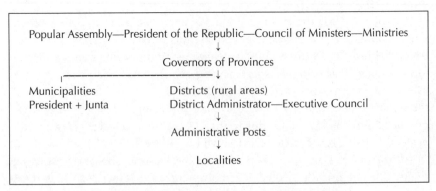

Figure 6.2. Schematic Representation of Current Administrative Units

tions. The result was surprising: the amount of taxes collected in many areas far exceeded previous amounts collected and/or announced by the district administrations, and this happened without raising tax rates. In the very first year of its mandate, the municipal council of Vilankulos, in Inhambane province, for example, was able to buy a tractor for use in garbage collection from its tax revenues. Streets were suddenly repaired, garbage collection improved, public gardens were cleaned, and urban buildings rehabilitated. Even more impressive, public issues were opened for debate and public opinion became important in the debates.

After the highly contested national elections of December 1999, the central government moved a few more steps closer to clarifying the status of rural areas. In July 2000, the Council of Ministers approved a draft law for districts that outlined areas of competency similar to those of the new autarchies but district administrations were *not* granted autonomy. As Joseph Hanlon explained with great clarity:

> The civil service's almost military command structure is continued in the new draft law. The district administrator is appointed by the Minister of State Administration and is "senior director" ("superior") of the territory. The administrator "represents the state and directs the execution of the government programme, the economic and social plan, and state budget in the district." The administrator is expected to carry out instructions from the provincial government and "is personally accountable" to the provincial governor for all administrative actions in the district (European, August 2000:4).

The districts were delegated responsibilities rather than independent decision-making powers as the next chapters explicitly show:

> The new law will explicitly give districts many of the same responsibilities as municipalities, such as for local streets, markets, cemeteries, rubbish collection, water and sanitation, public parks and sports grounds, etc. But district governments are also expected to carry out central government plans and provincial instructions, whereas elected municipal governments cannot be directed in the same way (European, August 2000:4).

Nominated by the Minister of State Administration, the district administrator, and his administration, was also directly subordinate to the Provincial Governor who represented the President of the Republic in the province. Directly under administrators, the chiefs of administrative posts, under the draft law, would be nominated by the Governor and confirmed by the Minister. Directly under them, the locality presidents would be nominated by the district administrator and confirmed by the governor. Just as in the present set-up, districts, posts and localities were strictly administrative bodies subordinate both to the province and national government. This draft law lay two years on the table awaiting discussion and approval by the Assembly of the Republic.

In October 2002, the Council approved an amended version of the draft law on State Local Bodies. Among the changes was the creation of the Office of Permanent Secretary at both provincial and district levels to oversee administrative functions. Another very significant change was the elimination of the proposed Consultative Councils to be set up at district level (discussed in the next chapter). This meant that there would be no channel of communication between government authorities and civil society in the rural areas other than that proposed in Decree 15/2000, which promised more a monologue than dialogue. It was predicted that the Assembly would consider the new version in early 2003.

To summarize: in the matter of changing its relationship to rural societies, the Mozambican government has moved both forward and backward since it took power from the Portuguese in 1975. Since 1994, however, it has to a great extent retreated, especially in the matter of decentralization. There were at least two ways to attempt to move decentralization forward in Mozambique. One had to do with pressuring for more rural district autonomy while the second had to do with empowering rural communities. In the 1990s many international and bilateral agencies chose the first path and invested in projects that focused on district-level planning. The next three chapters look closely at some of the more important ones as of the late 1990s and especially those, which also included a community participation or community planning aspect. A third alternative combining both approaches is discussed in the last two chapters.

Notes

1. In contrast to Alan Isaacman and, to some extent, Newitt, R. J. Barendse saw the prazos as the east African version of a system of landholding common to the Estado da India. "Portuguese territorial expansion in India and in Mozambique was based on exactly the same judicial arrangement, namely the emphytheutical holding (that is that land is granted by the king for one generation after which it reverts to the king). Instead, Africanists (like J. Isaacman) habitually argue the praca [sic] was a typical Portuguese East African arrangement. They see it as African law in Portuguese guise; basically land still belonged to the ancestor and thus the emphytheutical arrangement. Not so (at least not in the sixteenth/seventeenth century). It was an arrangement derived from Por-

tuguese (reconquista) law, which in India neatly dovetailed with the pre-existing judicial frame of the Gujarat sultanate (namely revocable jagiri holdings). Land-systems of the Gujarati sultanate differed from those of the Mughal Empire but that takes me too far" (http://www.H-Asia@H-Net.MSU.EDU, 20 August 2000, posted 21 August 2000).

2. I am grateful to K. P. Moseley for this reference. R. J. Barendse noted the difficulty historians have in capturing the essence of early Portuguese rule: "The Estado da India . . . was basically a central administration, 'out'-fortifications and factories, trading settlements . . . scattered market-places and 'rights' on market-places and fortified corrals [Barendse is here referring to the prazos] (in the Mozambique interior). And then a trade-network of a Portuguese warrior/merchant nation; some of those merchant settlements pledging allegiance to the Portuguese king. . . . Note that this is a flexible, in many ways very 'medieval' construction, which cannot conveniently be pressed into modern terms. Any modern term for a state implies boundaries and the Estado da India was in a way not thus 'fixed' (just like e.g. the Hansa or the Venetian 'oversea' in the thirteenth—fifteenth century). It was not an 'empire,' it was not a 'state' and it was certainly not a 'trade network.' There's a medievalist term for it: it was a 'dominion' but that does not strike much of a chord with modernist or early modernist readers. (Aah, academic boundaries—sadly the Portuguese expansion straddles the boundaries between 'Medieval' and 'Early modern' studies as much as it does those between Africanists and Asianists)" (http://www.H-Asia@H-Net.MSU.EDU, 20 August 2000, posted 21 August 2000).

3. AWEPA Peace Bulletin, no. 25, August 2000:4.

4. Zamparoni (2000) shows that Hindu, Muslim and even Goan settlers also faced discrimination that set them apart.

5. For even more detail, the reader is referred to Newitt (1995), which devotes more than one chapter on the various nuances in the colonial administration.

6. Dr. António Sopa of the Historical Archives of Mozambique told me that the research on the boundaries of regedorias had actually occurred earlier in the 1940s.

7. Portugal, 1967. Rafael Rosa Lôbo (1966) documented a sample of the internal criticism of so-called native policy within Portugal. One of the first critics appears to have been A. A. Pereira Cabral (1925) who recognized that transforming régulos into messengers of the colonial administration fundamentally weakened their prestige (Lobo, 1966:48). Lobo also cited the authors, António Marques and Manuel Dias Belchior, and the governors-general Bettencourt and Ferreira de Almeida (1966:64–66).

8. Personal Communication, November 2002.

9. See Geffray (1990), West (1998), and Alexander (1994) for alternative views.

10. Among other examples of similar fieldwork, see J. H. Bannerman's notes (1993) on the Gorongosa and Mossurize dynasties and Harry West's work (1998) on the power and authority relations on the Mueda Plateau in Cabo Delgado. See also JoAnn McGregor on Matutuíne and Namaacha districts in Maputo Province (1998) and M. Anne Pitcher (1998) on Monapo and Mecuburi districts of Nampula.

11. Artur and Virtanen note that "according to some estimates (Myers 1992, 10) they were still 'de facto' managing over three quarters of the agricultural land resource in the early 1990s" (Domingos do Rosário Artur and Pekka Virtanen, 1999:3).

12. AIM, *Edição no. 2293*, 16 and 17 September 2000.

13. Ministério da Administração Estatal (MAE) 1995:151, 152.

14. I am using the following definitions: *deconcentration* signifies the transference of central ministry functions to provincial and district directorates. The next step is the *delegation* of responsibilities; for example, the implementation of the Rural Water Policy of the Ministry of Public Works and Housing is with provincial directorates, which have been given a certain liberty to experiment with institutional forms. *Devolution* implies the transference of authority over certain areas of government. Federalism is the most advanced form of devolution. These definitions are adapted from Harry Blair, 1998, p. 1. In at least one version of the draft law on reform of local administration, MAE (1998) used the term "administrative deconcentration" to describe its intentions.

15. This section relies heavily on J. Guambe, 1996.

16. Titulo IV, Artigo 188, from MAE, 1998:20.

17. Lei no. 2/97, Artigo 6. See MAE, 1998, 24, 25.

18. As already noted, only 15 percent of the registered electorate participated.

CHAPTER SEVEN

INDER and Participatory Planning

The Planning Context

Up until the 1990s, planning at district level had never been given serious consideration or linked to planning with rural communities. While the Center for African Studies at the national university organized many rural surveys[1] in order to influence policy, most Mozambican planners and many donors understood planning as an essentially technical process best left in the hands of professionals. Investment planning had always been vertical in structure despite the fact that, in the early 1980s, the FRELIMO government established the principle that planning should begin at district level. Nevertheless, the National Planning Commission used the districts and provinces mainly to supply it with information and to communicate its decisions.

In the late 1980s and into the 1990s, the Commission evolved a number of planning instruments, including the Three-Year Rolling Public Investment Program (PTIP) and the annual Economic and Social Plan (both based, in principle, on the five-year government platform). The PTIP was theoretically the register of all government investment projects and programs in operation and in the pipeline. Initially, both instruments excluded the direct participation of provinces and districts. However, as a result of the post–civil war planning exercise in 1993, provincial administrations received a block investment grant to plan autonomously. This was included in the PTIP as the provincial program.

From 1997, provincial administrations also made annual economic and social plans.[2] However, under pressure from a number of donors from about

1998, ministries such as Health, Education, Agriculture, and Public Works (as regards roads and rural water) began to institute sector programs, which recentralized planning in these sectors. As a consequence provinces were not allowed to allocate investments in these areas. Since 1999, this has represented a significant decline in the amount of the block investment grant. Central line ministries, therefore, still retain the greatest influence on government plans even though they, too, had to make economic and social plans in order to substantiate their claims on the state budget. The Ministry of Plan and Finances (MPF), which absorbed the National Planning Commission, harmonized and synthesized provincial and sector plans into the national Economic and Social Plan. This it presented to the Assembly for approval.

In the late 1990s, personnel in the National Directorate of Plan and Budget of the MPF turned their attention to *district* planning. This was in the wake of donor-sponsored experiments in district-level planning (see below and next chapter) but mainly had to do with the creation of municipalities, which were given responsibility for their own planning and were also allowed to collect their own tax revenue. In order to avoid opening a development gap between districts and municipalities, the Ministry elaborated guidelines for district strategic planning. In September 1998, under the signatures of both the Ministry of Plan and Finances and the Ministry of State Administration guidelines were published for the elaboration of five-year District Development Plans, "in conjunction with civil society and the Provincial Government" (1998:preamble). Five-year district strategic plans were the basis for annual district social and economic plans. The guidelines included a short paragraph on civil society participation, which, in the Ministry of State Administration's perspective, was to be institutionalized in the form of *Consultative* Councils.[3]

> A new "district council" will be composed of the district government plus the president of any municipal council in the district, plus "community authorities" and representatives of economic, social and cultural organisations in the district. The district council will be a "consultative organ" convened by the district government, and will meet every three months (European, August 2000:4).

The fact that the proposed Councils would neither be elected nor their judgments binding meant that the government had little intention of democratizing the planning process. This fell in line with Mamdani's assertion that local African councils instituted under postcolonial systems have not been accountable to local peoples and Judith Tendler's point that they tend to be more representative of local power structures than of the general public.[4] Nor was the district planning initiative a decentralizing one. As the next chapter shows, the strategic plans developed by districts were still subject to negotiation with provincial administrations whose plans were, in turn, dependent upon line ministry and MPF approval. The initiative was thus aimed at *deconcentration* of the planning function. Even more crucial was the fact that no provision was made for the district to become a budgetary unit, which would have given their plans an independent status. "The territorial divisions of the MPF collect most taxes and fees, although the district administrator's department and some line agencies also collect revenue. Whilst all revenue is on [the State] budget (or should be) there are formulae in place permitting retention of a percentage by the local institution" (Jackson, 2002:10). In chapter 10 I propose expanding the percentages retained and extending the formula to include rural communities from whom the taxes are collected.

Bringing rural populations into the planning process was not just undermined by this political-administrative context but also by the difficult logistics prevailing in the countryside. For most of the war and even up until at least 1995, it was nearly impossible to reach the majority of people. When I arrived in Mozambique in June 1991, Maputo was an island. Heavily armed military escorts accompanied the movement of strictly necessary goods and people by road. Otherwise travel from a provincial capital to an outlying district or from Maputo to the interior was by small aircraft. Whole sections of the country were "no-go" RENAMO areas and only a few people, such as staff from the International Red Cross, were allowed to enter them. Bands of RENAMO troops emanated from these bases and made their unannounced attacks. Supplying internally displaced populations with food and other necessary items was a logistical nightmare. Moreover, beginning in 1991, the worst drought in living memory afflicted the country and the entire region of southern Africa. It is generally acknowledged that these conditions accelerated the willingness of the warring sides to reach a peace settlement. My own direct experience confirmed the desperate plight of rural Mozambicans in this period.

A trip to Boane, just across the Maputo river, which under normal conditions was a suburb of the capital, could only be undertaken in daylight because at night the area was under RENAMO siege. I went to see Massaca I and Massaca II, two refugee centers that had all the appearances of concentration camps in August 1991. People were living in tiny spaces with no room for privacy between families. They were barely able to sustain themselves on parched lands and were subject to terrible speculation by traders of basic consumer goods such as matches, soap, tomatoes, and so on. It was my first introduction to the horror war held for civilians.

A flight from the provincial capital of Tete to the district seat of Changara in September 1991, normally a fifty-minute drive, made it possible to visit one of the refugee camps for the district and witness the emergency feeding program for severely malnourished children sponsored by the international relief agency World Vision. It was on this, my first visit to the countryside, that I got an insight into the extent to which such nongovernmental organizations such as World Vision had taken the place of local government in administering services to people.

The next month I helped a rural survey taking place in Cabo Delgado and went deep in the bush on a sand road. In one Makonde village we were met by heavily armed militia who controlled this communal settlement. The situation was very tense as people complained of their abandonment.

A visit in September 1992 to a refugee camp based in a communal village near Vila Manica in Manica province revealed the breadth of the famine. The refugees there had not had a shipment of grain in six months and were reduced to foraging for wild roots and tubers. Children could not attend school because they were too weak to concentrate. Adults were thin as rods and some were severely stressed as relatives were dying. This scene was repeated in the worst hit areas throughout the country. The Resident Representative of the United Nations reported seeing people in Gaza eating the bark off of trees because the earth was scorched and trees stripped of their leaves. People began to leave RENAMO areas, which were among the hardest hit: they were extremely weak and nude for lack of clothing or with only bark cloth to cover them. Under these severe restrictions, both of the warring parties agreed to lay down arms.

With the greatest urgency the government began to consider what it could do to assist the millions of people dislocated in district and provincial seats, refugee camps and in neighboring countries to return to the countryside once the war was over and how best to help them begin the reconstruction process. In 1992, the National Planning Commission was mandated to gather information on the status of rural infrastructures and, in collaboration with provincial and district authorities and the planning departments of the national ministries, to produce a three-year National Reconstruction Plan (República de Moçambique, Fevereiro, 1992). The Commission decided that this was the moment to begin decentralizing the planning process and together with Provincial Governors it established and trained ten-person provincial planning brigades. At first it was hoped to send the teams to districts to gather first-hand information but this idea had to be abandoned because of logistical problems. Ten provincial "plans" accompanied the PRN, which the government presented to the Consultative Group of international donors in Paris in March 1993.

The Plan focused largely on the rehabilitation and reconstruction of infrastructure destroyed during the war. The only consultations with rural peoples about their needs or aspirations of which I am aware were the United Nations Development Programme's and UNICEF's brief but joint initiative in refugee camps in 1991. UNICEF also commissioned José Negrão to report on the plight of the worst affected women and children in refugee camps (Negrão, 1991). The National Emergency Relief Executive Commission (CENE) and the Department for Protection against Natural Calamities (DPCCN) sponsored the one-day visit to the refugee camp in Vila Manica, reported above, as part of a seminar on planning for the immediate post-war period.

The Plan received donor approval in Paris and some lukewarm support. Provincial plans were later integrated into the Three-Year Rolling Public Investment Program (PTIP) as a provincial component and this was the basis for the transfer of block investment grants noted above. The PRN was financed on a largely ad hoc basis, that is, as individual donors adapted parts of it to fit their own investment plans.

A number of donors adopted a frontal area approach to the rehabilitation of rural areas: they selected a geographical area in which to work and, with the government, drew up plans for integrated rural reconstruction programs. Although donors sent identification missions to work with government bodies in provincial and wherever possible in district capitals, it was still very difficult in the period 1993–1995 to visit rural communities even when there were intentions to do so. Among the donors sponsoring rural rehabilitation were the World Bank in the provinces of Zambézia and Sofala, the International Fund for Agricultural Development (IFAD) in Niassa, and the Norwegian Development Agency, NORAD, in Cabo Delgado. The United Nations Capital Development Fund (UNCDF) and later the Dutch government initiated programs in Nampula. Having operated in Manica since 1989, German Technical Cooperation began to assist Sofala and Inhambane as well. The Danish government gave support to Tete, and Italian Cooperation was much in evidence in Maputo and Manica provinces. In 1994, the European Union took a slightly different approach by sponsoring a micro-projects program for Gaza province. In this way, most of the country was covered with some kind of project or program to rebuild small-scale infrastructures in rural areas.

In the first phase, at war's end, most programs were called upon to provide emergency relief to communities in the process of resettlement. The United Nations High Commission for Refugees and the World Food Programme launched countrywide operations aimed at providing seeds and agricultural tools, blankets, used clothing, buckets, pots and pans, food and other essentials. Only later was it possible to begin to finance permanent basic infrastructure. Planning of basic needs with community participation, if it happened at all, generally began in the second phase, from 1995 onwards. This can be seen in the example of NORAD. In 1994, NORAD commissioned a planning exercise at national level using logical framework analysis in order to bring together the views of the various ministries that it sponsored to help rehabilitation in Cabo Delgado. When the program coordinator arrived in Mozambique, she led a team of ministry officials to visit rural areas in the province as a complement to the planning seminar. Later, in 1995, a local consulting firm in Cabo Delgado was engaged to do a rapid rural appraisal in the areas of concentration of the Program. In 1996, NORAD cosponsored a training program to encourage provincial and district officials to plan small-scale infrastructure with rural communities (discussed in the next section).

The relatively large rural rehabilitation projects were complemented by the work of over 180 international nongovernmental organizations (INGOs), many of which derived their operating funds from the major donors. Moreover, various United Nations agencies had efforts all over the country. The bulk of donor monies was, however, concentrated in *national* projects and programs, including road rehabilitation, major irrigation works, balance of payments support and sectoral investment programs. Even before the onset of peace, Mozambique's intake of donor assistance has been on the order of around U.S.$900 million and sometimes more than U.S.$1 billion per year.[5] (For an overall view of donor activity, see Joe Hanlon, 1998.) The next section reviews the experience of community planning of small-scale infrastructures in one of the major rural rehabilitation projects.

The Rural Rehabilitation Project of Sofala and Zambézia

In December 1990, the President of the Republic established the Institute for Rural Development, INDER, to give leadership on issues relating to rural life. INDER was placed formally under the Council of Ministers to give it distance from the ordinary business of ministries such as the Ministry of Agriculture and also to give it a direct opportunity to influence government policy-making as a recognized member of the Council. Its founding document, Presidential Decree no. 36/90, mandated INDER to contribute to "the decentralization of national government responsibilities to the provincial, district and locality levels." The Presidential Decree also gave it the duty to ensure *community participation* "so that the necessary qualitative and quantitative transformations come from within the community itself and have the impact of making the community its own agent of development." It left open the forms participation would take and how local administrations and communities would relate to one another.

Elaborated under the tutelage of INDER, the Rural Rehabilitation Project of Sofala and Zambézia (PRR) tried to provide an answer to both questions. The Project promoted a planning exercise that joined communities and provincial and district staff in the identification of small-scale social infrastructures. Moreover, by financing their implementation, the PRR became an important instrument of provincial investment planning in the two provinces. Yet, paradoxically, the availability of large amounts of financing—around ten million dollars for small infrastructures—undermined some of the more important aspects of community participation as shall be seen.

On February 25, 1993, the project document of the Rural Rehabilitation Project, Sofala and Zambézia (PRR) derived from the World Bank Staff Appraisal Report, described project objectives as follows:

> The overall objective of the project is to undertake pilot activities to support decentralized rural recovery, while simultaneously creating the capacity and procedures necessary to respond to the challenges of post-war national reconstruction. The project has four specific objectives: i) to build capacity in the institutions that will be responsible for post-war reconstruction and to develop procedures for decentralized rural development; ii) to secure information about land use and to develop policies to secure tenure security for smallholders; iii) to help households that have been displaced by the war restart agricultural production on their traditional lands; and iv) to improve the health and quality of life of rural households by increasing the coverage of the rural water supply (World Bank, 1993:i).

Of these four objectives, the first corresponded to what was called the Decentralization Component. The detailed description of this component foresaw two activities: firstly, capacity building and community-based investments and secondly, training mainly of government officials but also nongovernmental organization staff and community leaders. The formal activity of training included seminars to introduce the project, in-service training in the identification and design of small and micro-projects and several courses to help local officials and the private sector implement the micro-projects.

Although the Government of Mozambique and the World Bank signed the project document in April 1993, there was a lot of delay in launching the project on the ground. This was not unusual in large-scale projects. INDER hired the first personnel of the project management unit in 1993 but more than a year passed before it became possible to open an account in a commercial Mozambican bank. The first deposit of loan monies happened only in July 1994. This coincided with the period of post-war elections, a time when most provincial- and district-level cadres were absorbed in organizing and facilitating the electoral process. Even after the elections took place in October 1994 and the results were announced, the project could not begin until the new government was installed in March 1995. The start of the process of identifying small community projects began in April of that year with the proposal of a health post in the district of Mocuba, Zambézia. The pressure to disburse project monies had been building, from the provincial and district governments, from INDER, which wanted to demonstrate that it was doing something, and from the World Bank, which had its own internal pressures to palliate.

Under this mounting concern, the project administration urged the Agrarian Training Center (*Centro de Formação Agrária*), contracted by INDER to prepare and execute the training program, to fulfill its mandate. When it later became obvious that the center was unable to comply, a bid was launched to solicit trainers from the private sector. None of the bidders, however, understood the needs of the project. Under this constraint, the project administration began to accept proposals for small and microprojects from district administrations, provincial sector ministries, and the project's eight rural development agents, resident in what were at the time considered priority districts in the two provinces. According to the project's rural development agent resident in Buzi, Sofala, the typical pattern was for proposals to arise in meetings of the District Executive Council, at which he was invited to participate. The proposals were discussed, a consensus reached, and they were then transmitted to the provincial facilitation unit (PFU) in the capital of Beira. (There was also a PFU in Quelimane, the capital of Zambézia.)

From May to December 1995, conversations went on within INDER about the feasibility of organizing its own team to undertake the training activity. A pilot training took place in Buzi and Dondo districts in Sofala in November and December 1995. In February 1996, the PRR management unit together with NORAD agreed that INDER would provide training in participatory planning to provincial and district officials in Sofala and Zambézia, under World Bank sponsorship, and Cabo Delgado, under Norwegian government sponsorship. In 1998 the training was extended to the Niassa Agricultural Development Program sponsored by the International Fund for Agricultural Development (whose supervision was given to the PRR team).

Introduction to Participatory Planning

The principal form of training was a "course"[6] designated "Introduction to the Planning of Micro-Projects with Community Participation" for national, provincial and district level officials, the project's rural development agents[7] and Project Provincial Advisers, NGO staff, and community leaders. At the end of the training program, the course had been given twenty-six times[8] and resulted in two provincial-level teams of trainers and twenty-seven district-level "planning" teams in Sofala and Zambézia. The district teams included officials in the areas of Agriculture, Education, Health, Water, Roads and Social Action and sometimes personnel from nongovernmental agencies.

The "course" consisted of five and one-half days of intensive training. During the first morning a four-member multidisciplinary INDER team introduced the concepts of participatory rural appraisal. In the afternoon, the INDER team together with the district and provincial officials, the rural development agents and NGO staff split themselves into three or four multi-sectoral, multi-level teams, each with a local language capability. The teams prepared guideline questions in line with general topics to be put to rural communities who were then visited on the second, third and part of the fourth day.[9] In order to cover the districts as rapidly as possible, the course was given to officials from two districts at the same time.

Prior to the course, the INDER team and district administration officials visited the communities in order to explain to community leaders the purpose of the planning exercise and secure their authorization. This was generally given readily, although, one community in Zambézia denied permission to proceed with a similar training exercise despite the agreement of its régulo.[10]

On the second day, the three or four multi-sectoral teams met the "community"—that is, the people mobilized by the leaders—in plenary session. They explained the objectives of the training exercise, described the PRR and asked authorization of the community to proceed. The community was then split into several focal groups for the purpose of discussion. The groups generally represented elders and religious leaders, women, youth, and a residual group of "farmers." The discussions centered on general issues including the principal problems of the whole community and possible solutions. During the next day, the teams visited the homes of families selected by community leaders and repeated the process of open-ended questioning and discussion.

Each evening the teams synthesized their field notes and then proceeded as a group to analyze them. During the evening of the third day, they compiled this information in visual form in order to present it to the community on the following day. The purpose was to involve the plenary in analyzing the good and bad aspects of their situation, in discovering causes of major problems, prioritizing principal problems and deciding what type of infrastructure or basic service—a school, well, market, access road, and so on—might alleviate these problems. Attention was also paid to what the community might contribute toward the realization of these infrastructures and services.

After working with the community, the teams distilled the options resulting from the community consensus and put them on a matrix to compare with the PRR criteria. Points were awarded to the various options, the highest given to those that best fulfilled project criteria, such as community preference and contribution. This led to a decision as to which of the several options would become project proposals. On the fifth day, the INDER team introduced the district teams to simple guidelines for making project proposals and budgets.

On the final day, the district team presented a summary of all the work done in the community, including the plenary discussions and decisions, as well as the formal proposals to an enlarged meeting of the District Executive Council. This body included the district administrator and representatives of the line ministries plus other administrative bodies such as the police, and the Civil Registry. The council was enlarged to include representatives of the rural community in question and other civil society leaders. Council members including the community representatives vetted each proposal and determined which ones were then communicated to the project administration. This, then, comprised the participatory decision-making exercise introduced at district level for planning infrastructures.

The intention was to repeat the training two times in each district in order to place the teams on a solid footing but this was not carried out because the project ran out of time and funds. Five out of fifteen teams in Zambézia and six out of twelve teams in Sofala were trained twice. In three years of training, forty communities were reached in these two provinces and 116 micro-projects identified using the above-mentioned techniques. The expectation was that participatory planning would continue as the district teams gained in confidence, aided by the resident rural development agent for at least the life of the project. This was no doubt a naïve assumption given the vertical institutional structure as well as the natural reluctance of civil servants to change long-established habits.[11]

Nevertheless, the INDER staff members who embarked upon decentralized and participatory planning thought that they were helping to influence decentralization, which was under discussion at the highest policy levels, as has just been seen. The training in participatory planning did indeed have individual and institutional impacts, most of which were unforeseen and restricted to those districts with outstanding administrators, dynamic rural development agents and ambitious delegates from the provincial planning and finances directorates. Chapter 9 makes this point clearer. The next section from my field diaries gives a glimpse of how the planning exercise worked in practice.

Participatory Planning in Alto Lugela, Zambézia Province

Lugela district is situated in central Zambézia. On its southern edge, Alto-Lugela, is what remains of a "company town." Designated a locality,[12] its lush fields begin across the bridge over the Lugela and Licungo rivers. In colonial times, the area was the headquarters of the Namagoa Plantations Limited, a sisal plantation started during World War I with British capital.

Forced male labor had built the infrastructures of the plantation economy. The men of the area were also pressed into work on six-month "contracts" on the plantations while the women were obliged to grow cotton on small plots. They had also provided food for their families and sold cassava and cereals directly to Namagoa company, which provided meals as well as transport to the seasonal workers.

After independence, the government created a state farm to revitalize the economy but this ended in failure. Conditions on the farm were even worse for the workers than before and both cotton and sisal production dropped dramatically. In the 1990s, an Egyptian company, PIDICO, tried but failed to rehabilitate the enterprise. Despite the ups and downs in the plantation economy and the uncertainty over the future of Namagoa and the ownership of lands, many of the people of Alto-Lugela still remained on the small plots ceded to them by what they called the "Company" and hoped nostalgically for its reappearance.

When the INDER team arrived in February 1996 with eight district and provincial officials we were greeted by António Lopes Trigo, the newly appointed president of Alto-Lugela locality. A young man and somewhat new to the area, he was assisted by the secretary, Joaquim Gonçalves Madeira, an older man whose grasp of the local language and familiarity with the people was noticeably surer. The third person helping us was Isabel Siguiteiro Coroa, the local president of the Mozambican Women's Organization (OMM). She was a relatively young single mother, broadly representative of the many female-headed households found in the area.

Lopes, Madeira, and Coroa accompanied the teams to a large gathering nestled under the shade of several spreading mango trees, men to one side, women to the other. This was the area where community meetings were usually held. There were over one hundred people waiting. Introductions were made and much explanation given regarding our presence. It all seemed rather perfunctory but an air of curiosity and anticipation hung over the meeting. By the time we broke into smaller groups for focal group interviews, there were more than 150 people present. I was not prepared for my meeting with the women's group.

Pedro Semende, chief of planning for the Provincial Directorate of Education and Ernesto José, district director of Agriculture, and I were assigned to interview the women while other teams talked with community elders, traditional authorities and young people. Accompanied by Isabel Coroa, mute for the most part, we positioned ourselves in front of about fifty women. One by one, they recounted their dramatic and heart-rending stories: widows with no one to help them, divorced women with no other income but what they could dig out of the land, abandoned women with children to raise and no outside support. These were mainly older women, wrinkled, poorly dressed, emaciated.

Appalled, I asked how many were widows and there was close to a majority. Slowly, a story began to emerge of two migrations to the area: the first, in the early 1970s, because of employment offered by the Namagoa plantation; the second wave of people came, in the middle to late 1980s, looking for refuge from the civil war, which raged in Zambézia. Most of the women who had been talking were displaced persons, many of whom had lost husbands in the war. The one safety net all women had was land in contrast to custom in southern Mozambique where a widow is dependent upon her late husband's family and can lose everything, including land, house, possessions and children to his relatives. The land they occupied "belonged" to the extinct company for whom some of their husbands had worked. This particular group remembered nostalgically a time when Namagoa had bought their produce in exchange for basic consumer products. Some of these women had also participated at harvests in company fields, which gave them a small cash income.

After much coaxing, the women began to describe the general situation under which people lived in Alto-Lugela and the community's problems as a whole. Women were still responsible for cultivation but because males were "unemployed," they too helped in the fields. One major limitation was the condition of hand tools, most of which were worn out. Distributions of tools by the government and relief agencies had not reached many people; therefore families were working with old and insufficient tools. Another limiting factor for widows, abandoned and divorced women was a shortage of labor, especially if they had no children or only very young children. Certainly the greatest problem affecting everyone in the locality was the lack of an organized marketing system. Before the company store had weighed production on a scale and prices had been paid according to weight. People complained bitterly that now the only buyers were itinerant ones who measured produce in twenty-liter tins and paid ridiculously low prices.

Other problems included the sorry state of health services: basic medicines were not available, the prices charged were high and the location of the health post was not convenient. Many mothers mentioned that their children were not in school because of long distances to the four functioning schools. The women also expressed a desire for a community maize mill because they had to walk up to fifteen kilometers to the nearest mill.

We asked the women to rank these problems in terms of the most pressing and the following order obtained: new farming implements, more schools, a maize mill, and the need for a store.

The next day, our team went to Macuse, a small area in the south central part of Alto-Lugela, where we met the local secretary, Bernardo João, on our way to interview three families in their homes. João insisted on telling us Macuse's problems even though we were anxious to begin the family interviews. Surrounded by a number of men, he invited us to sit in the shade of a mango tree to listen to his catalog of difficulties. João repeated the need for new farming tools and added that there were not enough seeds for the next year's planting. Next, he mentioned that six hundred children in Macuse did not have access to schooling. The school that used to be there had been transferred to a place ten kilometers away, a distance too far for a small child to travel on a daily basis. Distance was also a factor for this community in regard to the health service.

João complained about the lack of a commercial outlet in the area. The government buyer, the Cereals Institute, only bought grain when a vendor had at least one ton and brought it to its office in Mocuba. This was the only way people could be assured of getting the government's minimum price. The "catch-22" was that there was no regular transport from Alto-Lugela to Mocuba or anywhere. João also wanted to see a number of improved wells because people used unsafe water from the Lugela river. A grain mill was needed and João also mentioned the unemployment problem for the men of Macuse.

The story recounted by the three families did not differ substantially but it was told in terms of each family's particular plight. The first family planted one and one-half hectares, the second close to four hectares, and the third, consisting of a poor elderly widow and her small niece, farmed a tiny plot. In the space of one short day, we had met representatives of the poorest, average and "wealthy" people of Alto-Lugela.

That night the INDER teams compiled the information gathered during the two days of interviews and represented it in verbal and graphic form. Armed with our flip charts and a sketch map of the area drawn by the community elders we set off the next morning for a final meeting with the people of Alto-Lugela. We were not prepared for the size of the meeting. Over four hundred people had come to review the information and prioritize their needs.

During the presentation of our "analysis," these were some of the comments we heard: "We are happy with what you saw in our community and we are going to improve even more." "Yes, we have had a good agricultural year, but what are our perspectives (regarding marketing)." "We are poor." "Many times, people come to talk to us, but nothing ever comes of it." "What about the Company? Isn't there anyone who can bring it back?" "PIDICO came and destroyed our land." There was applause following this comment. "We want to plant cotton in these lands." "We need a bus. Who can buy this for us? We can't buy one." "We are in great need of better medical services."

The discussion turned to prioritizing the major problems and it was a fierce, lively debate, with the following results: the need for new hoes and other small tools, the need for improved marketing, the need for better medical services, the need for more schools, the need for a maize mill, the need for improved wells.

The discussion then turned to solutions and the first topic was government distribution of tools, which had proved controversial in the past. Some people claimed that in previous distributions family members of those in charge of the distributions had been favored over the general population. Director José was visibly defensive at this accusation but he tried to assure people that he would look into the matter and provide as general a distribution as possible.

It was generally agreed that the INDER teams would ask the PRR to finance the rehabilitation of Alto-Lugela's marketplace. The idea behind this was that if producers brought their produce to a market and sold as a group instead of selling as individuals to itinerant merchants they could bargain for better prices. People said that they would be willing to contribute labor and local materials. They were also willing to contribute their time and energy to the building of school annexes if the PRR provided building materials and the government was able to provide teachers. Pedro Semende was optimistic about the latter possibility.

People also asked whether it was possible to get spare parts to repair the broken hand pumps on the wells throughout the locality and a conversation was promised with the Rural Water Program. Two hours passed before the map was finally presented to the community. This riveted the attention of everyone. There was widespread participation in correcting the map, adding all the different infrastructures, including the broken-down water pumps and semi-destroyed buildings. Armed with the community's list of priorities, consensus on some solutions including the contributions of the people of Alto-Lugela and a corrected map of the locality, the teams said their "good-byes" and invited community representatives to join the District Executive Council in decision making.

On the last day of the planning exercise, the district officials presented project proposals for the rehabilitation of the market place and for construction of two school annexes in the center of Alto-Lugela to the District Executive Council, which was enlarged for the occasion to include community representatives and the INDER teams. There was heated discussion on costs and on the possibility of securing teachers but once it was clear that budgets would be revised to meet actual costs and that the provincial government would provide teachers, the projects were approved. Director José promised to look into the matter of providing hoes.

A rough estimate of the total number of people who participated in this and similar planning exercises, including the rural development agents, the provincial level officials, the district teams and the community leaders was in the region of 560 in the two provinces.[13] Written evaluations of the training by trainees showed a very high appreciation of the utility of the course for their work.[14]

The Concept and Practice of Community Participation under the PRR
There was no definition or description in the project document regarding how communities were to participate in the Decentralization Component. Nonetheless it stated: "The new participatory rural development strategy reflected in the PRR allows community leaders an important role in project *implementation*" (sections 2.25 and 2.31, emphasis mine). For the project managers, community participation in project implementation was of utmost importance. In the first phase, from April 1995 until December 1996, community participation played an extremely significant role in the execution of primary schools, health posts, public markets, and so on. This was known as the phase of direct administration when communities organized themselves, with the help of the resident rural development agents, to provide local materials and unskilled manual work, all on a gratuitous basis.[15] It left the

Project open to the charge of reintroducing the colonial practice of "forced" labor.

In the second phase, when the decision was taken to use construction companies, communities were then expected to cofinance 10 percent of the costs. The 10 percent could come from three different sources: community contributions in materials and unskilled labor (later such things as food and lodging for contractors was included); community maintenance of the infrastructure; or government participation in the form of funds from the state budget. Negotiations regarding community contributions formed a large part of the dialogue between communities and district planning teams in the sessions dedicated to the priorization of community needs and the definition of responsibilities in the implementation of potential projects. It was the most difficult aspect of community planning. Novel and innovative forms of contribution evolved from these discussions. Nevertheless, no one knew how to quantify the various types of community coparticipation and so these values never entered into finalized project budgets. As the Project was coming to an end, project administrators were also very concerned about community participation in the maintenance of the completed infrastructures. It was generally recognized that not enough thought or training had occurred in this regard.

The question of ownership and maintenance was put to six community members in Muagiua, Zambézia, in 1999. Their answers were very revealing: while they expressed strong identification with the school and health center being built, they felt a certain helplessness in regard to how these would be maintained. However, one person asked whether it would be possible to allocate a part of the School Fund (*Caixa Escolar*), normally collected from each pupil. This comment showed an awareness of the difficulties of organizing and managing separate funds open to the possibility of pilfering among other problems. The suggestion to use an already established mechanism was a logical response to the problem posed.

The INDER trainers and their protégés, the provincial trainers, understood community participation in a much fuller sense: they wanted to see communities participate not only in the selection and implementation of projects—to a small extent achieved by the PRR—but also in their management and maintenance, and in the evaluation of the impact of the PRR on their communities. Their ideal was that communities should feel ownership of and responsibility for the constructed infrastructures. These were exaggerated expectations given the institutional context.

It would be difficult to characterize the planning exercises as either spontaneous or under community control. This was largely due to the procedures of the Rural Rehabilitation Project. To begin with, because the identification and building of small-scale infrastructures had begun before the participatory planning exercises, the communities visited had already formed an image of the Project and were "programmed" to ask for similar infrastructures. Moreover, the communities to be visited were picked by the district administrators. Communities were thus placed in the position of "beneficiaries" rather than initiators of the planning exercise. Had they been self-selecting, they might have been able to impose themselves on both the process and outcomes. In only one case did this happen: when the communities of Alto-Molocué anticipated the arrival of the INDER teams and began making bricks in anticipation that the PRR would build schools in those communities that had bricks ready.

Moreover, communities had no control over which of the priorities they identified would become a project. There were many steps before final approval: the matrix planning exercise, the decision of the Enlarged Executive Council at district level, the comments by the PRR provincial office, the compliance of the relevant provincial ministry delegation, and so on.

Communities also had no control over disbursement of the funds. A community committee was supposed to have been formed to accompany each project but as the PRR moved from using community labor to using private contractors, the community lost all opportunity to direct the work done. Most projects suffered more than a year and a half of delay, many due to problems caused by inexperienced or dishonest contractors. Communities thus lost their initial enthusiasm.

The infrastructures finally built were of the conventional type and many were beyond the financial and/or technical capabilities of the communities to support. The courses on Community Maintenance of Small Infrastructures tentatively planned were not realized because it became necessary to train contractors and candidates for the position of building inspectors.

Most of these problems could be traced to the anxiety to begin the Project before all of its components were in place, to the tendency to disburse extravagant sums and to overly bureaucratic disbursement procedures. When these obstacles became apparent, the PRR attempted to modify the amounts of money involved as well as its procedures.

District Development Funds

In March 1997, discussions took place within the INDER training team regarding this situation. One of the provincial trainers offered the suggestion that perhaps a special line of funding could be opened to finance very small initiatives within the capabilities of the Districts. The idea was not inconsistent with some of the small-scale projects listed in the project document (World Bank, 1993:Annex II-2:2). Moreover, sister rural rehabilitation programs sponsored by IFAD in Niassa and NORAD in Cabo Delgado had already begun to institute District Development Funds and the experience of Cabo Delgado proved particularly helpful.

In April 1997, the idea was presented to the project director, the president of INDER, and the World Bank team task manager, who discussed and approved it on an experimental basis. A year passed before the first District Development Funds (DDF) were introduced on a pilot basis in three districts in Sofala and three in Zambézia. The Funds financed only projects identified in participatory planning exercises. The district team and a community selected one or more micro-projects, which could be implemented within the district. This eliminated the need for negotiations with the line ministries at provincial level. *In this way, the Funds made autonomous investment planning at district level possible, even though on a very minor scale.* Such projects included the building of public markets, the training of traditional midwives, community reforestation, the promotion of small animal husbandry, the opening and rehabilitation of tertiary roads and the like.

The procedures for project approval also involved discussion within an enlarged district executive council and presentation to the provincial facilitation unit but this last step was only to ensure that the selected project fell within project guidelines. Disbursement was supposed to be immediate in order to ensure rapid implementation. Unfortunately, between April and June 1998, just as the first project proposals were approved, the PRR suffered a liquidity crisis and no funds were available for the next six to nine months, which considerably dampened enthusiasm in the new experiment. Administrators and district teams grew nervous and, in the case of Sofala, the administrators of Gorongosa and Cheringoma presented themselves to the provincial facilitation unit in Beira to plead their case.

Besides the initial liquidity crisis, a few other difficulties were experienced in establishing the Funds. District officials had difficulties because there were no banks in most districts. This meant traveling to the provincial capital every time a deposit or withdrawal had to be made and involved time and expense for which the Funds had made no provision. Not even the operational expenses of the participatory planning exercises were covered. Funds for travel to communities, for didactic materials, for per diems and other expenses were unavailable.

Moreover, there was not enough flexibility either in the amount of money in the Funds (an initial ceiling of U.S.$15,000) or in the eligibility criteria established for projects. Two out of the six communities visited in the experimental phase experienced notable and serious frustration because none of the priority needs they identified fit the criteria. In the first case, a small bridge needed repair on a vitally strategic road for the concerned community but the cost of rehabilitation exceeded the ceiling in the Fund. In the other case, the community expressed to the district team and training leaders that they felt the PRR was wasting the community's time if it could not respond to even one of its primary needs.

Nevertheless, the existence of the DDFs occasioned more than the usual level of activity in some districts. In the sister project in Niassa, where initial delays were minimal, DDFs revitalized the district administrations of Lichinga and Sanga and occasioned a beehive of activity. In the words of the administrator of Lichinga, this gave the administration the possibility "of gaining the confidence of the population." However, in Niassa, community involvement did not take place in any phase of the investment cycle. The Niassa experience is examined in more detail in chapters 9 and 10.

Overall Contribution to Decentralization and Reconstruction

Overall, the decentralization component of the PRR was an important instrumentality of decentralized planning in Sofala and Zambézia at the level of districts and provinces though not communities as has been seen. The District Development Fund was completely in the hands of the district administration. It allowed district administrators to gain self-confidence through direct assistance to communities in areas within their capacity and jurisdiction. District Funds gave administrations the opportunity to handle funds, contract public works and present accounts. It gave administrations the chance to show their capability to manage investment funds. Because it was not necessary to negotiate with the provincial representatives of the line ministries, the district administrations were for the first time, *on their own*, so to speak. They were accountable only to INDER in the matter of fund management. This was a good example of a central agency providing the means for increasing the role and capacity of local government to deal with "client" needs, the tri-directional dynamic that Tendler argues is essential to decentralization (1997:14 ff, 200 ff). Not all districts rose to this challenge, as discussed in chapter 9.

In regard to provincial planning, the PRR supplied around U.S.$1 million a year to each province and close to U.S.$2 million in 1999. Considering that central government transfers to provincial investment funds barely reached one million dollars a year, it is easy to appreciate the direct impact on provincial planning in Sofala and Zambézia. A relationship of trust and confidence gradually grew between the provincial facilitation units and various provincial directorates. In Sofala, both Health and Education directorates added their provincial investment funds to PRR funds and entrusted the facilitation unit with the planning and execution of the provincial PTIP in those sectors. Other sectors also collaborated to greater and lesser extents. Here a central agency can be seen as enlarging the capacities of the provincial level; in a not-so-small way, INDER facilitated decentralized planning in these two provinces.

In terms of project execution, the provincial facilitation unit gave technical assistance to the ministries at provincial level by expediting the implementation and monitoring of the larger micro-projects, from providing the terms of reference for infrastructural works and building specifications, to the launching of bids, the monitoring of the works in progress, and the training of construction companies and building inspectors. In the latter role, INDER helped create and heighten the capacity of the private sector in the two provinces. Before the PRR, there were hardly any construction companies worthy of the name. The several courses offered and the promise of public contracts caused many local businessmen to launch themselves into this sector. Tendler pointed to the stimulation of "civil society" as another aspect of the tri-directional dynamic (1997:200 ff).

In individual terms, the exposure of both provincial- and district-level officials to community consultation, through participation in the PRR training program, enlarged their knowledge of rural problems and community resources and enabled them to bring a broader perspective to planning, that is, an intersectoral rather than the typical sectoral view of Mozambican planning. It introduced them and communities as well to a more open decision-making process. And it had a small multiplier effect. In Zambézia, the provincial directorate of Plan and Finances also planned to train district officials in participatory methodologies. Helping to lead this process was a former member of the PRR provincial training team, now chief of the Plan and Budget department. In Milange district, the Danish nongovernmental organization, IBIS, incorporated PRR-trained district officials in its teams to lead participatory planning exercises throughout the district. In Gorongosa and Cheringoma districts in Sofala, German Technical Cooperation trained the PRR-trained district teams to lead the district strategic planning exercise and invited a member of the PRR provincial training team to help in the training. In Buzi, Sofala, Austrian Development Cooperation reinforced the role of the INDER-trained district team and the PRR provincial training officer became the counterpart for Austrian technical assistance.

The decentralization component of the PRR opened a small space for communities and multi-sector district teams to play a joint though limited role in district planning. At the same time, it financed some essential services for communities, in both human and material terms, in such areas as health, education, roads, water supply and so on. The building and/or rehabilitation of 109 primary schools, 31 health units, 167 wells and boreholes, 15 markets, among other small infrastructures, met many of the local needs identified in the National Reconstruction Plan. The next chapter looks briefly at several other important experiments in decentralized planning.

Notes

1. See CEA, 1981a, 1981b, for example.

2. A United Nations document questioned the independence of provincial planning: "Provincial Plans are essentially the result of a compilation of investments and activities, selected through a 'vertical' approach reflecting sectors' priorities. Little attempt is made to establish 'horizontal' linkages and to develop multiple-sector investment 'packages', in order to exploit synergy and maximize impact" (United Nations Capital Development Fund, July 1998:14).

3. The situation was that the Ministry of State Administration published the guidelines without consulting the Ministry of Plan and Finances. The guidelines were basically the same as those drafted by the Ministry of Plan and Finances but with some important changes relating to local participation, which the Ministry of State Administration had reduced to consultation. As just mentioned in the last chapter, the Ministry has now eliminated any reference to these Councils in the latest draft law on State Local Bodies. However, it appears that they will be maintained at least in the provinces about to receive World Bank sponsorship of the district planning initiative, possibly on an experimental basis (Personal Communication, November 2002). See the first section of chapter 8.

4. See Mamdani, 1996:102 ff and Tendler, 1997.

5. "After Sierra Leone, Mozambique is the most aid-dependent country in the world. Over the period 1987–95, it received more than US$8 billion of support in grants, credits and debt relief" (De Vletter, 1998:8).

6. The tradition in Mozambique is to call all training a course or seminar. This course was mainly a participatory rural appraisal exercise.

7. There were three in Sofala and five in Zambézia to cover the "priority" districts. Their terms of reference were later expanded and they were expected to cover the entire 27 districts.

8. As of April 1999, the same training had also been given, three times in Niassa under the auspices of the Programa de Desenvolvimento Agrário do Niassa and a number of times in Cabo Delgado under the Programa de Reabilitação Rural de Cabo Delgado.

9. As already noted in chapter 5, topics included the history, geography, environment, land use, general social and political organization of the community, and so on.

10. This instance in Mugema, in Alto-Molocué, Zambézia, is recounted in chapter 11.

11. Interview with the President of INDER, 1 April 1999.

12. Localities are units subordinated under administrative posts directly under districts. Districts normally have two to four administrative posts.

13. Some of whom received the same training twice, as already noted.

14. These written evaluations were reproduced in the reports on each of the training exercises.

15. Construction foremen, masons, civil engineers, building inspectors and so on were paid workers.

CHAPTER EIGHT

∾

Decentralized Planning: Various Donor Approaches in the Late 1990s

The Nampula Approach

In 1993, the Government of Mozambique signed an agreement with the United Nations Capital Development Fund to promote rural rehabilitation in the northern province of Nampula through the establishment of a Local Development Fund. This was a financial facility for creating small infrastructures, which was channeled through the provincial government for distribution at district level. What began as a mechanism for rehabilitating local communities later developed into a facility for training district officials.

In its initial phase, the project bore a certain resemblance to the PRR. For example, it also introduced participatory rural appraisals to allow communities to identify their needs and select possible solutions. Project proposals were also elaborated by district officials and sent to the Province for approval and insertion into the three-year rolling public investment program. There was also a separate project facilitation unit inside the Provincial Directorate of Plan and Finances. Here the similarities ended. The project operated on a much smaller scale in only three districts, Monapo, Muecate, and Mecuburi. After two years, it had financed only fifteen projects and disbursed less than U.S.$100,000.

In 1997, the organizational setup and objectives of the project changed fundamentally. The emphasis turned toward training district planners to enable them to orient public and private investment in local areas over the medium-term. Project staff melded into the Provincial Plan and Finances

Directorate in order to maintain provincial control over the planners.[1] Instead of separate planning processes for district projects and community projects, the elaboration of a five-year district strategic plan was seen as a way of blending the two.

The Ministry of Plan and Finances designated Nampula as the pilot province for the introduction of the new decentralized planning guidelines, referred to in chapter 6. This meant extensive training for district planning teams and district executive councils. District directors and other local officials also received exposure to some or all of the planning techniques. The approach, as in the PRR, was to train provincial level planning cadres first so that they could then train the district planning officers. During 1998, twelve provincial officers received training in four courses: Introduction to District Planning, Participatory Methods and Training Methods, Planning by Objectives, and Strategic Planning.

District officials received one year of training before they produced the strategic five-year plan, which consisted of a diagnostic of the district's resources, an identification of problems (thematic and areas) and a general development strategy. In 1998, participatory planning with communities continued and project proposals were fed into the provincial PTIP but the intention was to phase out the joint planning exercises and to organize popular participation around public meetings and consultative councils at district and sub-district levels.

The chief technical adviser to the training process had an interesting critique of participatory planning borne out of the original project's experience:

> What happens is that following various intensive and time consuming participatory exercises with people deemed to be sufficiently poor, a decision is made about something to be done. This invariably involves the spending of money and the continued participation by the beneficiaries. It is quite clear where the money has come from, and at the end of the process there is often some sort of formal thanks to the providers. This process raises a number of questions:
>
> - Extensive participation is often a prerequisite, yet the poorest of the poor are extremely busy people. . . . Is this participation sustainable? Or, as in the words of one local farmer is participation the punishment for being poor.
> - The government's role in this is negligible, yet it is the government who will often have to maintain and incorporate any infrastructure or service into its system. The population have not been empowered to dialogue with or pressure this government, or trained in how to get the best from

it. Is there any onus on the government to pay any attention to what happened? And will the population's response be any other than to hope for a return of the original providers? . . .

Some agencies tried to remedy this problem by working with the district government. This creates a different disempowerment in which district governments learn how to dialogue with and access agency funds but not how to dialogue and bargain within their own institutional setting with other levels of government. Nor do they learn how to relate and respond to community pressure (Jackson, 2002:14, 15).

He felt that the establishment of the consultative councils would be a way of starting a genuine political process at district level. In 1999, embryonic district councils were constituted in the three districts that began elaborating their first strategic plans. In principal, the process was to work in the following way: at the first meeting of the councils, the district administrator explained the objectives and process of the strategic planning exercise and initiated a preliminary discussion of district problems. At the second meeting, the councils discussed the general development strategy as it was being formulated. At further meetings, these bodies would comment on concrete activities and approve target areas where projects would be implemented during the five-year plan. Once the provincial level ministries approved the strategic plan, the district planning team would begin to make annual economic and social plans that pinpointed specific projects upon which the councils would also comment.

The chief technical adviser assessed the first meetings of the councils in this way:

The results were mixed. Perhaps the clearest success in post conflict reintegration came in Muecate district. Following the Consultative Council meeting one of the main local chiefs was interviewed. He testified that until the meeting he had been instructing the community not to get involved with the state at any level. He was awaiting reprisals from FRELIMO in revenge for the communities [sic] support for the opposition. For him the peace agreement was no more than an interval in a conflict that could begin again at any moment. However he said he had changed his mind since the meeting. Everybody was involved and respected each other. He now pledged to instruct the community to get involved and said that he himself would try to make this council work.

The clearest failure was in Mogincual district. There very few people turned up for the meeting and those that did believed it was a "project" type activity and were looking to get something out of it. When the traditional leadership found out that the meeting was under the auspices of the district government and not an international agency they stormed out, demanding payment for travel expenses and subsistence for the wasted journey. The other community representatives followed in solidarity and the event ended in acrimony and chaos (Jackson, 2002:16).

The monies to finance the district strategic plans came from the Local Development Fund that in 1999 now included Dutch government and United Nations monies. These funds were integrated into the provincial investment budget, to be used to finance the projects specified in the annual economic and social plans. The projects became the district component of the PTIP, administered under ordinary state budgetary procedures instead of being separately accounted for by a project unit. The amount set for each district was U.S.$75,000, five times the amount of the District Development Funds administered by the PRR. The Fund also covered the operating costs involved in identifying as well as implementing these investments.

By 2002, ten districts were to have received training, produced strategic plans, secured provincial approval and received investment funds. These ten plus the four districts covered by the Netherlands Development Organization (see next section) would cover the entire province.

SNV in Moma, Angoche, Mogincual, and Mogovolas Districts

In June 1995, the Netherlands Development Organization (SNV) signed a cooperation agreement with the Mozambique government for an integrated regional development program comprising Moma, Angoche, Mogincual, and Mogovolas districts of Nampula.[2] Planned for ten years, the program had two basic and separate components: district planning and community development. The first phase began in August 1998 and had among its objectives the elaboration of decentralized participatory planning methodologies as part of a coherent district planning framework, the promotion of village development committees and other consultative institutions with special emphasis on women's organizations.[3] Besides being very ambitious, the SNV organized a rather cumbersome bureaucratic administrative structure running parallel to the government's own structure. This was in contrast to the approach just described and opened questions about how the two experiments would operate side by side.

The planning component consisted of a regional planning unit, made up of an expatriate adviser, a Mozambican counterpart and the regional delegate of the Provincial Plan and Finances Directorate. There was also a steering council of the four district administrators to ensure the compatibility of the district plans and there were four planning officers, one in each district. A Local Development Fund of U.S.$75,000 for each district was a donation of the Dutch government. The resident project coordinator and staff in Nampula city managed the planning component.

In an interview, the program coordinator projected that the steering council would eventually expand to include civil society leaders from communities, churches, the private sector and other nongovernmental organizations, so that the four districts would also evolve district councils, in line with the strategic planning guidelines.

The community development component was composed of a unit for community development and had the services of a specialist, an assistant and sixteen United Nations volunteers in each of the administrative posts. Since the program provided each of the latter with a house and motorbike, there was concern that this aspect of the component would be a heavy burden for the Mozambican government to sustain once the project ended. But this should not have been the only subject of concern: as I argue in chapter 10, the introduction of "volunteers," "rural development agents," and the like was not only unnecessary but counterproductive to the goal of empowering communities.

The unit conducted participatory rural appraisals as a way of mobilizing communities to take their own initiatives in solving outstanding problems. According to the program coordinator, these local planning exercises resulted in a joint commitment between community and government. A local development committee was then formed consisting of the régulo, teacher, administrative post head, people from the private sector and women. The government formalized its commitment by inscribing the agreed projects in the district strategic plan. When I visited the project in 1999 only two local planning exercises had taken place.

The unit also dealt with community education regarding clean water supplies and dispensed credit to local women for income-generating activities. It may be that with time there will be a fusion of the district planning unit and community planning. However, given the commitment to cooperate with the Nampula experiment, just described, it was more likely that separate community planning will disappear.

Swiss Development Cooperation in Mecuburi District

Of the three initiatives in Nampula, the project supported by Swiss Development Cooperation in Mecuburi district had accomplished the most towards stimulating civil society involvement in planning by 1999. In its first phase, the project had also used participatory rural appraisal techniques to establish dialogues with rural settlements but in the second phase it chose to enable community and other groups to organize themselves in associations or nongovernmental organizations in order to accomplish specific goals. Moreover, it enabled government agencies to work more effectively with Mecuburi communities.

The two-person team that arrived during the second phase took the challenge of promoting civil society institutions in Mecuburi. They introduced a working methodology called *Pesquisa-Acção-Formação* (Research, Action, Training) to the institutions it both found and helped to create. The methodology involved finding adequate solutions to problems encountered in real-life situations (research) and defining concrete activities to test out solutions (action). This led to experience with which to confront new problems and find new solutions (training).[4]

The team found willing local partners in the administrator and the regional delegate of the Provincial Plan and Finances Directorate, both of whom were anxious to develop and try new strategies. Nevertheless, the team was also faced with a number of challenges. One was a number of requests from the district administration for help in resolving some basic problems of the district capital. Another was ongoing work with one or more communities previously approached through participatory rural appraisal techniques. The third was the introduction of the district strategic planning exercise and fourth was the arrival of a number of other international nongovernmental organizations, competing with each other and the Swiss team for projects and territories.

Given this situation, the team set out to create opportunities for contacts and collaboration between the SDC project and each of the key players in the district, beginning with the district administrator, the district planning team, the non-governmental organizations and the rural populations—organized in associations or other groupings. The team opened the prospect of cooperation among all of these players above all in the context of the ongoing strategic planning exercise through facilitating a networking exercise. One immediate result was the formation of what became the Network of Local Teams (*Equipas Locais em Rede*).

By March 1999 there had been seven meetings of the Network, which succeeded in coordinating activities, debating the district's strategic plan and offering financial support to certain projects, such as for access roads and several other smaller initiatives. The intention of the members was to keep meeting every forty-five days and to decentralize meetings from the district capital so as to include more people in the discussions at locality level, and wherever feasible to include *povoações/regulados*. A Fund for Civil Society Efforts, perhaps connected to the Network, was also under consideration.

The team also created chances for collaboration in the areas of food security, sustainable agriculture, marketing, land issues, and literacy training. In regard to the first and second areas, it initiated a dialogue with the director of the Provincial Directorate of Agriculture and Fisheries over how to reach Mecuburi communities. An internal debate within the directorate produced thirteen projects and SDC provided over U.S.$400,000 to finance them over a three-year period. The team also ran a training seminar for members of the provincial directorate, extension agents, and community leaders and engaged them in open discussions of more areas around which further training would take place. This seminar lasted three months. The eighteen participants were also trained in participatory training methods to promote this approach in their work with communities. The areas chosen for work in 1999 were: alternatives to slash and burn techniques, the multiplication of pigeon peas, and the promotion of small animal husbandry.

In regard to the problem of agricultural marketing, the SDC signed an agreement with the Cooperative League of the USA (CLUSA) to promote commercial associations in Mecuburi, which became the channel for the agricultural training just mentioned and literacy training.

In terms of land issues, the team negotiated accords with the Roman Catholic Diocese of Nampula, the Provincial Directorate of Agriculture, and a local nongovernmental organization, ASSANA, for the diffusion and debate of the new Land Law (discussed in chapter 11). The literacy program of ASSANA also broached the themes of land and food security.

In addition, the SDC supported a District Development Fund, which was called FUNIL, to finance district administration projects including the rehabilitation of the public gardens and electrification of the district capital. The latter project demonstrated the feasibility of civil society—government interaction where there was genuine need and interest. FUNIL provided the initial funds for a generator, while the administration and the town merchants set up a joint management board that had proven both ingenuity and sustainability at least up until March 1999.

The team left the project in 1999 but they expressed confidence that the project would continue through its local coordinators, including the regional delegate of the Provincial Plan and Finances Directorate and the Provincial Director of Agriculture with backup support from the Nampula office of SDC.

IBIS in Zambézia and Niassa

Zambézia

In January 1998, IBIS, a Danish nongovernmental organization, turned its project for building infrastructures in the Milange district of Zambézia into a local development program, involving rural communities and the district and municipal governments.[5] At the heart of this program was also a local development fund, divided unequally between communities, the district administration, the municipal government and the sectors at district level. In 1999, the total amount available in the fund for that year was close to U.S.$200,000, clearly too large to be sustainable.

Similar to the SNV program, this project included a rather large staff for one district, including a project director, a community development adviser, and a technical adviser. In regard to community projects, there was no attempt to follow government planning guidelines. Decisions on community projects were taken in participatory rural appraisal exercises combining the community with a district team led by the community development adviser. The project utilized the district planning team (including district personnel and Ibis project persons) trained by the PRR project. These decisions were not submitted to the district executive council or the provincial ministries for perusal, and the Provincial Directorate of Plan and Finances did not handle the funds. Rather project staff administered funds and implemented projects through its construction crew. This made for more rapid disbursal and implementation but it undermined local government and it did not empower communities. In relation to the latter, it substituted dependency on government with dependency on IBIS. In 1999, community projects amounted to U.S.$64,500.

The planning methodology used for the allocation of the rest of the funds, approximately U.S.$127,500 was completely different. It consisted of an annual seminar in which representatives of each sector, the district administration and the municipal government carried out a logical framework analysis, designed a number of projects and reached a consensus on the ones to be financed. The district submitted these projects to the Provincial Plan and Finances Directorate for inclusion in the PTIP.[6] Each agency managed its own projects, including the launching and adjudicating of bids. IBIS provided training and technical assistance to help it do this. For project execution, there was a technical unit, with a Mozambican civil engineer, who gave advice on budgeting, programming and technical matters. While this process helped district and municipal officials gain self-confidence in handling investment funds, there was also no attempt to link community development with district-level planning as the SDC Mecuburi project did.

Niassa

The IBIS project in Niassa was even more complex and it, too, divided community development from district planning. However the analysis and approach was completely different from that of its sister project in Zambézia because it treated community development as a training process to allow communities to do their own planning. Another difference was that the project operated on two distinct levels, provincial and in three districts. Moreover, unlike the project in Zambézia, it attempted to follow the Ministry of Plan and Finances guidelines for strategic planning in three districts.

The project had eight international advisers when I visited it in 1999; one in the two provincial planning units; one in the Provincial Directorate of Public Works and Housing, one in Agriculture and Fisheries, another in Culture, Youth and Sports, three in the districts, and a community development adviser. The following description outlines the methodologies used for both district planning and community development. These were interesting because of the large element of training that each involved.

A provincial team consisting of the coordinator-adviser, three people from the Provincial Directorate of Plan and Finances, three people from the Provincial Service for Physical Planning, and one person from the Provincial Delegacy of State Administration, led the strategic planning exercise. The function of the Provincial team was to train district teams, generally composed of district administration officials and directors of the ministries represented at district level.

The exercise took place in the following manner: first, the Provincial team held a meeting with the District Executive Council in order to explain the planning exercise. A district team was then selected and the provincial team explained the preliminary exercise and trained it to carry out a survey of all district resources, using survey bulletins and forms to guide the process. Both teams subsequently organized meetings with representatives from all sectors and segments of the population at which the planning exercise was explained and a preliminary discussion of district problems took place.

After completion of the survey, the provincial team led a planning workshop in which the district administration, the district directors, representatives of the population, political parties and so on discussed the district's problems in depth. This exercise involved fifty or so people for two to three days. The provincial team used maps to help people visualize district resources. The result of the workshop was a list of the district's priorities for one year. The intention was to extend this process gradually to produce a five-year indicative plan.

Finally, the plan entered the phase of negotiation at provincial level with the various ministries, which were solicited to contribute to it. IBIS contributed by financing the District Development Fund but other organizations were solicited to contribute as well. The IBIS project shared joint administration of the District Development Fund with the Provincial Directorate of Plan and Finances, which did the auditing. However, the IBIS adviser in each district handled community funds.

The community development component, assisted by a community development adviser and three trainer-supervisors, helped communities organize, articulate, and represent their needs at zonal and district levels. The initial methodology regrouped villages into various "traditional" territories (zones) and formed zonal committees with village representatives. (In Unango, this would have meant reforming Kalanje as a zone from the various communal villages such as Ilinga, Miala, and so on.) The assumption was that communities were ready for representative democracy but the reality in Niassa was found to be otherwise. Little more than extended families, in many cases, communities were not assertive because they lacked both forward-looking leadership and confidence. As a consequence, the community development adviser told me that he restructured both the plan of action and working methodology.

The new strategy turned on building confidence at village level. This was to be accomplished in various stages, the first of which was to explain to the village head the objectives of community planning, that is, identifying priorities, community contributions, and shortfalls in order to design projects. The second step was to hold the first of several village meetings at which the adviser, district supervisor, and district administration representatives were present, in order to explain the project and ask the community to select a village development committee. Once selected, the adviser and trainers trained the committee in the following skills: organizing meetings; obtaining a diversity of views in meetings; distributing responsibilities in committees; co-opting community skills through task forces; decision making; designing small projects; and conducting elections of delegates to zonal committees.

After completion of the training, a second village meeting was called during which the committee organized villagers to discuss problems first in small groups and then in the whole community to prioritize them. At a third meeting, the development committee assisted the community to devise solutions and contributions. Then the adviser, trainers, and the committee verified that solutions, inputs, and shortfalls were consistent with problems. In this way projects were finalized.

The only link between the community development component and the district planning process was through the zonal committee to which village representatives brought their community agenda, that is, those projects that could not be solved at community or district level and needed provincial level approval and inputs. The zonal committee was expected to negotiate which projects made their way to the district-planning workshop.

Besides the training already discussed, the IBIS project provided for courses in public accounting for district administrations and technical training related to community projects.

Irish Cooperation in the Province of Niassa

Financing from the government of Ireland was made available to the Niassa Province rather than to the national government of Mozambique. It was channeled directly through the Provincial Directorate of Plan and Finances for the purpose of supporting the provincial budget in various sectors such as education.

In 1998, the Irish Embassy entered a new phase of cooperation with the Province that aimed both at community development and support for strategic planning. As regards the latter, it was moving cautiously: in 1999, it financed a study on the question of micro-regions, that is, the grouping together of several districts to form a "natural" socio-economic unit and was awaiting the decision of the provincial government as to which micro-region it should support. The embassy was following with interest the Nampula approach in order to be in line with government policy when it finally initiated its own efforts.

The community development component, however, began an experiment to test community-planning methodologies in the village of Nzizi, in Muembe district. Before the experiment took place, a two-person Mozambican team went to Ethiopia to receive instruction in Community Organizing Leadership Training for Action (COLTA). It then formed a team of twelve members, consisting of seven community people chosen by Nzizi and five district officials,[7] to be trained in order to train others in the district in the COLTA methodology. The methodology consisted of five modules on: first, the concept of development; second, leadership; third, community organizing; fourth, project planning; and fifth, motivation for improving community objectives. The goal was to help communities organize themselves for taking responsibilities.

The group also received participatory rural appraisal training and, by 1999, had conducted four PRAs in villages in each of the administrative posts in Muembe. The Irish project team accompanied the first such exercise in Nzizi but the group led the other three appraisals on their own. The planning exercises with the communities resulted in a list of community priorities and a number of possible projects. The Irish project normally financed one of these projects and the list was registered with the district administration as a kind of community plan, which other potential partners were encouraged to support.

The Irish embassy financed a District Development Fund for Muembe in the amount of U.S.$60,000 (1998) of which 65 percent was earmarked for community-selected projects and 35 percent for district projects. In 1998, the district administration chose to rehabilitate administration buildings with its share of the Fund. The community of Nzizi chose, as its top priority, a grain mill. In order to receive a share of the Fund, Nzizi presented the proposal for the mill to the district administrator who then sent a formal letter of approval and the proposal to the Provincial Directorate of Plan and Finances for disbursement of funds. Budgetary procedures followed state procedures.

Responsibility for the implementation of the project was the community's. For its own part, Nzizi decided to contribute stones, bricks, and water for the construction of the building, which housed the mill. It obtained a blueprint from the Provincial Directorate of Public Works and designated a stonemason to construct it. Nzizi also selected the people to manage the mill. The person they selected to collect the milling fee was also a mechanic. The Embassy paid for his training in management practices. Nzizi solicited the District Development Fund for the money to buy the mill and asked the project adviser, of which there was only one, to buy the mill in neighboring Malawi.

The Muembe District Development Fund was in a provincial Bank under the watchful eye of the Provincial Plan and Finances Directorate. To withdraw money, two out of three signatures were necessary: the Provincial Plan and Finances director, the administrator of Muembe, and the head of the secretariat of the district administration. The community presented its receipts to them. The Embassy, the provincial administration, and the district people together reviewed the books every three months, as well as the status of all the Irish projects in Niassa.

Summary Analysis

In 1999 and the years leading up to it, most of the donors involved in investing in local areas focused on district strategic planning rather than on empowering communities to do their own planning. Some exceptions were the IBIS and Irish projects in Niassa. Nevertheless while both types of planning should go hand in hand, there is a need to emphasize community planning in the first instance. That this required going beyond consultation with "community authorities" and the establishment of consultative bodies such as consultative councils should be clear as these exercises were still fundamentally dominated by the top—by "urban" priorities and values.

One way to reverse this trend was to start the planning process with community demands rather than simply incorporate them at planning workshops, almost as an afterthought. A more radical approach, radical in the sense of going to the heart or root of the matter, was to let populations govern themselves. In chapter 10, I advocate reversing the normal planning procedure by letting rural peoples make their own plans, and inviting government or donor collaboration as needed, rather than the other way around.[8] This was also a key to governing agrarian societies and otherwise dispersed populations. Before entering into the argument, however, it is important to appreciate the concerns at provincial, district, and community levels of the people who participated in the experiments just described as well as to analyze what worked and did not work in these pilot projects.

Notes

1. Also in process, when I interviewed the head of the directorate in 1999, was the separation of the project execution unit from the Provincial Directorate of Plan and Finances and its establishment in the Provincial Directorate of Public Works and Housing. The minister of Public Works and Housing had asked the Nampula Directorate to pilot the creation of a technical unit (*Unidade de Apoio*) to facilitate the construction of public infrastructures for all ministries at provincial level. The Unit would gather civil construction personnel of all ministries and will train them. The UNCDF architect and another adviser would be responsible for helping to establish and guide the unit.

2. Also known as the MAMM programme from the initials of the four districts.

3. SNV, 1998:10.

4. This is a free translation of the description given in the team's final report: "As *iniciativas concretas constituem a oportunidade de enfrentar a realidade (acção), experimentar e validar soluções adequadas (pesquisa), e capitalizar a experiência para enfrentar novos problemas e novas soluções*" (Swiss Development Co-Operation, 1999:16).

5. I was unable to speak with project staff while in Milange as they were in Maputo. Thus the following was learned in discussions with the District Administrator and some of the district officials participating in the planning exercises.

6. According to the head of the plan and budget department, the IBIS project director, the community development adviser, and a member of the district administration simply presented information on the 1999 plan to the director of Plan and Finances.

7. The district officials included delegates from the ministries of Agriculture, Education, Culture, Youth and Sports, the head of the Administration Secretariat, and the head of the relevant administrative post.

8. There was a very tiny INDER project that may have originally been organized along these lines. The PROAREA project sponsored by the United Nations Development Programme in the province of Tete started the planning process with communities themselves. It too used UN volunteers but, apparently, certain communities were able to reverse the dynamic and to push the project into areas that best suited their priorities. I was unfortunately never in a position to evaluate the project. When I left INDER it seemed to be heading in the direction of a micro-business credit program.

~

CHAPTER NINE

Decentralized Planning: The View from the Field

Introduction to the Lower Levels of the Civil Service

When he took office in 2000, the Minister of State Administration found within the civil service a situation of proprietorial office holding not unlike that described in chapter 6. In an unusually frank statement to the press, he lamented, "The greatest enemies of the reform of the state apparatus now under way in Mozambique are the civil servants themselves." This was in an interview with the Mozambican News Agency (AIM), which went on to report that:

> Chichava said civil servants opposed reform because they feared losing the illegal earnings or illicit privileges that they have enjoyed up to now because of lack of discipline and control. . . . Chichava, who had been attending a Commonwealth conference on good governance, recognised that abuses of power have proliferated in the Mozambican state apparatus, including corruption in all sectors, theft of state funds, and the illegal use of public property, notably vehicles. . . . He said that since he took over as minister (in January) he has been working on a series of measures including drafting new legislation in cases where existing laws have loopholes or are outdated, in order to eliminate the evils or anomalies which give the state apparatus a bad name (Agência, 16–17 September 2000).

According to Judith Tendler (1997), mainstream development literature is very much of the same opinion. She, herself, disputed the charge that civil servants were the enemies of reform. This chapter shows that, at the lower levels of state administration, officials were eager for training and opportunities to broaden their work. Before relating the varied reactions of provincial and district officials to the opportunities opened by the various decentralized planning initiatives just described, it is necessary to try to understand the context in which they were operating at the time of my interviews with them at the end of the twentieth century.

Provincial-level officials were several levels removed from rural constituencies and constituted a body of professionals in the urbanized provincial capitals of Mozambique. Their identification with the urban milieu meant that they rarely reflected the concerns of rural areas. Moreover, they were one level below policymaking. This structural position, as middlemen, was an uneasy one. Rural rehabilitation and national reconstruction had given this level of government new life by opening doors to numerous sources of investment monies provided by the ever-growing number of projects sponsored by international agencies and nongovernmental organizations. Yet not all of these projects enlarged their scope of decision making in the way the PRR had. The issue of planning a component of the PTIP and the subsequent reduction of discretionary funds in the crucial areas of agriculture, rural water supply, education, health and roads greatly concerned provincial cadres. The sectoral investment programs imposed by donors in these areas narrowed what at first seemed to be an expanding opportunity to make an impact on provincial development and thus to exercise power.

Given the ambiguity of their situation, provincial officials considered further professional training of vital importance, as it provided one of the few avenues for promotion to the national level. Merit was not a consideration for promotion in the Mozambican civil service in 1999: what counted was formal education leading to degrees, certificates, and diplomas, and *cunha*, meaning contacts, favors, friends, including and, above all, having an influential *padrinho* or godfather. Some few provincial officials were absorbed by international agencies into the local administration of projects. This was one of the few other opportunities for personal advancement.

Exceptions to this thumb-nail profile of generally alienated provincial-level cadres could be found among the directors and supervisors of rural field workers, such as the head of community health services in the Provincial Directorate of Health, the head of adult education and literacy training in the Provincial Directorate of Education, the head of the program for low-cost sanitation, and so on, and also cadres from the Provincial Directorate of Plan and Finances delegated to a district. People in these positions were more often in direct touch with rural peoples and, *when given opportunities and means*, often showed enthusiasm and dedication in their work.

Their response to a seminar called in 1998 by the Provincial Directorate of Public Works in Nampula was a case in point. It was sponsored by the United Nations Children's Emergency Fund (UNICEF) to discuss ways of introducing a demand-based approach to clean water supplies with the promise that ways and means would be found to implement this approach. At the seminar were the above-mentioned heads of departments as well as representatives of nongovernmental organizations working with participatory approaches in the same sectors. Their reaction to the opportunity was impressive. They designed a strategy that involved the formation of a multi-sector provincial-level team to train and supervise multi-sector district-level teams in participatory planning not only of water supply but also community health, literacy, low-cost sanitation and so on. This would have involved themselves as well as field workers in working closely with rural peoples in the definition of basic needs.

The distinction between provincial-level officials that worked in close contact with rural peoples and those who did not became obvious in interviews with Manica Province officials on the subject of training needs in October and November 1999 (Galli, 1999c). Provincial heads of such ministries as Public Works, Agriculture, Social Action, Education, Plan and Finances, Physical Planning, and also certain heads of departments within them, demonstrated a remarkably different attitude to training from that of such officials as the head of the rural extension service and the head of the forestry service. Whereas the latter were very interested in instruction in participatory planning with communities and in the training of communities, the others were more apt to discuss formal education for their own staff.

At district level, the needs of communities and for practical, on-the-job training to work with communities were also uppermost in the minds of officials from all sectors. In Bàrué district, officials talked about several interesting ongoing community planning experiments in which they were already involved whereas in Machaze, which had very few projects of any kind, the district directors in agriculture and education brought up the question of participatory training strategies without any suggestion by the interviewer (Galli, 1999c).

The attitudes of district-level officials generally had to do with the lack of opportunities for having an impact either on policymaking or people's lives and even fewer chances for upward mobility. Instead, district officials were subject to frequent transfers, a horizontal movement from one district to another. District directors of the line ministries had a slightly greater chance of being promoted to positions at provincial level than did the field workers.

District administrators, under the Ministry of State Administration and the provincial governor, were the obvious exceptions to this career mode. In their districts, district administrators were kings; that is, they had a position of authority over their own staff and, to a lesser extent, over the district directors and their staff, and the auxiliary personnel such as the police force, civil registry, party officials, and so on. It was no wonder, then, that they looked somewhat askance at the municipal governments carved out of the urbanized areas in their districts. Of particular worry was the sharing of scarce tax revenues. It was rare to find a district administrator more interested in responding to rural interests than in tending to his own status, personal power and career. Some exceptions are pointed out in this chapter.

Because of their lowly position, district officials involved in extension work were the most sympathetic to the needs of rural populations. For this reason, it is not entirely unrealistic to think of them as potential "organic intellectuals" in Gramscian terms. These cadres generally showed much more interest in participatory planning methodologies than their provincial counterparts. What made them particularly enthusiastic about a training program, such as that provided by the PRR and other projects, was the hope that such programs would not only provide them with means to do their own jobs more effectively but also give them a chance to enlarge their tasks, to work as a team, and just possibly help them expand their career horizons. In a few instances, this was not mere illusion, as shall now be seen.

The following sections summarize how various provincial and district officials and district administrators in the Provinces of Zambézia, Nampula, Niassa, and Sofala viewed their situation in relation to the various decentralized planning experiments just described. The interviews were conducted in March and April 1999 and focused mainly on the Rural Rehabilitation Project (PRR). The chapter also analyses the human and institutional factors that contributed positively to district-level participatory planning as it had evolved until then.

Zambézia

At all levels of government, officials expressed concern over the reduction in investment funds in crucial sectors previously left to the discretion of provincial and district administrations, which was the immediate result of the recentralization of planning under sectoral investment programs in Agriculture, Health, Water, Roads, and Education as well as the announced closure of the PRR in December 2000. On the other hand, officials of the Provincial Directorate of Plan and Finances also worried about the injection of close to U.S.$200,000 in Milange by the IBIS project, which they thought would create an unsustainable precedent as well as foster regional imbalance.

District administrators were, moreover, preoccupied with the reduction of operating cost budgets, particularly in those districts that now had to share tax receipts with municipalities. There were two types of taxes collected at this level. The major one was the National Reconstruction Tax set in 1999 at between five and fifteen thousand *meticais* (approximately U.S.$.50–1.50) per able-bodied person of working age. This tax was divided among several bodies: 70 percent went to the national treasury, 25 percent to the district or municipality, and 5 percent to the tax collector (tax farmer). Other taxes were levied on property or economic activity. If the property (such as bicycles) or activity were in rural areas, the district administration still captured these taxes. If, however, the property or activity was in the urbanized area of the district capital, then the receipts went to the municipality. In Zambézia, this was the dilemma of Mocuba, Gùrué, Milange, and the provincial capital of Quelimane where municipalities had been created. The administrators of Mocuba, Gùrué, and Milange reported that, given the new situation, they did not expect to have sufficient funds for office supplies, diesel fuel, and the like. Although delighted to receive PRR and other project investment funds, they lamented that such funds did not always cover operating expenses. In regard to the question of participatory planning, they admitted not having taken full advantage of the opportunities afforded by having a team trained in participatory methodologies.

District planning teams had, for the most part, been neglected and not simply by administrators. Their utility had been little appreciated by district directors of line ministries and even the resident rural development agents ignored them. In the latter case, this had to do with structural limitations within the PRR, which had only budgeted for five rural development agents, one for each of what were known as priority districts. They were soon expected to cover all fourteen Zambézia districts. The rural development agents therefore had no time to accompany the teams nor did they have much interest in training them so that teams could replace them when the Project ended. What generally happened was that the rural development agent used one or other team member when he wanted to enter a community to check on a specific project. The teams as such were not generally used after the original one or two planning exercises in most districts. The experience of Milange where the team was absorbed by the IBIS project was the exception rather than the rule.

As a consequence, the rural communities I interviewed in Gùrué and Milange, where planning exercises had taken place, had not had further visits by the team as team, although individual members had passed by in the course of their regular duties. Members of these communities had trouble remembering the original planning exercise because of the slow response of the provincial facilitation unit in implementing the projects identified by the participatory planning exercise. Consequently, the school identified by Muagiua in May 1996 was only inaugurated in December 1998. The school identified by Tundo in August 1997 was still under construction when visited in April 1999.

The Gùrué "Success" Story

Of all the districts in Zambézia, the district, which had benefited the most from the PRR, was Gùrué. Close to U.S.$1,000,000 of the available U.S.$5,000,000 was solicited and successfully invested in the district.[1] The ex-administrator of Gùrué had his own personal formula for making the PRR work for the benefit of his district. Paraphrasing his words, he described his strategy in the following terms:

First, it was necessary to understand the objectives of the project. Then one needed to create basic working conditions for the resident rural development agent, which included providing housing and an office.

Next, it was important to develop a rapport with the agent in order to make him an agent of the district administration and a right hand man of the Administrator. This attitude was in marked contrast to other administrators who sat back and waited to see what the PRR could do for them.

Finally, it was fundamental to get all agencies, donor, and governmental together, to reach a common consensus on geographical areas and on sectors where projects were necessary; this meant creating a division of labor among the nongovernmental agencies.[2]

In the administrator's view, the training of a district team in participatory methodologies was important and made it possible for him to use the team to verify problems brought to his attention as well as to meet and discuss situations with communities.[3] As the person responsible for district development, he assumed the role of leader in the process which for him signified doing a diagnostic analysis of the district, understanding at first hand its problems, visiting communities and knowing how to select priorities and dialoguing with the various non-governmental organizations and program staff. As a result of his efforts, Gùrué's administration built, on the average, six primary schools per year and constructed five regional health centers.

As far back as 1995 the administrator had begun to pressure the PRR directors to decentralize funds to district level and therefore welcomed the District Development Fund even though the amount of funds was very limited. The successful completion of the projects selected by the community of Mucunha in April 1998 under the Fund had to do with taking the question of its management seriously. When, in late October 1998, the Provincial Facilitation Unit forwarded funds for three of the four projects, bids were launched. A Commission of Evaluation was established, including the administrator, the accountant, the district team leader and the director of Public Works and Habitation. They selected two contractors, one for the road and the other for small bridges and aqueducts to complete the road. A contract was signed, the work began, and everything, including paper work, was completed during November 1998. The community volunteered its labor.

Nampula

Provincial officials had the same preoccupations as in Zambézia. The chief of the Plan and Budget department noted that between 1993 and 1998 the tendency had been for the provincial investment budget to grow each year. By 1998, it had reached sixteen billion *meticais* (approximately U.S.$1,350,000) but in 1999 it was reduced to twelve billion *meticais* (less than U.S.$1,000,000) because of the recentralization of the planning process in the five sectors mentioned above. This had a significant impact on community planning. Paraphrasing the words of the head of the unit overseeing the decentralized planning exercise: schools, a water point, a health post/center, a principal road, and agricultural project were the first projects that communities requested. However, in light of recentralization, the district planning exercise could not respond directly to these needs; they now had to be negotiated with Maputo through the provincial directorates. He felt that this would have a demoralizing effect on district administrations and on district directors because it appeared to be a return to the past when there was little hope of a response from the center to their proposals. This perception rang true in light of my own personal experience on the provincial planning brigades during the national reconstruction planning exercise. After assessing needs, the discussion on proposals would begin. Inevitably officials would reach into their desks and take out dog-eared yellowed pages of proposals that had been previously submitted, rejected, re-edited and resubmitted. The experience of Mecuburi district was, perhaps, exceptional.

Mecuburi District

Along with the majority of administrators interviewed, the district administrator of Mecuburi worried about the dearth of funds for operating costs in his district. The strategic planning process had not yet been a drain on these resources because the bulk of the costs of the exercise were being borne by the Local Development Fund, financed by the Swiss Development Cooperation, and other external sources. The exercise conducted by the delegate from the Provincial Directorate of Plan and Finances with the district planning team covered all sectors and all needs. Moreover, the Mecuburi team, consisting of the administrator himself as coordinator, the district director of Health as assistant coordinator, the head of planning of Education, the head of accounting of the administration, all the heads of administrative posts, and the head of the secretariat, were able to negotiate relatively successfully with the relevant provincial ministries for additional investment funds for the priorities identified in the planning exercise.

Without a doubt, the presence of this dynamic and convinced administrator was a big factor in the success of Mecuburi, which was one of the first districts in Nampula and in the country to construct its own strategic plan. The process was also aided by a dedicated delegate from the Provincial Directorate of Plan and Finances who broadened the planning exercise to include elements from communities and various embryonic interest groups in Mecuburi.

The third factor was the catalyzing activity of the Swiss Development Cooperation team who together with the delegate, and with the blessing of the administrator, had helped bring together all the different partners in Mecuburi. Even though the planning process had started with a series of PRAs in individual communities, community participation was transformed into a consultative process. As already noted, the SDC team and the delegate inspired a series of meetings that were being decentralized to lower and lower levels from district to administrative post to locality and finally community level to widen and deepen the process of consultation thus aiding the formation of councils at these levels. As of April 1999, two public meetings of people interested in the strategic plan had been held in each of the four administrative posts and two meetings at district level.[4]

There were a number of similarities between the formula conceived and carried out by the administrator of Gùrué and the process slowly taking shape in Mecuburi. The similarities were: first, a dynamic administrator willing to experiment with new methodologies and test them to their limits; second, an administrator who used and encouraged the talented people in his administration such as the rural development agent of the PRR and his district directors, in the case of Gùrué, and the delegate from the Provincial Directorate and several of the district directors in the case of Mecuburi; third, in the case of Mecuburi, the delegate from the Provincial Directorate had no difficulty in advising and orienting the strategic planning exercise because he had a clear idea of what it was all about and was dedicated to seeing it work; the administrator of Gùrué showed this same quality of farsightedness and aggressiveness; fourth, a belief in community participation on the part of both administrators and a commitment to seeing that the results of participatory rural appraisals are concretized; fifth, the coming together of the various non-governmental organizations and other partners in the process of development and their willingness to discuss and participate in the implementation of the planning processes begun, in both districts.

Human factors were extremely important in these two cases, but as Tendler pointed out, leadership is not replicable on demand (1997:222–224). Therefore, in my suggestions for change in the next chapter, I focus on institutional arrangements that do not depend upon a far-sighted leader. In Gùrué, the transfer of the district administrator to another district could prove crucial but, in Nampula, the departure of the SDC team would only slow the process because the institutional framework had changed. The momentum created by the strategic planning exercise as well as the formation of the network of stakeholders and the dedication of the local coordinators should ensure that decentralized planning continued even if at a different pace.

Niassa

The adviser to the provincial director of Plan and Finances noted that the investment budget for the province was somewhat less than U.S.$500,000 in 1999. His principal worry was upgrading provincial-level planning officials to bring them in line with the new planning methodologies, particularly sector planners. This was being done through an extensive training program. As far as the districts were concerned, he personally felt that this would take a much longer time and noted that IBIS was working alongside the directorate to provide training in the Ministry of Plan and Finances guidelines. The IBIS planning adviser was also very conscious of the limitations of district-level personnel, most of whom had never received any training in planning.[5]

As already mentioned, the introduction of District Development Funds in the context of the Niassa Agricultural Development Program in Lichinga and Sanga districts had occasioned the identification of a large number of small projects during the course of its first year of operation. Both district administrators received this component of the program enthusiastically because it gave them the possibility of doing something positive and also visible in their areas. In 1998, both Lichinga and Sanga administrations successfully completed seven projects each. In the following year the Lichinga administration submitted ten projects for execution while the Sanga administration submitted seventeen projects. However, neither district administration had called the district planning teams into action. In Lichinga, moreover, administration staff alone managed the Fund contrary to the Fund's regulations, which specified that the district team leader had to be one of the signatories of the Fund. In Sanga, the team leader was also marginalized. Even more disheartening was the fact that *not one* of the communities, on whose behalf the twenty-seven project proposals were submitted, had been involved in the identification of the projects in question.

The relevance and importance of the projects to the rehabilitation of both districts was not in question. Neither did program staff nor communities complain. The irregularities in the Fund's management were due to its appropriation as an administration fund rather than as a community fund. This situation was avoided in the experiments, sponsored by the United Nations Capital Development Fund in Nampula, IBIS in Milange, and the Irish Embassy in Niassa, by simply dividing the district development funds into two parts, between the district administration and the communities. This lesson prompted one of the recommendations of the next chapter.

Sofala

The view from Sofala was both similar and yet more complex than that of the other provinces. In regard to the district planning teams, trained by the PRR, Sofala was the only province where these were taken seriously, in part because delegates of the Provincial Plan and Finances Directorate were present in the districts. In three of the four districts visited (Dondo, Nhamatanda, Gorongosa, and Buzi) in 1999, the teams were still functioning.

In Gorongosa, a German Technical Cooperation project to help district-level planning absorbed the INDER-trained team and gave it further training to carry out a district survey of resources. In Dondo, the team functioned largely because of the efforts of the Provincial Plan and Finances Delegate with the encouragement of the former administrator, now president of the newly created municipality.

In Buzi, the team benefited from the encouragement of the resident PRR agent and a particularly dynamic administrator and some small assistance from the Austrian Development Cooperation, detailed below.

In Nhamatanda, the story was different. The team had not had the support either of the PRR agent (resident in Gorongosa) or the administrator. It had all but disappeared, three of the four members having been transferred to other districts.

In regard to the functioning of the District Development Fund introduced by the PRR, Sofala's experience was similar to Zambézia's. Disbursement of funds and the opening of bank accounts were delayed by the late transference of funds from Maputo. However, there was a peculiarity in the disbursement in Sofala: funds were transferred for only one project out of the two or three identified in the three districts because of inaccuracies discovered in the budgets of a number of the projects.

Buzi

The evolution of the district development team in Buzi demonstrated the potential of the district team when taken seriously. It showed what encouragement, further training, and a little logistical help could accomplish. The support that the administrator had given to the participatory planning exercise and subsequently to the team was exemplary as was the guidance of the team under the resident rural development agent. The administrator, in his own words, had used the team to: first, monitor the projects identified by communities under the original and subsequent planning exercises; second, do surveys for other projects, such as the World Food Programme and Austrian projects; third, help in the preparation of proposals for the provincial PTIP; fourth, do data collection and information gathering for the District Executive Council; and fifth, begin the survey of district resources that would form part of the strategic planning exercise, taking place under the sponsorship of the Austrian Development Cooperation.

In the late 1990s, the Austrian Development Cooperation (ADC) began to provide a small amount of financial assistance which allowed the administration to transform the team into a Studies and Project Unit (*Gabinete de Estudos e Projectos*).[6] The administration itself provided office space for the team while the ADC provided office equipment in the form of desks and chairs, a telephone, chalkboard, typewriter, office materials, and a small fund for specified research. Beginning in 2000, it was expected that the ADC would provide a computer and photocopying machine, training in computer skills, per diems, and other costs related to the carrying out of the district survey. It would also cover technical assistance costs, if necessary.[7]

The administrator expressed the need for further training to develop the team and suggested a recycling in participatory and other facilitating methodologies, and also in monitoring and evaluation techniques. He also recommended a simple form of transport—motorbikes—to make the team more mobile and less dependent on lifts.

One of the most interesting developments that occurred in the Buzi "model" was the initiative on the part of the team to transfer its training to others in the district administration. On the very afternoon of my visit to Buzi—16 March 1999—two members of the team were about to begin a seminar on planning and data collection for eleven functionaries of all the different ministries represented in the district. The idea was to increase awareness of new methodologies and prepare officials who might, at a later date, be recruited to join the district development team, as its original members were transferred.

Notes

1. The two provinces together had close to ten million dollars allocated for microprojects.

2. A concrete example occurred in Muagiua in 1996. Of the five projects identified by the community and district team, three were financed by the PRR and the Administrator convinced Acção Agrária Alemã and IBIS to finance the other two.

3. The district team leader could not confirm this point. The other team members were not present in the district, which made it difficult to assess which perspective was more valid.

4. After approval by the Provincial Government, Mecuburi's strategic plan would be returned to a meeting of the District Consultative Council for final approval. The district planning team would continue to conduct PRAs in remote and deprived areas as a way of stimulating their interest and as a way of beginning the consultative process in them.

5. Niassa was not only the province where the government sent "undesirables," but it was also the province that had the least educated officials and the least technical assistance.

6. In 1998 ADC sponsored a district adviser; however, this person had not been effective.

7. Instead of a full-time adviser, ADC would cover the costs of short-term assistance, as required.

CHAPTER TEN

~

From Participatory Planning to Empowerment

The changes that took place in the planning context during the 1990s were considerable but also contradictory. "Decentralized" planning was in reality deconcentrated planning. Decision making in the five important sectors of Agriculture, Health, Education, Rural Water, and Roads was once more being centralized. The planning mentality had not yet evolved from blueprints and logical frameworks to open-ended dialogue, negotiation, and vision planning. The building of public infrastructures, although by no means exhausted in all districts or provinces, needed to be complemented by other types of public investment as the priorities of the countryside changed. The demand-based approach to government services, which gained acceptance in the adult education sector and was established in principle in the rural water sector, still needed to be implemented *and* extended to other sectors. Although struggling, the forces for democratic decentralization existed but they needed support.

A number of institutional factors[1] conspired against acceleration of decentralization in the late 1990s, including the uncertainty at the highest political levels over the future status of state local bodies, the general lack of vision of district administrations, the low level of education and training of district-level officials, the continuing tradition of centralization and hierarchy in government, and the discrimination against rural areas. None of these conditions had changed substantially at the time of this writing and the 2002 version of the draft law on state local bodies made it clear that the government was not even willing to create *consultative* councils at local levels. The only channel of communication it opened between itself and rural peoples was a very vaguely defined "consultation" between "community authorities" and lower levels of the administration. This had overtones of the meetings between regedores and colonial administrators known in some areas as *banjas*.

The following suggestions are based on the conviction that multi-sector district planning teams have the potential to become a key instrumentality not simply in the official deconcentrated planning process, where major donors have put their emphasis, but, more importantly, in awakening communities to their planning capacities. In Jules Pretty's words, this involved moving up the scale of participation from consultation to self-mobilization (cited by Gaventa, 1998:157). The district consultative council might have been the shaky first step toward mobilization in Muecate district in Nampula but this was not the same thing as self-mobilization. Moreover, such councils could prove counterproductive to empowerment because they included the administrator and administration officials as well as civil society leaders and "traditional authorities" in the discussion of district development. Depending upon the attitude of administrators, discussions could easily be dominated by them. Why not let civil society leaders discuss district issues by themselves?

The proposals that follow aim at restoring some balance in the institutional distribution of power among these groups. They focus on organizing planning first and foremost at community level and highlight the role lower level district officials and other potentially "organic intellectuals" could play to make this happen. The strategy involved firstly, a *multi-pronged training program* primarily for communities and local officials but also nongovernmental staff and local elites in order to secure them to the cause of generalized rural prosperity and, secondly, *an expanded planning process* including institutionalized Funds as a preparation for decentralized public investment planning in Mozambique.

Moving toward Empowerment

Many of the current rural development programs in Mozambique relied on outside community development agents to accomplish what district cadres including rural extension agents, rural water agents, community agents of the Social Action Ministry, adult education cadres, and community health agents should be doing and could be doing if they had some training and means. The government of Mozambique did not need a special agency for community development, nor outside community development workers, nor UN volunteers, all of which caused extra financial burdens, when it already had a group of officials who could also benefit from working in teams rather than alone.

This argument is similar to Judith Tendler's point that ordinary government officials can be transformed into dynamic change agents by giving them extra responsibilities and training to perform these, multiplying their tasks and affording them limited autonomy to accomplish them. Tendler (1997) showed that the adoption of this approach in Ceará in Brazil gave rise to heightened dedication on the part of functionaries and the establishment of rapport and trust in relations with their clients. A personal touch became one of the keys to better service delivery. Tendler underlined the similarity of this approach to best management practices in the private sector (1997:17ff).

The teams trained by INDER had not, in the main, been put to good use. One major stumbling block was the lack of awareness of their functionality, particularly on the part of district administrators and district directors. There were ways of overcoming this obstacle as shown by both the Irish Embassy and IBIS programs, which trained administrators, district directors, and heads of administrative posts as well as heads of planning at district level. The training was the same to enable everyone to experience the utility of the participatory planning, monitoring, and other methodologies for the routine work of their sector/administration.

Furthermore, the PRR provided almost no follow-up or logistical support to district teams, which had the effect of denying them an independent existence, flexibility, and maneuverability. The provision of basic office equipment, training materials, and transport in the form of two motor bikes could give such teams visibility and stimulate interest in and, one would hope, appreciation of their work. (See Leurs, 1998:127.) The extent to which the Austrian Development Cooperation's logistical support to the Buzi team boosted its credibility and self-confidence has already been noted.

Nor did the PRR fulfill its promise of a second round of training in participatory rural appraisal and other techniques because of a lack of time and money. In order to act as a viable alternative to community development agents and/or a core of decentralized planners, the teams needed retraining as well as training in other areas. *To what end?* This is the important question.

What should be the focus and objective of a district planning team? Most of the emphasis in Mozambique has been on creating a body of "professional" planners at district level reflecting the thinking and practice in the international development community. Considerable attention has focused on the Nampula project, whose emphasis was clear: to produce a five-year strategic plan at district level, and, in the process, train a semi-professional body of planners which consulted regularly if not frequently with rural community and civil society representatives. Given government hesitation to adopt even the consultative council as a form of dialogue with rural communities, the Nampula approach is the most progressive official experiment. Yet it still must be asked whether it is the best approach to decentralization and democratization. That it may be the only sanctioned approach is one thing, that it is the best approach is another. In my view, the Nampula experiment might, at best, lead to "better performance" to use Robert Putnam's criteria. That is, it could lead to demands by community authorities on behalf of their communities for better services and it might lead to some accountability on the part of government officials but, although this would improve the situation of rural communities, it would not lead to empowerment nor a more equal distribution of power.

In a World Bank publication Deepa Narayan (1995) provided a powerful rationale for empowerment and a clear conception of what it requires:

> In many countries, limited government success in managing natural resources, providing basic infrastructure, and ensuring primary social services has led to the search for alternative institutional options. In recent years, a shift has occurred away from supply-driven toward demand-driven approaches, and from central-command-and-control to local management or co-management of resources and services. This shift is intended to increase efficiency, equity, empowerment, and cost effectiveness. . . . One of these options is community-based development. The experience in community-based development is substantial, both about what works and what does not. From this experience it is clear that there is no single model appropriate for all places and times. Supporting community-based development on a large scale requires new institutions, which support:
>
> - Adoption of goals and processes which strengthen the capacity of a community, its networks or groups, to organize and sustain development and its benefits;
> - Reorientation of bureaucracies to support community empowerment and investment in social capital through user participation in decision making including rule formulation; and
> - Achieving a match between what people in a community want and are willing to pay for and manage, and what agencies supply (1995:5).

The INDER experience with participatory planning showed that, for the most part, Mozambican rural communities were not organized internally to discuss and resolve their needs on an open, regular, institutional basis. This did not mean that they did not know their needs or that they lacked a decision-making process. Part 1 gave two examples of community organization around important problems: the questions raised by the people of Ilinga with the district administration when the cadastral agency cadres planted concrete pillars in the middle of community lands instead of consulting elders over community boundaries and those raised by Massoane with the administrator of Matutuíne over the electrified fence erected by the Elephant Coast Company on community lands, also without proper consultation.

Nor does it mean that communities are unable to meet the challenge of open discussion and decision making. As seen, a deeply divided community such as Ilinga was able to mold an "imposed" process to its own requirements. When prompted to debate problems, communities had no difficulty, apart from some initial reluctance to do this in front of strangers. What was lacking was an institutional framework that made open discussion involving men, women and where appropriate children a normal occurrence.

As Ilinga and Massoane showed, community-wide opinion was easily aroused in extreme circumstances, but open discussion needed to be encouraged around more routine everyday problems, such as uncontrolled cutting down of trees or unguided burning during the dry season, or improving water supplies and community health through better hygiene, having first aid kits and basic medicines, organizing around marketing or the supply of basic consumer goods, cleaning and maintaining a sports field, and organizing a football team. There was no lack of awareness of these problems, but a lack of open community debate and resolution. The district consultative councils were not the places for these issues to be addressed; the place was within the communities themselves and the question was how to stimulate this. If only one issue were debated and a common solution agreed—requiring little or no outside help—the process would boost community self-confidence and make it easier for a community to raise and solve more problems.

The approaches being developed by IBIS and the Irish Embassy in Niassa and HELVETAS in Matutuíne had this in mind. They relied on building confidence. The facilitation methodologies developed in Mecuburi by the SDC team and put into practice on a regular basis by the delegate of the Provincial Directorate of Plan and Finances were giving good results. Thus putting aside temporarily the question of producing a district plan, it could be argued that one of the key functions of a multi-sectoral district team was promoting and supporting community and group organization, including user groups, producer groups, consumer groups, brick-making groups, community development committees, and marketing cooperatives.

This role has normally been seen as the function of nongovernmental organizations, particularly the international non-governmental organizations

(INGOs), but not all have had this as their purpose. Tendler provided evidence, from many sources, that international nongovernmental organizations suffer from centralization, top-down approaches, and inflexibility (1997:214–221). This was because "many development NGOs are more accountable to their external donors than to the communities they serve" (Lisa Vene Klasen, cited by Chris Alden, 2001:151). Tendler argued that it is better to put efforts into government reform since governments are capable of even better relations with communities than INGOs. Furthermore, government structures are more likely to endure than INGOs dependent as they are on dwindling foreign assistance.[2]

Implicit in this analysis is the necessity for extended training of an entirely different and broader nature to allow district teams, first of all, to act as a channel of communication for information flowing in both directions; secondly, to orient communities towards problem solving rather than waiting for solutions from the outside; thirdly, to give technical assistance in terms of help in articulating needs and formulating project proposals; and fourthly, to stimulate community self-organization. In other words, in their dialogue with communities district teams should be trained as *facilitators* rather than as simply planners in the professional sense. This had more to do with "good talk" in Michael Bell's analogy for democracy than with good management practices, as Tendler argued.

The role of district teams should be that of Gramsci's "organic intellectual."[3] In his analysis of how to integrate rural southern Italy into the industrializing society of his time, Gramsci highlighted the special significance of what he called "organic intellectuals": instructed and enlightened persons and groups who worked alongside of workers and peasants in articulating and defending their interests, who capacitated and trained them and who helped to open spaces for advancing political struggle. This was not as idealistic as it may seem. Those who doubt that low-level officials are capable of playing this role should consult Diana Hunt's article on participatory planning in eastern Kenya (1999). Hunt found that in Ishiara, an area within Mbeere district, the lowest level of administrators "often act as intermediaries between local people and the administration" (1999:19).

One recommendation, therefore, is for broader, deeper and joint training for both officials and community leaders on the model of the Irish Embassy project in Niassa since the primary objective is not simply *community development* as the result of a strategic plan but *community self-management*, that is, bringing the planning process to the community itself. This is a distinctly different approach from that being tested in Nampula. It involved the district teams in assisting communities with simple planning techniques rather than doing the planning for them. Joint training of local-level cadres and community-selected persons could encourage a heightened sense of trust and confidence between them especially as it led to passing the initiative to communities themselves.

Others who should be included in an extended training program are political leaders such as district administrators and other locally influential people, to make them aware of and, one would hope, supportive of a new approach and thus to create a network of stakeholders, available to give advice and assistance. Since these are the people who would have been incorporated in the consultative councils in a national program of deconcentrated planning and are included in the Nampula experiment, the sooner that they are involved in understanding what an enlarged planning process could mean for themselves and the district the better.

The example is Mecuburi, where there has been active stimulation of civil society organization around a district fund and available technical assistance. The extended training program together with an extended District Development Fund (see below) could serve this purpose. Nevertheless, one does not need to be overly optimistic or idealistic about district realities. Governments do not normally give away power, which explains the backtracking of the Mozambican government. Thus the training program needs to be understood as a preparation for political struggle, that is, as a means for instilling in communities the confidence to demand services, not simply on the basis of what a leader says but as a result of community-wide planning and the knowledge that authority derives from the people themselves. For this reason the training syllabus is all-important.

The content of a training program for rural communities, political leaders, government officials, and nongovernmental organization staff should include: a discussion of the Constitution and particularly people's rights under it; an explanation of the revised Land Law; national development objectives and an exchange of views on the specific meaning of development for the peoples of the area; instruction in the methods used for project selection; in basic project management functions, including the rules and regulations of tendering, budgeting, and so on; tuition in organizational abilities, such as the conduct of meetings, skills for negotiating with different groups of people and communications skills in general; training in basic numerical and accountancy skills and also methods of monitoring and evaluation. (See also Belshaw, 1988:101–102.)

On the basis of the results obtained in Masvingo, Zimbabwe, Training for Transformation techniques could be a focal part of the specific program for community leaders and district teams.[4]

The Importance of Community and District Funds

The dialogue with communities needs to go one step further, in light of the government's move to stimulate tax collection by making régulos tax farmers. As part of the training program, communities should be encouraged to survey and *pool* some internal resources. The former president of INDER suggested using the same mechanism as local tax collection for raising community monies.[5] If each family normally paid ten thousand *meticais* (approximately 80 cents in 1999) per year for national reconstruction, then it could be levied another ten thousand *meticais* for community development.

An alternative proposal would be to retain in the community and in the district a healthy portion of government taxes.[6] I explore this idea only in regard to rural communities as the emphasis here is on community empowerment. I was informed that this would not be possible because the first tax was considered a national sovereignty tax and thus must go to the Treasury. However, this is exactly the point: the struggle for autonomy and self-management is essentially a matter of sovereignty, that is, of defining it on a federal rather than unitary basis. Sharing the national sovereignty tax might be one way of reconciling rural communities to their would-be rulers, particularly at national level. It might even yield more taxes!

A community multi-purpose fund, under the tutelage of a *locally selected* development committee, would thus be available for simple maintenance of infrastructures or seed capital for the construction of an infrastructure, or to buy a stock of medicines or to launch an income-generating activity, a cultural activity, and so on. With the assistance of the district team and as a result of community-wide discussions, a subgroup could produce a diagnostic analysis of common resources and a forward-looking plan for community management and development. This would constitute a new power basis from which to deal with district administrations and the district planners.

The above suggestion finds resonance in Hunt's analysis of the decentralized planning process instituted in Kenya in the 1980s called District Focus for Rural Development. In theory, it was based on a bottom-up consultative exercise beginning at sub-location level (SLDC), from there to location level (LDC) and then to divisional level and finally to district level. Development Committees were set up at each level and were supposed to co-opt local community leaders including representatives of cooperatives, nongovernmental organizations and self-help groups. Proposals were mooted at each level and those approved were passed from one level to another and to result in a five-year plan. There was, however, very little funding put at the disposal of Districts which ended up, just as in the case of Mozambique, having to go cap in hand to the line ministries or to international aid donors.

This was demoralizing. Hunt found that

> among SLDCs and LDCs that perceive only poor chances of success in bidding for the small sums available at District level, committee motivation and performance is likely to be low—unless at these levels members are reoriented towards greater emphasis on self-sufficiency: to identification and implementation of, and resource mobilization for, local development initiatives which are possible without substantial external financial assistance (1999:7).

The experience in Ishiara was somewhat different because of the collaboration between low-level officials and ordinary people and the people on the Sub-Location Development Committee. Once proposals were agreed in the Committee, local people participated with in-kind resources and also with cash donations to implement them. "Committed use of SLDCs as an active discussion forum for planning local development may then depend more heavily on access to a development budget (1999:19)." Hunt suggested the levying of a tax for this purpose.

In order to accomplish all of the above, *time* was required to build the necessary confidence and trust within Mozambican communities. It cannot be expected that many communities would be able to reach all of these goals within three years, the normal time frame of most development projects, or five years, the time frame of the Assembly of the Republic and government. However, if only a few communities were able to establish a fund, organize one or more activities, and produce a simple plan within these time frames, this would provide an example for other communities to follow. The government needed to resist the multiple pressures from donors, particularly the World Bank, and rivaling ministries alike to rush into a *definitive mold* of local government and deconcentrated planning. Perhaps the current hesitation of the government to commit itself to a nationwide program based on the Nampula project will give everyone the chance for second thoughts on how to proceed. It has already led the World Bank to "retreat from a national strategy in which a bank loan is available nationwide to a project in four provinces financing district level investment from a provincial fund," which hopefully means that experimentation will continue and perhaps there may be a space for new models to be tried (Jackson, 2002:20).

Part of the incentives and stimulation for community organization, tax collection and participatory planning would have to be an expanded version of the District Development Funds. A module of the training program should be dedicated to providing information about District Development Funds and the procedures for gaining access to them, one new aspect of which could be a "matching grant."[7] Community proposals would have to demonstrate the availability of internal resources for implementing and supporting a project, the existence of a community group to implement and sustain the proposed activity, and some progress towards the indicated goal. One role of the district planning team might be to assist communities and subgroups in formulating their ideas in order to qualify for this funding.

In regard to the Fund itself, the question of *sustainability* must be squarely addressed. The principal objective of such Funds should be training—of those who direct and manage the finances (including the areas of accounting, launching of bids, management principles, etc.) as well as the communities, groups and cooperatives who request access to the funds (project planning, accounting, management, etc.). As such, the amount of money available should not, in the first instance, exceed the capacities of district officials, groups and communities to implement initial development objectives. Amounts could be expanded as capacities grow. The aim of an extended training program is to upgrade capacities on a continuing basis.

Replenishment of the Fund should also be linked to performance in accounting, management, and fund-raising. As more taxes were raised, districts should have more monies for investment funds. As locally raised taxes replaced donations (from donors) and government transfers, the authority of taxpayers and the régulo as tax collector as well as the independence of districts would grow proportionately. Combined with direct elections of administrative officials, power relations between communities and district governments as well as between rural district governments and the national government would begin to change radically.

In regard to Fund regulations, another recommendation is to have three windows in order to accommodate the various local constituencies. The first window for *community initiatives* should include very flexible project criteria. It is not advisable to include projects that would normally enter into the PTIP or require provincial, national, or even local council approval as this would defeat the primary purpose of the Fund which is to help communities gain self-confidence in their ability to solve problems with little outside help.[8] The value of this window should remain relatively small and there should be an upper limit for funding any one proposal in order to encourage a large number of proposals to be funded and also to encourage maximum rather than minimum contributions from the communities.

The second window is for *operating costs* to supplement tax collections for a short period, so that administrations could dedicate themselves to community investment and not be tempted to divert community funds.

Above all, it is advisable to expand the coverage of District Development Funds to include a window for *district administration investment*. This was similar to the practice of the Funds sponsored by IBIS, the Irish Embassy, SNV and the Swiss Development Cooperation. Such funds acted as a stimulant to district administrations to think about the development of their district.[9] They have also prompted the private sector to organize itself to implement district projects, which benefit not only communities but also themselves. In Mecuburi, it was decided to electrify the district capital and the merchants of the town contributed directly to the project, not only funds but also services. They organized the distribution of electricity, the collection of funds for maintenance, and the management of the simple system. Eligibility criteria would have to be well defined in order to avoid abuse and guarantee that the general welfare is the main objective. These projects would be the obvious objects of district council deliberation.

Dividing the Funds into three parts would also have the secondary effect of preparing the psychological as well as material groundwork for strategic district planning to become more than a paper exercise because districts will have the possibility to take care of some of their immediate needs and communities will begin to organize themselves, and thus be ready to discuss broad developmental goals at locality, administrative post, and district levels. Once immediate concerns are addressed, the planning exercise would be able to focus on truly strategic issues such as increasing the productivity of communities, protecting and enhancing natural resources and transforming resources into income, and improving the quality of life.

In summary, the above suggestions for advancing towards a relatively democratic decentralization process included the reinforcement of communities as a *preparation* for self-management through a multi-faceted training program including communities, multi-sectoral district planning teams, district administrations, and civil society leaders. The second aspect was the introduction of the demand-based approach to the community element of the District Development Fund. Parallel to this was the identification of small-scale interventions solely by the district team in concert with the district council and the provision of operating expenses for all these processes.

Notes

1. In direct reference to Mozambique, Marc Wuyts commented, "semi-autonomous projects compete material resources and skills away from regular state employment without much prospect of such projects becoming self-sustainable in the absence of the continued infusion of foreign aid (cited in Alden, 2001:97)."

2. It should probably be pointed out that Amílcar Cabral's analogy of "class suicide" is also not applicable in describing the relationship between district field

workers and rural communities because it would be stretching a point to define these workers as "petite bourgeoisie." They are more likely to be the sons and daughters of rural cultivators who have acquired a basic education. This is why I prefer the term "organic intellectual."

3. See AGRITEX, 1998. See also Gaventa, 1998.

4. Interview with the President of INDER, 1 April 1999. See also Robert Leurs, 1998.

5. I am here adapting ideas discussed with Custódio dos Mocudos in 1999.

6. The following ideas were developed in conjunction with the PRR Project Manager and the President of INDER (since 2000, Vice Minister of Agriculture and Rural Development). Responsibility for errors in presentation, however, is mine alone.

7. This was not to suggest that District Development Funds would be given in exactly the same measure as community funds. Nevertheless, community funds and other contributions in labor, materials and so on would have to be transparent and also committed.

8. Remote communities with problems of access should be given priority as should the building of access roads. It would be advisable to continue to conduct participatory rural appraisals in areas that have yet to be reached by any development activity.

9. Vicente Paulo explained that in Mecuburi, some district officials looked with suspicion on the participatory planning process and considered all those involved as agents of RENAMO but gradually this resistance disappeared, especially with the introduction of the district fund, FUNIL, which was placed in the hands of the administration.

CHAPTER ELEVEN

~

Land and Power

Much more basic to power relations than planning development projects is control over land. It is the essence of sovereignty, which, over the course of several centuries, was progressively robbed from Mozambican populations. Established communities' claims to land are relatively long-standing ones. In the four communities described in part 1, the dynasties had been established at least in the nineteenth century and were at least in their second generation before the Portuguese attempted to govern them. Bannerman's study of land tenure in Manica province shows that the bases of these claims include guardianship and husbandry of the land:

> Under the rulers of all of these states were sub-rulers, who were essentially land chiefs. In the south of the Province they were called Nhamasangos (literally ruler of the woodland). These sub-rulers allocated land to people whom they ruled and a cultivator who could only be evicted if he misused the land or deserted it held this land. These sub-rulers also gained their legitimacy by their control over rain cults, officiating at rain making ceremonies, which were held in places held to be sacred. Grazing, hunting and fishing rights were communal, though in the case of hunting the sub-rulers—or in the case of valuable commodities such as ivory—the rulers were entitled to portions of the animals killed. Other ruling dynasties were connected with wider territorial cults, which often had ecological overtones, for example in the use or control of fires and the protection of forest. Much of the ruling dynasty's raison d'etre had to do with the control of land as well as the control of cults associated with ancestral land spirits (Bannerman, 1993:9).

Bannerman's findings mirror the account of a Mossurize settlement head's duties given by Seven's sons in chapter 3.

Parker Shipton reminds us that the question of land tenure involves more than simple control over economic resources, that is, persons, places, and things; it also involves identities. Land has an emotive as well as economic significance. The definition of what constitutes territory and life space is, therefore, neither simple nor straightforward.

This chapter again takes up the question of discourse over rural areas. Just as those who defined the regedorias and thus created a political reality that did not necessarily conform to historical realities, those who defined and implemented the Land Law have the power to determine the future status of Mozambican rural communities. "Who gets to control the language, the translations, the mapping, the demarcations? These controls legitimize or delegitimize units of aggregation, kinds of rights or ways of land use or they justify appropriations and expropriations" (Shipton, 1994:348–49). As shall be seen, the control over discourse was an essential part of the ongoing struggle in Mozambique.

Spatial occupation has to do with social organization. All over Africa, Shipton found that "a tendency to cluster in lineage-based settlements, however old the idea may be, seems now to be a quite contemporary adaptation to competition for land" (1994:356). However, the social as well as physical spaces of settlements are not wholly discrete as "people move in and out as borrowers, land clients, or quasi-members" (1994:353). According to Shipton, it was even difficult to define landholding (or tenure) for there were so many diverse forms, many of which were neither communalistic nor individualistic in essence. "Overlapping and interlocking rights in land are part of whatever a people deem their social fabric, whether woven around kinship, bureaucratic hierarchy, age grading, or other principles" (1994:349). The living held the land in trust for the dead and yet to be born.

What is straightforward and apparent is that African land rights differ from property rights as understood in Europe or North America. The specific rights and duties of use, transfer, administration, access, occupation, and reversionary control were not the same. According to Shipton, there were not even pure patrilineal and matrilineal patterns, although male and female sorts of property were sharply discrete in inheritance or devolution.

Colonial Land Policy

Under colonialism, the Portuguese not only deprived Mozambicans of their sovereignty, that is, the right to determine the specificity of rights over land, but also superimposed their own, European, definitions of land tenure. Narana Coissoro (1964) documented the evolution of the colonial land regime. He described three periods.

In the earliest period of contact, the Portuguese acquired land by various means including individuals buying land, the cessation of certain areas by the ruler Monomotapa to the Crown of Portugal, and the concessions of lands by the Crown, including prazo lands and *sesmarias* (a type of land grant). The buying and negotiation of land with Monomotapa had been necessary because the Portuguese could not match his power. Conquest over land chiefs was much easier.

The second period of occupation, according to Coissoro, began after the fall of the Gaza empire in 1895. The defining moments of the second period included:

The *Carta de Lei of 9 May 1901* was the first attempt by the Portuguese to systematize landholding. All land not in private hands was defined as State property. The law established a classification of land types and the rules by which concessions were granted.

The *Regime Provisório para a Concessão de Terrenos do Estado na Província de Moçambique*, 9 July 1909, set forth conditions for state concessions, recognized indigenous lands and classified them and set forth the principle of native reserves.

Decree 3,983, 16 May 1918, institutionalized native reserves distinguishing them from State lands that could be contracted, rented, or sold. It defined the jurisdiction of the central government and that of the governor-general of each province.

The *Colonial Act*, 8 July 1930, forbade the concession of certain State lands and the creation of new Companies or sub-concessions of lands.

Lei 2,001, 16 May 1944, fixed the upper limit of five thousand hectares for each concession; this could be extended to fifteen thousand with permission of the ministry of colonies. Even larger tracts could be rented.

In regard to native land rights, the first two laws of 1901 and 1909 recognized native institutions and gave Mozambicans full property rights after twenty years of uninterrupted production or residence, including the ability to sell their land and buy other lands but such properties were restricted to two hectares per adult. Shortly thereafter, even these rights were suppressed. Mozambicans were subordinated to the governor-general of each province according to the Portuguese Constitution. The second article of Decree 3,983 declared that natives could never have individual property rights.

Under Salazar, the *Estatuto Político, Civil e Criminal dos Indígenas*, 1929, defined a special native property regime and customary rights. The *Estatuto dos Indígenas Portugueses das Províncias da Guiné, Angola e Moçambique*, 1954, placed the reserves within the public domain; within them, natives had the right of occupation, use, habitation, and pasturage. In order to acquire the title of private property, a native had to renounce his/her customary rights and leave the reserves. Natives could buy vacant lands and acquire title after ten years. The reserves could also be divided so long as the parcels were less than one hectare.

Only in 1961 was this last statute revoked and consequently the reserves abolished. As pointed out in chapter 6, the regedorias were then integrated politically under Portuguese administrative laws as autarchies (*autarquias*) but their lands were still defined as under the customary regime and therefore inalienable and not subject to mortgage. Finally, the Land Concession Regulation permitted the transformation of customary lands into private property at the end of ten years if authorized by the governor and the governing council.

Postcolonial Land Administration

After independence, one might have expected that authority over land would have been recognized as belonging to those occupying and working it and that an attempt might have been made to right colonial wrongs by returning property, plantations and the like to the dispossessed. Despite the help of régulos in areas of conflict, FRELIMO chose to ignore their local authority and instead to follow a centralized model of land administration, not dissimilar to that of the Portuguese. In certain areas, it even dispossessed rural dwellers (see below, for one such example). In 1979, all land was nationalized. *Lei 6/79* vested all property rights in the State, which determined land usage. All concessions of land rights were usufruct rights requiring state approval. There was no guaranteed security of tenure for rural communities. Unlike the Portuguese, FRELIMO recognized no formal right of private property for anyone.

The new Mozambican government was not alone in taking the path of centralization. Similar to other militant nationalist movements, it "pursued reform in both civil society and Native Authority, deracializing the former and detribalizing the latter" but such policies "degenerated into a centralized despotism, the other and more unstable variant of the African state" (Mamdani, 1996:300). According to Mamdani, this happened because the political link forged between rural peoples and urban leaders was transformed into a coercive relationship.

Doubt has been cast upon the success of FRELIMO in melding urban and rural interests even during the liberation struggle. A recent book, *Mozambique: The Tortuous Road to Democracy*, tries to lift the veil from the official portrait of FRELIMO as a united movement of urban elites and rural fighters (Cabrita, 2000). It argues that, as a political force, it was split internally between factions vying for leadership, and that even Eduardo Mondlane was unable to control dissent. Factionalism related not only to regional antagonisms (southerners versus northern and central peoples) but also to questions of strategy and financial backing, Nkrumah versus Nyerere, the United States versus the Soviet Union, and so on. The author portrays Mondlane as an intellectual unable to reach out and establish a rapport either with Mozambican students receiving education at the movement's headquarters in Tanzania, or with the rural rank and file fighting the Portuguese on Mozambican soil.

Samora Machel, who replaced Mondlane after the latter's assassination, was said to have depended mainly on coercion to unify the movement. After independence, Machel led the country towards "centralized despotism." He showed no mercy toward local authorities. In the village where he later built his villa, the régulo was subjected to maltreatment after the war for independence. This same régulo had suffered torture and imprisonment from the Portuguese as a FRELIMO collaborator. This was not a unique situation in the 1960s and 1970s.

The alienation of FRELIMO from rural Mozambique is perhaps most clearly seen in the very areas from where not only Samora Machel but also the present leader, Joaquim Chissano, originated. The Chòkwé district of the southern province of Gaza had been a relatively privileged area in comparison with most others. It received considerable Portuguese and FRELIMO investment from the 1950s through the 1990s, but continual expropriation and maladministration of land has also been a major source of discontent and fragmentation of the societies that live there.

The following glimpse of the district's social economy is based on notes derived from conversations with leaders of two distinct communities during two separate visits in 1995:

> The social history of Chòkwé district in the twentieth century has been one of systematic land expropriation. People recalled five major periods during which expropriations took place: Portuguese domination until the 1950s; the irrigation scheme and the *colonato* (settlement scheme); nationalization of the irrigation works under FRELIMO and the communal villages; the bankruptcy of the state enterprise and land distribution; the 1991/1992 redistribution. Thus,

in every generation of families that lived on the irrigation scheme—today called "the Perimeter"—there has been a major upheaval. Displacement was also common outside the Perimeter.

Xilembene

Xilembene, an administrative post of Chòkwé district, covers 589 km.[2] and contains two localities, Xilembene and Chiduachine. The following information covers Xilembene.

Conversations with some of the former "traditional" authorities indicated that during the colonial times the "traditional" area of Xilembene had been divided into eight *regulados* or clan territories, governed by a number of families, most prominent of which were the Khossa, which governed three of the eight territories. Under the colonial administration, a Portuguese administrator of what became known as the *Baixa do Limpopo* (Limpopo Valley) adapted the so-called native structure for purposes of governance as follows: the paramount leader *Hosi* was known by the Portuguese as Régulo; he was aided by a prime minister, known in Changaan as *nduna*. The régulo also consulted a council of elders, known in Changaan, as *ndota* (the ancients being known as *madodas*) on all-important decisions. Below the régulo was the *chefe de terras* (*nganakana*) and below him, the *chefe de povoação* (*muliume*) and directly below him, the *chefe de família* (*munumuzana*). The Portuguese added a number of other ranks.

Some of the main functions of the "traditional" power structure were land distribution, settlement of disputes, seed distribution for planting in times of drought, conducting religious ceremonies, the principal one of which were ceremonies for rain and so on. On top of these tasks, the Portuguese added regulation of the movement of people, regulation of the productivity of people, including the mobilization of labor gangs for work on infrastructures, or on colonial farms, tax collection and so on.

During the last days of the colonial empire, the Portuguese secret service, PIDE, rounded up the régulos of the area and put them in prison in a suburb of Maputo where they underwent a certain amount of torture being accused of collaboration with FRELIMO. It is important to emphasize that after independence these same people were repudiated by FRELIMO as collaborators with the Portuguese and their powers were stripped as new administrators were installed.

During the interview, the former chiefs did not dwell upon the Portuguese expropriations to build the Perimeter but rather excoriated FRELIMO for the land expropriation of 1975 when the government took over almost all of the irrigated land and put it under the state enterprise known as CAIL (Complexo Agro-Industrial do Limpopo). These same people recognized that FRELIMO admitted its error in 1983 and began a process of redistribution of the land but they noted that the first redistributions were minor (on the order of one hectare to all of the workers of CAIL who had been owners of generally larger plots before the expropriation) and they noted that subsequent redistributions were only partially just, that there were injustices committed in regard to distributions to some "private" farmers and in regard to the joint ventures (LOMACO and João Ferreira dos Santos). It was stressed that the latest redistribution of 1992 was done by a local commission headed by the president of the locality aided by a number of local people. One of the interviewees had been picked to represent the "private" sector rather than his chiefly position. He felt that the exclusion of "traditional" authority from the decision making had deprived the commission of knowledge and legitimacy.

Chate

Chate is one of a number of communal villages built in 1977 after a major flood of the Limpopo river. It is situated outside the Perimeter, twelve kilometers from one of the principal canals. Before the construction of the village, the population lived in settlements in a more or less dispersed fashion near the Limpopo. The area chosen for the site of the communal village had been under the direction of Chate Mabundo, a land chief. A majority of the population of Chate was from his area but people from the chieftaincies of Chilengue and Mavalene also joined them. All three communities had formerly lived under the dominion of the Hosi by the name of Eduardo Cuna (an uncle of the defunct President Samora Machel). It should be noted that the people of these three areas had no choice in the matter of resettlement; they were told by the government (led at the time by Machel) to leave their homelands and build this village. It is also important to understand that, by 1977, Srs. Cuna, Mabundo, Chilengue, and Mavalene no longer had official power over the settlement of their peoples. Local authorities appointed by the government had replaced them.

The contemporary displacement from lands did not cease. In the 1980s, two joint ventures between the government and the London company, Lonhro, and between the government and the Portuguese company João Ferreira dos Santos were formed. The venture between the government and Lonhro, known as LOMACO, took over part of the lands belonging to the people of Chilengue without offering compensation to them. The latter venture known by its initials, JFS, made a contract with the people of Chate. In return for the land taken by the company, JFS provided irrigation on seventy-five hectares near the village. The conditions for exploitation of this plot, however, reduced the population to the status of unskilled seasonal laborers. In the eyes of the population the terms of trade were decidedly unfavorable.

The example of Chate showed that land expropriation has been accompanied by robbing people's status, first, as independent self-governing peoples and, secondly, as independent producers.

One of the *root* causes of second-class citizenship and poverty in Mozambique can be traced to enclosures such as the ones described above and in part 1. While the Portuguese were among the first to move people off their lands, the post-independence government followed suit. The two most important policies provoking rural dislocation were the forced movement of peoples into communal villages and the conversion of large areas, usually former colonial plantations, into giant state farms. In the 1980s and 1990s enclosure accompanied the most recent war. The greatest beneficiaries have been government and military officials, private entrepreneurs, and large enterprises. In 1993, a year after the war ended, Gregory Myers found:

> In Chòkwé District, Gaza Province, several hundred families have recently been displaced from their land by "new" private interests and by the expansion of a joint venture enterprise. Many of these family farmers claim to be refugees returning to their "home" lands, others are part of a large population that remains displaced by war, drought and government policy. In the first instance, a "retired" general from the Mozambican army acquired a lease at the Provincial government in Xai-Xai without consultation at the district or local level of government. The families on his land were forced to move—creating another level of displacement. . . . In the second case, the joint venture enterprise LOMACO has either acquired new land, or begun to exploit previously acquired land, in the district that was occupied and farmed by smallholders. . . . In Niassa Province, it has been reported that an individual has acquired the concession to an entire district for mining exploration. . . . These cases are not isolated, and they are not diminishing. . . . The data we have gathered suggests that, at a minimum, rights to nearly 3 million hectares have already been conceded, acquired or reactivated. However, we believe that the actual figure is 2.5 to 3 times larger. And it is important to restate that this represents the best land in the country (Myers, 1993:1-4).

The land grab has not stopped. In 1999, José Negrão wrote about the foreign demand for land in Mozambique: "During the past few years, a significant increase in the demand for land has been observed in Mozambique. . . . the demand for land by capital from South Africa and Zimbabwe quickly led to" requests for many thousands of hectares of land and "a hoarding of land by Mozambicans" who envisaged that they could sell it to foreigners (1999:2). In 2002, Joe Hanlon reported: "the land grab continues. Senior people in government, the military and party obtain land and either bypass the consultation procedures completely, or use the district administrator to force through a token consultation. Often they consider it a right attached to the post, to ensure themselves something for their retirement. District administrators have extensive power and have used it to obtain land for themselves, or to force outside investors to take local partners" (2002:14).

The government *actively* encouraged foreign investment in land. In one of the most highly publicized cases, the government entered an agreement with the South African Chamber for Agricultural Development in Africa to form a joint venture known as the Mosagrius Development Corporation and conceded 550 thousand acres, mainly in Majune and Sanga districts of Niassa. One of the consequences of this concession, namely the demarcation of community lands in Ilinga, has already been noted in chapter 1. President Chissano for Mozambique and President Mandela for South Africa signed the protocol in May 1996. This same protocol also ceded two hundred and fifty thousand hectares surrounding an irrigation system developed with Italian bilateral assistance in the Sabie river area for private exploration.

In May 1998, the government entered into an agreement with the MADAL company and its partner, the Niassa Investment Company, regarding the land management of around 3,900,000 hectares in northern Niassa. Another well-publicized concession, cited in chapter 4, went to the Blanchard Mozambique Enterprise for 236,000 hectares covering practically the entire district of Matutuíne in Maputo province.

On February 24, 2001, *Agence France Presse* reported that "the Mozambican government has granted a concession to a South African firm to promote conservation and tourism in a wetlands and coastal region, including part of the ocean, the company involved said on Sunday. Christine Donaldson, spokeswoman for the Vilanculos Coastal Wildlife Sanctuary development, said the 30,000-hectare sanctuary lay within the southern area of the Bazaruto Archipelago World Heritage Site, in Mozambique's Inhambane province. In what Donaldson described as a world first, the concession extends into the ocean, up to the 20-meter depth line." This was the largest concession of a coastal region made by the government to a private company. Most concessions, however, were for smaller areas and went relatively unnoticed. What made these large concessions problematic, from the government's perspective, was that this type of concession led to relatively little investment.

The Land Tenure Center of the University of Wisconsin kept a record of the *applications* for land concessions, which amounted to additional millions of hectares. One of their publications gave the following data: in Nampula, 1,350 requests for concessions were outstanding amounting to more than four hundred thousand hectares.[1] In Zambézia alone, nearly two million acres, or about 20 percent of the province's land area was under application for concession. In Maputo, the corresponding figure was five hundred thousand hectares. From 1989 to 1998, over 1,300 concessions were sought in Manica province, covering almost two-fifths of the total land mass.[2] These were requests for agricultural use of the land and did not include requests for concessions for cattle raising, tourism, hunting, mining, or forestry. For example, in Bàrué district, concessionary companies involved in the exploitation of game, timber, and mineral resources were working in the northwest and other parts of the district. This was also the case in Gorongosa as in most areas of Mozambique.

Throughout the country numerous concessions were granted to large and small logging companies. Precise and comprehensive data was hard to come by because the various provincial cadastral agencies used differing land categories and did not always maintain their records up to date. Nor were they always forthcoming with information. Moreover, much illegal activity occurred in regard to the granting of concessions and the unauthorized exploitation of natural resources. At the national level, as of 30 July 1997, there were twenty requests for long-term forestry concessions for a total of approximately one million hectares. However, the requests at provincial level were for even greater areas: in Zambézia alone over one million hectares (out of a total of three million hectares of forestland) and almost a million hectares in Cabo Delgado (out of a total of a little over two million hectares) were requested.[3] The provincial applications were for short-term licenses, which meant that investors were not likely to be very interested in investment and the rational exploitation of these resources.

Reform of the Land Law

Concern over the disposition of state farms and the need for a transparent land policy led the Land Tenure Center to propose to the Ministry of Agriculture a series of studies and conferences on land.[4] This was supported by a grant from the United States Agency for International Development (USAID). Later, the United Nations Food and Agriculture Organization (FAO) gave technical assistance in land use planning. The first conference in 1992 included scholars from countries in southern and central Africa that had undergone land reform and gave Mozambicans the chance to make comparisons regarding different policy approaches. The second conference in 1994 opened the question of a reform of the Mozambican land law and included representatives from all levels of government and civil society, from ministers to provincial governors to district directors of Agriculture to farmers themselves. A memorable speech was given by a farmer from Chate who brought into focus the use of child labor in LOMACO fields bordering the village. International donors were also invited to participate. A third conference in 1996 debated the draft proposal of a new Land Law and transmitted participants' comments to the inter-ministerial commission responsible for the final proposal.

There was a concerted attempt on the part of the government to solicit opinions and widespread commentary on the Land Law. Seminars were held within government agencies and at provincial and district levels. This was the first and only policy deliberation open to the public that I witnessed in nine years of living and working in the country and its importance cannot be doubted.

Contrasting positions developed. First of all, there were those who felt that a private property regime and an open land market would best serve agriculture and promote investment in land. They were opposed by those who argued that smallholders and rural communities in general needed to be protected against land speculators and that this was best accomplished by leaving land under state management. The hypocrisy of the latter position was that the state had never done much either to protect smallholders from speculators or to invest in the land occupied by them. In a very perceptive analysis, José Negrão argued that the resulting Land Law was a compromise between those concerned about commercial interests and those worried about secure access to land for rural communities.[5]

In a seminal article on African land tenure policy as a whole, Jean-Philippe Platteau (1996) deconstructed the first of these positions, which he called the evolutionary theory of land rights, and denounced the second stance involving state protection. He demonstrated that commercial interest has generally been a chimera and that state intervention had normally been prejudicial to small landholders. As a third option, he defended the importance of indigenous land institutions.

Platteau's critique was based on the following observations of the history of land policy in Africa: first, the move toward more formal individualized land rights through registration of titles, open land markets and so on often created risks and uncertainty especially for women or poor people who were not able to afford the titling process, as well as ignorant people who had not heard about the process and others. Second, governments had trouble keeping records up-to-date; that is, recording all rights accurately, keeping track of all transactions and so on. Third, the formalization of land rights could negate traditional institutions that provided a certain amount of economic security and helped to hold differentiation in check.

Fourth, titling processes were generally manipulated by elites who were not necessarily entrepreneurial in practice. The motives for land purchases could be mixed: as a step on the political ladder; as a hedge against inflation and so on. Therefore, open markets did not necessarily stimulate land transfers from less to more dynamic agents. It did, however, imply a transfer of wealth to this group and could cause costly conflict. Moreover, new property owners were often a pampered elite requiring subsidies and special treatment. Platteau explained that the data on the relationship between land rights and land improvements and between land rights and improved yields was inconclusive. Finally, land disputes had not diminished in countries where a program of systematic titling of all farmlands was in effect.

In addition to these considerations, Platteau noted that creation of a market for land resulted in a highly constrained market as the experience of Kenya and elsewhere showed. Before a piece of land could be sold, all members of a family had to be consulted and give consent. This was due to the social, ritual, affective, and political meanings attached to land and also enduring kinship and ethnic ties. Local communities also opposed alienation because they appreciated the insurance function of land. Most land sales were desperation acts.

Platteau also referred to the costs related to formalizing individual property rights, which were not simply search, enforcement, and litigation costs but also involved social costs. When alienation of land violated deep-rooted norms, there were many additional costs in terms of sabotage, looting, burning, and theft. There were many types of resistance to strangers who settled in foreign areas, which led to costs of protecting property, labor-shirking, labor supervision costs, and so on.

Finally, Platteau felt that the evolutionary theory overlooked the fact that the state was not a neutral force and it had a policy agenda of its own. It might not, therefore, react in the rational way assumed by the evolutionary model.

Platteau therefore arrived at the following conclusion: if one removed the obligatory titling process from the formulation of the evolutionary theory, then its propositions were tenable since customary rights were changing under the pressure of growing land scarcity towards individualization of tenure rights and the transferability of land. State intervention therefore became unnecessary.

A keen observer of land tenure in Mozambique, Bannerman confirmed that this indeed was the case:

> It has been estimated that 80 percent of the land in Moçambique is cultivated in terms of customary rights, though these rights may vary from one ethnic group to another, they will be fairly similar. It should be pointed out that ideas of the western concept of ownership have often been incorporated to a greater

or lesser degree into customary rights of ownership. Where land is held by customary right, the landowner may on occasion try and get legal title to the land (1993:15).

Platteau's preferred land policy accorded with the recommendations of this study—to allow the maximum amount of flexibility and autonomy to local levels. "What the region requires is a pragmatic and gradualist approach that re-institutionalizes indigenous land tenure, promotes the adaptability of its existing arrangements, avoids a regimented tenure model, and relies as much as possible on informal procedures at local level" (1996:74).[6]

Not surprisingly, the new Land Law reaffirmed centralized state control over land. Article 3 confirmed that the land was "state property and cannot be sold, or in any way mortgaged or pawned." Thus, it rejected outright the evolutionary approach but neither did it "institutionalize indigenous land tenure" as communities were dependent upon the state for land use rights (titles). Some of the more important provisions were as follows: articles 6, 7, and 8 defined the public domain, excluding any and all land use or enjoyment rights, however, article 9 provided for the licensing of certain activities in these areas. Article 13 reconfirmed the public cadastral service, DINAGECA, as the state agency in charge of the titling process and provided for local authorities to submit an opinion on requests for a concession as well as consultation with resident communities on the occupancy status of the land under request. According to article 22 provincial governors were able to authorize land grants up to one thousand hectares, and the minister of Agriculture between one and ten thousand hectares. Requests for land of more than ten thousand hectares had to be authorized by the council of ministers.

While continuing with a centralist model of land administration, article 13 made provision for communities to defend their land rights while article 24 gave them certain responsibilities regarding natural resources. This was the basis of the historical compromise referred to by Negrão. Article 24 also gave rural communities responsibilities in regard to the resolution of internal conflicts. Moreover, it required consultation on applications for concessions on the land that they occupy, and in the delimitation or demarcation of their territories.

The new law recognized smallholders' rights to land through occupation and communities' rights through informal, customary forms of evidence. Moreover, land could be registered in the name of a local community as well as an individual. Article 13 stated that ten consecutive years of land occupation were sufficient for a community or an individual to obtain title.

Nevertheless, as the analysts of the Land Tenure Center pointed out, small-holder security depended above all upon the willingness of government officials to implement the new law and the capacity of individuals and communities to demand their new rights and responsibilities.

Lei no. 19/97 was a framework law and required general as well as some specific legislation to make it operational. For example, in regard to specific pieces of legislation, the Commission on Judicial Matters, Human Rights and Legality (*Comissão dos Assuntos Jurídicos, Direitos Humanos e de Legalidade*) pointed out that the entity identified as "local community" was a new concept to Mozambican jurisprudence and needed definition. A parliamentary majority agreed with this suggestion and therefore affixed an amendment to the government proposal.

Land Tenure Center Concerns

Draft regulations published in July 1998 were the subject of analysis by the Land Tenure Center, which made concrete suggestions aimed at clarifying them. In regard to the concept of the public domain, which gave the state the power to declare land unavailable for exploitation, the Center felt that the different expropriation criteria needed to be spelled out (Kloeck-Jenson et al., 1998:3). It also called for community consultation before land was expropriated. Moreover, the Center called for reexamination of the prohibition of *all* land use rights in all categories of the public domain (1998:5). And it felt that there was need to clarify the question of compensation in regard to expropriation, especially the issue of a "just" compensation in order to make the state hesitate before declaring land under the public domain. It also worried that land destined for tourism would be included in the public domain although this was not mentioned in either the land law or the regulations.

The Land Tenure Center pointed out the need for a clearly specified appeals process in regard to all state decisions regarding titling or expropriation. It suggested a separate chapter on appeals in the regulations. It also recommended precise stipulation of the different land use categories because of the confusion within the cadastral agency on this matter.

In regard to the responsibilities of rural communities, the Land Tenure Center felt that the regulations should detail each area of competency as a guide to the state agencies with whom communities would work on such matters as the titling process, natural resource management, conflict resolution and so on. For example, in the process of consultation on titles, it was not clear whether communities could veto an application for land. The Center also requested clarity and detail on how communities would be represented in each area of competency. For example, in the question of titling, a minimum of three community members would sign its opinion but it remained unclear who these members should be. Without guidelines on the mechanism for selection of these members, the possibility existed for unrepresentative members to be nominated. The perspectives of women members of communities were of particular concern. The Center had its own suggestions as to the mechanism of selection and land management.

The Center also raised questions on whether a community would be required to delimit or demarcate its land in order to establish its claim to its territory. Demarcation, a longer more expensive but more accurate process in determining boundaries, was required for individual titles, but the simpler process of delimitation was being bruited for community registration of their lands. However the draft regulations offered no clarity on these matters.

The Center also brought forward the issue of how the state would interpret the criteria of customary norms and practices in regard to defining community lands. The Center itself felt that a strict interpretation associated exclusively with "traditional" authorities would be too confining and that adaptations across time should be considered. It was also necessary to specify which agency would take the decision on whether land was occupied on the basis of customary norms or whether the norms were constitutional.

In regard to conflict resolution, the Center demonstrated the need to make clearer the criteria of "occupation" versus temporal precedence of acquired rights. Finally, the question of how pending requests for concessions would be handled was a matter of great concern to the Center, which argued that they should be subject to the new land law, in particular, the consultation process with local communities.

The final regulations approved by the Assembly of the Republic in December 1998 showed that the arguments of the Land Center had made a certain impact. The question of pending concessions was resolved and requests for concessions were made subject to the requirements of the titling process. The question of the criteria for declaring areas in the public domain was to be dealt with in a separate regulation. Presumably, this would also include a decision on the question of whether communities would be included in these decisions and, perhaps, clarify the question of compensation.

There was no separate chapter on an appeals process, probably the most serious omission in the regulations, nor was there a clarification of land use categories. Moreover, the question of more clarity on the principles of conflict resolution does not appear to have been resolved. Finally, no more detail was offered on community responsibilities. However, the regulations referred to the necessity of editing a Technical Annex to detail the methodology of registering and titling of community and individual lands.[7]

The Technical Annex, in effect since March 2000, distinguished between delimitation and demarcation and defined a delimitation process that communities could use to register their lands with the national cadastral agency.[8] On the subject of community representation, Artur and Virtanen noted that the Draft Technical Annex supported de facto recognition of customary authorities provided that they had the support of the local population (1999:4). They also noted that there was support from the Campanha Terra (see below) for an alternative, which was a land council at district and/or administrative post level. "This would be composed of representatives from the main local interest groups, and thus it would facilitate the participation and articulation of views of a larger cross-section of the population than a chief or headman alone—or even a council of elders" (1999:4). I comment on these proposals below.

Implementation of the New Land Law

The concern of the Land Tenure Center over how the Land Law would be interpreted at local levels was entirely justified. The worry that the processes of community consultation and titling might not be taken seriously, either by communities themselves because of internal conflict or by state officials at local levels because of neglect, corruption or simply the lack of ability to reach communities with the necessary information or by investors for lack of interest, was not simply academic. In one of the last documents he wrote, Scott Kloeck-Jenson (1998) addressed these issues. His suggestion was for a set of procedures for community consultation in regard to the titling of its own land and in response to requests for a portion of their land. Kloeck-Jenson was particularly concerned that communities be given ample notification and time to select their representatives, to discuss issues internally, and to negotiate them with district officials and outside investors. He felt that a series of public community meetings were necessary to accomplish these purposes and he stressed the importance of written documentation not only of the proceedings of these meetings but also the decisions taken.

Kloeck-Jenson (1999) alluded to the need for the cadastral agency to have guidelines. He stressed the importance of uniform procedures as a regulatory mechanism on the actions of the provincial level officials of this agency. For example, he says: "The primary problem that could emerge with the issue of representation is that the selection process may not be sufficiently transparent. It has been reported in some provinces that SPGC [the provincial cadastral service] and/or district administration personnel have been 'consulting' local communities simply by finding three to nine community members to affix their signatures to an *edital* [official notice or order] document. Such a procedure provides no guarantee that these individuals understand what they are signing or that other community members view these individuals as legitimate representatives of their interests" (1998:3). And "the depositing of documents with the community will help to prevent an unscrupulous state official from submitting a false document" (1998:4). Such precautions were not out of line with local realities.

My own personal experience in 1997 with national and provincial officers of the cadastral agency (DINAGECA) confirmed the need for regularized procedures and monitoring of them. In anticipation of the new Land Law, the Cadastral Agency made efforts to prepare itself for its new role of helping communities register their land. In a pilot activity, the agency attempted to delimit lands in the Vilankulos area of Inhambane province and admitted to having difficulty communicating with local villagers.

My INDER colleague and I were invited to help train provincial cadres of this service in participatory methodologies that would facilitate their dialogue with communities. It was decided that the second trial run of the delimitation process would use participatory methodologies and that the training would take place in the district of Alto-Molocué in the north of Zambézia province. Officials from several provinces were joined together.

It became immediately obvious why the cadastral personnel had difficulty speaking with local peoples. First of all, the reputation of the agency was very dubious. The then head of the Surveying and Cadastral Department of DINAGECA, who formally opened the various meetings with district administration personnel and community representatives, openly acknowledged that there had been dishonesty in land deals and promised a new beginning, which the pilot activity of delimitation was supposed to demonstrate. It was difficult to know whether his audience believed him. If the audience did indeed have doubts, subsequent experience proved them right. Hanlon reported corruption in the provincial delegations of DINAGECA in 2002 and cited no less than the head of the Technical Secretariat of the Inter-Ministerial Commission to Revise the Land Law as having complained of "the lack of transparency in the cadastral services" (2002:15).

In a subsequent meeting with the community chosen for the pilot exercise, open distrust of the motivations behind the delimitation was expressed and the more influential members of the community vetoed the proposition. The régulo who had already agreed to it, felt compelled to follow the community's will. The process of selecting a community for delimitation began all over again.

A second reason for concern over the sincerity of the cadastral personnel was the attitude the majority of provincial officers showed toward the training exercise. Most of them were more interested in learning how to operate small Global Positioning System handsets (GPSs) than they were in participating in the community consultation. While all were obliged to attend the training sessions on participatory methodology, only two of the seven provincial and national officials volunteered to work with the community in the delimitation exercise.

The third reason to doubt the seriousness of the personnel was occasioned by the manner in which the national officers chose to carry out the actual exercise of delimitation. During the first meeting of the whole community, long discussions between community elders including a man identified as the régulo produced a sketch map of the territory. Much to their chagrin, DINAGECA officials discovered that the area was larger than expected and would take longer to survey with the GPSs than had been originally programmed. Consequently, the head of the Surveying and Cadastral Department took the decision to ignore the elders in favor of working with FRELIMO party officials, that is, the local administrators of the area in the exercise of confirming the boundaries of the map that had been drawn. When it was discovered that the area was indeed large and that the party officials did not have the necessary information to confirm some of the boundaries, this same official took the arbitrary decision to delimit a part of the territory. The part that was delimited conformed to one of the electoral constituencies that had been drawn for the 1994 presidential elections! These political boundaries were hardly representative of the territory or life space of that community.

A fourth reason to wonder about the good faith of the DINAGECA personnel had to do with the delimitation of Mosagrius lands in Niassa which occurred at the same time as the Alto-Molocué exercise and was supervised by the same national director of the Surveying and Cadastral Department.[9] In that exercise, there was no consultation either with the district administration in Sanga or with the community of Ilinga, as already reported in chapter 1. This was not out of ignorance because the Land Law had already passed the Assembly of the Republic and because INDER had paid for this exercise.

INDER had asked that the participatory training exercise be combined with the delimitation in Niassa but the national director had diverted the training team to Alto-Molocué. In terms of documentation, the record of the Niassa delimitation was very poorly reported whereas there was a full account of the procedures and techniques used in Alto-Molocué as well as a full explanation of the results and an accompanying socio-economic study of the community delimited (República, 1997). This happened, however, under the guidance of the INDER technicians.

Therefore, while appreciating the need for procedures, guidelines, and participatory methodologies [10] my own experience pointed to the importance of communities being able to defend themselves against malpractice. While the first community we met in Alto-Molocué was able to say "No" to delimitation, a more productive position would have been for the community leaders to negotiate the terms of the exercise and to supervise it every step of the way. However, this required that communities know their rights and responsibilities and have faith in the government agency promoting these rights. Kloeck-Jenson's recommendations were a preliminary step in that direction. An alternative strategy would be to train communities to do their own delimitations.

Campanha Terra

Isolated initiatives by nongovernmental organizations, such as HELVETAS in Matutuíne, ORAM, CONCERN, and ANDA in Manica and other provinces, the SDC team in Mecuburi, and the Irish Embassy in Muembe, attempted to strengthen the capacity of individual rural communities. In 1998, the *Campanha Terra* (Land Campaign) was launched, not by the government but by a concerted effort of civil society organizations. Headed by José Negrão, professor at the Universidade Eduardo Mondlane and rural historian,[11] it incorporated over two hundred nongovernmental organizations in a movement to publicize the new Land Law in every district in the country. In the first year alone, nearly U.S.$200,000 was raised, mainly from the Swiss Development Cooperation and the Danish aid agency, DANIDA. With this money, the National Committee, which consisted of Negrão as national coordinator and an executive secretary, contracted a team of specialists to produce a manual on the content of the Land Law and six booklets on main issues in order to harmonize the messages in the publicity campaign.[12]

A theater group helped produce radio plays based on the six booklets in Portuguese and a variety of local languages. A national seminar was organized and then seminars were held in the ten provinces by July 1998. At the provincial level, provincial committees brought the information to district and community levels. It is important to underline that the Land Campaign used lower level state functionaries and personnel of the nongovernmental organizations to facilitate the dissemination of information and discussion at village level,[13] the strategy recommended in chapter 10.[14] According to one of the participants in the campaign, the organizations involved in Campanha Terra understood that they and other institutions would not be able to defend smallholders' rights, that only smallholders themselves could do this. Defense of community rights and responsibilities thus required community organization and a relatively open decision-making process, as argued in the last chapter in regard to issues of investment and development. These community mechanisms need not be separate since the question of land management was intimately tied to that of investment and rural development, a point also made by Negrão (1999).

Negrão outlined an optimistic and radical vision of natural resource management, which involved the sharing of land between commercial interests and communities in what he saw as an interactive partnership. In his own words:

> The application of the interactive model of community/private sector partnerships within the same overall land areas is directly related to the adoption of a new rural development paradigm, which implies an increase in the rural families economic returns as a result of private sector investments in land, with the security of land tenure to both rural households and private investors. . . . The adoption of this paradigm has implications for the land tenure system because such an approach incorporates both the family and the private sector. The tenure system should lead to their closer integration and the transformation of the rural families into business enterprises or, at least, promote the productive interaction of the two sectors within the same geographical area. It should be an interactive model of land use in the same physical area. Only the adoption of an interactive model will allow for growth in household savings and investment, combining household food production with the creation of additional cash income sources that are less time consuming and provide higher returns. . . . However, the application of the interactive model of land use in the same physical area depends on the creation of forms of partnership between the two parties, which allow for investment in production, the sharing of the returns and the maintaining of part of them for the community. Private sector profits could, for instance, be reinvested in local credit targeted at increasing and diversifying smallholder production. Such an approach requires a tenure system, which permits interaction between family and commercial sectors and promotes both private and public investment in lands within the same physical areas. The development of these partnerships would not be possible in a tenure system based on a dualistic segregation of commercial and communal sectors. The rights and responsibilities created by the new land law in Mozambique provide the opportunity for testing this model, given a genuine political interest and available finances in developing suitable institutional arrangements to implement the law (1999:13).

Negrão's elaboration of a new basis for rural development did not mean that he ignored political economic realities whereby the State and the individuals associated with it, including functionaries, generals, speculators of different kinds profited from land concessions, in the manner of "proprietorial office holding." He noted that such "deals" were done without consulting the people on the land and without even taking their interests into account. In his model, communities replaced the State in negotiations with commercial interests but, before this could happen, the capacities of communities to undertake such negotiations had to be reinforced, hence the Land Campaign. "For transformation to take place it is necessary that the producers increasingly assume decision making roles, which implies a change in the role of the State from simply defining partnerships to promoting and introducing incentives for community/private sector partnerships. This is one of the motivators of participation on the free market and in just competition. The civil society organizations should also assume their role as facilitator of the growth and consolidation of local institutions" (Negrão, 1999:11).

In his argument, Negrão did not confront the question of how to modify the behavior of the State and those benefiting from the present situation. Nor did he tackle the problem of how communities were to counterbalance the power of the State or the economic power of speculators and investors or how to counteract an alliance between these interests. These were important issues and could not be resolved simply by framework legislation. In the final analysis, everything depended upon implementation that, in turn, meant appealing not simply to the good will but also the interests of all parties involved. Perhaps, Negrão, as Platteau, hoped that potential investors as well as the State would learn from others' experience regarding the efficiency costs of *not* bringing local peoples into the investment process. As seen above, the costs related to titling were not simply search, enforcement and litigation costs but could also involve social costs. When land alienation violated deep-rooted norms there were many additional costs such as protecting property from sabotage, looting, burning and theft as well as resistance of all kinds such as labor-shirking which brought labor supervision costs and so on. In other words, partnerships between commercial interests and communities might be more profitable in the long run, if not in the short-term. The fall of the Blanchard Mozambique Enterprise was a case in point.

The question is how to incorporate communities into the investment process without violating deep-seated customs. Whether one liked it or not, this means confronting the issue of the role and authority of so-called traditional authorities. The most sensible thing to do was not only to recognize customary authorities, *when legitimized by their populations*, as suggested in the

Technical Annex, but *also* to institute a land management council at district and/or lower levels, as each had a part to play in managing natural resources or resolving disputes at administrative post and/or district level.

The experience of Serra-Chôa in Bàrué was instructive:

> The customary authorities in Mozambique have turned out to be a relatively efficient, and in many remote areas the only existing local institution to deal with conflicts over natural resources. This is true despite the post-independence Frelimo policy to demolish these institutions and to create an alternative form of "popular justice." Especially peasant-peasant type of conflicts are handled almost exclusively by these authorities in many rural areas, even though the recent civil war and related population movements have weakened the basis of this authority to some extent. With respect to peasant *vs.* commercial farmer type of conflicts the customary authorities seems to be less effective on their own, even though their participation in collaboration with state authorities is still crucial. In conflicts between commercial farmers or those and the state, customary institutions have only a marginal role if any (Artur and Virtanen, 1999:7, 8).

Artur and Virtanen then go on to recommend:

> Our study also shows that locally based customary institutions are quite flexible, and there are some signs that they are presently finding new ways to adapt to the changing socio-political situation. There is also some proof that some accountability mechanisms like the right of the population to dismiss an unpopular or incompetent office holder are still functioning. However, while the role of customary authorities in the prevention and management of local level resource conflicts should be recognised by state authorities, we do not recommend a restoration of the colonial regedoria system. The historical developments have been quite dissimilar in different parts of the country, and consequently also the local legitimacy of these institutions at present varies from place to place. Customary authorities can also have a role in modern local institutions like management councils, which should not become the privilege of locally unrepresentative state and party officials. All those supposed to represent the local interests must be subject to explicit approval of the intended beneficiaries, that is the local population (1999:8).

This approach, combining "traditional" authority *wherever appropriate* with representation of a broad spectrum of civil society interests in land management councils, could go some way to bridge the gap between rural and urban interests at local levels in Mozambique. As argued throughout this book, everything depended upon who controls the selection process. If the rural population were allowed to select its representation in its own way, such councils would open the way for *deliberative* councils and local autonomy at district level equal to that of the existing municipalities.

On a wider scale, the conferences, seminars, meetings, and Campanhas at national, provincial, and district levels were a mere beginning but could provide that all-important first step towards creating a broad-based civic community bridging the rural-urban gap. A possible second step was the proposal to transform the existing Technical Secretariat into a Network on Land and Natural Resources (*Rede de Terras e Recursos Naturais*).[15]

Notes

1. See Scott Kloeck-Jenson, 22 December 1998, and also Scott Kloeck-Jenson, John Bruce, and Susanna Lastarria-Cornhiel, September 1998 (known hereafter as Kloeck-Jenson et al.). Joe Hanlon recorded that "By the end of 2001, of the live applications [for land use titles], 4336 were approved, 225 rejected and 322 remained. . . . (2002:9).

2. Eliseu et al., 1998:34–44.

3. The data is from Scott Kloeck-Jenson, 22 December 1998.

4. This was the Land Tenure Center Project-Mozambique which became intimately involved with the drafting of the new Land Law and Draft Regulations as well as establishing a training program for students and researchers on land questions, setting up and supporting the *Núcleo de Estudos sobre a Terra e Desenvolvimento* (NET or Nucleus of Studies on Land and Development) at the Universidade Eduardo Mondlane, Maputo, advising and consulting on land issues, and maintaining a specialized library and information center. The staff led first by Gregory Myers and later his student, Scott Kloeck-Jenson, included Julieta Eliseu, Paulo Ferro and others were among the most informed persons in Mozambique on land issues. Others include José Negrão who led the NET. Scott Kloeck-Jenson merits special notice not only for his scholarliness and dedication but also for his willingness to discuss and share his information. From the footnotes to this chapter, one will be able to appreciate my debt to him and to Gregory Myers. Tragically, Kloeck-Jenson and his family died in a motor accident in June 1999.

5. José Negrão detected a number of intermediate positions as well: that "the management of land has to be implemented at the local level and thus a national policy does not make sense"; that "title deeds should immediately be issued to everybody"; that "communities are the landowners and can negotiate land ownership with the investors"; that "land in the family sector should be demarcated in order to protect it"; that "land should be privatized but private hoarding and speculation controlled" (1999:3).

6. I have summarized at length Platteau's arguments in order to demonstrate that he does not advocate demarcation of community lands as a mainstay of an African

land tenure system. One of the main commentators on land tenure in Mozambique, José Negrão incorrectly identified Platteau with this position. Negrão argued that while demarcation can both guarantee access and promote community development, it can also mean a confinement of rural communities to reserves reinforcing what he calls structural dualism and I have identified as apartheid and second-class citizenship. A policy of widespread demarcation might also foster land conflict where none existed in the present open boundaries. Moreover demarcation was an expensive process and the same purpose could be served by delimitation which local communities themselves could, with training, initiate and carry through. However the same arguments applied to delimitation as well as demarcation. INDER colleagues felt that delimitation should only be encouraged in areas where there were substantial land competition and potential conflict and thus was used as a process to negotiate boundaries. As shall be seen in the text, Negrão was not in favor of strict demarcation even in this case as he felt that communities as well as communities and commercial interests should share natural resources.

7. This was in draft form by June 1999.

8. FAO consultant, Chris Tanner, defined the participatory diagnosis methodology as allowing "communities to define themselves" (2002:24). Paul Anderson described it in these terms: "the delimitation procedures include at least a minimal form of territorial mapping called an *esboço* (sketch-map), defined in the Decrees and Regulations (1999) as 'a drawing, at a conventional scale, of the configuration of the piece of land, containing drawn or written references sufficient (*tendentes a*) to locate it on the Cadastral Atlas, including, when necessary, the geo-referencing of points and/or boundary lines not visible on existing [l:50,000-scale] topographic maps.' The sketch-map is not required to have a known projection, standard cartographic symbols, ground surveying, nor geo-referencing for metes and bounds descriptions of features such as road junctions and stream courses that are on topographic maps. The sketch-map and a required descriptive narrative (*memória descritiva*), plus other documents signed by community leaders, are considered to be sufficient to comply with the delimitation requirements. To obtain an adequate 'sketch-map,' any combination of mapping techniques can be used" (Anderson, 2000). In the same paper, Anderson proposed still another methodology for delimitation, which he tested in a peri-urban area near Maputo in 1999 and 2000. It was mainly a technical exercise rather than a planning or grass roots organizing one. Tanner's enthusiasm for participatory diagnosis is wisely tempered with an assessment of the political difficulties of getting it implemented.

9. In 2002 the same director was on record favoring large-scale foreign investment in agriculture over smallholder development (Hanlon, 2002:2, 34).

10. Here it may be appropriate to add that I compiled a rudimentary manual for INDER and DINAGECA, *O Guião para o Reconhecimento de uma Comunidade Rural Moçambicana*, INDER, October 1997.

11. Professor Negrão is one of the most prominent authorities on the question of rural societies and their development in Mozambique.

12. The six areas around which the booklets were developed were land rights, demarcation of land, women and land, partnerships on the land, urban land rights, and conflict resolution.

13. The specific target group for the *Manual to Better Understanding of the New Land Law* "were the literate population at the district level: professionals, civil servants and workers from the organisations which joined the Land Campaign. It will be the task of the latter groups to take the Land Campaign to the village level, where they will act as facilitators of the individual and collective understanding of the messages. . . . The role of the campaign 'activist' was defined as one of facilitator of group dynamics and as a vehicle for the return of information to the communities" (Negrão, 1999:16, 17).

14. From Mozambique, a number of suggestions have been proposed to follow up this Land Campaign strategy. They also echoed the strategy recommended in chapter 10. Among these was the creation of District Delimitation Funds to enable communities to pay the costs of delimitation and the training of "facilitators, extensionists and para-legals" to increase the "level of organization of communities" (cited in Hanlon, 2002:33).

15. Hanlon's excellent summary (2002) of the recent land debate gives details on all of these proposals.

Epilogue

The peasant question in Italy is historically determined, it is not a generalized peasant and agrarian question.

—Gramsci, 1987:139.

The end of World War II along with the movements to end colonialism and worldwide oppression prompted governments (and international agencies) to endorse a variety of rural policies that were supposed to soften the worst effects of capitalism, keep producers on the land, and prevent rebellion. De Janvry (1981) records the numerous reforms undertaken in Latin America: in the 1940s, the strategy was *community development* while, in the 1950s, policies focused on technology transfer through *rural extension*. In the 1960s some land reform was attempted but more attention was given to *Green Revolution technologies*. In the 1970s, governments gave lip service to *integrated rural development* while, in the late 1970s and early 1980s, they espoused the doctrine of *basic needs*. None of these policies worked to the benefit of the majority of small producers. Throughout the period, national and transnational agribusiness penetrated Latin American agriculture causing widespread dislocation and new tenure relationships. Thus, in the 1990s, reformist policies centered on *micro-credits* for those forced off the land into the urban "informal economy." Micro-credits were also made available to a privileged few in rural areas seeking to diversify their livelihood or looking for alternative employment.

Portugal, too, invested in *community development* and *rural extension* for Mozambican producers, particularly in commercial crop-growing areas. Examples included both the unsuccessful cotton experience of Unango and the successes of Gorongosa and even Mossurize as well as the settlement schemes for rice growing promoted in Matutuíne and Chòkwé. However, the more progressive of these Portuguese policies were a matter of too little, too late. The least progressive—the aldeamentos—were devastating; they paved the way for the newly independent Mozambican government's policy of throwing caution along with reform to the wind as it hurried the disappearance of what was and is still called "the family sector" through the establishment of communal villages, cooperative production, and giant state farms. When these experiments failed, the Mozambican government succumbed to international donor pressures to invest in resettlement and reconstruction via *integrated rural development* projects in Niassa, Zambézia, Sofala, and other provinces and in *Green Revolution technologies* in Niassa, Nampula, and Manica and other areas. The move towards *micro-credits* cannot substitute for a rural credit policy as part of a coherent rural development strategy.

Nevertheless, despite hundreds of millions of donor dollars poured into it since 1987, the Ministry of Agriculture and Rural Development still has no rural development strategy. Chris Tanner (2002) added his criticism of the persistent dualistic mentality in the higher echelons of decision making: despite, or perhaps, because of the recognition of community land use rights in the new Land Law, government officials are publishing a National Land Management Policy that could preempt local land policymaking. They are also preparing a National Land Use Plan under which areas for investment purposes are pre-selected rather than negotiated with communities (Tanner, 2002:51). The Minister of Agriculture and Rural Development openly favors a "big project" approach; that is, foreign capital investment on an industrial scale, the revival of medium-to-large plantations and out grower schemes for smallholders, a position he maintained in spite of the recent collapse of some ventures. Among the cotton concessionary companies, LOMACO is reported to have failed while João Ferreira dos Santos (JFS) was reported to be in financial crisis.[1]

Within the Ministry, there were divergent positions, one of which urged state intervention in favor of the more entrepreneurial smallholders, a kind of model farmer approach. This would entail state subsidized credit as well as other inputs to this group since private banking tended not to lend to rural areas. The tobacco growers in Ilinga, Kanda's prolific male and female maize-growers, and the cattlemen and women of Chaiva showed that potential entrepreneurs did exist in rural communities. The National Peasants Union

(UNAC), however, is said to argue for a less differentiated, smallholder approach.

While these elites engaged in debate, most people worked the land in the absence of significant productive investments favoring *their* development. As the stories of Unango, Mossurize, and Matutuíne show, smallholders largely fend for themselves, which often means crossing borders in order to obtain necessary consumer items as well as capital goods. The Cereals Institute no longer guarantees prices and was so starved of credit that it hardly functioned during the late 1990s. Private rural traders also suffered from the credit crunch. The lack of stable marketing outlets within the country has generally discouraged producers from expanding production beyond what donors and the government term "subsistence." Nevertheless, people do not see themselves as subsistence producers. All who can, market what they can as part 1 has shown. The increasing amounts of crops brought to market since the late 1990s is ample proof of this situation. The general state of low accumulation is therefore not because smallholders conform to some Chayanovian conception of peasantry or live in a "natural" or "moral community"; it has mainly to do with the lack of credit and productive investments in their vicinity, such as access roads, marketing outlets, rural industry, such as in packing and processing, and yes, even plantations.

If the majority of Mozambican producers do not fall neatly either into the categories of subsistence farmers or small commodity producers for lack of secure market opportunities, those who have left the land for work elsewhere likewise resist the category of proletarians. DeVletter found that even the most proletarianized—those in South African mines for ten years or more— are not about to give up their land and their relation to it.

> To almost every miner, Mozambique is and will continue to be home. The overriding reason is that their *machamba* [field] is there. Sometimes little more than a rural piece of ground from which the vast majority of Mozambicans eke out their subsistence, the *machamba* represents something more fundamental than a source of food. It is the traditional right of every male or female Mozambican . . . to acquire land. Access to land is the common thread between rich and poor. More than anything else it brings some psychological sense of equality, nationhood or ethnic commonality (DeVletter, 1998:28, 29).

Yet, however attached to their land, it is important to understand that rural Mozambicans do not, in principle, oppose outside investment and would happily co-exist with investors, so long as these respect customary procedures governing the land[2] and bring employment that would help young people integrate in the countryside. Referring to people's expectations of the activities of the Elephant Coast Company, a report of HELVETAS' work in Matutuíne stressed: "The population awaits the start-up of activities in order to obtain jobs (expectations) and to improve their living standards" (1999:11). HELVETAS and the Swiss Development Cooperation in Mecuburi were among the few agencies in Mozambique dedicated not only to helping communities understand their rights under the Land Law but also preparing them to deal with potential land conflicts and with investors. That rural communities are open to negotiation, if this is done with respect and on a more or less level playing field, was one of the many insights gained from four years of participatory planning.

In our interviews, summarized in chapter 5, people often mentioned "employment" or "industry" as one of the needs of their community. The current disillusionment with independence and nostalgia for colonial times among rural peoples can be explained in terms of the closure of numerous employment opportunities[3] and, most importantly, the breakdown of the marketing system. The government's failure to facilitate the flourishing of small to medium-sized traders—and not peoples' attitude towards markets—contributes directly to the current state of rural poverty. In terms of the commoditization of productive forces and proletarianization, O'Laughlin is right: "Though wage labour is neither inevitable nor irreversible, the historical processes of commoditisation that have turned labour into a potentially salable commodity and hence underlie the development of wage-labour relations, proletarianisation in its broader sense, *are* irreversible" (2000:31). Rural peoples have accepted this fact; what they resent is the lack of opportunities to participate in these processes on their own terms.

People who ignore history are condemned to repeat its mistakes. The Mozambican political economy has again opened to "western" forces and capital and has been rewarded by being considered a "showcase" nation, an advertisement for the so-called Washington Consensus.[4] Alongside generous flows of loan and grant money, there has been an outpouring of international investment in hydroelectric schemes, irrigation projects, heavy industry, energy development, mining, and land. In a manner reminiscent of the 1890s, large concessions have once again been granted to agribusiness, for tourism and settlement schemes, for timber and mining purposes, for South African and now Zimbabwean farmers, but this only signified losing once again control of the destiny of the economy to outside forces and, more importantly will only create more rather than less poverty. As one Mozambican expressed it: "Who will resolve the problems of this country—foreign investors or the people who are here? Big investors are not the answer. We have to analyse our own history. The reality of the past ten years is that foreign investment is not protecting and creating jobs. But how do we create small investors when there is no access to banks and credit, to cheap inputs and water, to roads, etc.? Peasants don't produce because there is no market" (quoted in Hanlon, 2002:7).

Some forms of capital investment posed the threat of marginalizing some Mozambicans on their own land. The examples given in chapters 1 and 4 of Mosagrius and the Elephant Coast Company have not materialized but those mentioned in chapter 11 might. It is still too early to predict the impact of the Zimbabwean farmers wanting to establish themselves in Manica province. In 2001, a second group of sixty-three farmers requested no less than four hundred thousand hectares in concession. Anticipating situations of land conflict, the government said it would limit the amount of land it will grant.[5] The Agriculture minister promised that no Mozambican's land would be taken from him or her. However, it is well known that there is no land that does not belong to someone in Manica.

Physical displacement may, however, not prove as threatening to the majority of Mozambicans as other forms of exclusion. Marginalization in today's globalized political economy takes the form of economic exclusion: cheap food is imported from foreign rather than domestic sources in the areas undergoing industrialization. Thus, as Armando Bartra reminds us, globalization robs some small producers even of their statute of exploitation. "In the system of big capital, the worker who does not generate profit has no destiny or reason to be" (Bartra, 2000:1).

In the current rebirth of the old colonial sugar and tea plantations, new technologies mean fewer workers hired than in the past. In still other areas such as Kanda in 1996, petty commodity producers struggled to find buyers for their produce and, when they did, faced the humiliation of prices that did not or hardly covered their production costs. In cotton-growing areas, monopoly buyers enforced unfavorable terms of trade driving many to abandon this profession, while a privileged few in Nampula formed sellers' cooperatives to try to redress this situation. Nevertheless "the daily struggle of the organized small producers is not a simple fight over surplus value which can be resolved by displacing intermediaries or getting access to 'just markets' and selling at super-prices; it is not a dispute over the rate of exploitation but rather a life and death struggle for pertinence and dignity; for recognition as producers. . . ." (Bartra, 2000:4). The despair engendered by this latest form of exclusion was poignantly expressed in the meeting in Massoane.

But who cares? Nationally and internationally, the focus of reformist policies is on the urban informal economy, which is seen as the refuge of the rural exodus. What greater proof exists that reformist policies continue to fail rural peoples? Herman de Soto asks us to recognize the capital created by the ingenuity of those who have left rural areas. But what about rural peoples when given half a chance? James Scott eloquently overstates the economic case for rural development:

> The long-term survival of certain human institutions—the family, the small community, the small farm, the family firm in certain businesses—is something of a tribute to their adaptability under radically changing circumstances. They are by no means infinitely adaptable, but they have weathered more than one prediction of their inevitable demise. The small family farm, by virtue of its flexible labor (including the exploitation of its children), its capacity to shift into new crops or livestock, and its tendency to diversify its risks, has managed to persist in competitive economies when many huge, highly leveraged, mechanized, and specialized corporate and state farms have failed. In a sector of the economy where local knowledge, quick responses to weather and crop conditions, and low overhead (smallness) are more important than in, say, large industry, the family farm has some formidable advantages (1998:354).

Fundamentally, the agrarian question in Mozambique as elsewhere is not just a matter of economics: of whether it is best to empty the countryside because of the comparative advantage of grain production in the United States, Canada, India, Australia, or Argentina as per liberal economics, or whether semi-proletarianization is more advanced, in terms of capitalist development, than petty commodity production as per "socialist" economics. The agrarian question has to do with *who* decides: whether those who live in rural areas are to be allowed to participate in the building of their own and the common future. And *on what terms*: as urban immigrants? As seasonal workers? As small-scale producers? Or as people who have the opportunity as well as the right to define themselves and the destiny of their space and their country on a more or less equal basis with others? If national and international policymakers cannot admit this possibility, they must ask themselves whether Mozambique can afford the luxury of wasted people or empty spaces as people flee the countryside.

As mentioned in the Introduction, this is not only Mozambique's problem. Jules Pretty shows that rural Europeans and Americans share a similar dilemma:

> The 20th century's period of remarkably successful agricultural growth brought great social change in rural areas throughout Europe. In the quest for greater food production, landscapes, rural livelihoods and farming systems have all been progressively simplified. In every European country, farms have become

both fewer in number and larger during this century. . . . These changes have left very different landholding structures in each European country. . . .

Many argue that progressively larger farms are an economic necessity. They permit economies of scale to be made and they enable more efficient producers to take over or absorb the operations of smaller more "inefficient" producers. But small farms provide other benefits to society. They employ more people than do larger farms. Small farms contribute to both rural social capital and natural capital. Their greater on-farm diversity maintains both plant and animal biodiversity; they are more efficient users of energy; and they tend to have a better record with animal welfare. But larger farms receive most from public subsidies.

A different but equally damaging problem is that of land abandonment. The regions most prone to population decline have been rural Ireland, parts of Scotland and Wales, central France, most of Italy and Greece, and Spain and Portugal. Generally there has been very little population decline in England, Germany, Belgium and The Netherlands. There are at least 56 million hectares of low-intensity farmland of high biodiversity value in Europe. Their value is maintained by the practice of farming—and when farmers leave, the value declines significantly. . . . Fewer farms, fewer jobs and larger-scale farming operations have also played a rise in the rise of rural poverty and the lack of services. A quarter of rural households in the UK are living on or below the official poverty line. Endemic poverty means a lack of food for some, particularly amongst old people. It means a lack of affordable housing, few job opportunities and inadequate childcare facilities. Many people are active in the informal economy. . . .

The result of this poverty, deprivation and declining services is the gradual unraveling of communities. Although there has been an increase in material affluence, this is not linked to social, cultural and spiritual strength. Throughout the world, external agencies have routinely undermined social capital in order to encourage economic "development." It may not be intentional, but the effect of doing things for people, rather than encouraging or motivating them to act as much as possible for themselves, is substantial. All of this has led to a decreased capacity amongst local people to cope with environmental and economic change. As once thriving communities are plunged into dependence, so people have increasingly lost a sense of belonging to, and commitment for, a particular place. This spiral of decline in local communities has diminished social capital. Continuity of individual farms is held dear by many farm families. Most wish to see their children as successors. Yet, in the EU, as a whole, there are more than four million farmers over the age of 55. A quarter are now past retirement age, and only 8 per cent are under 35. . . . There is also a growing dislocation between generations, with the young perhaps never appreciating what a sense of community may feel like. Almost every rural area in Europe is getting older. The young have fewer opportunities and so get less involved in community life. In some regions, the exodus of rural youth has virtually become an epidemic.

Another result of the decline of social capital arising from changes in farming is a marked increase in mental distress amongst farmers. In Britain, farmers and farmworkers are two and a half times more likely to commit suicide than is the rest of the population. In France, suicide rates amongst both men and women are highest in rural communities and fall steadily with increasing size of village and then town. This is the exact opposite of the reported situation at the turn of the century—with the highest rates recorded in cities. According to research in the US, as communities become economically depressed and people emigrate, so those who remain become more prone to mental ill-health (1998:221–223).

Space belongs or ought to belong to the people who occupy it, work it, or live in it. The previous pages have shown that fundamental instability and enormous social as well as economic costs occur when people are prevented from defining and using their living space as they feel best. People either move or rebel. This is one of the more obvious lessons of Mozambican history.

But there are other lessons as well including the fallibility of overly centralized planning born out of the presumption of superior knowledge on the part of an educated elite. The ongoing struggle in Mozambique over territorial rights may have begun with colonial enclosures but they continued with policies that defined where people lived as well who they were/are. Postcolonial governments have not given up that pretension. James C. Scott (1998) has called this almost universal process of enclosure "the creation of state spaces," by which he means the deliberate simplification of social life by bureaucrats in order to open communities to easy taxation collection, agricultural appropriation, military recruitment and other manipulation. As does Pretty, he contrasts state spaces, state simplifications, with the diverse, scattered and complex living spaces of rural populations and also the rich social intercourse and networking of multifaceted urban neighborhoods.

This book has argued that it is time to reverse this process and to address the question of balance between state and community spaces. And it has proposed a way of doing so. Scott also offers a number of suggestions to policymakers:

> *Take small steps.* In an experimental approach to social change, presume that we cannot know the consequences of our interventions in advance. Given this postulate of ignorance, prefer wherever possible to take a small step, stand back, observe, and then plan the next small step. . . . *Favor reversibility.* Prefer

interventions that can easily be undone if they turn out to be mistakes. . . . *Plan on surprises*. Choose plans that allow the largest accommodation to the unforeseen. In agricultural schemes this may mean choosing and preparing land so that it can grow any of several crops. . . . *Plan on human inventiveness*. Always plan under the assumption that those who become involved in the project later will have or will develop the experience and insight to improve on the design (1998:345, the emphasis is mine).

This book offers two more lessons: first, *let people do their own planning* in regard to those problems and resources that are closest to them and over which they need to have control. Democratization of the planning process by decentralizing it to the lowest living spaces in order to include the widest possible participation is empowering as well as productive. Mike Bell defines democracy in terms of "good talk." Some of the participatory planning exercises of the PRR were examples of good talk but communities normally had only one such experience. This was not enough to instill a feeling or desire for more of the same. Good talk has to become a habit.

Moreover, *good* talk can only take place between equals or rather people who accord each other relatively equal standing. In the training for participatory planning, the attitudes of openness, flexibility, humility, and above all, listening were stressed with those representing government in the dialogue with rural communities. These were people who, in the context of a command economy, had been trained to issue orders, the opposite of "good talk." Thus, the need for extensive retraining but this also applied to communities used to receiving orders. They needed to know that, since the end of war, a new context has been created and, moreover, to understand that their opinions are important.

This book has argued that the lowest level of state officials would be the most receptive to the habit of democracy, particularly those who work closest with rural populations, those in extension, in such areas as public health, social work, adult education, agriculture, and so on. As already noted, this contention is similar to Judith Tendler's point that ordinary government officials can be transformed into dynamic change agents by giving them extra responsibilities and training to perform these, by multiplying their tasks and affording them limited autonomy to accomplish them. Tendler underlined the similarity of this approach to best management practices in the private sector (1997:17 ff).

My recommendations, however, have little to do with management and everything to do with political organizing. They are based on the observation that the lowest civil servants are closer to rural peoples than are the more urbanized provincial and national officials and the typical non-governmental organization staff. Yet they, too, need to be reminded of their common social origins. As part of the process of grass roots organizing, they need to rid themselves of the stereotype of backward rural peoples just as rural peoples have to be reminded of their own political interests in order not to be blinded by those who would lead them in the interest of exploiting them (Gramsci, 1987:139, 140, 143ff). For these reasons, the proposed training program begins with discussions of individual and community rights and the meaning of development for the participants.

Most importantly, "good talk" has to lead to decision making and an assumption of responsibility for decisions. Talk by itself is empty; hence the need for Development Funds. Bringing decision making to those with the knowledge and capability of carrying out decisions is empowering but, because central governments are not prone to letting power go, communities may have to form associations and alliances to demand a say in governance and, more to the point, to take power over their living space. A training program by itself cannot bring this about but it could lead to the self-confidence required to jump-start the process.

The second and final lesson is to *take the long view*. Time is necessary to allow people to get accustomed to taking decisions and responsibility for their decisions. Time is necessary for training and retraining where necessary, for self-training, that is learning from mistakes and so on. A hopeful and more just vision of the future calls for promoting democratic spaces at local levels so that rural peoples can organize themselves to articulate their aspirations and demands not simply for resources but also partnerships with potential investors. This is the essence of citizenship. A slow confidence-building process and the concurrent extension of networks and alliances first at local, then provincial and national levels could open this possibility.

Through a detailed historical exposition, this book has engaged the battle of discourse for the purpose of changing how rural peoples are perceived. It has tried to demonstrate their capacities and resilience but, more importantly, it has opened a small space for rural Mozambicans to speak for themselves. Is anybody listening?

Notes

1. The information in this and the following paragraph come from an informal talk by Joseph Hanlon to the Britain-Mozambique Society on 14 May 2002 at the School of Oriental and African Studies, University of London.

2. Although I have no information regarding the terms upon which the recent settlement of white Zimbabwean farmers in Manica Province has been made and would normally be suspicious about the following, it is interesting to note that the current Agriculture Minister reported: "The peasants are satisfied," he said, "because each of the Zimbabweans has created between 40 and 60 jobs. They've brought work, they've brought development and a market, and people now have money. They've brought a whole new dynamic" (AIM no. 211, Mozambique-news@geo2.POPTEL .org.uk, 10 July 2001).

3. DeVletter gives some idea of the current employment situation: "The active labour force is currently estimated to be about 8 million, of which only 17 percent are officially in wage employment. Since the early 1980s, the number of people in wage employment has dropped considerably, initially because of economic stagnation and war. After 1987, significant retrenchment (estimated at about 100,000) took place through enterprise restructuring and privatization" (1998:8).

4. Joe Hanlon (1996) and Chris Alden (2001) provide an overview and an interesting critique of international intervention.

5. AIM no. 211, Mozambique-news@geo2.POPTEL.org.uk, 10 July 2001.

Appendix

ILINGA

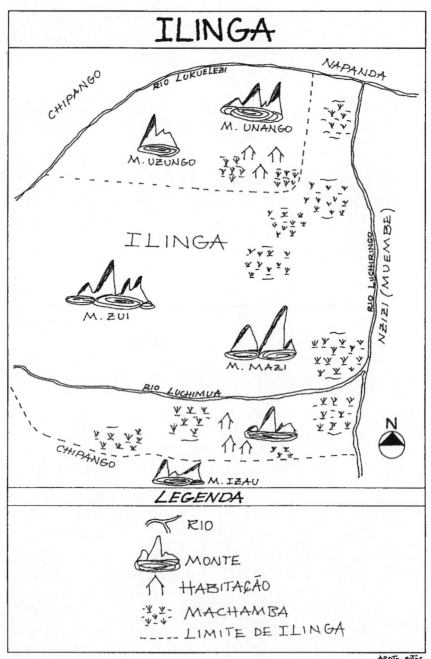

Map 6. Ilinga

KANDA

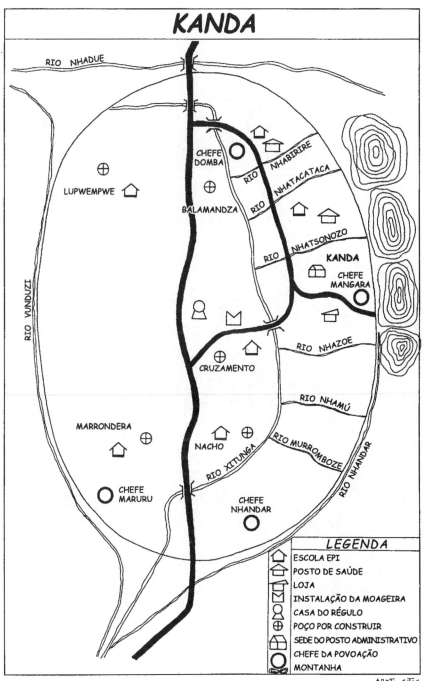

RIO NHADUE

RIO NHABIRIRE
RIO NHATACATACA
RIO NHATSONOZO
RIO NHAZOE
RIO NHAMÚ
RIO MURROMBOZE
RIO XITUNGA
RIO NHANDAR
RIO VUNDUZI

LUPWEMPWE

CHEFE DOMBA

BALAMANDZA

KANDA
CHEFE MANGARA

CRUZAMENTO

MARRONDERA

NACHO

CHEFE MARURU

CHEFE NHANDAR

LEGENDA

ESCOLA EPI
POSTO DE SAÚDE
LOJA
INSTALAÇÃO DA MOAGEIRA
CASA DO RÉGULO
POÇO POR CONSTRUIR
SEDE DO POSTO ADMINISTRATIVO
CHEFE DA POVOAÇÃO
MONTANHA

ARQTE SITOE

Map 7. Kanda

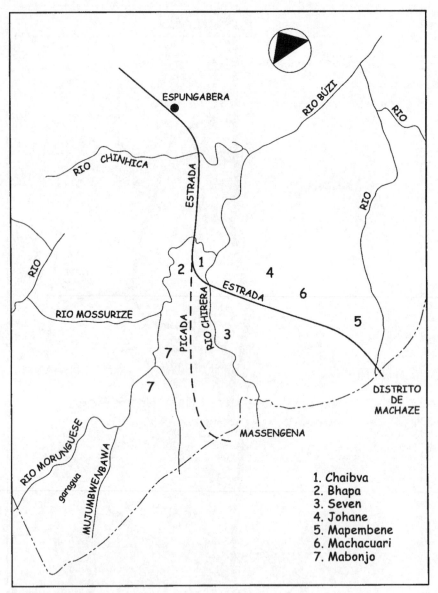

RIO CHINHICA

ESPUNGABERA

RIO BÚZI

RIO

ESTRADA

RIO

RIO

2   1

4

RIO MOSSURIZE

ESTRADA

6

RIO CHIRERA

PICADA

5

3

7

DISTRITO
DE
MACHAZE

7

RIO MORUNGUESE

garagua

MUJUMBWENBAWA

MASSENGENA

1. Chaibva
2. Bhapa
3. Seven
4. Johane
5. Mapembene
6. Machacuari
7. Mabonjo

Map 8.   Chaiva

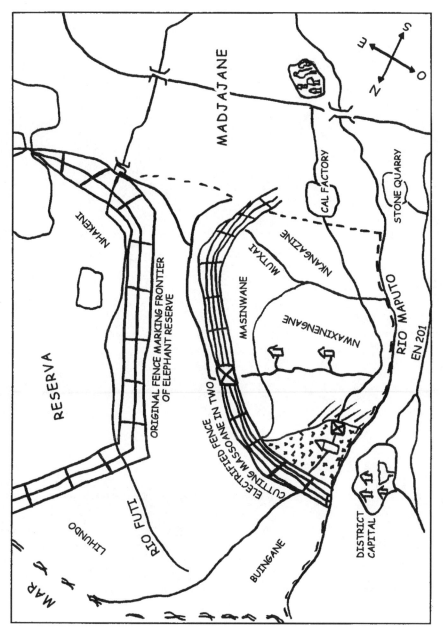

Map 9. Massoane Including a Part of Madjajane

Bibliography

Primary Sources

Documents from the Arquívo Histórico de Moçambique

Abdallah, Y. B. *Os Yao*. Translation of the 1973 English edition by the Arquívo Histórico de Moçambique. Maputo: Universidade Eduardo Mondlane, 1983.

Arquívo Histórico de Moçambique. Projecto de Recolha de Fontes Orais de História, Secção Oral (oral interviews led by G. Liesegang with the help of Teresa Oliveira). July 17–19, 1981.

Baptista, J. R. *Caminho de Ferro da Beira a Manica: Escurções e Estudos, effectuado em 1891 pelos officiães da Companhia Mixta de Engenharia Expedicionaria a Moçambique*. Lisboa: Imprensa Nacional, 1892.

Boletim Oficial, no. 1 (1 January 1877).

———. no. 4 (22 January 1877).

———. no. 11 (18 March 1877).

———. no. 13 (26 March 1877).

———. no. 19 (7 May 1877).

———. no. 22 (28 May 1877).

———. Special Supplement (30 June 1877).

———. no. 28 (9 July 1877).

———. no. 45. *Relatório do Governador do Districto de Lourenço Marques no Anno Económico de 1876 a 1877*. (28 October 1877) continued in no. 46 (12 November 1877), no. 47 (19 November 1877), no. 48 (26 November 1977), no. 49 (3 December 1877).

———. no. 52. *Relatório do Districto de Lourenço Marques Relativo ao Anno Económico de 1877 a 1878*. (30 December 1878).

———. no. 1 (6 January 1879).

——. no. 2 (13 January 1879).

——. no. 3 (20 January 1879).

——. no. 4 (27 January 1879).

——. no. 7 (17 February 1879).

——. no. 10 (10 March 1879).

——. no. 11 (17 March 1879).

——. no. 12 (24 March 1879).

——. no. 12 (11 March 1882).

——. no. 13 (18 March 1882).

——. no. 14 (25 March 1882).

——. no. 15 (1 April 1882).

——. no. 16 (8 April 1882).

——. no. 44. *Relatório do Governo do Distrito do Lourenço Marques referido ao anno 1884–85*. (31 October 1885).

——. no. 4. Governador do Distrito de Lourenço Marques. *Relatório referido ao anno 1885 a 1886*. (22 January 1887).

——. no. 20 (14 May 1887).

——. no. 3. *Relatório do Governo do Districto de Lourenço Marques referido ao anno economico de 1886–87*. (21 January 1888).

——. no. 15, III Serie (11 April 1953).

Colonia de Moçambique, Província do Niassa, Inspecção dos Serviços Administrativos e dos Negócios Indígenas. *Correspondência recebida durante a inspecção ordinária na Província do Niassa, em 1943*. Typescript. Caixa 95.

——. *Relatório e documentos referentes a inspecção ordinária feita na Província do Niassa, 1938–40* (Inspector Administrativo, Capitão Armando Eduardo Pinto Correia). Governo Geral, Caixa 96.

——. *Inspecção Administrativa Ordinária na Província de Niassa, segunda parte, Relatório do Inspector Capitão Carlos Henrique Jones da Silveira, 1944*. Typescript. Caixa 97.

——. *Relatório da Inspecção Ordinária ao Distrito do Lago da Província do Niassa, 1950–51* (Inspector Administrativo, Manuel Metello Raposo de Liz Teixeira, Intendente do Distrito). Typescript. Caixa 99.

Colonia de Moçambique, Inspecção dos Serviços Administrativos e dos Negócios Indígenas. *Inspecção às Circunscrições de Mossurize, Manica, Gorongosa e Chimoio, 1957, por Júlio Leite Pinheiro*. Typescript. Caixa 40.

——. *Inspecção Ordinária à Circunscrição do Mossurize, Março de 1954 à Maio de 1959, por Augusto do Sacramento Monteiro*. Typescript. Caixa 54.

——. *Inspecção Ordinária à Circunscrição do Mossurize, Novembro de 1967 a Janeiro de 1968, por António A.S. Borges*. Typescript. Caixa 54.

——. *Relatório da Inspecção Ordinária à Circunscrição da Gorongosa, 3 de Julho a 7 de Agosto de 1967, por António A.S. Borges*. Typescript. Caixa 52.

Colonia de Moçambique, Direcção dos Serviços de Administração Civil, Inspecções, Inquéritos e Sindicâncias. *Relatório da Inspecção ordinária ao Concelho de Lourenço Marques e Circunscrições de Marracuene e Maputo.* 1950. Typescript. Caixa 1473.

———. *Relatório da Inspecção ordinária ao Concelho de Lourenço Marques e Circunscrições de Marracuene e Maputo.* 1954. Typescript. Caixa 1473.

———. *Relatório da Inspecção ordinária ao Concelho de Lourenço Marques e Circunscrições de Marracuene e Maputo.* 1960. Typescript. Caixa 1476.

———. *Relatório da Inspecção ordinária à Comissão Municipal.* 1969. Typescript. Caixa 1476.

Companhia de Moçambique. *Relatório do Governador do anno 1901.* Caixa 1.

———. *Relatório do Governador do anno 1902.* Caixa 1.

———. *Relatório do Governador do anno 1903.* Caixa 1.

———. *Relatório do Governador do anno 1904.* Caixa 1.

———. *O Território de Manica e Sofala e a Administração da Companhia de Moçambique (1892–1900). Monographia para ser presente ao Congresso Colonial promovido pela Sociedade de Geographia de Lisboa em 1901.* Lisboa: 1902.

———. *Respostas ao Questionário Etnográfico, elaborado por Gustavo de Bivar Pinto Lopes.* 1928.

Companhia de Moçambique, Repartição do Gabinete, Processos Confidencias, 1903–1942. Letra I-12. *Indígenas implicados na Revolta do Barué,* vol. 1. "Declaração do Nhamanda." 4 September 1917. Caixa 75.

———. "Depoimento de três irmãos." 5 June 1917. Caixa 75.

———. "Declaração dos Inhacuauas." 2 January 1918. Caixa 75.

———. Letra I-13, *Inquérito às Causas da Revolta do Barué, 1918,* vol. 1. "Carta da Repartição do Trabalho Indígena à Governador." 6 December 1917. Caixa 75.

———. "Carta do Governador ao Chefe do Posto de Macequece." 21 February 1918. Caixa 75.

———. "Carta do Governador ao Governador-Geral, Lourenço Marques." 2 March 1918. Caixa 75.

———. "Carta do Chefe do Posto de Macequece ao Governador." 5 February 1918. Caixa 75.

———. "Depoimentos." 7 October 1917. Caixa 75.

———. *Boatos sobre os movimentos Indígenas, 1927–1930,* 2 vol. B-10. Caixa 57.

———. *Reorganização Administrativa da Circunscrição do Barué, 1921–1922,* vol. 1. Caixa 87.

———. Processo-19, Letra-R, 1921–1922. *Revolta do Barué.* Caixa 87.

———. Processo-15, Letra G, 1923. *Boatos de Nova Rebelião,* vol. 1. Caixa 58.

Companhia de Moçambique, Secretaria-Geral, Processos Confidenciais, 1897–1942. *Boatos de Revolta Indígena no Barué, 1920–1925,* vol. 1. Caixa 2.

———. Processo no. 2. (8 January 1924). "Cartas de 1922 e 1923." Caixa 2.

———. Processo no. 154. 1925. Caixa 2.

———. *Revolta do Barué.* Caixa 11.

———. "Carta do Director de Negócios Indígenas ao Governador da Companhia de Moçambique." (22 November 1935). Caixa 8.

Companhia de Moçambique, Secretaria Geral, Relatórios. *Relatórios do Governador do Território.* 1917 and 1918. Caixa 8.

Companhia de Moçambique, Secretaria Geral, Relatórios, Circumscripção da Gorongoza. *Relatórios.* 1894 and 1896. Caixa 259.

——. *Relatórios Semestrais.* 1900. Caixa 259.

——. *Relatórios annuais e mensais.* 1905–1907. Caixa 187.

——. "Resumo do Arrolamento de palhotas e recenseamento da população indígena no ano de 1913." Caixa 189.

——. *Relatórios Anuais da Circunscrição da Gorongoza.* 1919–1923. Caixa 190.

——. *Recenseamentos da População Indígena.* 1919–1923. Caixa 190.

——. *Relatórios semestrais.* 1920. Caixa 190.

——. *Relatórios de Cobrança de Imposto de Mussoco.* 1921 and 1922. Caixa 190.

——. *Relatórios anuais da Circunscrição da Gorongoza.* 1924–1929. Caixa 191.

——. *Relatórios trimestrais.*1925–1927. Caixa 191.

——. *Recenseamentos da População Indígena.* 1926–1929. Caixa 265.

——. *Relatórios anuais.* 1932–1936. Caixa 192.

——. *Recenseamentos da População Indígena e Arrolamento de Palhotas.* 1932–1941. Caixa 192.

——. *Relatórios de Cobrança de Imposto.* 1934 and 1942. Caixa 192.

Companhia de Moçambique, Secretaria Geral, Relatórios, Circumscripção de Mossurize. *Relatório Annual de 1897.* Caixa 259.

——. *Relatórios annuais.* 1901–1904. Caixa 259.

——. *Relatórios mensais.* 1903–1905. Caixa 259.

——. *Relatórios annuais.* 1904–1908. Caixa 260.

——. *Relatórios annuais.* 1909–1911. Caixa 26.

——. *Relatórios da Circunscrição de Mossurize: Anual e Semestrais.* 1913–1917. Caixa 262.

——. *Arrolamento e recenseamento da população, Mossurize.* 1915 and 1916. Caixa 262.

——. *Relatórios mensais.* 1912. Caixa 262.

——. *Relatório do Recenseamento e Arrolamento do Ano de 1916, Mossurize.* Caixa 262.

——. *Relatório Anual e Relatórios Mensais.* 1918. Caixa 263.

——. *Relatório do Recenseamento da População Indígena e Arrolamento de Palhotas, Circunscrição de Mossurize.* 1918. Caixa 263.

——. *Relatórios anuais e mensais.* 1919–1925. Caixa 263.

——. *Relatório da Cobrança do Imposto de Palhota de Ano 1919.* Caixa 263.

——. *Recenseamentos da População Indígena e Arrolamento de Palhotas.* 1919–1923. Caixa 263.

——. *Relatórios anuais e mensais.* 1926–1930. Caixa 264.

——. *Recenseamentos da População Indígena e Arrolamento de Palhotas.* 1927–1930. Caixa 264.

——. *Relatórios anuais e mensais.* 1931–1934. Caixa 265.

———. Recenseamentos da População Indígena e Arrolamento de Palhotas. 1931–1933. Caixa 265.

———. Relatórios anuais e mensais. 1935–1938. Caixa 266.

———. Recenseamentos da População Indígena e Arrolamento de Palhotas. 1936–1938. Caixa 266.

———. Relatório de Cobrança do Imposto de Palhota. 1935. Caixa 266.

———. Relatórios anuais e mensais. 1939 and 1940. Caixa 267.

———. Recenseamento da População Indígena e Arrolamento de Palhotas. 1939–1942. Caixa 267.

Companhia do Niassa. Occupação das Terras do Mataca: primeiros relatórios. Lisboa: January 1913.

———. Relatórios e Memórias sobre os Territórios pelo Governador Ernesto Jardim de Vilhena. Lisboa: "a Editora," 1905.

Coutinho, João D'Azevedo. A Campanha do Barué em 1902. Lisboa: Ministério da Marinha e Ultramar, 1904.

Districto de Lourenço Marques. Relatórios das Circumscripções, 1909–1910. Lourenço Marques: Imprensa Nacional, 1910. Cota B225.

———. Relatório das Circumscripções, 1911–1912. Lourenço Marques: Imprensa Nacional, 1913. Cota B198.

———. Relatório das Circunscrições, 1913–1914. Lourenço Marques: Imprensa Nacional, 1915. Cota B199.

Fundo da Administração do Concelho do Maputo. Administração, vol. 1. Cotas 1–3, 8, 21–23, 45, 47–49, 52, 56, 57, 59, 65.

———. Tribunais Indígenas. Cota 425.

———. Livros de Registro. Cotas 675, 482, 483.

———. Orçamento e Contas. Cota 341.

———. Educação e cultos. Cotas 286, 288, 289, 292.

———. Fomento. Cotas 225–235, 214, 214–220, 192–195, 273–274.

———. Curadoria e Negócios Indígenas. Cotas 78–79, 111–114, 119–123, 138, 140, 143, 144, 150.

———. Fazenda. Cotas 175–185.

Fundo do Governo do Distrito da Beira. Correspondência. May 1967. Caixa 735.

———. Censo Geral da População. 1945–1968. Cota 735.

———. Comércio. 1942–1972. Cotas 737–743, 743 A.

———. Demarcação. 1946–1957. Cota 750.

———. Relatórios. 1972. Cota 230.

Fundo do Governo do Distrito de Lourenço Marques, Processos. Administração, Pedidos de autorização para posse de armas. 1947–1948. Cotas 3, 4.

———. Limites de Regedorias e postos, 1949–1962, vols. 1–3. Cota 1.

———. Associações, vol. 17. Cota 51–52.

———. Autoridades Tradicionais, vol. 1. 1969. Cotas 162–160.

———. Actas de Juntas Locais. 1970, 1972–1974. Cotas 145 and 154.

———. Trabalho e Acção Social, Autoridades Gentilicas. 1948–1956. Cota 407.

———. Recenseamento. 1948–1957. Cota 419.

———. Política Indígena, vol. 1. 1951. Cota 413 (408).

———. Comércio, Demarcação e Concessão. 1947–1969. Cota 459 (453).

———. Povoações Comerciais. 1948–1960. Cota 482 (479).

———. Reservas Indígenas. 1956–1960. Cota 483 (475).

Fundo do Governo-Geral, Relatórios, Província de Manica e Sofala, Inspecção dos Serviços Administrativos e dos Negócios Indígenas. *Relatório da Inspecção Ordinária as Circunscrições de Buzi, Chemba, Cheringoma, Chimoio, Gorongosa, Manica, Marromeu, Mossurize, Sena, Sofala.* 1943–1944. Cota 177.

———. *Relatório das Inspecções Ordinárias as Circunscrições de Chemba, Cheringoma, Sena, Marromeu, Gorongoza, Manica e Mossurize, do Distrito da Beira.* 1946. Cota 219.

Fundo do Governo-Geral, Relatórios, Província de Sul do Save, Inspecção dos Serviços Administrativos e dos Negócios Indígenas. *Inspecção Ordinária as Circunscrições de Marracuene e Maputo.* 1943. Cota 152.

Fundo do Governo-Geral, Relatórios. Maputo. 1943. Caixa 152.

———. Conferências dos Administradores. 1947. Caixa 149.

———. Agricultura. 1927. Caixa 23. 1940–1944. Caixa 178.

———. Caminhos de Ferro. 1906. Caixa 2.

———. Economia Rural, Conferência. 1949. Caixa 280.

———. Delimitação de fronteiras. 1951. Caixa 380.

Fundo do Governo-Geral, Relatórios, Comissão Reguladora da Importação da Província de Moçambique. *Elementos para a elaboração do Relatório da Sua Excelência o Governador-Geral referente ao ano de 1953.* Lourenço Marques: December 1955. Caixa 2088.

Fundo do Governo-Geral, Relatórios, Comissão Técnica de Planeamento e Integração Económica (Moçambique), Serviços Privativos. *Planeamento Agrário de Moçambique: Relatório do Grupo do Fomento Agrário.* Lourenço Marques: 1965. Caixa 2088.

Fundo do Governo-Geral, Relatórios, Direcção dos Serviços de Economia e Estatística Geral. *Relatório da Visita de Inspecção aos Distritos de Tete e do Niassa em 1964.* Typescript.

Fundo do Governo-Geral, Relatórios, Governo do Distrito do Niassa, O Niassa, *Relatório Anual de 1970.* Caixa 2097.

Fundo do Governo-Geral, Quartel-General no. 5, Processos. "Carta do A. A. Pereira Cabral a Chefe da Repartição do Gabinete." 10 August 1918. Caixa 65.

———. *Inquérito às Causas da Revolta do Barué.* Pasta 15.

———. "Carta do Governador Pery de Lind." 24 November 1917.

———. "Carta do Governador Pery de Lind." 21 December 1917.

———. "Carta do Chefe do Gabinete Pompeu de Mierles Garrido." 4 March 1918.

———. Telegram of 25 February 1917.

———. Telegrams of 11, 16, 21 and 26 April 1917.

———. Telegrams of 5, 24, 29 June 1917.

———. Telegram no. 1175 of 27 December 1917.

———. Telegram of 25 June, 1918.

Fundo do Governo do Distrito da Beira, Anexo I. *Relatórios, 1954–1972*. Caixas 16, 17, 18.

———. Gremio dos Produtores de Cereais do Distrito da Beira. *Relatório e contas de Gerência do ano de 1955*. Beira: 1956. Caixa 16.

———. "Carta, 23 de Maio de 1967, do Governador Manuel de Sousa Teles a Director Provincial dos Serviços de Fazenda e Contabilidade em Lourenço Marques." Caixa 735.

Fundo do Seculo XIX, Governo do Districto de Lourenço Marques. Correspondência de Bom Successo (Salamanga), Maputo. 1888–1894. Sala 8, Caixa 101, Maço 1 (1).

———. Correspondência do Governo da República Sulafricana Transvaal. 1879, 1887–1899, 1885–1899. Maço 1 B a 3, Maço 2, Maço 3 (1).

———. Informações das concessões. 1871–1893. Sala 8, Caixa 1, Maços 1(1) e 2.

———. Maputo, Administração. 1894–1904. 11–89, A a 8.

———. Macassane, Posto Militar. 1896–1898. 11–1115 A j 9.

———. Telegramas recebidas do Bella Vista. 1898. 8–4, Maço 3 (12).

———. Fazenda, Feitoria de Lourenço Marques. 1851. 8–6, Maço 2 (8).

———. Marracuene, Correspondência da Maputo. 1896–1900. 8–14, Maço 3 (4), B e 3.

Fundo do Seculo XIX, Lourenço Marques. Correspondência para Direcção Geral do Ultramar, 1881–1895 and 1892. 8–150, Maço 2 (5) and Maço 3 (2), B e 1.

———. Requerimento 2o Cabo, no. 13 do Poletão da Polícia de Maputo. 1896. 8–137, Maço 1 (11), B d 4.

———. Informações Annuais. 1851 and 1875. 8–134, Maço 3 (1) B d 3 and Maço 3 (2).

———. Mapas dos preços dos generos. 1856. 8–134, Maço 2 (5).

———. Termos de vassalagem. 1882. 8–134, Maço 1 (1) B d 3.

———. Informações mensais. 1875, 1879, 1881, 1885. 8–133, Maço 3 (2).

———. Arrolamento/Cobrança. 1882, 1887, 1891. 8–128, Maços 1 (2) and 3 (3) B d 2.

———. Correspondência, repressão da revolta, Maputo. 1894. 8–128, Maço 1 (10) B d 2.

———. Delimitação da Fronteira/Transvaal. 1888, 1894, 1896–1899. 8–127, Maços 3 (1), (2) and 2 (4).

———. Correspondência da Bruheim em Macassane. 1894. 8–121, Maço 1 (10) B d 1.

———. Mossurize–Bilene. 8–120, Maço 3 (5 and 6) B c 5.

———. Correspondência Missão S. António Macassane. 8–110, Maços 1 (1 and 2) B c 4.

———. Escola Primária. 1895. 8–109, Maço 3 (6).

———. Administração. 1898–1900. 8–108, Maços 1 and 2.

———. Administração. 1895–1897. 8–107, Maço 2.

———. Bela Vista. 1890–1894; Bom Successo. 1888–1894. 8–107, Maço (1 and 2).

Governo do Território da Companhia de Moçambique. *Relatório da Circunscrição da Gorongoza, Ano de 1922*. 1922.

Governo do Território da Companhia de Moçambique, Direcção dos Negócios Indígenas. *Relatório da Inspecção Ordinária à Circunscrição de Mossurize, Setembro de 1940.* Caixa 267.

Governo do Território de Manica e Sofala, Companhia de Moçambique. *Relatório do Governador do Território, 1917.* Caixa 8.

Governo do Território de Manica e Sofala, Companhia de Moçambique, Circumscripção da Gorongoza. *Relatórios annuais e mensais.* 1908–1910. Caixa 188.

———. *Relatórios anuais e semestrais.* 1911–1916. Caixa 189.

———. *Relatórios do Recenseamento da População Indígena na Circunscrição da Gorongoza.* 1914 and 1915. Caixa 189.

———. *Cobrança do Imposto do Mussôco em 1916 na Circunscrição da Gorongoza.* Caixa 189.

———. *Relatório da Cobrança do Imposto de Palhota de Anno 1914.* Caixa 189.

———. *Recenseamento da População Indígena e Arrolamento de Palhotas.* 1913–1915. Caixa 189.

Governo do Território de Manica e Sofala, Companhia de Moçambique, Direcção dos Negócios Indígenas. *Relatório da Inspecção Ordinária à Circunscrição de Mossurize.* Setembro de 1940. Caixa 267.

Governo-Geral da Província de Moçambique. *Relatórios do Distrito de Lourenço Marques, 5a Circunscrição (Maputo), Ano de 1915–16.* Lourenço Marques: Imprensa Nacional, 1918. Cota B200.

Governo-Geral da Província de Moçambique, Inspecções, Inquéritos e Sindicâncias aos Serviços. *Inspecção à Circunscrição de Sanga.* 1971. Caixa 33.

———. *Inspecção à Circunscrição de Mossurize.* 1954. Caixa 19.

———. *Inspecção à Circunscrição de Mossurize.* 1968. Caixa 19.

———. *Inspecção ao Concelho de Manica e Chimoio e as Circunscrições de Mossurize e Gorongosa.* 1954—1957. Caixa 19.

Governo-Geral da Província de Moçambique, Intendência dos Négocios Indígenas e de Emigração. *Relação dos Regulados, Régulos, Chefes, Indunas, Cábados e Cabos das Diversas Circunscrições dos Distritos de Lourenço Marques e Inhambane e da Companhia de Moçambique ao Sul do Paralelo 22°.* Lourenço Marques: Imprensa Nacional, 1914.

Governo-Geral da Província de Moçambique, Inventário dos Relatórios das Inspecções Ordinárias, 1936–1974, Manica e Sofala/Beira. *Circunscrição da Gorongoza.* 1967. Caixa no. 52.

———. *Circunscrição de Mossurize.* 1954–1959, 1968. Caixa 54.

———. *Circunscrição de Mossurize.* 1955. Caixa 40.

———. *Circunscrição de Mossurize.* 1954–1957. Caixa 41.

Machado, J. *Questões Africanas: Maputo–LM–Mossamedes.* Lisboa: Sociedade de Geographia de Lisboa, 1889.

Ministério das Colonias, Junta das Missões Geográficas e Investigações Coloniais, Instituto Geográfico e Cadastral. *Carta da Colonia de Moçambique: Carta no. 12: Lourenço Marques.* 1951.

———. Cartas no. 26, 27: Sanga and Unango. 1951.

———. Carta no. 6: Mossurize, Chaiva. 1951.

———. Carta no. 17: Kanda. 1951.

———. Mapa no. 11: Tete, Barué, Milange, Sena. 1946.

———. Cartas no. 31, 32: Mopeia. 1946.

———. Carta no. 49: Montepuez. 1944.

———. Carta no. 43: Gurué. 1941.

———. Mapa no. 12: Maputo. 1947.

Ministério do Ultramar, Junta das Missões Geográficas e de Investigações do Ultramar. *Carta da Província de Moçambique.* 1971.

Ministério do Ultramar, Missão Inquérito Agrícola de Moçambique. *Recenseamento Agrícola de Moçambique, Manica e Sofala,* vol. VII. Lourenço Marques: 1964.

———. *Recenseamento Agrícola de Moçambique, Distrito da Zambézia,* vol. VI. Lourenço Marques: 1964.

———. *Recenseamento Agrícola de Moçambique, Lourenço Marques,* vol. XI. Lourenço Marques: 1966.

———. *Recenseamento Agrícola de Moçambique, Cabo Delgado,* vol. II. Lourenço Marques: 1963.

———. *Recenseamento Agrícola de Moçambique, Niassa,* vol. V. Lourenço Marques: 1964.

Monteiro, Aurélio Antunes da Silva. *Direitos e Deveres das Autoridades Indígenas do Distrito de Tete, Província de Moçambique.* Lourenço Marques: Imprensa Nacional, 1924.

Nogueira Guedes, Albano. *Nótulas de um Expedicionário.* Beira, 1963.

Noronha, Eduardo de. *A Rebelião dos Indígenas em Lourenço Marques.* Lisboa: Tipographia do Jornal–O Dia, 1894.

———. "Lourenço Marques e as suas Relações com a Africa do Sul." *Boletim da Sociedade de Geographia de Lisboa,* no. 2, 15a serie. Lisboa: Imprensa Nacional, 1896.

Portugal, Província de Moçambique, Direcção Provincial dos Serviços Geográficos e Cadastrais. Folha no. 102: Maputo, Carta de Portugal. 1966.

Portugal, Província de Moçambique, Serviços de Centralização e Coordenação de Informações. *Prospecção das Forças Tradicionais, Manica e Sofala.* 1967.

Portugal, Província de Moçambique, Direcção de Agricultura e Florestas. *Inquérito por Mostragem à Agricultura Indígena, 1954–1955, primeira parte: Distritos de Lourenço Marques e Gaza.* Lourenço Marques: Empresa Moderna, Ltd., 1958.

Portugal, Província de Moçambique, Manica e Sofala, Direcção dos Serviços dos Negócios Indígenas, Secção A, Administração, Administração da Circunscrição da Gorongosa. "Respostas dadas aos quesitos da Circular no. 3.885 pelo Administrador Manuel Arnaldo Ribeiro." 13 de Agosto de 1954. Caixa 135.

Portugal, Província de Moçambique, Inspecção dos Serviços Administrativos e dos Negócios Indígenas. *Inspecção Ordinária ao Concelho de Lourenço Marques e as Circunscrições do Maputo e Marracuene.* 1954. Caixa 1473.

———. *Inspecção Ordinária à Circunscrição do Maputo e seus Postos Administrativos de Catembe, Catuane, Inhaca e Manhoca.* 1960. Caixa 1476.

———. *Relatório da inspecção ordinária ao Concelho do Maputo e seus postos administrativos de: Catembe, Catuane, Inhaca e Manoca.* 1965. Caixa 1476.

Portugal, Província de Moçambique, Inspecção dos Serviços Administrativos. *Relatório da Inspecção Ordinária à Circunscrição da Gorongosa.* 1965. Caixa 52.

Portugal, Província de Moçambique, Direcção Provincial dos Serviços de Planeamento e Integração Económica da Província de Moçambique. *Estudos 13: Divisão Administrativa de Moçambique, por Regedorias.* 1970.

———. *Niassa.* 1971. Caixa 100.

República Portuguesa, Estado de Moçambique, Direcção dos Serviços Geográficos e Cadastrais. Folha no. 22: Montepuez. 1973.

———. Folha no. 41: Vila Junqueiro. 1972.

———. Folha no. 21: Namuno. 1973.

República Portuguesa, Estado de Moçambique, Instituto Nacional de Estatística. *IV Recenseamento Geral da População—1970: Resumo Geral.* 1970.

Ribeiro, José Caramona. *Sumários do Boletim Oficial de Moçambique, anos 1855–1965.* Lourenço Marques: 1966.

Seyrig, Henri. *Rapport sur la Situation actuelle e l'Avenir possible du Prazo de Gorongosa.* Lisboa: 1897.

Vilhena, Ernesto Jardim de. *Relatórios e Memórias sobre os Territórios.* Lisboa: Companhia do Nyassa, 1905.

Post-1975 Government Documents

Arquívo Historico de Moçambique, Secção Oral, *Projecto de Recolha de Fontes Orais de Historia.* Niassa: 1981.

Comissão das Terras, Secretariado Técnico. *Informação ao Seminário Nacional sobre Gestão e Ocupação de Terras pelas Comunidades Locais.* Maputo: August 1998.

Extra, "Anteprojecto da Lei de Terras em Debate Público." Edição Especial, no. 17. (June 1996).

———. "Que Lei de Terras para Moçambique: Conferência Nacional sobre Terras e Projecto de Lei de Terras." Edição Especial, no. 19. (October 1996).

Guambe, J. E. "Evolução Histórica do Processo de Descentralização em Moçambique." Maputo: Ministério da Administração Estatal, November 1996.

Instituto de Desenvolvimento Rural (INDER). *O Fundo de Desenvolvimento Distrital e Instrucções para a sua Utilização.* Maputo: February 1998.

———. *Diagnóstico Participativo de duas comunidades, Tundo e Simbe, Província de Zambézia.* R. E. Galli with Romão Cossa. Maputo: July 1997.

———. *Diagnóstico Participativo de dois bairros, 4 de Outubro e Rua Domingos, do distrito de Nhamatanda, Sofala.* R. E. Galli and Inácio Sitoe. Maputo: May 1997.

———. *Diagnóstico Participativo de Maleia, Namacurra e Dugudiua, Nicoadala, Província de Zambézia.* R. E. Galli with Inácio Sitoe. Maputo: March 1997.

———. *Diagnóstico Participativo de três distritos, Montepuez, Namuno e Balama, da Província de Cabo Delgado.* R. E. Galli with Judite Muxlhanga, Inácio Sitoe and Ofelia Simão. Maputo: December 1996.

———. *Diagnóstico Participativo de duas comunidades, Intama e Natelaca, no distrito de Alto-Molocue, Zambézia*. R. E. Galli with Inácio Sitoe. Maputo: October 1996.

———. *Diagnóstico Participativo de dois regulados no distrito de Mopeia, Província de Zambézia*. R. E. Galli with Judite Muxlhanga. Maputo: August 1996.

———. *Diagnóstico Participativo de Muagiua, Gurué, e Hapala, Ile, Província de Zambézia*. R. E. Galli with Judite Muxlhanga and Inácio Sitoe. Maputo: July 1996.

———. *Diagnóstico Participativo Rural de Kanda, Gorongosa e Pungué, Nhamatanda, Província de Sofala*. R. E. Galli with Judite Muxlhanga, Leya Bila and Inácio Sitoe. Maputo: June 1996.

———. *Diagnóstico Participativo dos distritos de Mocuba e Lugela, Zambézia*. Judite Muxlhanga, R. E. Galli, Leya Bila and Isabel Cossa. Maputo: March 1996.

———. *Diagnóstico Participativo dos distritos de Buzi e Dondo, Sofala*. R. E. Galli with Judite Muxlhanga, Leya Bila and José Mate. Maputo: December 1995.

———. *Diagnóstico Rápido Rural do distrito de Mossurize, Manica*. R. E. Galli with Isabel Cossa, Sara Algy, and Romão Cossa. Maputo: October 1995.

———. *Estudo Sócio-Económico do Distrito de Gorongosa, Província de Sofala*. R. E. Galli with Judite Muxlhanga, Isabel Cossa and Tiago Luís. Maputo: July 1995.

———. *Diagnóstico Participativo nas Comunidades de Nhataca e Nhandemba, Distrito de Gorongosa, Sofala*. Inácio J. Sitoe and Isabel Cossa. Maputo: July 1997.

———. *Levantamento Rápido e Participativo do Posto Administrativo de Changalane, 13 à 17 de Março de 1995*. Maputo: 1995.

INDER/UNICEF. *Estudo Sócio-Económico de Base nos Distritos de Ile, Namacurra, Báruè, Manica, Massinga e Panda*. Draft document. Maputo: July 1995.

Programa dos Orgãos Locais, Projecto dos Distritos Pilotos. "Atribuições e Competências das Administrações de Distrito e Respectiva Forma de Organização." Draft proposal. Maputo: April 1997.

Republic of Mozambique, Ministry of Agriculture and Fisheries, Directorate of Economics. *Smallholder Cash-Cropping, Food-Cropping and Food Security in Mozambique*. Working Paper no. 25. 17 June 1997.

Republic of Mozambique, Ministry of Agriculture and Land Tenure Center. *Proceedings: International Workshop on Land Policy in Africa*. Maputo: 18–20 February 1992.

República de Moçambique. *Decreto Presidencial, no. 36/90. Boletim da República*.

———. *Regulamento da Lei de Terras: Decreto no. 16/87. Boletim da República*.

———. *Lei no. 2/97. Artigo 6. Boletim da República*.

———. *Lei no. 9/96. Boletim da República*.

———. *Plano de Reconstrução Nacional 1994-96*, vols. I and II. Maputo: December 1993.

República de Moçambique, Comissão Inter-Ministerial para a Revisão da Legislação de Terras. *Propostas para um Programa de Delineação das Comunidades Locais*. Proposal presented to the National Seminar on Community Land Delimitation and Management, Beira, Sofala, 12–14 August 1998.

República de Moçambique, Comissão Nacional do Plano, Direcção Nacional de Estatística. *Relatório sobre os Resultados Finais do Inquérito às Famílias na Cidade de Maputo*, vols. I and II. Maputo: September, 1993.

República de Moçambique, Comissão Nacional do Plano, Direcção Nacional de Planificação. *Plano de Reconstrução Nacional: Documento Orientador*. Internal document. Maputo: February 1992.

República de Moçambique, *Pacote Autárquico*, brochura I. 1998.

República de Moçambique, Ministério da Administração Estatal, Núcleo de Desenvolvimento Administrativo. *Autoridade e Poder Tradicional*, vol. I. Maputo: November 1995.

———. *Anteprojecto/1: Princípios e normas de organização e funcionamento dos órgãos locais do Estado*. Draft proposal. 1998.

República de Moçambique, Ministério da Agricultura. *Bases para uma Política Agrária*. Maputo: September, 1992.

República de Moçambique, Ministério da Agricultura, Departamento de Estatística. *A Preliminary Analysis of the Size of Land Holdings in the Family Sector in Moçambique*. Maputo: May 1994.

República de Moçambique, Ministério da Agricultura, Direcção Nacional de Economia Agrária. *A Socio-Economic Survey in the Province of Nampula: Cotton in the Smallholder Economy*. Working Paper no. 5e. Maputo: January 1992.

———. *Diagnóstico da Estrutura, Comportamento e Desempenho dos Mercados Alimentares Rurais de Moçambique*. Relatório preliminar no. 19. 4 July 1995.

República de Moçambique, Minstério de Agricultura e Pescas, Direcção Nacional de Geografia e Cadastro (DINAGECA), Serviços Provinciais de Maputo. *Carta da Concessão do Blanchard Sodetur*. no date.

República de Moçambique, Minstério de Agricultura e Pescas, Direcção Nacional de Geografia e Cadastro (DINAGECA). *O Primeiro Relatório sobre a Delimitação das terras comunitárias na comunidade de Mucorro-sede, no distrito de Alto-Molocué, Província de Zambézia*, com a colaboração do INDER. Maputo: December 1997.

———. *Relatório: Trabalho de Delimitação das Terras Comunitárias, Província de Niassa, Distritos de Majune e Sanga*. Maputo: 1997.

República de Moçambique, Ministério de Plano e Finanças, Direcção Nacional de Plano e Orçamento. "Planificação Provincial." Memorandum à Directora Nacional. 7 July 1998.

República de Moçambique, Ministério de Plano e Finanças, Unidade de Alívio a Pobreza. "Avaliação da Rede de Protecção Social em Moçambique." Por Vitoria Ginja e Iain McDonald. February 1995.

República de Moçambique, Serviço Provincial de Planeamento Físico de Manica, Secção Técnica. *Carta do Distrito de Mossurize: Chaibva*. October 1995.

República de Moçambique, Serviço Provincial de Planeamento Físico de Zambézia. *Lugela: plano de recuperação*. Quelimane, Zambézia: June 1991.

República Popular de Moçambique. *Legislação sobre o uso e aproveitamento da terra*. Maputo: Imprensa Nacional de Moçambique, 1987.

Other Documents

Actionaid Mozambique. *Participatory Rural Appraisal: Ndixe and Gimo Ocossa Villages, Nhongonhane Localidade, Marracuene District, Maputo Province*. Report by Martin

Whiteside, Ivone Pascoal, Julia Ussey, Georgina Mugawa, and Roberto Luís. Maputo: October 1995.

Centro de Estudos da População. *A Pobreza em Moçambique: um estudo participativo sobre a pobreza, relatório resumo, 1a fase.* Elaborado por Yussuf Adam, Humberto Coimbra e Dan Owen. Maputo: 5 December 1995.

Conferência Nacional de Terras. "Documento de Trabalho." Maputo: 5–7 June 1996.

———. *Debate do Ante-Projecto de Revisão da Lei de Terras: Relatório do Secretariado Técnico.* Maputo: 5–7 June 1996.

Fok, Michel. "The Cotton sub-sector in Mozambique: Institutional Diversity, Performance and Prospects for Improvements." Draft prepared for the Ministry of Agriculture and Fisheries. Maputo: May 1995.

German Technical Cooperation (Deutsche Gesellschaft fur Technische Zusammenarbeit, GTZ). "Re-Integration and Re-construction Programme Sofala, PRRS-GTZ Sofala: Programme Brief and Concept." Draft. Beira: May 1995.

German Technical Cooperation (Deutsche Gesellschaft fur Technische Zusammenarbeit, GTZ), Manica Agricultural Rural Reconstruction Project. "Mossurize District, Re-Integration, Resettlement and Reconstruction Project." Draft. Chimoio: September 1995.

———. *A Prefeasibility Study of the Introduction of Coffee, Tea and Fruit Production in Mossurize District in Mozambique: final report.* Prepared by Agricultural and Rural Development Authority. Chimoio: October 1993.

———. *Projecto de Reintegracao (sic), Reassentamento e Reconstrução do Distrito de Mossurize.* Chimoio: September 1993.

Kappel, Rolf. *Monitoring Adjustment and Rural Poverty in Mozambique: Results from the Swiss Monitoring Programme in the Province of Cabo Delgado, 1990.* Preliminary version prepared on behalf of the Swiss Development Co-Operation. Zurich: August 1991.

———. *Ajustamento e Pobreza Rural em Moçambique.* Zurich: September 1992.

Land Law, Law no. /97. English translation of Land Law submitted to the Mozambican Parliament for final approval 31/7/97 by Jennifer Garvey. Maputo: Land Tenure Center, August 1997.

Lundin de Coloane, Irаê Baptista. *Um Estudo Sócio-Antropológico Sobre Alguns Aspectos Referentes ao Projeto Namuno II.* Maputo: August 1992.

MOLISV. *Apoio à Reinserção de Deslocados, Refugiados e Desmobilizados no Distrito de Mossurize: Relatório Final.* Maputo: 1995.

Operação das Nações Unidas em Moçambique, Gabinete de Coordenação da Ajuda Humanitária. *Movimentos Populacionais no Pós-Guerra em Moçambique.* Maputo: June 1993.

Programa de Reabilitação Rural do sul de Cabo Delgado. *Estudo Sócio-Económico, Diagnóstico Rápido Rural Participativo,* vols. 1 and 2. Pemba: 1996.

Programa de Segurança Alimentar, Ministério de Agricultura/Michigan State University, Equipa de Pesquisa. "Padrões de Distribuição de Terras no Sector Familiar em Moçambique." Paper presented at the National Land Conference in Mozambique, 25–27 May 1994.

Resistência Nacional Moçambicana, *Programa e Estatutos do Partido*, n.d.
SNV, "The MAMM Programme." Maputo: April 1998.
Swiss Development Co-Operation (SDC), Moz. 44. "Apoio as Iniciativas Locais e Empowerment na Província de Nampula." Maputo: March 1999.
United Nations Capital Development Fund, Project of the Government of the Republic of Mozambique. "Support to Decentralized Planning and Financing in Nampula Province." MOZ/98/C01. 28 July 1998.
United Nations High Commission for Refugees (UNHCR). *Reception and Reintegration of Returnees in the Central Region: Fact Sheet.* Chimoio: 25 April 1995.
———. *Chimoio, 1995, Quick Impact Projects.* Maputo: 4 September 1995.
Universidade de Eduardo Mondlane, Faculdade de Agronomia e Engenharia Florestal, Departamento de Produção e Protecção Vegetal. "Estratégias de Geração de Renda das Famílias Rurais e Suas Interacções com o Ambiente Institucional Local." Elaborado por Bart Pijnenburg et al. Maputo: June 1999.
World Bank, *Rural Rehabilitation Project: Mozambique.* Washington, D.C.: 25 February 1993.
———. *Mozambique: Restoring Rural Production and Trade,* vols. I and II. Washington, D.C.: 1990.
———. *Poverty Reduction Framework* Paper. Washington, D.C.: 1990.
———. Office Memorandum. "June 4 Version of Mozambique Draft Land Law." Restricted circulation: n.d.

Secondary Sources: Books, Dissertations, and Articles

Abrahamsson, Hans, and Anders Nilsson. *Mozambique: Macro-economic Developments and Political Challenges in the Nineties.* Working Paper no. 4. Uppsala: The Scandinavian Institute of African Studies, 1994.
Adam, Yussuf. "Papel e Importância dos Sectores Sociais na Agricultura." Paper presented at the 2nd Seminário sobre o Estudo do Sector Agrário, Maputo, 16–20 April 1990.
Adam, Yussuf and H. Coimbra. "A Pobreza Num Distrito Rico: Chibuto, Província de Gaza." Maputo: Centro de Estudos da População, Universidade de Eduardo Mondlane, March 1996.
———. "A Pobreza no Distrito de Macossa: uma interpretação e sugestões para a acção." Maputo: Centro de Estudos da População, Universidade de Eduardo Mondlane, March 1996.
Agência de Imprensa de Moçambique (AIM, Mozambique News Agency). *Report.* 9 July 1997.
———. *Edição.* 16 and 17 September 2000.
———. Issue. 16-17 September 2000.
———. *Edição.* 10 July 2001.
———. *Report.* 17 December 2001.
AGRITEX. *Learning Together through Participatory Extension: a Guide to an Approach Developed in Zimbabwe.* Harare: GTZ and IT Publications, 1998.

Alberto, M. S. *Os Negros de Moçambique: Censo Etnográfico*. Lourenço Marques, 1947.

Alden, Chris. *Mozambique and the Construction of the New African State: From Negotiations to Nation-Building*. Basingstoke and New York: Palgrave, 2001.

Alexander, Jocelyn. "Land and Political Authority in Post-War Mozambique: Notes from Manica Province." *Second National Land Conference in Mozambique: Briefing Book*. Maputo, 1994.

Almeida d'Eça, Vicente. "Considerações gerães sobre história colonial." *Boletim da Sociedade de Geographia de Lisboa* 1, 2, 7–12 (1901, 1903). Lisboa: Imprensa Nacional.

Alpers, Edward. "The Role of the Yao in the Development of Trade in East Central Africa, 1698–1850." Doctoral Dissertation, University of London, 1966.

———. "Trade, State and Society among the Yao in the Nineteenth Century." *Journal of African History* 10, no. 3 (1969): 405–420.

Amaral, Manuel Gomes da Gama. *O Povo Yao: subsídios para o estudo de um povo nordeste de Moçambique*. Lisbon: Instituto de Investigação Cientifica Tropical, 1990.

Anderson, Paul. "Mapping Land Rights in Mozambique." *Photogrammetric Engineering and Remote Sensing* 66, no. 6 (June 2000): 769–775.

Arnfred, Signe. "Notes on Gender and Modernization: Examples from Mozambique." Mimeo, 1990.

Arnold, Anne-Sophie, "Missions, African Religious Movements and Identity in Mozambique, 1930–1974." Draft manuscript, 1991.

Artur, Domingos do Rosário and Pekka Virtanen."The Role of Traditional Authority in Conflict Resolution in Mozambique: a Case Study from Serra-Chôa, Bárue District." Paper presented at the Workshop of Integrated Analysis and Management of Renewable Natural Resources in Mozambique, 7–11 June 1999.

Axelson, Eric. *Portuguese in South-East Africa, 1600–1700*. Johannesburg: Witwatersrand University Press, 1960.

———. *Portuguese in South-East Africa, 1488–1600*. Johannesburg: C. Struik (pty) Ltd., 1973.

Baez, P. *Analysis of Relevant Institutions in Gorongoza*. Harare, 1993.

Bannerman, J. H. "Community-Based Natural Resource and Land Use Management and Community Development." Draft document prepared for German Technical Cooperation (GTZ), Chimoio, Mozambique, 1997.

———. "Land Tenure in Central Moçambique, Past and Present." Chimoio: MARRP/DPA, 1993.

Barendse, R. J., "Commentary." Posted on the H-Asia@H-NET.MSU.EDU (20 August 2000).

Bartra, Armando, "Milpas del Milenio: A donde Iran los Excluidos si el sistema que los Excluye es Global y esta em Todas Partes?" Paper presented at the X World Congress of Rural Sociology, Rio de Janeiro, 30 July–5 August 2000.

Beach, D. *The Shona and their Neighbours*. Oxford: Blackwell, 1994.

———. *The Shona and Zimbabwe, 900–1850: An Outline of Shona History*. London: Heinemann, 1980.

Belshaw, D. G. R. "Linkages between Policy Analysis, National Planning and Decentralized Planning for Rural Development." In *Training for Decentralized Planning*. Rome: Food and Agriculture Organization, 1988.

———. "Decentralized Governance and Poverty Reduction: Comparative Experience in Africa and Asia." Paper presented at the Public Administration and Development Jubilee Conference, St. Anne's College, Oxford University, 12–14 April 1999.

Bernstein, Henry. "Concepts for the Analysis of Contemporary Peasantries." In *The Political Economy of Rural Development: Peasants, International Capital, and the State*, edited by R. E. Galli. Albany: State University of New York Press, 1981.

Berry, S. *No Condition Is Permanent: The Social Dynamics of Agrarian Change in Sub-Saharan Africa*. Madison: The University of Wisconsin Press, 1993.

"Best of Times, Worst of Times." *The Sunday Times*, 5 August 2001:15.

Betto, Frei. "Interview." In *A Democratização Inacabável: as Memórias do Futuro*, edited by J. Rossiaud and Ilse Scherer-Warren. Petrópolis: Editora Vozes, 2000.

Billing, K. *Final Report: Preliminary Survey to Establish the Requirements for the Initial Phase of the Re-Integration and Reconstruction Programme–Sofala*. Harare: Price Waterhouse, December 1993.

Blackburn, James, and Jeremy Holland. *Who Changes? Institutionalizing Participation in Development*. London: Intermediate Technology Publications, 1998.

———. *Whose Voice?* London: Intermediate Technology Publications, 1999.

Blair, Harry. *Spreading Power to the Periphery: An Assessment of Democratic Local Governance*. www.usaid.gov.html (September 1998).

Bowen, Merle. *The State Against the Peasantry*. Charlottesville: University of Virginia Press, 2000.

Bravo, Nelson Saraiva. "Esboço político, histórico, administrativo e ethnográphico da Circunscrição Civil do Báruè." *Anuário da Escola Superior Colonial*. Lisboa: 1937.

Brouwer, Roland. "Setting the Stake: Common and Private Interests in the Redefinition of Resources and their Access in the Machangulo Peninsula, Mozambique." Unpublished paper, Maputo: Universidade de Eduardo Mondlane, 1998.

Bryce, Gartrell. "Land Tenure and Cadastral Issues in Nicaragua." www.spatial.maine.edu/Landtenure/gartrell.html (4 July 1999).

Cabrita, João. *Mozambique: The Tortuous Road to Democracy*. Basingstoke and New York: Palgrave, 2000.

Cappelen, Adne. "Credit Policy, Macroeconomic Adjustment and Growth." Unpublished research paper. Oslo: June 1992.

Carrilho, J. L. "Sobre as principais necessidades do Distrito de Tete." *Boletim de Sociedade de Geographia de Lisboa* 4, 33 serie (April de 1915): 137–161.

Castells, Manuel. *The Power of Identity*. Oxford: Blackwell, 1997.

Centro de Estudos Africanos. *O trabalhador sazonal na transformação duma economia de plantações*. Maputo: Universidade de Eduardo Mondlane, 1981a.

———. "Já não se batem": a transformação da produção algodoeira. Maputo: Universidade de Eduardo Mondlane, 1981b.

———. Plantações de Chá e Economia Camponesa. Relatório A. Maputo: Universidade de Eduardo Mondlane, 1982.

Chambers, Robert. Rural Development: Putting the Last First. London: Longman, 1983.

———. Whose Reality Counts? Putting the First Last. London: Intermediate Technology Publications, 1997.

Chilcote, Ronald H. Transição Capitalista e a Classe Dominante no Nordeste. S. Paulo: Editora da Universidade de São Paulo, 1991.

Cogill, Bruce. "National and Individual Food Requirements: Common Questions and Misconceptions." Draft document, Maputo: UNICEF, 1993.

Coissoro, N. O Regime das Terras em Moçambique. Lisboa: Instituto Superior de Ciências Sociais e Política Ultramarina, 1964.

Community Organising and Leadership Training for Action (COLTA). Organise your Community: A Community Organisers Training Manual. Sidama, Ethiopia: n.d.

Coupland, Reginald. Livingstone's Last Journey. London: Readers Union/Collins, 1947.

Cunha, J. M. Silva. O sistema Português de Política Indígena. Coimbra: Coimbra Editora, Limitada, 1953.

De Janvry, Alain. The Agrarian Question and Reformism in Latin America. Baltimore: Johns Hopkins University Press, 1981.

DeVletter, Fion. Sons of Mozambique: Mozambican Miners and Post-Apartheid South Africa. South African Migration Project, 1998.

Dias, Jorge. "Estruturas socio-económicas em Moçambique." In Moçambique: curso de extensão universitário, ano lectivo de 1964-65. Universidade Técnica de Lisboa, Instituto Superior de Ciências Sociais e Políticas Ultramarina, 1964.

Dowbor, Ladislau. Oral presentation to the Escola de Formação dos Governantes. Fortaleza, Ceará, Brazil: 18 September 2000.

———. "Governabilidade e Descentralização." Perspectiva 10, no. 3 (Jul/Sep 1996).

———. Introdução ao Planejamento Municipal. S. Paulo: Editora Brasiliense, 1987.

Du Plessis, W. "Historical Overview: Evolution of Land Tenure Systems in South Africa." www.spatial.maine.edu/Landtenure/abstracts/duplessis.html (1999).

Eagleton, Terry. The Idea of Culture. Oxford: Blackwell Publishers, 2000.

Effler, D. "Profil da area de Chaibva, posto administrativo de Chiurairue, Distrito de Mossurize." Unpublished document prepared for the German Technical Cooperation, 1995.

Eisenstadt, S. N. Revolution and the Transformation of Societies: A Comparative Study of Civilizations. New York and London: The Free Press and Collier Macmillan, 1978.

Ellert, H. Rivers of Gold. Gweru, Zimbabwe: Mambo Press, 1993.

Environmental Insecurity and Conflict Resolution Project (Mozambique). Final Narrative Report, Project no: 97-89200-01, implemented by Helvetas Moçambique. IDRC, April 1999.

European Parliamentarians for Southern Africa. *Mozambique Political (formerly Peace) Process Bulletin,* 1993–present.

Fals Borda, Orlando. *Knowledge and People's Power: Lessons with Peasants in Nicaragua, Mexico and Colombia.* New Delhi: Indian Social Institute, 1987.

"Farmeiros Zimbabweanos instalam-se em Manica." *Noticias,* 9 January 2001.

Feliciano, José Fialho. *Antropologia Económica dos Thonga do Sul de Moçambique.* Estudos 12. Maputo: Arquívo Histórico de Moçambique, 1998.

Ferreira, A. "Promoção Social das Comunidades Rurais Africanas de Moçambique com Base no Desenvolvimento Comunitário." In *IV Jornadas Silvo-Agronómicas* (pp. 95–108). Chianga, Angola: Direcção de Agricultura e Florestas e Instituto de Investigação Agronómica de Angola, October 1963.

Figueiredo, L. A. de. "Notícia do Continente de Mossambique e abreviada relação do seo Comercio." Lisboa, 1 December 1773. In *Fontes para a História, Geografia e Comércio de Moçambique,* edited by Luiz Fernando de Carvalho Dias. Lisboa: 1954.

Fox, J. "Mapping Customary Lands: A Tool for Forest Management." Paper prepared for the Association for Asian Studies, Boston, Mass., 23–27 March 1994.

Galli, R. E. "FRELIMO's Socialist Experiment in Agriculture." A review of Merle Bowen. *The State Against the Peasantry,* H-Net Review, 25 October 2000.

———. "Rural Communities and Community Development in Mozambique: A Historical Perspective." In *Grassroots Organizations, Decentralization and Rural Development,* edited by H. Holmen and E. Luzzati. Turin: ILO, 1999a.

———. "Community Participation and Empowerment in the Development of Mozambique: Recommendations for the Future." Maputo: INDER, May 1999b.

———. "Elementos para a Elaboração de uma Estratégia de Capacitação em Desenvolvimento Rural para a Província de Manica." Chimoio: República de Moçambique, November 1999c.

———. "Drought, Resettlement and Food Security in Mozambique." Unpublished memorandum. Maputo: Social Dimensions of Adjustment Project, June 1993.

———. "Winners and Losers in Development and Anti-Development Theory." In *Rethinking the Third World: Contributions Towards a New Conceptualization,* edited by R. E. Galli. Washington, D.C. and London: Crane Russak, Taylor and Francis, 1991.

———. and Jocelyn Jones. *Guinea-Bissau: Politics, Economics and Society.* London and New York: Frances Pinter and Columbia University Press, 1987.

Gaventa, James. "The Scaling Up and Institutionalizing of PRA: Lessons and Challenges." In *Who Changes?,* edited by J. Blackburn and J. Holland, London: IT Publications, 1998.

Gebauer, Herman. "The Subsidized Food Distribution System in Mozambique and Its Socio-Economic Impact." Mimeo. Maputo: July 1991.

Geffray, C. *A Causa das Armas em Moçambique: Antropologia de uma Guerra Civil.* Paris: Karthala, 1990.

Giddens, Anthony. "Reith Lectures." BBC Radio 4 Homepage, www.bbc.co.uk .html (1999 Reith Lectures).

Gilbert, Jess. "Participatory Democracy and Democratic Planning in the Work of Carl C. Taylor, New Deal Rural Sociologist." Paper prepared for the Rural Sociological Society meeting, Toronto, Canada, August 1997.

Graig, Cary, and Marjorie Mayo, eds. *Community Empowerment: A reader in Participation and Development.* London and New Jersey: Zed Press, 1995.

Gramsci, Antonio. *A Questão Meridional.* Rio de Janeiro: Paz e Terra, 1987.

Green, Reginald. *Poverty Assessment Paper.* Maputo: Social Dimensions of Adjustment project, Mozambique, 1989.

———. *The Reduction of Absolute Poverty: A Priority Structural Adjustment.* Brighton: Institute of Development Studies, University of Sussex, 1991.

Griffin, Keith. *The Political Economy of Agrarian Change.* London: Macmillan, second edition, 1979.

Guedes, Armando Marques. "Organização Administrativa de Moçambique." In *Moçambique: curso de extensão universitário, ano lectivo de 1964–65.* Lisboa: Universidade Técnica de Lisboa, Instituto Superior de Ciências Sociais e Políticas Ultramarina, 1964.

Guyer, J., and Pauline Peters, eds. "Conceptualizing the Household: Issues of Theory and Policy in Africa." Special edition, *Development and Change* 18, no. 2 (April 1987).

Guyer, Jane. "Household and Community in African Studies." *African Studies Review* xxiv, nos. 2/3 (June–September 1981): 87–137.

Hafkin, N. J. "Trade, Society and Politics in Northern Mozambique, c. 1753–1913." Ph.D. dissertation. Boston: Boston University Graduate School, 1973.

Hall, M. "The Mozambican National Resistance Movement and the Reestablishment of Peace in Mozambique." London: Center for African Studies, SOAS, 1991.

Hall, M. *The Changing Past: Farmers, Kings and Traders in Southern Africa, 200–1860.* Cape Town and Oxford, David Philip and James Currey, 1987.

Hanlon, Joseph. "The Land Debate in Mozambique: Will Foreign Investors, the Urban Elite, Advanced Farmers or Family Farmers Drive Rural Development?" Research Paper. Oxford: Oxfam, 2002.

———. ed. *Mozambique Peace Process Bulletin,* Issue 25 (August 2000).

———. *Peace without Profit: How the IMF blocks the rebuilding in Mozambique.* London and Oxford: Heinemann and James Currey, 1996.

Hedges, David. "Trade and Politics in Southern Mozambique and Zululand in the early eighteenth and nineteenth centuries." Ph.D. dissertation. London: School of Oriental and African Studies, University of London, 1978.

Held, David, et al. *Global Transformations: Politics, Economics and Culture.* Cambridge and Oxford: Polity Press and Blackwell, 1999.

HELVETAS. "Relatório da Formação da Equipe da HELVETAS em Metodologias Participativas: Pesquisa-Acção em Massoane, 13-17 de Abril de 1998." Matutuíne e Maputo: 19 April 1999.

Hermele, Kenneth. *Mozambican Crossroads: Economics and Politics in the Era of Structural Adjustment.* Bergen, Norway: Chr. Michelsen Institute, 1990.

Hunt, Diana. "'Community Development,' Participatory Planning Structures and Local Development Initiatives—with reference to Mbeere, eastern Kenya." Paper presented at the Public Administration and Development Jubilee Conference, St. Anne's College, Oxford University, 12–14 April 1999.

Instituto Nacional de Planeamento Físico. *Proposta de Projecto, "Região de Lúrio," Distritos de Cuamba, Gúruè e Malema.* Maputo: 1994.

Interview with Herman de Soto. *Business Report*, BBC World Service, 9 September 2000.

Isaacman, A., *Mozambique: The Africanization of a European Institution: the Zambesi prazos, 1750–1902.* Madison, Milwaukee and London: The University of Wisconsin Press, 1972.

Isaacman, A., and Barbara. *The Tradition of Resistance in Mozambique: Anti-Colonial Activity in the Zambesi Valley, 1550–1921.* London: Heinemann, 1976.

Ishemo, Shubi Lugemalila. *The Lower Zambezi Basin in Mozambique: A Study in Economy and Society, 1850–1920.* Aldershot: Ashgate, 1995.

Jackson, David H. "Local Governance Approach to Social Reintegration and Economic Recovery in Post-Conflict Countries: The View from Mozambique." Discussion Paper, 2002.

Johnston, H. H. *Livingstone and the Exploration of Central Africa.* London: George Philip and Son, 1891.

Kearney, Michael. *Reconceptualizing the Peasantry: Anthropology in Global Perspective.* Boulder, Colo.: Westview Press, 1996.

Kloeck-Jenson, Scott. "Analysis of the Parliamentary Debate and New National Land Law for Mozambique." Maputo: Land Tenure Center Project-Mozambique, September 1997.

———. "Locating the Community: Local Communities and the Administration of Land and Other Natural Resources in Mozambique." Paper prepared for the International Conference on Land Reform, Cape Town, December 1997.

———. "A Brief Analysis of the Forestry Sector in Mozambique with a Focus on Zambézia Province." Draft paper. Maputo: Land Tenure Center Project-Mozambique, 22 December 1998.

———. "Consulting Local Communities in Mozambique: Issues of Representation, Process and Documentation." Maputo: Land Tenure Center, June 1999.

Kloeck-Jenson, Scott, with John Bruce and Susanna Lastarria-Cornhiel. "Analysis of the July 1998 Draft Regulations for the Land Law in Mozambique: A need for more Specificity." Maputo: Land Tenure Center Project-Mozambique, September 1998.

Koch, Eddie. "'Nature has the Power to Heal Old Wounds': War, Peace and the Changing Patterns of Conservation in Southern Africa." In *South Africa in Southern Africa: Reconfiguring the Region,* edited by David Simon. Oxford: James Currey, 1998.

Lastarria-Cornhiel, Susanna. "Impact of Privatization on Gender and Property Rights in Africa." Paper prepared for GENDER-PROP and E-mail conference, May–December 1995.

Leurs, Robert. "Current Challenges facing Participatory Rural Appraisal." In *Who Changes?*, edited by J. Blackburn and J. Holland. London: IT Publications, 1998.

Li, T. M. "Images of Community: Discourse and Strategy in Property Relations." *Development and Change* 27, (1996): 501–527.

Liesegang, G. "Nguni Migrations Between Delagoa Bay and the Zambezi, 1821–1839." *African Historical Studies* III, no. 2 (1970): 317–337.

———. "Lourenço Marques antes de 1895." *Arquívo*, no. 2 (October 1987): 19–75.

———. *A História do Niassa, c. 1600-1920.* Typescript, Maputo: AHM, n.d.

Lippman, Hal, and Barbara Lewis. "Democratic Decentralization in Mali: A Work in Progress." USAID/CDIE Impact Evaluation, number 2, 1998.

Livingstone, David. *Missionary Travels.* London: Wardlock, 1910.

Livingstone, David and Charles Livingstone. *Narrative of an expedition to the Zambesi and its tributaries and the discovery of Lake Shirwa and Nyassa, 1858—1865.* London: John Murray, 1865.

Lôbo, Rafael Cárcomo de Almeida Rosa. "As Autoridades Tradicionais e a Organização das Regedorias de 1961." Dissertação. Lisboa: Universidade Técnica de Lisboa, Instituto Superior de Ciências Sociais e Política Ultramarina, 1966.

Manning, Carrie. "Constructing Opposition in Mozambique: Renamo as Political Party." *Journal of Southern African Studies* 24, no. 1 (March 1988): 161–189.

Maples, Ellen. *Journals and Papers of Chauncy Maples.* London: Longmans, Green and Co., 1899.

Mamdani, Mahmood. *Citizen and Subject: Contemporary Africa and the Legacy of Late Colonialism.* Princeton, London, Kampala, and Cape Town: Princeton University Press, J. Currey, Fountain Publishers and David Philip, 1996.

Marrule, Higino et al. "Changing Agricultural Market Policies in Mozambique: Insights from Empirical Information on Farmer and Market Behavior." Paper presented at the Seventh Annual Conference on Food Security Research in Southern Africa, Victoria Falls, Zimbabwe, 28–30 October 1991.

Marsden, Terry. *Rural Restructuring: Global Processes and their Responses.* London: Fulton, 1990.

Martins, Coronel Azambuja. "O povoamento indígena de Moçambique: considerando a família e os agrupamentos." Memórias e Comunicações apresentadas ao Congresso Colonial (IX congresso), Tomo II, II Secção, Lisboa, 1940.

Martins, José de Souza. "O futuro da sociologia rural." *Estudos Sociedade e Agricultura* 15 (October 2000): 5–12.

Martins, Monica Dias. "Açucar no Sertão: a Ofensiva Capitalista no Vale do Curu." Ph.D. dissertation. Fortaleza: Depto. da Sociologia, Universidade Federal do Ceará, 2000.

McGregor, JoAnn. "Violence and Social Change in a Border Economy: War in the Maputo Hinterland, 1984–1992." *Journal of Southern African Studies* 24, no. 1 (March 1988): 37–60.

Medeiros, Eduardo. *História de Cabo Delgado e do Niassa (c. 1836–1929).* Maputo: 1997.

Mitchell, J. Clyde. *The Yao Village: A Study in the Social Structure of a Nyasaland Tribe.* Manchester: Manchester University Press, 1956.

Mooney, Patrick. *My Own Boss? Class, Rationality and the Family Farm.* Boulder, Colo. and London: Westview Press, 1988.

———. "Class Relations and Class Structure in the Midwest." In *Studies in the Transformation of US Agriculture,* edited by Eugene Havens and Howard Newby. Boulder and London: Westview, 1986.

Myers, Gregory. "Land Tenure Development in Mozambique: Implications for Economic Transformation." Report prepared for the German Technical Cooperation and the University of Wisconsin Land Tenure Center, September 1995.

———. "Competitive Rights, Competitive Claims: Land Access in Post-War Mozambique." *Journal of Southern African Studies* 20, no. 4 (1994): 603–632.

———. "Land Tenure and Resettlement in Post-War Mozambique: Capacity and Individual Choice." Land Tenure Center, University of Wisconsin, 18 September 1992.

———. "Confusion, Contradiction and Conflict: Land Access in Mozambique in the Post-War Period." Land Tenure Center, University of Wisconsin, September 1993.

———. "Agricultura e desintervencionamento das empresas agrárias estatais em Moçambique." *Extra,* no. 9 (1992).

Myers, G., Julieta Eliseu, and Erasmo Nhachungue. *Case Studies of Land Access in the Post-War Period.* Maputo: Land Tenure Center and Ministry of Agriculture, December 1993.

Myers, G., and Ricky Weiss, eds. *Second National Land Conference in Mozambique: Briefing Book.* Maputo: Land Tenure Center Collaborative Project, 25–27 May 1994.

Myers, G., Harry G. West, and Julieta Eliseu. *Land Tenure Security and State Farm Divestiture in Mozambique: Case Studies in Nhamatanda, Manica, and Montepuez Districts.* Research Paper no. 110. Madison, Wis.: Land Tenure Center, January 1993.

Narayan, Deepa. *Designing Community Based Development.* Participation Series, Paper no. 007. Washington, D.C.: World Bank, Social Policy and Resettlement Division, Environment Department, June 1995.

Negrão, José. "Land and Rural Development in Mozambique." Paper presented at the Workshop of Integrated Analysis and Management of Renewable Natural Resources in Mozambique, 7–11 June 1999.

———. "Mulheres em Situação Difícil." Maputo: UNICEF, 1991.

Neil-Tomlinson, B. "The Mozambique Chartered Company, 1892–1910." Ph.D. Dissertation. London: School of Oriental and African Studies, University of London, 1974.

———. "The Nyassa Chartered Company, 1891–1929." *Journal of African History* 18, no. 1 (1977): 108–128.

Newitt, M. D. D. "Mozambique." In *A History of Postcolonial Lusophone Africa,* edited by Patrick Chabal. London: C. Hurst, 2002.

———. *A History of Mozambique.* London: C. Hurst, 1995.

———. *Portuguese Settlement on the Zambesi: Exploration, Land Tenure and Colonial Rule in East Africa.* London: Longman, 1973.

Nilson, Anders. "Legitimidade de Economia, Conflito e a Guerra." In *Autoridade e Poder Tradicional* I. Maputo: Ministério de Administração Estatal, 1995.

Noticias, 20 September 2000.

———. 28 November 2000.

O'Laughlin, Bridget. "Proletarianisation and/or Changing Rural Livelihoods: Forced Labour and Resistance in Colonial Mozambique." Working Paper 12. Manchester: University of Manchester, Institute for Development Policy and Management, June 2000.

———. "Past and Present: Land Reform in Mozambique." *Review of African Political Economy*, no. 63 (1995): 99–106.

———. "Interpretations Matter: Evaluating the War in Mozambique." *Southern African Report* 7, no. 3 (1992): 22–33.

Orta da Encarnação, José. "Organisation Économique, État et Symbolique dans les Sociétés Shonas." These de doctorat em sociologie. Louvain: Université Catholique de Louvain, March 1995.

Osorio, João de Castro, and João F. Rodriguês. "Integração dos actuais régulos na obra administrativa nas colonias de Angola e Moçambique." Memórias e Comunicações apresentadas ao Congresso Colonial (IX congresso), Tomo II, II Secção, Lisboa, 1940.

Pelissier, René. *História de Moçambique*, vols. 1 and 2. Lisboa: Imprensa Universitária, 1988.

———. *Naissance du Mozambique: Résistance e Revoltes Anticolonials (1854–1918)*, Tome 2. Orgeval, France: Pelissier, 1984.

Pequenino, Fernando. "O Papel das Autoridades Linhageiras e/ou Régulos na Implementação da Nova Lei de Terras." Paper presented to the Land Seminar of Zambézia, Mocuba, 4–5 June 1997.

Pinhal, Euclides Mendes. "Aspectos da Divisão e Ocupação Administrativa em Moçambique a Norte do Zambeze, 1885-1910." Dissertação de licenciatura. Lisboa: Universidade Técnica de Lisboa, Instituto Superior de Ciências Sociais e Política Ultramarina, 1971.

Pitcher, M. Anne. "Disruption without Transformation: Agrarian Relations and Livelihoods in Nampula Province, Mozambique, 1975–1995." *Journal of Southern African Studies* 24, no. 1 (March 1998): 115–140.

Platteau, J-P. "The Evolutionary Theory of Land Rights as Applied to Sub-Saharan Africa: A Critical Assessment." *Development and Change* 27 (1996): 29–86.

Potts, Deborah. "Worker-Peasants and Farmer-Housewives." *Journal of Southern African Studies* 26, no. 4 (December 2000): 807–832.

Pretty, Jules. *The Living Land*. London: Earthscan, 1998.

Price Waterhouse Agriculture. *Relatório sobre a comercialização dos cereais*. Harare: December 1993.

Putnam, Robert. *Comunidade e Democracia: a experiência da Italia moderna*. S. Paulo: Fundação Getulia Vargas, 1996.

Ranger, Terry. "Territorial Cults in the History of Central Africa." *Journal of African History* XIV, no. 4 (1973): 581–597.

Rennie, J. K. "Christianity, Colonialism and the Origins of Nationalism among the Ndau of Southern Rhodesia, 1890-1935." Ph.D. dissertation. Northwestern, Ill.: Northwestern University, 1973.

Ribeiro, Francisco dos Reis. "Alguns Aspectos da Ocupação e Divisão Administrativa de Moçambique a Sul do Zambeze, 1885–1910." Dissertação de licenciatura. Lisboa: Universidade Técnica de Lisboa, Instituto Superior de Ciências Sociais e Política Ultramarina, 1972.

Rita-Ferreira, A. Os Africanos de Lourenço Marques. Lourenço Marques: IICM, 1967–68.

Said, Edward. Cultura e Imperialismo. São Paulo: Companhia das Letras, 1995.

Salbany, A. "Desenvolvimento Comunitário." In IV Jornadas Silvo-Agronómicas (pp. 55–63). Chianga, Angola: Direcção de Agricultura e Florestas e Instituto de Investigação Agronómica de Angola, 15–20 October 1963.

Samaje, J. A. "Administração Local do Estado (1975–2002): O Caso de Chinde." Dissertation. University of Eduardo Mondlane, 2002.

Sayagues, Mercedes. "Mozambique's Not So Sugary, Daddy." Electronic Mail and Guardian, 15 May 1998.

Schoonmaker-Freudenberger, Mark. "Resource Management and Planning Study." USAID/Senegal, 31 March 1993.

Scott, James C. Seeing Like a State. Yale Agrarian Studies Series. New Haven, Conn.: Yale University Press, 1998.

Shanin, Teodor, ed. Peasants and Peasant Societies: Selected Readings. Harmondsworth, N.Y.: Penguin Press, 1971.

Shipton, P. "Land and Culture in Tropical Africa: Soils, Symbols, and the Metaphysics of the Mundane." Annual Review of Anthropology 23 (1994): 347–377.

Shipton, Parker, and Mitzi Goheen. "Understanding African Land-Holding: Power, Wealth and Meaning." Africa 62, no. 3 (1992): 307–324.

Silva, J. Oliveira da. Da Urgência de Reformas em Moçambique. Beira: Edição de "Notícias de Beira," 1962.

Simon, David, ed. South Africa in Southern Africa: Reconfiguring the Region. Oxford, England, Athens, Ohio, Cape Town: J. Currey, Ohio University Press, David Philip, 1998.

Sinclair, Paul J. J. "Space, Time and Social Formation: A Territorial Approach to the Archaeology and Anthropology of Zimbabwe and Mozambique, c. 0–1700 AD." Doctoral dissertation. Uppsala, Sweden: University of Uppsala, Department of Archaeology, 1987.

Smith, Alan K. "The Peoples of Southern Mozambique: An Historical Survey." Journal of African History XIV, no. 4 (1973): 565–580.

———. "The Struggle for Control of Southern Moçambique, 1720–1835." Ph.D. dissertation. University of California, Los Angeles, 1970.

Sopa, António Jorge Diniz. "A Resistência em Moçambique: o Caso de Barué." Typescript. Maputo: n.d.

———. "Achegas para o Conhecimento da Pequena Agricultura Colona no Território de Manica e Sofala." Typescript. Maputo: n.d.

Stedile, João Pedro. "Interview." In A Democratização Inacabável: as Memórias do Futuro, edited by J. Rossiaud and Ilse Scherer-Warren. Petrópolis: Editora Vozes, 2000.

Tanner, C. "Law-Making in an African Context: The 1997 Mozambican Land Law." FAO Legal Papers Online 26. www.fao.org/legal/prs-O1/1po26.pdf. 2002.

Taylor, Stephen. Shaka's Children: A History of the Zulu People. London: HarperCollins, 1995.

Tendler, Judith. Bom Governo nos Trópicos. São Paulo: ENAP, 1997.

Theal, George McCall. Records of South-Eastern Africa, vol. I. London: Government of the Cape Colony, 1898.

University of Wisconsin-Madison, Land Tenure Center. O Disinvestimento das Empresas Agrícolas Estatais em Moçambique: Conflitos de Propriedade e Questões Ligadas à Nova Política de Acesso à Terra, o Caso da Região de Chokwe. Prepared for USAID-Maputo and the Ministry of Agriculture, Mozambique, May 1992.

Vail, Leroy, and White Landeg. Capitalism and Colonialism in Mozambique: A Study of Quelimane District. London: Heinemann, 1980.

Vail, L. "Mozambique's Chartered Companies: The Rule of the Feeble." Journal of African History 17, no. 3 (1976): 389–416.

Waller, Horace. The Last Journals of David Livingstone in Central Africa, from 1865 to His Death. London: John Murray, 1874.

Wallerstein, Immanuel. The Modern World-System: Capitalist Agriculture and the Origins of the European World-Economy in the Sixteenth Century. New York: Academic Press, 1974.

Weber, Max. Economy and Society, vol. 1. Berkeley: University of California Press, 1968.

Wegher, P. Luís. Um Olhar sobre Niassa. Maputo: Paulinas, 1995.

Weimer, Bernhard. "Interrogações de um observador privilegiado." In Moçambique: dez anos de paz, sobre democracia, governação e reforma, edited by Brazão Mazula. Maputo, 2002.

West, Harry G. "'This Neighbor is not my Uncle!': Changing Relations of Power and Authority on the Mueda Plateau." Journal of Southern African Studies 24, no. 1 (March 1998): 141–160.

Whiteside, Martin, compiler. Diagnóstico (Participativo) Rápido Rural: Manual de Técnicas. Maputo: Comissão Nacional do Meio Ambiente, March 1995.

Williams, Raymond. Culture and Society, 1780-1950. New York: Columbia University Press, 1958.

Woodhouse, P., H. Bernstein, and D. Hulme, eds. African Enclosures?: The Social Dynamics of Wetlands in Drylands. Oxford: James Currey, 2000.

World Bank. Voices of the Poor. vols. 1 and 2. Washington, D.C., March 2000.

Worsfold, W. Basil. Portuguese Nyasaland. London: Sampson Low, Marston and Co., 1899.

Wunsch, James. "Towards a Political Economy of Decentralization in Africa: Policies, Institutions, Interests and Consequences." Paper presented at the Public

Administration and Development Jubilee Conference, St. Anne's College, Oxford University, 12–14 April 1999.

Wuyts, Marc. *Camponeses e Economia Rural em Moçambique.* Maputo: Centro de Estudos Africanos, Universidade de Eduardo Mondlane, 1978.

Zamparoni, Valdemir. "Monhés, Baneanes, Chinas e Afro-maometanos: colonialismo e racismo em Lourenço Marques, 1890–1940." *Lusotopie 2000* (2000): 191–222.

Index

233–36; inter–generational conflict in, 42, 132, 150; soil erosion in, 150

communities, rural: demarcation of, 43–44, 133–34, 157–59, 237, 243, 245–47 (*see also* land); economic activities of, 141–46 ; economic and social infrastructures in, 149, 153, 181–83; emancipatory pathways for, 7–8, 166, 202–3, 223, 262–64 (*see also* empowerment and social struggle); gender divisions of labor of, 144–46, 180; nature and definition of, 5, 19; need for organization of, 7–9, 153–54, 196, 200–201, 220–21, 248, 264; and partnerships with private investors, 248–51; planning by, 153–54, 202–3, 217–27 (*see also* community participation; planning, community); political structure of, 136–38; problems of resettlement of, 149–50, 172–74, 180–83; religion and customs of, 147–48; responses to economic opportunities, 4–5, 19, 135, 256–60; size and types of, 132–33; social organization of, 4, 11, 138–41; social tensions within, 150, 180, 221. *See also* Alto-Lugela; Chaiva; Chòkwé; Kanda; Ilinga; Massoane; Mozambique, population; training; Yao

community authorities, 9–10, 156, 203, 218

community development. *See* rural development, rural rehabilitation projects

community participation 5, 40–45, 131, 169–89, 191–203, 205–16, 217–27; conflicting concepts of, 183–85; critique of, 192–93. *See also* consultative councils; Institute for Rural Development and Planning

community self–management, 9, 17, 154, 203, 222, 227, 241, 244–51. *See also* empowerment; land; planning; rural communities; sovereignty

Companhia de Gorongosa, 55–57

Companhia de Moçambique (Mozambique Company), 12, 17–18, 80, 156; benefits under, 85–87; brutality of, 86; conditions of work and pay under, 58, 84–85; corruption under, 86–87; forced labor under, 58–59, 61–62, 82–85; lack of investment under, 57, 62–63, 81, 89–91; original capital of, 55; profits of, 63, 82, 85; sub-concession of, (*see* Companhia de Gorongosa); tax-farming arrangements of, 80, 86–87

Companhia do Niassa (Niassa Company), 12, 17, 156; insufficient capital of, 27; forced labor under, 29–30; promotion of commodity production under, 30; rule of, 27–30, 35; taxation under, 28–29; violence, of, 28–29

Companhias Majesticas. *See* Companhia de Gorongosa; Campanhia de Moçambique; Companhia do Niassa; Zambézia Company

CONCERN, 247

concessionary companies: Blanchard Mozambique Enterprise, 125, 237, 249; Buzi Sugar Company (Companhia Colonial de Buzi), 84, 104n16; Companhia Nacional Algodoeira, 64; João Ferreira dos Santos, 32, 235–36, 256 (*see also* cotton cultivation); LOMACO, 235–36, 238, 256; MADAL Company, 27, 237; Mosagrius Development Corporation, 27, 44, 237, 245, 259; Namagoa Plantations, Ltd., 179–80; Niassa Investment

About the Author

Rosemary Galli is the coordinator of the sociology module of the Master's Program in Development Management sponsored by the International Labour Organization (ILO) and the University of Torino, Italy. She has authored five other books including the edited works, *The Political Economy of Rural Development: Peasants, the State and International Capital* (1981) and *Rethinking the Third World* (1992), as well as *Guinea-Bissau: Politics, Economics and Society* (1987 with Jocelyn Jones) and *Guinea-Bissau* (1990). Her research, mainly on agricultural policy and rural development, has ranged over a number of countries on three continents including Italy, Colombia, Nigeria, Guinea-Bissau, as well as Mozambique. She has worked as a consultant for many of the major development agencies and was an adviser to the government of Mozambique during the 1990s.